Woman's Being, Woman's Place

A Publication in Women's Studies

Barbara Haber, Series Editor

Edited by
Mary Kelley

Woman's Being, Woman's Place:
Female Identity and Vocation
in American History

G. K. Hall & Co.,   Boston, Massachusetts

Copyright © 1979 by Mary Kelley

Library of Congress Cataloging in Publication Data

Conference on the History of Women, St. Paul, 1977.
    Woman's being, woman's place.

    1. Women—United States—History—Addresses, essays,
lectures. 2. Women—United States—Social conditions—
Addresses, essays, lectures. I. Kelley, Mary, 1943- II. Title.
HQ1410.C64   1977   301.41'2'0973   79-15436
ISBN 0-8161-8324-4

This publication is printed on permanent/durable acid-free paper
MANUFACTURED IN THE UNITED STATES OF AMERICA

Contents

Acknowledgments

A volume such as this is a collective endeavor that presupposes and draws heavily upon a network of scholars and a legacy of research. The contributions made by others have been many, and the debts incurred just as numerous. Certainly the most obvious was the contribution of those involved in the Conference on the History of Women: all but two of the essays included in this collection were originally presented as papers at the meeting held in October of 1977. The Women Historians of the Midwest, the Chicago Area Women's History Conference, and the College of St. Catherine made possible a stimulating conference in which 160 participated and 800 attended from nearly every state in the country. Unlike participation and attendance which can be easily measured, other indicators of a meeting's significance defy quantification but are no less important. Perhaps this Conference's greatest contribution lies in that which it so clearly encouraged—a community of scholars committed to the study of women's past. Just as important was the response of those whose individual contributions appear in the volume. Their cooperation, enthusiasm, and dedication made my experience as an editor a pleasure. To others there are debts as well. From her initial suggestion that a collection of essays be published to completion of the volume, Mary Grace Smith's help and patience have been important. Gail Patten's encouragement as a friend, her skill as a typist, and, not the least, her wit have lightened many a task. And more than anyone's, Robert Kelley's support has sustained me throughout.

MK

Introduction

Women's history is still recent history. That some individuals might misinterpret my observation illustrates the point. Obviously, I do not mean to say that in actual fact the history of women is not as ancient as the history of men. But little time has passed since the printed history of women and thus our knowledge of women's history amounted to little more than a blank page. Even less time has passed since historians' reading of women's past was either absorbed under the rubric "mankind" or captured in the adage that, unlike that of men, "all women's experiences in all time are all the same." With footnote, article, and monograph, historians in the last two decades have come to recognize and study the influential role played by gender in the past. And besides the most obvious determinant affecting women's lives, namely historical period, other factors such as race, class, ethnicity, and religious affiliation have become more readily identified and isolated leading to an increasing awareness that, as in the case of men, women also have had disparate as well as shared experiences.

As the twenty essays in this collection illustrate, the historian in a sense must always begin with either a blank page or an undifferentiated past. The primary focus of most of the essays is the experiences and responses of white, middle- and upper-class American women. But a suggestion of commonality and the attempt to generalize are combined with the discovery and recognition of manifold factors that contributed to divergent experiences and lead to findings as complex as the lives of women themselves. Varied in perspective and periods studied, the essays do share a concern with society's conceptions and expectations regarding the middle- and upper-class woman's being and place. Certainly the most dominant of these was based upon the assumption that women were different from men in more than a biological sense and that these differences made a singular role and status as wife and mother within the home proper and inevitable. Both perspective and practice attempted to divide the world into the feminine and masculine with clearly designated traits, functions, and activities assigned on the basis of gender. A glance at phenomena as diverse as antebellum educational policies, images of women in late nineteenth-century painting, and silent screen heroines of the Twenties indicates how pervasive and influential this perspective was: all manifest the belief that women possessed characteristics that were not only innate but which fitted them for a special function in society and barred them from others.

One would expect that the needs and interests of a Victorian lady dedicated to wifehood and motherhood would stand in contrast to those of a twentieth-century working woman. Just as clearly, the life of a black female slave in antebellum South Carolina would hardly be the same as that of her white, middle-class contemporary in Boston. But if Victorian, middle-class women were universally confronted and singularly affected by rigid, gender-based conceptions, expectations, and practices, regarding their nature and role, their experiences and responses were hardly simple or uniform. An Elizabeth Cady Stanton could oppose her society's premises and urge that women be perceived as individuals with the same rights and responsibilities as their male counterparts, while wives and mothers participating in the late-nineteenth-century women's crusade for temperance could find in these same premises motivation and means to expand women's influence and role beyond the traditional domestic boundaries. Women directly involved in challenging the separation of spheres by gender could offer an alternative conception that freed women from restrictions inherent in this narrowly construed sense of being and place. Stanton and other nineteenth-century feminists, for example, developed an ideology which defined women and men as citizens of the Republic with dual, overlapping roles in the family and society. A century later, echoes of this ideology could be heard in the demand that women be accorded the same opportunities in employment as men. That the arguments were similar suggests a continuing tradition in a twofold sense: women still protested their secondary status, while segments in society sought to restrict women to that status.

In part, the choice of essays for this volume was dictated by the subjects chosen and issues raised by the papers given at the Conference on the History of Women held in St. Paul, Minnesota, during the fall of 1977. But the decision to restrict the focus of this collection has emerged as well from the belief that a volume analyzing the lives of white, middle- and upper-class women from colonial times to the present not only could provide coherence for the reader, but also would isolate significant issues in the history of these American women. The issues explored most generally are: socialization as a process which influenced the lives of women and was in turn shaped by women; wifehood and motherhood as an identity and vocation to which women responded in myriad ways but which had a profound impact upon their self-perceptions; and the emergence of women from the home.

As critical to historians as the findings of their research is the preliminary question of approach. What sources and methodologies have been developed to uncover and explicate women's past? Phrased differently, what strategies have been adopted for a search that cannot be adequately pursued solely within the constraints of conventional historiography? The essays in the first part of the volume address themselves explicitly to these questions, while those in the second part suggest the many paths open to historians. Underlying all of these essays are realizations pertinent for an understanding of women's past. Perhaps most important is the recognition that the private as much if not more than the public sphere has provided a basic context for women's lives. Not surprisingly, this fact has necessitated a search for materials that would illuminate a part of existence previously deemed inconsequential. Personal documents have proved particularly helpful in this regard. Letters, diaries, and journals can provide the basis for analysis of the individual experience of a Louisa Catherine Adams or the general experience shared by women involved in the migration westward. Just as significant are more familiar public documents. Already basic sources for research on other subjects, these data can yield insights about women's past as well: wills left by husbands and renunciations of the dower made by wives are only two examples of documents that can shed light upon the legal and societal position of women.

Directly related to acknowledgment of the private sphere as most critical, has been recognition that wifehood and motherhood have strongly influenced the content and character of women's experiences. Such is especially true for the white, middle-class women who are the focus of this collection. Harriet Beecher Stowe, for example, merged private conviction with public pronouncement in her glorification of women's role within the home. Stowe's experience as a wife and mother, however, was one in which expectations clashed with reality. The result was a life riddled with conflict and a series of novels and short stories reflecting tensions and contradictions. Others such as Juliette Low and Julia Ward Howe experienced similar conflicts. In each of their cases, a type of resolution was achieved—for Low it came through a leadership of the Girl Scouts that, in opposition to notions of female helplessness, dependence, and passivity, promoted strength, independence, and self-reliance as characteristics to be identified with women; and for Howe it came with a feminism predicated upon the potentialities and responsibilities of women's domestic vocation. Different circumstances and resolutions notwithstanding, the experiences of Stowe, Low, and Howe testify to the importance of wifehood and motherhood as a source of identity as well as vocation. The fact that the prescribed role generated conflict raises the question of whether the ideal was beyond human reach or the domestic identity and vocation were too circumscribed, rigid, and dependent upon the performance of others.

Conflict, tension, and uncertainty were not the exclusive lot of wives and mothers. Indeed, similar ambivalence can be seen in the lives of those who deviated from these expected roles. Against the background of early childhoods that allowed and even encouraged the development of traits irrespective of gender, stress, and conflict were encountered as early as adolescence. Considered the stage in maturation during which attributes of womanly behavior could and should be inculcated, adolescence for women promised a period of confrontation between antithetical pressures. Just as self-reliance, already developed within the personality, would be opposed to dependence, so individual assertion was checked by the demand for female submissiveness. Conflict was not necessarily resolved in adulthood. In fact, it was intensified for some women whose deviance was symbolized by their spinsterhood and whose lives oscillated between involvement in the sphere beyond the home and retreats into unwedded domesticity.

The attempt to ascertain the degree of conformity or deviance in the history of middle- and upper-class American women is to acknowledge that these women, indeed, were confronted with the omnipresent expectation that they fulfill the role of wife and mother within the home. But theoretical polarities do not presuppose the existence of automatons, whether in a traditional or radical mold. The responses of Louisa Catherine Adams did not duplicate those of Harriet Beecher Stowe, anymore than Elizabeth Cady Stanton's did Willa Cather's. To claim otherwise would be, to paraphrase Voltaire, to play another trick upon the female dead.

MARY KELLEY
Hanover, New Hampshire
12 January 1979

Part One

Sources and Methodology

Introduction

Exploring the range of approaches to women's experiences in the past, the essays in this section have a primary concern with sources and methodology. Historians involved in research on women have drawn upon previously neglected sources, experimented with analytical techniques, and looked to various disciplines for theory pertinent to an understanding of women. Paralleling the course taken by the "new social history," historians have applied statistical techniques and social theory to data, if not as disparate as the temporal and the eternal, at least as varied as municipal tax lists and church membership records. Whatever the data, technique, or theory, those involved in this approach have sought to establish the broad patterns of women's lives as well as to record changes in those patterns over time. Others have chosen personal documents with letters, diaries, and journals predominating. The objective has been to recover a knowledge of women's consciousness. Constructive and continuously innovative use of both avenues can provide an understanding of women's past that approaches the complexity and fullness of the lives of women themselves.

The essays by Joan Hoff Wilson and Kim Lacy Rogers are illustrative of the first approach. Aptly titled "Hidden Riches: Legal Records and Women, 1750–1825," the focus of Wilson's essay is twofold. Beginning with an analysis of legal records themselves, Wilson draws attention to the opportunites and warns of the pitfalls in the use of such materials. Hers is an analysis that cautions historians about both sources and methodology. Obstacles are inherent in the documentation itself. Not only is the evidence easily subject to misinterpretation, but the records themselves are rarely complete in the colonial and early national periods. Skills, both legal and quantitative, are at least desirable and perhaps necessary because the evidence must be placed in the context of the structure and procedures of the law, and the data must be evaluated to determine the extent to which it is complete and thus representative. The methodology chosen can also obscure more than it illuminates, especially with regard to women. Whether "internal" or "external" in their approach, legal historians, generally, have considered women only tangentially. The same cannot be said for socioeconomic historians who have turned to legal records for demographic and other quantitative information about women. They, however, are vulnerable on other grounds in that their conclusions can be biased due to ignorance of either the legal processes or the inherent limitations of legal evidence.

Nonetheless, historians with both legal and quantitative training can uncover the "riches" about women "hidden" within legal documents. Such can be seen in the second part of Wilson's essay which concerns the legal and societal position of women from 1750 to 1825. Exploring a previously neglected source, namely renunciations of dower, Wilson focuses upon the tendency on the part of women to renounce their dower rights and thereby convey to others property that was legally theirs. The striking increase in renunciations in the late eighteenth century leads Wilson to conclude a general decline in female social power—and, as Wilson notes, it was, ironically, a decline accomplished by apparently voluntary, legal means.

A case study in the quantitative approach to legal records, Kim Lacy Rogers' essay looks to probate records for insights about values and practices associated with widowhood in seventeenth-century New England. Intensive analysis of records of Essex County, Massachusetts, and the Hartford District of Connecticut between 1638 and 1681 reveals that husbands and courts protected the wife but preferred to lodge eventual control of the estate with male descendants. Granted the right of administration of estate and awarded land, along with other forms of property, a widow's actual control of such property was circumscribed. Ownership eventually rested in the hands of sons or grandsons who were accorded control once they came of age. The woman who survived her husband, however, did receive protection through a process in which inheritances were made conditional upon the heirs' continued support of the widow. Rogers' exploration of widowhood not only probes the motivations of the husbands and the courts who served in their stead but deals with the implications for women generally in a male-dominated society.

The essays written by Lillian Schlissel and Katharine T. Corbett shift to an alternative approach in the study of women. Placed against the background of individual and historical circumstances, personal documents are rich with insights concerning the content and character of women's lives in the past. Letters, diaries, and journals offer the possibility of a sustained, intimate recounting of an individual's actual experience, as well as the opportunity to examine the response to that experience. Equally important, female consciousness receives consideration. Women's perceptions of reality are revealed as well as how and why these perceptions differed from those of male contemporaries.

Just as Wilson offers a balanced commentary in regard to other sources, so

Schlissel points to the possible pitfalls as well as the opportunities involved in research based on personal documents. Taking diaries as an example, Schlissel notes that historians examining these records of response to a particular moment must decide whether they are singular or whether they are part of a configuration encompassing disparate accounts. Historians must also try to determine why diaries do not explore particular issues. It is almost expected that a nineteenth-century diary would contain little discourse on sexual relations, but information may also be lacking on other, seemingly more likely topics. The motivations of the diarists must be considered as well. The unquestioned assumption that diaries are, however private, completely unself-conscious ignores the fact that they may be consciously designed for more public purposes. The diary may serve as a vehicle for self-justification. It may as well be a chronicle of a family with an end that is more hagiographical than historical. The historian, as Schlissel says, must "learn to read the obscured patterns."

Diaries kept by nineteenth-century women on the Overland Trail are a case in point. The subject of Schlissel's essay, these diaries are examined in terms of three topics which underline the challenges inherent in the use of such materials. The diaries are replete with commentary concerning both women's response to the prospect of the journey west and their experiences once the journey was underway. And yet these women remained silent about the times when, their husbands gone, they had to assume full responsibility for the household. Diaries, then, reveal much, but they conceal as well.

Drawing upon memoirs as well as letters, Katharine T. Corbett's essay is a case study of the consciousness of Louisa Catherine Adams. Virtually forgotten by historians who have preferred to study her mother-in-law, Abigail Adams, the English-born Louisa offers an equally valuable, albeit starkly different, perspective. While Abigail personified Republican Motherhood, Louisa felt herself an alien in her family and society. Louisa's alienation did not stem from a rejection of cultural dictates concerning women. Indeed, she was fully committed to wifehood and motherhood as her only valid role and considered domesticity her appropriate setting. Rather, Louisa's disillusionment and despair were the fruits of a genuine but unsuccessful attempt to fulfill the role.

Of course, the reasons for Louisa Adams' demeaning of self, her sense of failure, derived in part from her individual personality, the relationships she formed, and the circumstances of her Life. Louisa considered herself an alien in every sense of the term. Caught between two worlds she felt herself neither English nor American. Adams perceived herself as a republican expatriate and yet found republicanism in practice, repugnant. She prided herself on having developed the qualities expected of an upper-middle-class English-woman only to find that her accomplishments were inappropriate for

America. Nor did her relationship with her husband augur well for achievement of identity as an Adams. More generally, John Quincy seems to have wanted his bride to become a Republican Mother and play a critical if limited role politically, whereby she was accorded the responsibility for rearing sons and disciplining husbands in the virtue necessary for the maintenance of the Republic. If that theoretical model were not sufficiently demanding for Louisa, there was always the more imposing and formidable figure of her mother-in-law. Clearly, Louisa Adams was drawn to neither the model nor its personification in Abigail Adams. Possessing pluck and integrity, she also refused to be intimidated by her husband or slavishly to follow his admonitions. The cost, however, was great. Louisa forsook what little possibility there might have been for a comfortable place in the Adams' circle and an intimate, satisfying relationship with John Quincy. Her relationships with her children brought more sorrow than satisfaction. The significance of Louisa Adams lies not so much in the experience of failure as in her ability to articulate that experience. Here too lies the significance of personal documents. Taken together, the memoirs and letters of Adams shed light upon the role played by large numbers of women, the inherent strains in that role, and its effect upon the conception of self.

Joan Hoff Wilson

Hidden Riches: Legal Records and Women, 1750-1825

More than ever before historians are using legal records as principal sources for socioeconomic studies of the colonial and early national periods.[1] This trend is somewhat surprising given the deteriorating condition of the originals and the often poorly catalogued and unorganized state of microfilmed projects. Furthermore, published legal series are usually so selectively edited that they do not provide the data now required by social historians. Municipal tax lists and probate records from county court houses in the form of wills, inventories, and accounts of administration of estates are the easiest to locate and consequently contemporary legal and social historians have conducted most of their research in these documents. Yet they are seldom complete for any town or region—even for relatively short periods of time. Understandably, such fragmentary evidence has produced uneven scholarly results, especially with respect to women.

Leaving the question of incomplete documentation aside, there are other reasons for the erratic quality of recent scholarship employing legal documents which relate to women. All hinge on several basic historiographical problems encountered when working with such data. Often technical legal knowledge and quantitative skills are essential to assess accurately how complete and thus how representative existing records are. Moreover, while detailed information about the procedural and substantive aspects of early legal structures exists, that information must be reassessed as applied to women. Finally, general schools of thought explaining developments in American law have to be taken into consideration to understand why

[Professor of History at Arizona State University, Joan Hoff Wilson is engaged in a study of the impact of the American Revolution on the legal status of women. Wilson's publications include *American Business and Foreign Policy, 1920–1933, Ideology and Economics: U.S. Relations with the Soviet Union, 1918–1933*, and *Herbert Hoover: Forgotten Progressive*. Her recent article, "The Illusion of Change: Women and the American Revolution," was awarded the 1977 prize of the Berkshire Conference of Women Historians.]

specialists have traditionally not investigated the early legal or socioeconomic status of women.

County court records illustrate these standard historiographical problems, while they simultaneously constitute a major "hidden" source of information about women. Because county or sessions courts existed in all of the original colonies except South Carolina, they tended to assume similar functions up and down the coast. They had both appellate and original jurisdiction and were originally staffed by "commissioners" and later by so-called justices of the peace who were not necessarily men with formal legal training before the middle of the eighteenth century. This was probably just as well because these courts often assumed more administrative functions than common-law and equity actions. They not only handled the probate matters historians are now studying with renewed vigor, but they also made a variety of regulatory and licensing decisions.[2] One study of early justice in Massachusetts lists the duties of the county courts as

> probate and administration, apportionment of charges for the
> repair of bridges, provision for the maintenance of the ministry,
> punishment of interference with church elections, punishment of
> heretics, ordering highways laid out, licensing of ordinaries,
> violations of town orders, regulating wages, settlement of the poor,
> settlement of houses of correction, licensing of new meeting houses
> and punishment of vendors charging excessive prices.[3]

In considering the specific duties of the county courts, it is also necessary to determine the significance to women of any changes over time in the functions and accessability of such judicial bodies. During the first half of the eighteenth century, for example, some colonies automatically assigned court costs to criminal defendants whether or not they were found guilty. Naturally, such a practice encouraged greater use of local courts both as a substitute for gratuitous private violence and for legitimate self-help. From a structural point of view there is little doubt that the voluntary, community-oriented county court system, as it had developed by the first half of the eighteenth century, offered women more opportunity to initiate civil actions and to utilize civil procedures than the more streamlined, impersonal, and professionalized modern legal system that began to emerge after 1787.[4]

Obviously, the legal status of women cannot be disassociated from meaningful access to the services provided by the prevailing judicial structures. Recent legal research has indicated that the independent, local courts of government were gradually transformed first into courts of law in the 1750's and 1760's and then, after the Revolution, into specialized governmental agencies performing limited routine, standardized functions.[5] The modern legal system based on centralized authority, specialization, and adherence to common-law standards of judicability ultimately replaced the undifferentiated community controlled judicial means of "conserving the peace" represented by the county courts of the colonial period. Consequently, it is entirely possible that the county courts better met the legal needs of women (and other disadvantaged groups) *before* 1776 than afterward.

Another matter of principal importance for studying women and the law lies in the fact that the historiography of American law remains largely in the hands of legal historians with law school training. This has resulted in the tendency to isolate and analyze an autonomous sphere of phenomenon known as "the law," which somehow lies outside "the society."[6] Such subordination of legal history to common-law tradition, legal fictions, and appellate court decisions has in turn led to the subordination of judicial matters affecting women because they seldom contributed to major changes or landmarks in legal history. It is characteristic of these traditional legal historians, writing what has been called "internal" legal history, to regard women as inferior or unimportant legal entities by common-law standards.[7] Practitioners of a more broadly based brand of "external" legal history, which takes into account societal influences upon the development of American law, are also generally guilty of this gender-biased approach. With the exception of Richard B. Morris and George L. Haskins, established legal historians most valued for their "neo-progressive, external" approach, namely, James Willard Hurst, Lawrence M. Friedman, Morton J. Horwitz, William E. Nelson, and Mark Tushnet give short shrift to women, if they consider them at all. At best there are perfunctory discussions by these authors about marriage and divorce laws, dowry and dower customs, and of course, sexual crimes involving women, such as fornication resulting in illegitimate children. In contrast to slave studies, for example, which struggle with the difficult question of the "transition from an analogical to a categorical system" of constitutional law for determining race relations, little has been done to investigate gender relations along these same, potentially fruitful, lines.[8]

Whether practitioners of "internal" or "external" legal history, the historians involved in research on the colonial and early national periods have concentrated their efforts upon the increased benefits of Lockean liberalism that accrued to a relatively small number of free, white males. At the same time, those adopting an "external" approach have also, along with a number of other colonial historians, consciously or unconsciously applied modernization theories to these years.[9] Unfortunately, modernization processes not only often operate in mysterious ways known only to modernization specialists, but they almost always ignore or negate the experiences of women. However one may view the concepts about modernization which have been developed by social scientists over the last twenty years, they have not been systematically applied to women in the eighteenth and nineteenth centuries.

One reason for this is that advocates of the modernization approach seldom ask themselves: were women subjected to the same set of transitional economic forces and sociopsychological pressures as men on the so-called road to modernity? Most history texts and monographs about early American history implicitly answer this question affirmatively. Indeed, this is one of the best preserved illusions of scholarship dealing with the colonial and revolutionary periods. Yet, the first leg of the journey of women into the modern world contained some distinctly different emotional and intellectual experiences, a decrease in high-status socioeconomic functions, and fewer liberalizing political-legal benefits than it did for men. This is not to say that it is wrong or inferior *not to be modern* or that modernization *theories* cannot be defined by other than male standards.[10]

In fact, one of the greatest societal setbacks for women was a direct result of legal modernization induced by new private and public laws which appeared in the United States in the first three decades of the nineteenth century. Relying largely, but not exclusively, on Blackstone's *Commentaries* as a guide in the training of professional lawyers, in reaching court decisions, and in drafting new laws, the American legal profession began to construct a new rationale for the common law because the Revolution had undermined some of its former legitimacy. Morton J. Horwitz has noted that from 1780 to 1820 judges began to abandon the eighteenth-century, natural-law concept of law and to view it as an instrument for achieving policy goals.[11] (Please note that this theoretical development took place at approximately the same time the county courts were undergoing their final transformation into administrative units with limited legal functions. It constituted in essence the ideological analogue to the structural changes then occurring in the American legal system.)

During the course of early nineteenth-century changing legal reforms, this abandonment of natural law as a theoretical base for reforming postrevolutionary American law also insured the likelihood that women's legal rights would not be given much attention by lawyers or judges. Natural-law and other Enlightenment theories, which had played such an important role in justifying rebellion against England, had also allowed such writers as Condorcet and Mary Wollstonecraft to argue for equality of the sexes.[12] Simultaneously as the legal profession abandoned natural-law theories in favor of an instrumental approach, just as political theorists, educational reformers, and those few advocates of women's rights at home and abroad adopted them to argue for greater equality between men and women.

Horwitz argues that "an instrumental perspective on law did not simply emerge as a response to new economic forces in the nineteenth century. Rather, judges began to use law in order to encourage social change...." At the same time lawyers began to play a more important role than juries in private lawmaking through their influence over state legislatures and judicial decisions. Lawyers thus defeudalized economic relations among men. But they left intergender economic relations in a feudal condition that may have been slightly worse than during the colonial period in part because of their disdain for equity procedures. [13] Consequently, legal reforms of first private and then public law were considerably less liberalizing for female than for male citizens, especially in the area of contractual relationships.

This is not to say that the colonial period represented a millennium for women's rights. What legal leniency existed arose out of economic necessity and the numerical scarcity of women in the New World—not any fundamental change in the patriarchal attitudes that had been transplanted from Europe. Moreover, equity as opposed to common law juris prudence figured as a determinant of the civil capacities of women. Among other things equity procedures provided a means for bypassing "the irrationality of the common-law status of married women. . . as the economy became more commercial." And although it appears that wealthier women were the main beneficiaries of this separate form of jurisprudence designed to achieve justice when common-law legal procedures proved inadequate, my own research is beginning to suggest that equity procedures, other than for the creation of property trusts for married women, affected more female civil actions than previously thought. Equity in essence represented a vehicle for law reform because it allowed for the defeudalization of real property by removing common-law disabilities for both men and women. In their haste to reform the laws of the new nation, the importance of equity as an agent for change and justice was lost upon a postrevolutionary generation of lawyers and judges as they turned from the original natural-law foundation of the common law to a unitary foundation for both statute law and common law. [14]

At first glance the regression in the legal status of women so evident by the end of the first half of the nineteenth century appears to have been reflected primarily by the codification of American law beginning in the 1820's and 1830's. Codification was a movement away from private law in the direction of public law based on state statutes. This also meant a more strict application of common law to women in private litigations. Codification was a "top-down" approach which simply consolidated the gradual erosion in the legal status of women by promoting rigidity through uniformity. Events leading up to codification were both more subtle and complex than it first appears. There was a stage between the end of the Revolution and the beginning of codification in which private contract law in particular began to reflect the breakdown of colonial customary law and conduct, especially at the county court level. At the same time there was a concerted effort to rid the United States of the feudal vestiges of English law such as equity trusts which had formerly protected the property of married women. Most important, there was also increased commercialization and the beginning of industrialization in the United States during this same period. As private law began to reflect a conscious tendency on the part of early United States federal judges and lawyers to use the law as a means of reform, it conveniently met the needs of early American entrepreneurs—but not generally of women.

Regardless of the exact motivation of these legal practitioners, the results were the same—customary, extralegal circumventions of laxly applied common law, for both men and women, became a less likely means of settling disputes, especially those involving property, as the courts literally began to make new private laws. Since women had already lost a number of property rights through loss of equity procedures, renunciations of dower, inheritance patterns, and other means[15] by the time of the Revolution, they were considered marginal actors at best in this process after the Revolution. Under Jacksonian democracy a popular antipathy developed toward both the legal profession and its manipulation of common law in postrevolutionary courts. This sentiment gave rise to the codification movement. Instead of democratizing American contract law or the legal system in general, however, all codification did was freeze the process where it was. Women had been "frozen out" so to speak even before codification began. Moreover, codification not only procedurally transferred authority from the courts to the legislature, it fostered significant substantive changes in the slowly evolving constitutional status of women.[16] While the power of judges and lawyers to influence private law through court decisions may have been reduced by the codification process, the result was that public laws in the form of state statutes misleadingly appeared impartial and above petty political and economic interests. In fact, this *public law* simply institutionalized a legal and economic male elite that had already been created by the early postrevolutionary changes in *private law*. Rather than achieving a redistribution of wealth or even more proprietary rights for women, Jacksonian codification concretized existing inequalities between rich and poor men, and between men and women in general.

Given the complexities of these juridical developments as well as the standard biases of legal historians, one must look to the socioeconomic specialists, most of whom do not have formal legal training, for demographic and other quantitative information about women between 1750 and 1825, if the "hidden riches" of colonial legal documents are ever to be fully utilized and placed in proper historical perspective. While traditional legal historians have concentrated on codification, appellate case-law, and the autonomous existence of a continuous body of law, most demographers and socioeconomic historians seldom have demonstrated these same proclivities. This frees the latter from the propensity to write history solely from the perspective of a lawyer, but it can lead to an antilegal or extralegal approach. Sometimes questionable conclusions are reached either out of ignorance of judicial processes, or out of the inherent limitations of court records—or both. It is not that every historian who wants to use legal documents must become a bonafide lawyer. But James Willard Hurst has aptly noted that such historians probably do need at least a year of formal legal training in order

> to read statutes, court opinions, and administrative rules and order
> with an eye to defining precisely what is being done or decided, to
> detect fictions or questions—begging, or loose or slippery concepts,
> to identifying overt or unacknowledged judicial notice or facts
> underlying rules of law, and to marking the presence of pattern,
> trend, or jumble, as the case may be, in the course of legal action.[17]

I would add that they also need such training in order to retain a basic legal perspective about the documents themselves in the course of their research. This is particularly true of demographers and other historians who use quantification in their work. The simple fact is that with few exceptions, colonial legal records specifically relating to women remain quantitatively scarce. Also, equity, rather than common-law jurisprudence, often governed the legal existence of colonial women even though only seven colonies had separate chancery courts. This meant, among other things, that womens' civil rights were determined by paralegal means like writs or commissions of *dedimus protestatem.*[18] These were issued or established in the colonies by chancery courts or their equivalents enjoining the person or persons named to perform certain legal acts. For example, most of the numerous renunciations of dower, which took place in the eighteenth century, were heard by commissions established through the procedure of *dedimus protestatem.*

Since equity jurisprudence also included divorce, most bodies with authority to end marriages evolved in this paralegal fashion before being given statutory legitimacy. Therefore, in considering changes in divorce patterns from 1750 through the first quarter of the nineteenth century, historians must be aware of the structural origins of, as well as the revolutionary hostility toward, those colonial bodies performing such quasi-chancery court functions in the New World. Consequently, any increase, for example, in the number of divorces granted just before, during, and after the American Revolution must take into consideration the defensive position of those performing what were in essence equity functions. As Stanley N. Katz has pointed out, it was not equity law that was disputed in the last half of the eighteenth century as much as it was the courts or paralegal bodies that dispensed equity.[19] Increases in divorces after the Revolution did not, therefore, necessarily reflect any more progress in the legal status of women than did the renunciations of dower which drastically reduced female economic power.

Equity jurisprudence operated like a two-edged sword as far as early American women were concerned. It provided them with some redress from the injustices of the common law, like the protection of property of wealthier women after marriage through special trusts, but it could be utilized in negative ways as well. Decline in equity procedures constituted a particular hardship on widows who were more likely to take advantage of antenuptual agreements upon remarrying than young women marrying for the first time. The virtual elimination of certain equity trusts (and dower rights) in some states led inexorably to Married Women's Property Acts beginning in the second quarter of the nineteenth century. These did not simply codify procedures as once thought, but attempted to avoid such specific disabilities inherent in premarital trusts established under equity as the absence of legal ownership and use of property. The Married Women's Property Acts, in turn generated more demands for a broadening of female civil liberties following the Civil War and led to several negative Supreme Court decisions which were not overturned until the 1960's and 1970's. An examination of the evolution of the legal fiction of marital unity leads to a similar constitutional pattern. For example, a Supreme Court case touching peripherally on the constitutional limits of state divorce laws, *Dartmouth College v. Woodward,* 17 U.S. 518 (1819), cannot be fully understood without a general review of the common-law marital prototype from 1750 to 1825 and beyond.[20] Constitutional attitudes toward women did not emerge full-blown with only sporadic Supreme Court decisions. They evolved structurally substantively at local and state levels after 1787.

The subsystem of extralegal privileges and paralegal procedures, within which American women operated from colonial times, by its private and informal nature mandated to them an inferior status that was reinforced by early constitutional developments. Changes in this female substructure of law can only be accurately gauged in retrospect. Because the Constitution did not guarantee women the same fundamental, unalienable rights it did men, their constitutional history has been one of a series of attempts to compensate for this oversight. Women represent a classical example of constitutional neglect. Moreover, their constitutional development did not suddenly begin with commonly cited post-Civil-War cases involving voting and professional rights. Because there were probably more significant Supreme Court cases which negatively affected women in the last quarter of the nineteenth century than at any other time, it is all the more important to understand the civil capacities of women prior to these landmark decisions.

Thus, in documenting a decline in the legal status of women between 1750 and 1825, I first looked at specific activities in which women engaged;[21] then I studied their treatment under equity jurisprudence; and finally I have begun to look at significant structural changes in the legal system. Employing all of these approaches, I have become more and more aware that women were more often ignored in the formation of the new laws and courts of the nation than they were consciously discriminated against by paternalistic Founding Fathers.[22] In short, then, the ultimate determinants of the negative impact of the American Revolution on the legal status of women rests less with an accounting of isolated juridic actions of women and more with the gradual erosion of access to equity procedures and with the restrictions placed upon the functions of county courts as the modern legal system emerged.

If these multifaceted aspects of equity jurisprudence and other structural considerations such as the changing status in, and accessability of, the county courts, are not carefully analyzed by demographers and socioeconomic historians, final conclusions may display exaggerations or misrepresentations about the presumed legal rights of women or their general societal condition. These interpretative pitfalls may increase to the degree that the legal origins of the data are all but destroyed or forgotten in attempts to distill and abstract them for computer analysis. Recent attempts to improve the quality of legal history by merging the disciplines of history and law have not, therefore, overcome this tendency to subordinate legal matters affecting women because they seldom constitute juridical landmarks. Although demographers and socioeconomic historians have uncovered new data about women from legal documents, their evidence is still too incomplete and fragmentary to allow for more than tentative regional or township comparisons.[23] Moreover, the general paucity of records about the civil and criminal actions of women in certain colonies and states between 1750 and 1825 places the legal status of women precariously close to being permanently beyond the reach of historians regardless of how sophisticated their methodology or intense their motivation.[24]

Even if one is dealing with all existing records relating to a particular type of legal action by, about, for, or against women—for example, tax lists, deeds, licensing, fiduciaries' accounts, marriage agreements, divorce decrees, wills written by women or naming them as executrixes, guardianships, and fornication or bastardy convictions (or other criminal prosecutions)—one is usually studying relatively few cases.[25] The most sophisticated quantitative methods cannot extract representative information from a dozen or fewer cases covering century-long periods. Probate information on women is usually so incomplete compared to the actual number of decedents that it is often an exercise in quantitative futility to attempt estimates and interpretations from such data.[26] How statistically and substantively significant, for example, can figures be that offer for a one-hundred-year period only twenty-six examples of Pennsylvania colonial women being appointed as sole executrixes from a list of wills that is probably already more than seventy percent incomplete? Or what about the significance of the fact that six percent of approximately 440 wills of colonial Georgia were written by women? (Ironically, this percentage is approximately the same as some New England and Middle colonies whose early probate records did not suffer the ravages of the Civil War as did those of Georgia.)

Despite the minute amounts of most legal data relating to women quantitative methodology probably remains one of the most innovative and rewarding approaches for analyzing such records if one wants to uncover not only the societal status of women, but also to approximate what female self-perceptions may have been. It is also possible that quantitative techniques combined with legal structural analysis will provide that still missing link in a new conceptual framework for the general writing of women's history. These lofty goals cannot be accomplished, however, without greater legal *and* quantitative expertise on the part of historians. If we are to uncover maximum information about colonial women from legal records we cannot afford to ignore either methodological approach—out of ignorance or indifference.

Let me now suggest some ways to proceed. Unlike some legal historians, I do not consider the criminal justice system the "key intercept between law and society."[27] Such an assertion seems especially questionable in the case of women. Civil regulations touched the lives of many more married and single women than did the criminal codes between 1750 and 1825. These years were also ones of periodic economic, as well as political upheaval. My own research shows that under such circumstances there was a tendency in all of the colonies for criminal actions to take a back seat to civil ones. Therefore, it is through the study of civil procedures and adjudication of civil cases that we will find the most revealing information emerging about public policy affecting the legal and societal status of women. Outside of the licensing of marriage, it would be profitable to draw up a hierarchical list of civil actions in which a substantive number of women engaged. Significance could be based initially on either percentages of women compared to men when both could entertain a particular action, or it could be based on those cases where women primarily initiated the cause for action or where they were subjected to certain gender-based statutory or customary legal practices under law or equity. Such an ordered list would satisfy the lawyer's penchant for meaningful judicability; the quantifier's search for substantive numbers; and the socioeconomic historian's desire to show the interaction between the judicial system, mainstream values, and institutional developments. I am not saying that we will be completely satisfied with any single hierarchy of civil actions, but this multilevel, systematic approach would eliminate the current haphazard tendency to concentrate on the bizarre or unique female cases, especially in the field of criminal justice, or on the random concentration of civil actions that one may accidentally come across in the course of one's research and be tempted to analyze out of context. It should also encourage historians of women to be less traditional in their choice of legal activity and to broaden their interpretations of such activities.

In particular, there is one specific kind of civil action that women engage in more often than any other except marriage, namely, the act of renouncing their dower rights at some point during marriage before the death of their husbands. These renunciations would logically head any list of civil actions in which a substantial number of women engaged.

Technically, under common law the dower came to be defined as

> an estate for life—in the third part—of the lands and tenements—
> of which the husband was solely seised either in deed or in law—at
> any time during the coverture—of a legal estate of inheritance—in
> possession—to which the issue of the wife might by possibility
> inherit and which the law gives—to every married woman... who
> survives her husband—to be enjoyed by such woman... from the
> death of her husband—whether she have issue by him or not—
> having for its object the sustenance of herself, and the nurture and
> education of her children, if any;—and the right to which attaches
> upon the land immediately upon the marriage, or as soon after the
> husband becomes seised—and is incapable of being discharged by
> the husband without her concurrence.[28]

This meant that at common law in England a widow was entitled to a life interest in one-third of the land held by her husband at *any time* during the marriage. In actual practice in colonial America, however, dower rights were usually abrogated or limited to one-third of the real property held by the husband at the time of his death.[29] Unless there was considerable wealth in the family the dower rights of most widows were not adequate for their support. The dower became an even less adequate source of basic support for widows in the course of the late eighteenth and early nineteenth centuries as renunciations increased and more legal estoppels were placed on the types of land subject to dower right claims. Moreover, from the middle of the eighteenth century dower rights were increasingly regarded as "a dormant incumbrance on a title," that is, as hindrances to land development.[30] Their reputation also suffered from the strong revolutionary rhetoric against equity-dispensing courts as a form of British tyranny.

It is not surprising to find a series of obscure, but effective, state court decisions undermining the right of dower by 1825 because it operated "as a clog upon estates designed to be the subject of transfer."[31] One of the earliest antidower decisions came in Pennsylvania, which had an unusual colonial history of *not* guaranteeing women their dowers if their husbands died in debt. Thus, in *Graff v. Smith's Administrators,* 1 Dallas 484 (1789), the Pennsylvania Supreme Court presaged other findings undermining dower rights in Massachusetts, Virginia, and New York.[32] In other words, dower rights did not facilitate land speculation and improvement, or payment of debts, especially after 1800, when the American economy began to develop at an accelerated pace.

Having said this about the declining favor in which dower rights were viewed by the American legal profession from 1750 to 1825, what additional insights can be obtained from quantitative analysis of the numerous cases of renunciation of dower, which occurred in the original colonies and new states? A random sampling and computer analysis of over five thousand cases of renunciations of dower from representative areas (an estimated twenty to thirty thousand such documents were recorded between the middle of the eighteenth century and the end of the first quarter of the nineteenth century) revealed an alarming tendency on the part of women to convey to others property that was legally theirs. Dower rights represented the largest source of "hidden riches" that colonial women possessed. Their renunciation indicates a general decline in female power—a decline that took place through apparently voluntary, legal means.

For example, from 1726 to 1787 there were 1,931 recorded cases of women renouncing their dower rights in South Carolina alone. Fifty-two percent of all these renunciations took place between 1761 and 1787—the years of greatest revolutionary upheaval. All of these conveyances by women were made, according to the offical testimony, without "compulsion, dread or fear from their husbands." Whether this is true or not these transactions represent a drastic decline in the property controlled by wealthier women in South Carolina by the end of the revolutionary period. There is strong indication from a regional and townlot breakdown that many of the large South Carolinian estates controlled by men as of 1800 were built on the basis of these renunciations. In the case of the Loyalists, less conclusive figures suggest that they tried to preserve their land from confiscation by the Patriots through conveyance by renunciation of dower rights to those not suspected of disloyalty to the revolutionary cause.

Not all of the dower right lands went to men, however. Between 1726 and 1787, 124 women received land from other women through dower renuncia- tions. While this is only six percent of the total number for these years, some female kinship patterns emerge from these figures. Most of these female recipients of renounced acreage and townlots turn out to be sisters-in-law, widowed mothers and unmarried sisters—in that order, with sisters-in-law clearly the dominant group. These ostensibly voluntary conveyances of property from married women to married or single women should not be interpreted as an example of female bonding. Rather, the estate patterns, which are reflected even in these few cases where land is conveyed to women, seem to be dominated by the male members of the two families involved. Widowed mothers and unmarried sisters received scattered portions of townlots exclusively, while sisters-in-law received contiguous improved and unimproved acreage.

The economic reality is clear even if the exact state of mind of these women who were renouncing their dower rights is not. How much duress or pressure they were under remains open to speculation. By renouncing such lands while their husbands were alive and relatively young, these women were reducing what they were entitled to inherit upon their spouses' deaths except for what was provided them through wills or intestacy laws. No amount of dowry that they brought to their marriages, or antenuptial agreements could make up for this kind of property loss during marriage.[33] Combined with figures showing diminished inheritance patterns for widows throughout the eighteenth century, these ostensibly innocuous renunciations have produced an impressive amount of information about the economic condition of an important group of colonial women on the basis of legal and quantitative analysis.[34]

"Hidden riches" clearly abound in the legal records about colonial women for those historians who want to take the time to do such painstaking research and to develop legal and quantitative skills for analyzing the riches. In the case of renunciations of dower not only do the documents themselves constitute a previously untapped rich source of socioeconomic data about women, but also the equity nature of conveyance of property through the dower right raises the possibility that equity procedures may have affected a wider cross-section of early American women than previously thought. Thus, in a double sense dower renunciations represent "hidden riches" from colonial legal records about women.

Notes

1. Edmund S. Morgan, *American Slavery American Freedom: The Ordeal of Colonial Virginia* (New York: W.W. Norton, 1975), p. 441; Lawrence M. Friedman, *A History of American Law* (New York: Simon and Schuster, 1973), p. 220; David E. Narrett, "Preparation for Death and Provision for the Living: Notes on New York Wills (1665–1760)," *New York History* 57 (October 1976): 419; Gloria L. Main, "Notes and Documents: Probate Records as a Source for Early American History," and Daniel Scott Smith, "Underregistration and Bias in Probate Records: An Analysis of Data from Eighteenth-Century Hingham, Massachusetts"—both in *William and Mary Quarterly* 32 (January 1975): 89–110; James K. Sommerville, "The Salem Women at Home, 1660–1777," in *Eighteenth-Century Life* 1 (Summer 1974): 11–21.

2. Friedman, *History of American Law*, pp. 35, 37; James W. Ely, Jr., "American
   Independence and the Law: A Study of Post-Revolutionary South
   Carolina Legislation," *Vanderbilt Law Review* 26 (1973): 958–62;
   Hendrik Hartog, "The Public Law of a County Court: Judicial
   Government in Eighteenth-Century Massachusetts," *American Journal of
   Legal History* 20 (1976): 282–329.
3. Friedman, *History of American Law*, p. 35.
4. Richard B. Morris, "Legalism versus Revolutionary Doctrine in New England,"
   New England Quarterly 4 (April 1931): 195–215. Roscoe Pound wrote
   the first work on *The Formative Era of American Law* in 1938. Also see
   his, *Administrative Law* (Pittsburgh: University of Pittsburgh Press,
   1942). For detailed descriptions about the differences between "a modern
   positivist jurisprudence that considers law the command of a soverign
   and unitary state" and local legal institutions of the colonial period which
   were "regarded as independent recipients of constitutional power and
   authority," see Hartog, "The Public Law of a County Court"; David
   Roper, "Society and Law before the Formative Era," *Reviews in
   American History* 5 (June 1977): 180–85; Harry N. Scheiber, "Back to
   'The Legal Mind'? Doctrinal Analysis and the History of Law," *Reviews
   in American History* 5 (December 1977): 458–65; and Friedman, *History
   of American Law*, pp. 32–49, 93–137.
5. The periodization cited here is from Hartog, "Public Law of a County Court,"
   p. 327. Throughout his article Hartog documents in detail how the
   "conception of undifferentiated judicial government that underwrote the
   power of a sessions court over county affairs gradually unravelled and
   was replaced by a modern conception of county government as an
   administrative agency." He further notes how the transformation was "in
   seemingly direct opposition to the ideological and constitutional struggle
   of revolutionary America to confirm the independent authority of local
   institutions against the will of the soverign" (p. 284). There was no place,
   he concludes, in postrevolutionary America "for a discretionary problem
   solver... committed to an undifferentiated conservation of the peace" (p.
   328). The work of the county courts prior to 1750 "stands as a public
   manifestation of the private needs of its public" (p. 328) and as such
   "depended on the allegiance of a local public. But by the late eighteenth
   century that allegiance was not forthcoming.... A local public had grown
   unresponsive to the values represented by an undifferentiated judicial
   government. And so that older conception of a judicial government of
   county life was replaced by a bureaucratic model of county government,
   by a conception of an institution responsible only for specific categories
   of county action and administration" (p. 329). Hartog describes the
   integrated jurisdiction of the average county court as a continuum: "At
   one extreme stood each purely administrative business as petitions to
   build roads or the repair of county buildings, at the other extreme were
   particular cases of violent or economic crime. But in the middle lay the
   great majority of the business of the court; and in the middle categories

like administrative or criminal were mixed and had only a technical meaning. Much of what we think of as the criminal practice of the court fell directly within this middle ground of moral and regulatory 'order'" (p. 323).

6. Robert W. Gordon, "Introduction: J. Willard Hurst and the Common Law Tradition in American Legal Historiography," *Law and Society Review* 10 (Fall 1975): 9–10; Morton J. Horwitz, "The Conservative Tradition in the Writing of American History," *American Journal of Legal History* 17 (1973): 275–94.

7. Gordon, "Hurst and the Common Law," *passim;* Morton J. Horwitz, "The Rise of Legal Formalism," *American Journal of Legal History* 19 (1975): 251–64; Joan Hoff Wilson, "Women's History in the Colonial and Revolutionary Periods," paper delivered at the annual meeting of the Organization of American Historians, April, 1977, and Wilson, "The Legal Status of Women in the Late Nineteenth and Early Twentieth Centuries," *Human Rights* (ABA) 6 (Winter 1976): 125–34.

8. Richard B. Morris, *Studies in the History of American Law* (New York: Octagon Books, 1974; reprint of the original 1958 edition), pp. 126–200; George L. Haskins, "Reception of the Common Law in Seventeenth-Century Massachusetts: Case Study [of Dower Rights]," in George Athan Billias, ed., *Selected Essays: Law and Authority in Colonial America* (Barre, Mass.: Barre Publishers, 1965), pp. 17–31. The consideration given by Friedman to the legal status of women in his *History of American Law* is far superior to Hurst's in *Law and Social Process in the United States* (New York: Da Capo Press, 1972). Neither of the two most recent publications by lawyers in the field of late eighteenth- and early nineteenth-century legal history focus on the specific procedural and substantive changes in the new laws of the land except perfunctorily to note the undermining of the right of dower through court decisions after 1800. See Morton J. Horwitz, *The Transformation of American Law, 1780–1860* (Cambridge, Mass.: Harvard University Press, 1977), pp. 56–58 and William E. Nelson, *Americanization of the Common Law: The Impact of Legal Change on Massachusetts Society, 1760–1830* (Cambridge, Mass.: Harvard University Press, 1975), pp. 9, 48, 228n175, 249n34, 253n100. Mark Tushnet's study of American slave law does not discuss any legal distinctions based on sex, not even the obvious question of miscegenation. See: "The American Law of Slavery, 1810–1860, A Study in the Persistence of Legal Autonomy," *Law and Society Review* 10 (Fall 1975): 120–84. For an attempt to compensate for these omissions with respect to free, white women see Albie Sachs and Joan Hoff Wilson, *Sexism and the Law: A Study of Male Beliefs and Legal Bias in Britain and the United States* (London: Martin Robertson and Co., 1978).

9. Modernization theories were first applied to developing nations in an attempt to anticipate changes and reactions to modern technology and the introduction of western social and political concepts. For bibliographies

and explanations of these theories see: *A Conference Report on The Role of Ideas in American Foreign Policy* (Hanover, N.H.: University Press of New England, 1971), pp. 54–58; Nancy F. Cott, *The Bonds of Womanhood* (New Haven: Yale University Press, 1977), p. 3; Richard Jensen, "Modernization and Community History" (unpublished Newberry paper), January, 1978. These theories are currently undergoing very critical scrutiny, especially when applied generally to broad periods of early American history. See: James A. Henretta, "Modernization: Toward a False Synthesis," *Reviews in American History* 5 (December 1977): 445–52. Henretta's piece is a critique of one recent example of applied modernization, thinking namely, Richard D. Brown, *Modernization: The Transformation of American Life, 1600–1863* (New York: Hill and Wang, 1976).

10. For example, if one uses as a reference point Kenneth A. Lockridge's idea that modernization requires a diversity of worldly experience on the part of individual members of society, there is no doubt that before and after 1776 women did not participate enough in conflicts over land, religion, taxes, local politics, or commercial transactions to be as prepared as men for the beginnings of a modern, pluralist society. It is not surprising, therefore, that women of the colonial and revolutionary periods did not demonstrate "acceptance of diversity, the commitment to individual action in pursuit of individual goals, the conception of politics as an area where these goals contest and the awareness of a national government which is at once the source of political power and framework for an orderly clash of interest." These, according to Lockridge, are the characteristics of "modern man." And indeed they are, because he is not using the term "man" in any generic sense. Women are simply not included in these descriptions of early modernization. See: Lockridge, "Social Change and the Meaning of the American Revolution," *Journal of Social History* 6 (Summer 1973): 404, 426, 427, and Gordon Wood "Rhetoric and Reality in the American Revolution," *William and Mary Quarterly* 23 (January 1966): 31, *passim*.

11. Horwitz, "The Emergence of an Instrumental Concept of American Law, 1780–1820," in Donald Fleming, ed., *Law in American History* (Cambridge, Mass.: Harvard University Press, 1971), pp. 24–25, 74, 291, 452–57.

12. For a discussion of Enlightenment theories in relation to women see: Linda Kerber, "The Republican Mother: Women and the Enlightenment, an American Perspective, *American Quarterly* 28 (Summer 1976): 187-205, and Abby R. Kleinbaum, "Women's History: Enlightenment Historiography," unpublished paper presented at the annual meeting of the American Historical Association, December 1975.

13. Horwitz, *Transformation of American Law*, pp. 17-18, *passim;* Peggy A. Rabkin, "The Silent Feminist Revolution: Women and the Law in New York State from Blackstone to the Beginnings of the American Women's Rights Movement" (Ph.D. dissertation, State University of New York,

Buffalo, 1975), pp. 31, 147; and Nelson, *Americanization of the Common Law,* pp. 165–174.

14. Rabkin, "Women and the Law in New York State," pp. 31, 40–52. *passim;* Joseph H. Smith and Leo Hershkowitz, "Courts of Equity in the Province of New York: The Crosby Controversy, 1732–1736," *American Journal of Legal History* 20: 192–226.; Mary Beard, *Woman as Force in History; A Study in Traditions and Realities* (New York: Macmillan, 1946), pp. 133–44, 158–9; Marylynn Salmon, "Equity or Submersion? Feme Covert Status in Early Pennsylvania," in Carol Ruth Berkin, ed., *Women of American History* (Boston: Houghton Mifflin Co., 1979), pp. 92-113.

15. For a loss of equity procedures see: Rabkin, "Women and the Law in New York State, " pp. 27–52; Marylynn Salmon, "Protecting the Widow's Share: Equity Law and Women's Property Rights in Early Pennsylvania," Norman Basch, "In the Eyes of the Law: The Legal Fiction of Marital Unity," and Joan Hoff Wilson, "The Legal Legacy of Mary Ritter Beard"—The last three were delivered as papers at the Fourth Berkshire Conference on the History of Women, August, 1978. For renunciations of dower see below; for declining female inheritance patterns see Joan Hoff Wilson, "Illusion of Change: Women and the American Revolution," in Alfred Young, ed., *The American Revolution: Explorations in the History of American Radicalism* (DeKalb, Illinois: University of Northern Illinois Press, 1976), pp. 416–17 notes 91–92. One example of "other" ways in which women lost property rights after the Revolution can be seen in Georgia where the well-established landgrant system for women was replaced by a more male-oriented lottery system by the early nineteenth century. See: Lee Ann Calwell Swann, "Landgrants to Georgia Women, 1755–1775," *Georgia Historical Quarterly* 61 (Spring 1977): 23–33, and Lottery Records, Land Division, Georgia Department of Archives and History, Atlanta.

16. Horwitz, *Transformation of American Law,* p. 259; Eric Foner, "Get A Lawyer!" *New York Review of Books,* April 14, 1977, p. 38; Tushnet, "American Law of Slavery," p. 135.

17. Hurst, "Legal Elements in United States History," in Donald Fleming and Bernard Bailyn, eds., *Law in American History* (Boston: Little, Brown and Company, 1971), p. 13.

18. Joseph Story, *Commentaries on Equity Jurisprudence as Administered in England and America* (Boston: Charles C. Little and James Brown, 1839), 1: 62. *Dedimus protestatem* literally means "we have given power." In English law it meant a writ or commission issuing out of chancery, empowering the persons named therein to perform certain acts, as to administer oaths to defendants in chancery and take their answers, to administer oaths of office to justices of the peace, etc.

19. Stanley N. Katz, "The Politics of Law in Colonial America: Controversies over Chancery Courts and Equity Law in the Eighteenth Century," in Fleming and Bailyn, *Law in American History,* pp. 259, 282; Nancy F.

Cott, "Divorce and the Changing Status of Women in Eighteenth-Century Massachusetts," *William and Mary Quarterly* 33 (October 1976): 589; Helena Mast Robinson, "The Status of the Feme Covert in Eighteenth Century Virginia," (M.A. Thesis, University of Virginia, 1971), pp. 19–21; Robinson, "'Under Greet Temptations Heer': Women and Divorce in Puritan Massachusetts," *Feminist Studies* 2 (1975): 183–93; Norbert B. Lacy, "The Records of the Court Assistants of Connecticut, 1665–1701," (M.A. Thesis, Yale University, 1937).

20. Rabkin, "Women and Law in New York State," pp. 1–90, *passim;* John James Park, *A Treatise on the Law of Dower; Particularly with a View to the Modern Practice of Conveyancing* (Philadelphia: John S. Littell Publishers, 1836), p. 3; Salmon, "Protecting the Widow's Share"; Sachs and Wilson, *Sexism and the Law,* pp. 77–125, 210–224; Basch, "The Legal Fiction of Marital Unity."

21. Wilson, "Illusion of Change," pp. 385–445; Sachs and Wilson, *Sexism and the Law,* pp. 69–80.

22. Rabkin, "Women and the Law in New York State," pp. 1–20, 114–28; Horwitz, *Transformation of American Law, passim;* Nelson, *Americanization of the Common Law, passim;* Cott, *The Bonds of Womanhood,* pp. 1–18; Keith N. Melder, *Beginnings of Sisterhood: The American Woman's Rights Movement, 1800-1850* (New York: Schocken Books, 1977), pp. 4–7.

23. For a general discussion of the historiographical and methodological problems facing those who try to write interdisciplinary legal history see the unpublished work in progress by Sandra F. Van Burkleo, "'An Independence Beggarly and Barren': Kentucky Land Politics, Depression, and the Case of *Green v. Biddle,"* especially draft pages 10–28. Recent quantitative studies of note include: Douglas Greenberg, *Crime and Law Enforcement in the Colony of New York, 1691–1776* (Ithaca, N.Y.: Cornell University Press, 1976); Michael Stephen Hindus, "Prison and Plantation: Criminal Justice in Nineteenth-Century Massachusetts and South Carolina" (Ph.D. dissertation, University of California, Berkeley, 1975); Hindus, "Black Justice Under White Law: Criminal Persecutions of Blacks in Antebellum South Carolina, *Journal of American History* 63 (1976): 575–99; Suzanne Lebsock, "Women and Economics in Petersberg," (Ph.D. dissertation, University of Virginia, 1977); Kim Lacy Rogers, "Relicts of the New World: A Survey of the Conditions of Widowhood in Seventeenth-Century New England," Joan R. Gundersen, "'In the Name of God, Amen': Wills, Women and Property in Virginia," and Lyle Koehler, "Women in Work and Poverty: The Difficulties of Earning a Living in Early Puritan New England," all three papers were delivered at the Conference on the History of Women, October 1977.

24. Greenberg, *Crime and Law in New York,* pp. 39, 69; Carole Shammas, "The Determinants of Personal Wealth in Seventeenth-Century England and America." *Journal of Economic History* 17 (September 1977): 679.

25. For the relatively small number of criminal cases see Michael Stephen

Hindus, "Prison and Plantation"; Greenberg, *Crime and Law in New York*. Samples of wills from Hingham, Massachusetts, from 1730 to 1786 reveal only six percent written by women for a total of ten in all. A probate sample from Tidewater, Virginia, from 1660 to 1677 revealed that only three percent of the women went through probate. See Smith, "Underregistration and Bias in Probate Records," p. 104, and Shammas, "Determinants of Personal Wealth," p. 679.

26. Although the limitations and biases of male probate records have been extensively analyzed by demographers, I have read only one article that categorically refused to compute a probate coverage estimate for women "because information about sex ratios, the free female population, and the proportion of married to unmarried women [was] so sketchy...." See Shammas, "Determinants of Personal Wealth," p. 679.

27. Hindus, "Prison and Plantation," p. 5.

28. Park, *A Treatise on the Law of Dower*, p. 3.

29. Haskins, "Case Study [of Dower Rights]," pp. 19–23; Charles M. Scribner, *A Treatise on the Law of Dower* (Philadelphia, 1864–67), 2 vols., *passim;* Robinson, "Status of the Feme Covert," pp. 23–26.

30. Alexander Keyssar, "Widowhood in Eighteenth-Century Massachusetts: A Problem in the History of the Family," *Perspectives in American History* 8 (1974): 114–119. Also see the "life estate" or "annuity" tables computing the gross value of a widow's dower right in Scribner, *Treatise on Dower*, 2: 767–69; Park, *A Treatise on the Law of Dower*, p. 2; Nelson, *Americanization of the Common Law*, p. 9.

31. Horwitz, *Transformation of American Law*, p. 58.

32. Some later cases were: *Conner v. Shepherd*, 15 Mass. 164 (1818); *Braxton v. Coleman*, 9 Va. (5 Call) 433 (1805); *Webb v. Townsend*, 18 Mass. (1 Pick) 21 (1822); *Ayer v. Spring*, 9 Mass. 8 (1812), and the following New York decisions: *Humphrey v. Phinney*, 2 Johns. 484 (1807); *Dorchester v. Coventry*, 11 Johns. 510 (1814). See Scribner, *Treatise on Dower*, for other negative holdings on dower.

33. Dowries usually took the form of livestock, household items or cash. While such goods look impressive when subjectively compared to lands given to sons they fall far short of constituting equal economic distribution between the sexes, contrary to the claims of a few demographers. See Narrett, "Preparation for Death," p. 422.

34. Since multivariate analysis is required to analyze the differences between women engaging in various civil actions up and down the east coast, I am using Multiple Classification Analysis (MCA) instead of standard multiple regression because so many of my independent variables are categorical in nature. This quantitative method allows me to avoid the problem of multicolinearity without having to create dummy variables. South Carolina dower records can be found in the South Carolina Department of Archives and History, in the record of the Court of Common Pleas.

Kim Lacy Rogers

Relicts of the New World: Conditions of Widowhood in Seventeenth-Century New England

Richard Window died in Gloucester, Massachusetts in 1665. He willed his wife Bridgett "al her wearing cloathes," a bed, a rug, and bolster "which she brought with her: and one Iorn pot: and one bras pot: whith al other things that are left: which she brought with her: of her houssal Stuff...." He named his daughter Ann his "Soule Ex-sectetrecks" and lawful heir of an estate valued at £213 25s. 6d. In April of 1666 the widow Bridgett appeared before the Essex County Quarterly Court to claim that she had brought an estate worth £40 to her marriage with Window. Since his death she had received only 30s. a year, "she being now aged and not able to work for her maintenance, and James Stephens, the overseer, not providing her even with bread or beer." Her petition, "that she had been left in a poor condition, her husband having disposed of his estate by will to his children," was referred by the General Court to the Salem Quarterly Court. The magistrates, "understanding" that Window had ordered that a cow be given to his wife after his death—though this had not been mentioned in his will—directed the administrators "to deliver that cow or another cow as good to said Bridgett." When Bridgett Window died in 1673, she left a small estate of £26 1s.1d. to her son-in-law, Nicolas Wallington, his children and to her son James Travers.[1]

Bridgett Window's petition of 1666 was one of several she made before the courts and Essex County. The widow of Henry Travers of Newbury was the second wife of Richard Window when the couple married in 1659. In 1661, she appeared before the General Court to contest the provisions of Travers' will, written before he had gone to sea in 1648. In this document, Travers had left his daughter Sara a cow and "hefer," and his son James, then two years old, his house and lands. In Bridget Window's first petition, she complained that he had given the child

[Kim Lacy Rogers is a doctoral student at the University of Minnesota. She has also done field work for the Women's History Sources Survey. Her dissertation concerns desegregation of schools and public facilities in New Orleans.]

two steers and foure akers of upland & eight akers of marsh and all the household stuffe we had, onely he gave me a bed & a coverlet which was very meane, and also I and my children was very meane in apparell: and this was the whole estate of my husband, I had not so much as a house to dwell in and left me also five pounds in debt.[2]

The Ipswich Quarterly Court had granted administration of Travers'estate to Bridgett in 1659, allowing a total of £20 to be paid to daughter Sara Wallington and her husband, and £30 to go to James Travers when he was to come of age. The rest of the estate of £92 was awarded to the widow, with "the land to stand bound for the children's portion." Richard Window repeated the guarantees of his predecessor to James Travers in his will probated in 1666, leaving him the £30 "which the Honnored Court was pleased to allow him out of his father's inheritance which lies in Necheles Waringtans hands which is his portion." Bridgett Window and her son petitioned the General Court in 1666 to transfer the case concerning Travers' will to the Ipswich Quarterly Court. That Court "saw no cause to alter the order made in Sept., 1659, for disposing of the estate."[3]

The reasons behind Bridgett Window's "poor" and "mean" legacies from the wills of two husbands can only be guessed. Perhaps she was a scold, or was improvident. Neither husbands nor courts seemed inclined to trust her with much property. Bridgett Window's story is an exceptional one. Most widows appearing in the probate records of Essex County, Massachusetts, and the Hartford District of Connecticut between 1638 and 1681 acted as administrators of estates, and inherited considerable amounts of estate capital. What the wills of James Travers, Sr., Richard Window, and Bridgett Window do suggest is a hierarchy of concerns evident in the majority of wills written in the towns of these two areas in the years studied. Probate records reveal that although most widows were granted rights of administration of estates and were awarded land, moveables, stock and household goods, their actual control of such property was limited. Ownership of fields, houses, and other means of production eventually rested in the hands of sons and daughters of property owners, demonstrating the priority of direct succession of valuables within a nuclear family. Householders and their courts exhibited a preference for awarding sons or grandsons legal inheritance and adminis-tration of estates whenever such young men were of age. Within the limitations imposed by these priorities, widows were granted property rights, ownership of livestock, and produce in ways that guaranteed continued service and obligation by family members.

In an effort to discover the material peripheries as well as the social values and practices associated with widowhood in New England, I examined 431 probated estates from Essex County and 149 from the Hartford District. Property owners whose estates were probated, and who left widows, appear in these records. Documents with incomplete information were excluded.[4] The Essex County records consist of 240 estates determined by wills, and 191 intestate cases for which no valid wills existed and in which courts distributed property among widows and their children. From the Hartford District, 103 estates with wills and 46 intestate cases were examined. The years chosen provide a glimpse of the property arrangements and social preferences expressed by several generations of householders and their courts in an early period of community settlement and growth. Economic and institutional development progressed differently in the two areas. According to William Davisson, Essex County was a commercialized region by 1680; its market, Salem, was "tied to international trade." Most of the county population of 12,461 "lived in or near towns."[5] A diversified economy is reflected in the various occupations and investments cataloged in the probate records. The Hartford District was dotted by small agricultural towns settled by men and women who had left Massachusetts for a complex of economic and religious reasons. If Linda Auwers Bissell's conclusions concerning Windsor can be applied to other towns in the Connecticut River Valley, it may well have been 1800 before this area attained the economic diversity that characterized Essex for at least half of the period studied.[6] A generational difference in the experiences of settlement, institutional stability, and economic development marked the lives of the property owners of Essex and Hartford. That they and their courts displayed a consistency of pattern in awarding land, capital, and care to their widows indicates a singular set of attitudes and assumptions about the role of women within early colonial families. (See Tables I and II.)

Wills and intestate cases involving women from both areas reveal a remarkable consistency in the administration and inheritance of property over the years studied. In general, courts followed the practices of husbands when awarding the administration and inheritance of property to relicts. Through the years, the single most important factor in determining a widow's treatment was age, an additional factor being the number and ages of children. The younger a man died, the younger his children were likely to be. Under such conditions, the widow was far more likely to control an estate

Table I. Age Distribution, 18-70 Years.

Essex: Total Age Distribution, 1640-1681			Hartford District: Total Age Distribution, 1640–1681		
18–25 Years:	62	(14.4%)	18–25 Years:	10	(6.7%)
25–45 Years:	167	(38.8%)	25–45 Years:	75	(50.3%)
45–70 Years:	201	(46.7%)	45+ Years:	64	(42.9%)
TOTALS:	430	(99.9%)	TOTALS:	149	(99.9%)

Table II. Chronological Age Distribution, 1640-1681 (Read down)

Essex County

YEARS	N	18–25	25–45	45+
1640–1645	9	3 (4.8%)	4 (2.39%)	2 (0.09%)
1646–1650	25	6 (9.67%)	13 (7.78%)	6 (2.98%)
1651–1655	32	3 (4.80%)	19 (11.37%)	10 (4.90%)
1656–1660	38	6 (9.67%)	19 (11.37%)	13 (6.46%)
1661–1665	52	6 (9.67%)	19 (11.37%)	27 (13.40%)
1666–1670	61	7 (11.30%)	19 (11.37%)	35 (17.40%)
1671–1675	96	14 (23.20%)	30 (17.90%)	52 (25.80%)
1676–1680	107	17 (27.40%)	37 (22.15%)	53 (26.30%)
1681	10	0	7 (4.10%)	3 (1.40%)
TOTALS:	430	62 (100%)	167 (100%)	201 (100%)

Hartford District

YEARS	N	18–25	25–45	45+
1640–1645	8		5 (6.00%)	3 (4.68%)
1646–1650	13		7 (9.30%)	6 (9.30%)
1651–1655	19	1 (10%)	11 (14.60%)	7 (10.90%)
1656–1660	12	1 (10%)	6 (8.00%)	5 (7.80%)
1661–1665	22	2 (20%)	10 (7.50%)	10 (15.60%)
1666–1670	18	1 (10%)	11 (14.60%)	6 (9.30%)
1671–1675	15		5 (6.00%)	10 (15.60%)
1676–1680	29	3 (30%)	14 (18.60%)	12 (18.70%)
1681	13	2 (20%)	6 (8.00%)	5 (7.80%)
TOTALS:	149	10 (100%)	75 (100%)	64 (100%)

and to retain large portions of estate capital, than was an older woman with grown sons or sons-in-law. (See Table III.) In Essex County, the widow was named sole executrix by 53 percent of all husbands who left wills, and appointed sole administrator in 86 percent of all intestate cases. She was made coadministrator in 15 percent of all wills, and in 7 percent of all intestate cases. In the Hartford District, 51.5 percent of wills named widows sole executrixes, and another 5 percent named them coexecutors. The courts appointed 76 percent of widows of intestate cases sole administrators, and 2 percent as coadministrators. (See Figures 1 and 2.)

The higher proportion of widows involved in intestate cases who were named sole administrators was primarily a factor of their age. These widows' husbands were much younger than were men who wrote wills, and their children too young to manage financial affairs. Courts guaranteed these children their "portions" upon reaching a majority, usually age twenty-one for sons, and eighteen, or age of marriage, for daughters. Fully 66 percent of

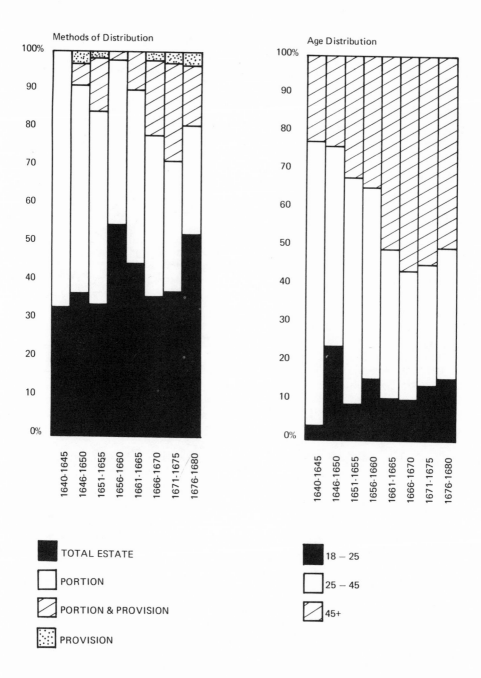

Figure 1. *Essex County, 1640–1680, Distribution of Estates*

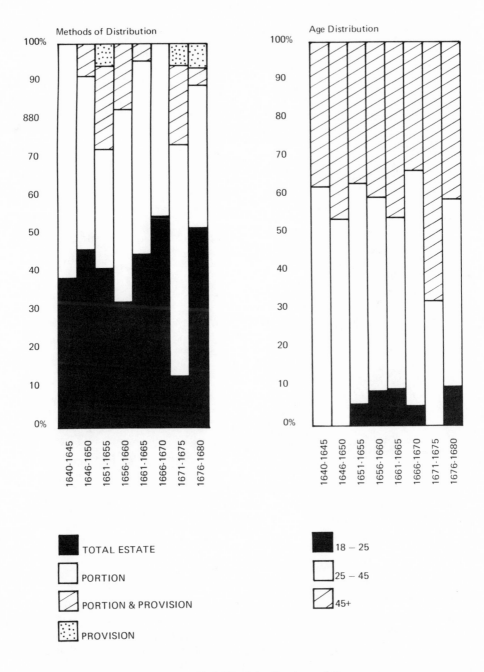

Figure 2. Hartford District, 1640–1680, Distribution of Estates

Table III. Wills and Intestates, 1638-1681

	Essex County, Mass. N = 431		Hartford District, Conn. N = 149
	WILLS		
Total:	240 (55.6%)	Total:	103 (68.6%)
Sole Executrix:	129 (53%)		53 (51.5%)
Co-administrator:	36 (15%)		5 (4.9%)
Land Inheritance:	192 (80%)		88 (85.4%)
Total Estates:	77 (31.3%)		45 (43.6%)
Portion:	101 (42%)		40 (38.8%)
Portion & Provision:	55 (22.9%)		14 (13.6%)
Provision:	5 (2%)		4 (3.8%)
	INTESTATES		
Total:	191 (44.31%)	Total:	46 (31.3%)
Sole Administrator:	165 (86.3%)		35 (76.08%)
Co-administrator:	14 (7.3%)		1 (2.13%)
Land Inheritance:	136 (71%)		40 (85.10%)
Total Estates:	100 (52%)		19 (40.43%)
Portion:	76 (39.9%)		27 (51.5%)
Portion & Provision:	5 (2.6%)		– (0%)
Provision:	1 (.05%)		1 (2.34%)

Essex County's intestate widows were either childless or had very young children. Most of the estates appearing in intestate records were small, valued well below the mean of each decade studied. The mean value of probated estates of Essex County was £177 for the first decade examined. Nine of the eleven intestates recorded fell below the mean. Four were valued between £50 and £100, and four below £50. Such estates as that of John Pease of Salem, who died in 1644, illustrate the sparse surroundings experienced by many families. Pease's estate was worth £39, and included a house, barn, and eleven acres of ground valued at £11. The livestock "five ewe goats and three lambs," was deemed worth £3 6s.; some "swyne" were valued at £1 6s. 8d. Household goods were few. Pease left a widow, Marie, and four children.[7]

The fact that widows of intestate estates tended to be made sole administrators and tended to inherit greater proportions of estate capital than women whose husbands left wills indicates that the courts understood and provided for the younger, poorer widows' need to control even scant resources in order to secure financial survival. A young widow would need whatever property existed as a second dowery to aid her in the acquisition of another mate whose labor would be required to maintain these primarily agricultural estates. (See Figure 3.)

Intestate records also feature young widows of wealthy men, some of whom were granted assistance in the administration of complex estates by kinsmen or family friends.[8] This was particularly true when an estate involved commercial investments. These women were usually awarded major portions of estate capital "for the bringing up of the children," with courts reserving guarantees of legacies to be inherited when sons and daughters came of age.[9] If the widow remarried a short time after her husband's death, the court often awarded administration of the estate to the new spouse.[10] Widows with grown sons or married daughters were often appointed joint administrators with their sons or sons-in-law—especially if the court deemed a young man the eventual heir of the estate.[11] Exceptions, of course, existed. Elizabeth, widow of Salem merchant John Turner, was appointed administrator of an estate valued at £6788 in 1680. The estate was awarded to her for the upbringing of at least four of her five children. Turner's property included numerous commercial and marine investments. Legacies were to be dispensed to the children as they came of age, but the record suggests that the widow Elizabeth enjoyed a great deal of control over an extensive and complex array of property.[12]

Evident from an examination of administration is the crucial relationship of a woman's age to her chances of inheriting and controlling property. (See Tables IV and V.) Householders and courts preferred to insure inheritance through males, and were careful to specify the double portion traditionally given eldest sons in English common-law practice. When responsible male relatives were present, they were often appointed to assist young widows. Surely, relicts were granted more extensive control over estates, and larger

Table IV. Control of Estate and Age, Executors

Essex County

AGE	WIDOW	WIDOW & OTHER	OTHER	TOTAL
18-25	59 (95%)	2 (3%)	1 (1.6%)	62 = 100%
25-45	139 (83.2%)	12 (7.1%)	16 (9.5%)	167 = 100%
45+	97 (48.25%)	37 (18.4%)	67 (33.3%)	201 = 100%

Hartford District

AGE	WIDOW	WIDOW & OTHER	OTHER	TOTAL
18-25	8 (80%)		2 (20%)	10 = 100%
25-45	51 (68%)	3 (3.9%)	21 (27.6%)	75 = 100%
45+	29 (45.3%)	3 (4.68%)	32 (50%)	64 = 100%

Table V. Age and Inheritance of Land, 1640-1681

Essex County

AGE	LAND	NO LAND	TOTAL
18–25	34 (55%)	28 (44%)	62 (100%)
25–45	142 (85%)	25 (14.97%)	167 (100%)
45+	151 (75.12%)	50 (24.87%)	201 (100%)

Hartford District

AGE	LAND	NO LAND	TOTAL
18–25	9 (90%)	1 (10%)	10 (100%)
25–45	65 (86.8%)	10 (13.15%)	75 (100%)
45+	53 (82.8%)	11 (17.18%)	64 (100%)

guarantees of property in the absence of these younger and older men. Whenever estates had not been previously divided among children, and when sons and sons-in-law were available, property owners and their courts preferred to insure the inheritance of land and capital through the young men of the family. Such arrangements often involved elaborate divisions of fields, livestock, utensils, and household space.

A majority of men who possessed land willed it to their widows; intestate courts almost always awarded some portion of whatever land existed in an estate to the relict. Land was willed in the form of rights to house, houselot, and/or agricultural property of marshes, uplands, orchards, and gardens. It was given to widows in 80 percent of the wills in Essex, and in 71 percent of intestate cases. In the Hartford District, 85 percent of wills and intestate judgments awarded land of varying value and size to widows. Many of the smaller intestate estates did not include land. Women who were willed land seldom received rights to sell or dispose of it. The man who left his wife property to be enjoyed during her widowhood always specified the heir after her death or remarriage. Husbands frequently specified that, should the widow remarry, generous holdings willed to their wives would shrink to a legally guaranteed "widow's third" of the husband's personal property and real property. Estate property would then pass to specified sons, daughters or grandchildren, as it would at the widow's death.

According to Alexander Keyssar, Massachusetts law granted the widow of an intestate "one-third of her husband's personal property forever and one-third of his real property, lands and houses, as a life estate or dower." If the real estate were not divisible, the widow could be given "in a special and certain manner, as of a third part of rents, issues, or profits" of the estate. A widow could not legally sell property; under English common law, she "could not be an heir," and had "no rights of succession." Keyssar sees the widow's

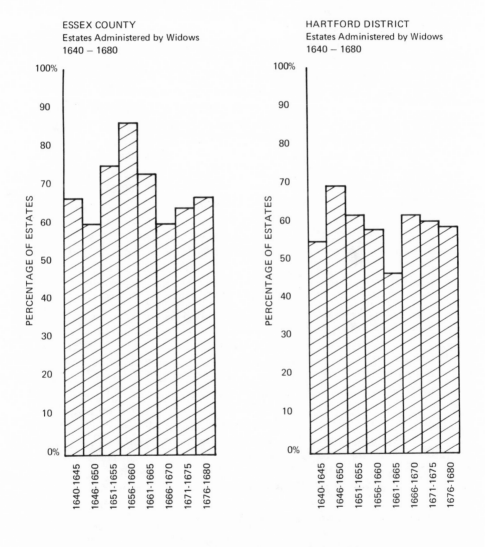

Figure 3. Essex County and Hartford District, Estates of Which Widows were Sold Administrators

thirds "in real property [as a] kind of trust fund, designed to give her support while protecting the estate and line of succession." He notes that provisions in Connecticut as well as Plymouth Colony closely resembled those of Massachusetts.[13]

The inheritance of land, and the appointment as administrator of an estate, varied according to a woman's age, the size of the estate, and the gender and age of living children. The evidence indicates that this was due to the preference for awarding young male heirs the administration and possession of estate property. The methods by which such possession and control were granted young men usually involved obligations to support and assist the widow—whether she was his mother, mother-in-law, or, occasionally, his grandmother. Widows were maintained by four general arrangements: total estate, portion, portion and provision, and provision.

Widows inheriting total estates received property ranging in value from the tiny estates of the very young—sometimes as little as £10—to estates over £1000—such as the £1600-estate willed by Governor John Endecott of Boston and Salem to his wife Elizabeth in 1666.[14] Widows with grown children, whose husbands had previously awarded grown sons and daughters their inheritances, were most frequently willed total estates by husbands, or granted them by courts. Since in so many of these cases sizable amounts of property had not been accumulated, or had already been awarded in inheritances, estate values were frequently low—below or slightly above £200. One such estate belonged to Lawrence Leach of Salem, aged eighty-five when he willed his wife a total estate of £138, from which £50 was owed in debts. Their house and two acres of land were valued at £30, a mill listed at £40, a "Basket with other lumber" worth 5s. The "2 Cowes, a heyfer & a Calfe" were assessed at £12, and "5 small swine" at £4. Household goods were spare, and included two feather bolsters, three feather pillows, a coverlet, two rugs, two blankets, a featherbed, and two flock beds. The couple had two pair of sheets and "3 pillow beares," and one single sheet. Their bedstead and chest were valued at £1 10s. Cooking utensils included three dishes, three old brass kettles, and a skillet, a "Chafindish & 1 Candlestick, 2 Iron pots & a skillet.[15] Total estates were granted to widows in 31 percent of Essex County wills, and in 52 percent of intestate inheritances. The larger proportion of total estates awarded through intestate proceedings reflects the ages of the women as well as the size of the estates themselves. Some 44 percent of Hartford District wills awarded widows total estates, and court proceedings granted 40 percent of intestate widows total estates. Courts often awarded total estates to young widows "for the bringing up of the children."

Similar proportions of widows were granted portions of estates, usually amounting to the legal "widow's third" of valued estate properties, and often more. Widows with adolescent children, or with grown sons and daughters awaiting inheritance, were often left portions by husbands and courts. Some 42 percent of Essex wills, and 39 percent of those of Hartford, specified portions as widows' inheritances. Intestate courts awarded 40 percent of Essex cases, and 51 percent of Hartford cases portions of estates.

Widows with numerous grown children were maintained by portion and provision in 23 percent of Essex wills, and 13.6 percent of those of the Hartford District. By this method, a woman was left a portion of an estate's moveable property, rights to a room in her husband's house, and a guarantee of services to be performed by the son or sons with whom she would live during her widowhood.[16] Sarah Short, wife of Henry Short of Newbury, Essex, was cared for in this way. In 1673, she was willed £100, "to be paid out in stock," and £8 per year, "part in good marchantable wheat and part in good marchantable barley or barley malt." She was willed a third of the household goods, and was granted the "new parlour for her own use withall furniture within with free egresse and regresse...." Her son Henry was to keep two cows for her, wintering them at his own expense, and was to fetch and cut wood for his mother, and maintain any swine and fowl she chose to keep. The widow Sarah was also willed the use of a small garden, two rows of apple trees, a horse "at her command and one to attend her as she hath occasion," and free "egresse and regresse into the Bakehouse for Bakeing and Washing." All of this was conditional. The estate, worth £1842, had housing, barns, orchards, and lands valued at £1250. Except for ten acres willed to the daughter Sarah, the son Henry was heir to this property. Henry Short specified in his will that the provisions of comfort and service depended on the widow's assent to "quit her clayme to any thirds of my housing or lands."[17] This was common practice among men who maintained their widows by portion and provision, reflecting a conviction that economic decisions should be made by young men whom they named their heirs.

Portion and provision was a method by which men willed their wive's services rather than control of major shares of land and capital, reserving for young men the privileges of estate management. It was a method favored by men with five or more grown children. In Essex County, children appeared more numerous in the records of men who chose portion and provision, than in the wills of those who left their widows total estates or portions (Figure 4). Fifty percent of these Essex men mentioned grandchildren in their documents. This indicates that these property owners retained control over lands, buildings, and productive capital until death. In many of their families, at least some grown sons and daughters had not been awarded full inheritances, and remained dependent upon the fathers who bound them into service to their mothers in return for eventual autonomy.

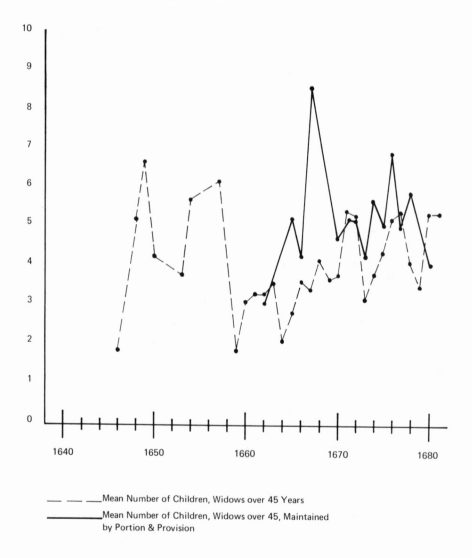

— — — Mean Number of Children, Widows over 45 Years

Mean Number of Children, Widows over 45, Maintained
by Portion & Provision

Figure 4. Essex County, 1640–1680, Children and Widows Over 45

Precise motivation for the choice of portion and provision is not always clear. The elaborate nature of the prescriptions points to differential treatment of family members, to the rewarding of favored children and grandchildren, and, sometimes explicitly, to the slighting of others. Tension and conflict are often suggested by a writer's compulsion to detail every comfort that a widow might enjoy in a dwelling almost certainly shared with a daughter-in-law. Often included in guarantees of service to widows were special rewards for favored heirs—the sons, sons-in-law, or grandsons appointed executors of estates.[18] The favoritism expressed in the special treatment of a grandson often seemed a function of a couple's age, and of the previous division of an estate. In such instances, the grandson was obligated to live with his grandmother, and to maintain estate property. These arrangements were not without potential conflict. William Clark, Sr., of Haddam, willing an estate of £412 in 1681, ordered that his grandchild Thomas Hubbard be at the disposition of the widow, and taught to read and write. If "son" Hubbard "make any trouble about him," warned the old man, "he shall satisfy for his bringing up."[19] Thomas Lee of Ipswich, leaving an estate of £198 in 1662, named his grandchild Richard Lee heir to half of his estate, obligating him to live with his grandmother until age twenty-two—"if she willed it." If the widow did not prefer this arrangement, Richard was to be bound out until age twenty-two, at which time he would inherit his portion.[20] The records indicate that the grandson named heir usually lived with his grandparents at the time the husband wrote his will. The absence of any mention of a child's mother in these crucial documents implies that such a favorite was at least a partial orphan before he was named an heir.

Still other evidence of conflict and differential treatment appears in other portion-and-provision documents. Thomas Treadwill, Sr., of Essex, ordered his widow "not to bring in my sister Bachellor to molest the familye."[21] Thomas Wells of Ipswich granted his youngest son Thomas £250 when he would come of age, enjoyment of the parlour chamber of his dwelling, with liberty for firewood "until he marrye," the possession of all books "bought for his use," and £20 "for his chardges of going to the college and for books and apparrell." Wells also arranged for the education of his daughter Hanah by "Misteris Marye Rogers of Rowley" until her marriage. Wells had eight children. Apparently four were married. His eldest son Nathaniel was named executor of the will and eventual heir to the estate valued— before legacies—at £1040.[22]

Portion and provision may thus be seen as a method that allowed property owners to bind their sons in service to their wives and their works, to guarantee the physical rights and comforts of widows in potentially anxious domestic situations, and to attempt the resolution of existing family conflicts by legally prescribing differential rewards to deserving family members. It was a method by which estate land was guaranteed to male heirs, whether these were sons, sons-in-laws, or grandsons. And it provided a widow with that which she may have needed most: financial support, physical comfort, and household privileges. That the documents sometimes bristle with wrathful prose is not surprising: many of these men seem to have been prosperous patriarchs, domestic tyrants bent on insuring their widows the privileges and domestic autonomy enjoyed in an active married life.

The intestate courts of Essex awarded only 2 percent of the widows appearing before it portion and provision, and the Hartford District courts awarded none. Depending as this method did on the guarantee of an heir's labor, it was seldom a desirable option for a court. Most intestate widows had underaged children rather than grown sons. In Essex, over 80 percent of widows with grown children were willed their estates; 30 percent of these women were cared for by portion and provision. In the Hartford District, over 89 percent of widows with grown children received inheritances through wills, and 20 percent were maintained in this fashion.

A final method by which a tiny number of women were maintained was that of provision. Used infrequently, it implied care and service by sons, and no property in the form of moveable goods or stock. Only 2 percent of Essex wills stipulated this care, and courts assigned it only once (.5 percent). In Hartford, 4 percent of wills specified provision, and the courts awarded it once. Provision left widows considerably less potential leverage within families. It appears to have been used when the widow was aged, infirm, or senile—when she was no longer capable of ordering the details of her life.

The proportions of widows acquiring land declined in Essex County and the Hartford District after 1665 (Figure 5). Fluctuations within that decline, and in the proportion of widows awarded sole administration seems related to the age and economic structures of the probated population. Essex was settled earlier than Hartford; accordingly, it contained a higher proportion of older widows who were less likely to control land than were the relatively younger widows of the Hartford District's probates.

Essex County, a rapidly growing agricultural, mercantile and maritime district in this period,[23] also had a higher proportion of very young widows listed in its probates than did the Hartford District. This was particularly evident in the first two decades examined. Thus, very small estates appeared in greater proportion in Essex probates than in those of the Connecticut towns. Over 76 percent of Essex widows inherited estates valued under £200 between 1640 and 1650 (Figure 6). Over 75 percent of these women had underaged children. And even though the percentage of estates awarded as total estates is nearly identical for the two five-year periods of 1640–45 and 1646–50, the proportions of probated wealth are not. Total estates granted

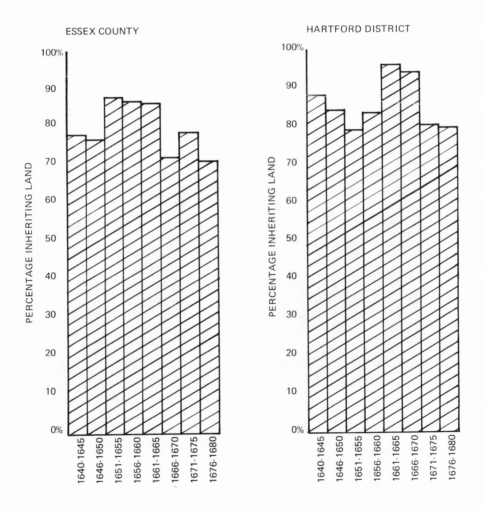

Figure 5. Essex County and Hartford District, Land Inheritance of Widows

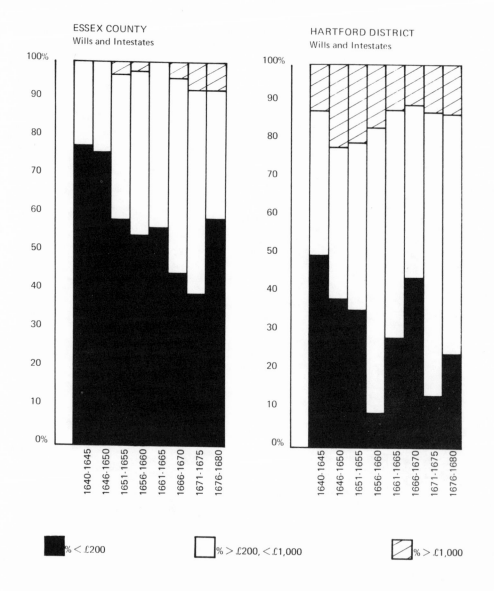

ESSEX COUNTY
Wills and Intestates

HARTFORD DISTRICT
Wills and Intestates

% < £200   % > £200, < £1,000   % > £1,000

Figure 6. Essex County and Hartford District, Estate Values

to the very young (who made up 24 percent of the widows between 1646 and 1650) represented less than half the proportional value of total estates dispensed during the previous six years—when those in the youngest group were only 4 percent of the widows appearing in Essex probate records (Figures 1, 2, 7). Wills listing adult sons and daughters increased after 1665, and with them the percentage of probated wealth dispensed through portion and provision. Larger percentages of older widows corresponded to their declining acquisition of land. (See Figure 8.) In the diversifying economic world of Essex County, several trends appeared. Widows' chances of inheriting all or major portions of extensive estates diminished. In these probates, as in others, wealth corresponded with age. Widows old enough to enjoy the benefits of capital accumulation stood little chance of exerting much control over lands, investments, and great numbers of livestock. (See Figure 9.)

There were exceptions. Widows of merchants and ministers, often owners of estates valued near or over £1000, were frequently granted total estates, or major portions. Even among these women, inheritance seems to have been a function of their childlessness, or of previous dispensation of estate property to heirs. Mary Rogers of Rowley, Massachusetts, was willed an estate valued at £1661 by her husband, the Reverend Ezekiell Rogers. Mary Rogers was charged with the education of at least one of the daughters of the prosperous Thomas Wells of Ipswich. Her husband's will listed no children. Of four merchants with grown children, two left widows total estates, one a considerable portion of an estate worth £2050 in 1674, and one, portion and provision. These widows most often inherited capital in the form of rights to housing and land, rather than the control of investments. Elizabeth Price, widow of Salem merchant William Price, was willed a major portion of his £2058 estate in 1674. Her share included a house and houselot valued at £400, and lands valued at £600. She was to live in the dwelling with her son John, who was to manage the estate. She was also directed to pay out "a portion... what she think meet, to Wm Price ...according as he shall behave himself."[24]

Data from the Hartford District reveal similar trends, altered slightly by different geographic and economic circumstances. Settled after 1635, the Connecticut communities were populated largely by people who had migrated first from England to Massachusetts Bay. A prominent complaint of many Connecticut settlers was that their original land grants in Massachusetts had been too small for comfortable maintenance.[25] These communities bore characteristics of frontier towns; the probates lack the clusters of very young widows, very old, and very poor that appear in the Essex documents. Between 1636 and 1650, only two men mentioned grandchildren in wills probated in the Hartford District. Between 1651 and 1655, six out of thirty-

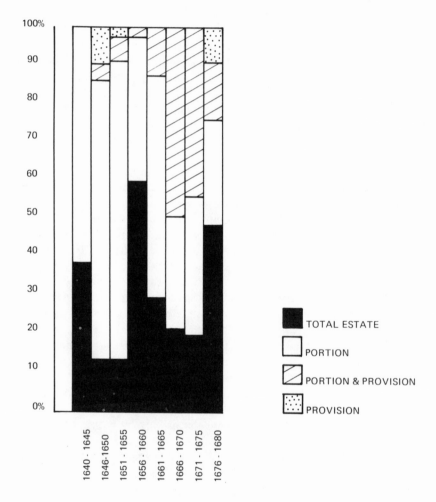

Figure 7. *Essex County, Probated Wealthy, Methods of Distribution*

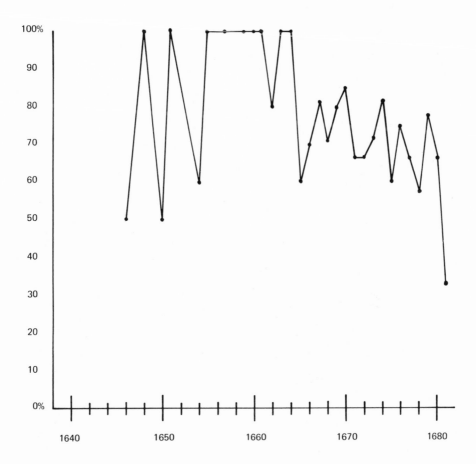

Figure 8. Essex County, Land Inheritance by Widows

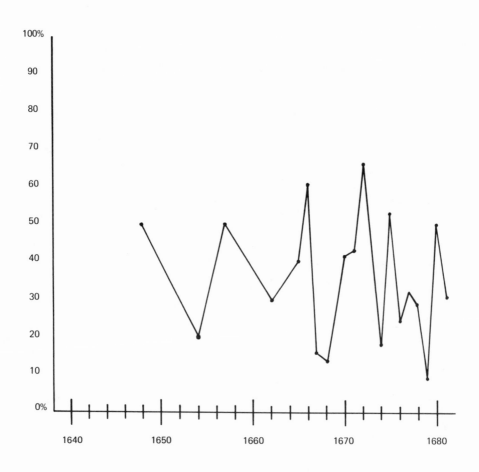

Figure 9. Essex County, Portion and Provision Inheritance by Widows

one estates probated were left by men who left legacies for grandchildren. During this period, the proportion of estates valued below £200 was far lower than that of Essex, reflecting, perhaps, the opportunities attendant with first land grants in new communities, and the access to courts enjoyed by the prosperous. The paucity of small estates may have been a consequence of less formal arrangements made by families for whom visits to the magistrates would have involved financial and geographic inconvenience.

In Hartford probates, control of land shared the same relationship to age and wealth as it did in the Essex documents. When women with young children constituted half of the widows of the probates—as they did between 1640 and 1655—total estates and portions dominated the patterns of property distribution. Between 1666 and 1670, 66 percent of widows documented had underaged children. In that period, 55 percent of all widows were granted total estates, which also accounted for 55 percent of the probated wealth distributed in that period (Figure 10). Not surprisingly, 45 percent of estates probated were worth less than £200, a percentage unmatched since 1640–45, when half of the estates presented to the court were valued under £200. When portion and provision was most frequently used, the proportion of wealth distributed by that method far exceeded the proportions of widows maintained by its guarantees. Between 1671 and 1675, when 78 percent of Hartford's widows had grown children, over 22 percent of these women were maintained by portion and provision. Their husbands' estates accounted for over 33 percent of the community's probated wealth.

Patterns similar to those of Essex County emerged, but they were bound by different constraints. More of Hartford's older widows received land than did those in Essex. The probated population appeared more prosperous in these Connecticut towns (Figure 10). The scarcity of very small estates corresponds with Linda Auwers Bissell's findings on Windsor, Connecticut. That town featured a persisting population characterized by inclusion in the community's original land grant, family ties within town, and participation in church activities.[26] Probate records confirm this portrait of prosperous persisters. Estates valued below £200 constitute a smaller proportion of probate records in the Hartford District than they do in Essex County. The Connecticut River towns also had proportionally more estates valued over £1000. Such data accord with Bissell's judgment that the economically disadvantaged of Windsor migrated throughout this period to newer communities in search of opportunity. If this occurred throughout the Hartford District, young men and couples may have migrated until able to find and claim a sufficient stake for future prosperity, whether in the form of a land grant of some other option. The age structure drawn from the Hartford District's probates reflects the demographic truism that people migrate at times or life changes: hence the scarcity of the very young, and the

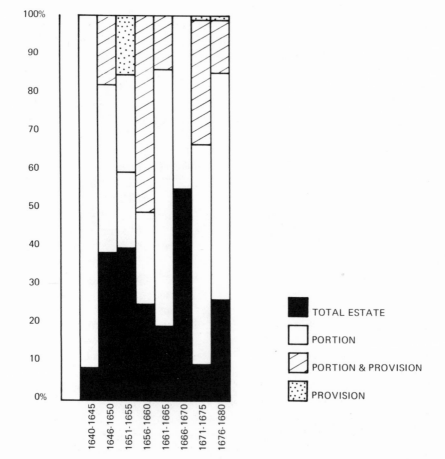

Figure 10. Hartford District, Methods of Distribution

very old, in these early documents.

Although a majority of widows in the areas examined received estate capital in fairly stable patterns, widows of the Hartford District had greater access to land, moveables, and administration than did the women of Essex. This was perhaps due to the relatively less settled and commercialized economy of the Connecticut River Valley in the first generations after settlement. Davisson suggests that agriculture held less importance in the economy of Essex County in the decades preceding 1680.[27] If this is true, the privileges associated with rights to land may have had less value than those granted in an area more dependent upon agriculture. Too, land might have been more available to the men of the Hartford District, who could thus have divided it among wives and children with greater frequency and generosity.

Despite differences in inheritance, it is clear that the majority of widows represented in the probate records of these two areas inherited control of estates and received advantageous proportions of estate capital. Substantial numbers of widows received control of their financial affairs after their husbands' deaths. For many, this must have been more of a burden than a blessing: many hardships must have beset a young woman with four small children and an estate valued below £30. For the twenty-nine Essex widows whose records indicate remarriage within months of their husbands' deaths, economic pressure must have been a consideration in some of these hasty unions. Twenty were left holdings valued below the mean of all estates probated in that five-year period. Ten of these women had five or more children; twenty-three received their property through intestate proceedings. One such woman was Sarah Lampson, who remarried within months of her husband's death in 1659. She was awarded a portion of her husband's £111-estate by the court, the rest reserved for her eight children.[28] Hartford probates detail similar situations: nine out of nineteen widows who remarried quickly after their husbands' deaths had five or more children. Seven had estates listed below £200. A woman such as Ann Hillier, widowed in 1655, faced a desperate future. Her husband left property worth £39, which the court divided among the widow and her eight children. Twelve of the women who remarried hastily had received their property through intestate decisions.[29]

We cannot precisely determine the economic power and personal autonomy of colonial widows from this study of probates. Women left total estates and portions were addressed in language similar to that used by men who bequeathed their wives portion and provision inheritance. In wills that framed the latter, the privileges of widows, legacies to family members, and obligations of sons or grandsons were much more painstakingly itemized, perhaps because the widow was to share her home with the family of an heir. Perhaps, too, the numerous children listed in these wills had long engaged in rivalry over the undivided estate, which created the necessity for careful delineations of legacies by their tenacious fathers. The elaborate descriptions of rights awarded widows may well have been a recognition of and accommodation to the territoriality of family members anxious to possess valued household items and limited spatial resources. The widows who were granted horses, fowl, cattle, gardens, flax and rights to parlours, bakehouses, kitchens and cellars were assured domestic prerogatives, and, thus, a certain amount of control within the household and family. Such rights were guarantees of continued economic and familial function within domestic hierarchies arranged with great care by their husbands—men who often dispensed praise, blame, and differential rewards in their wills. These rights and legacies must have amounted to a widow's continued control over crucial aspects of a woman's sphere—the household and family. This was true for women who received portion and provision dispensations, and even more pronounced for women given total estates or portions.

Property owners and their courts entrusted women with economic control over lands and goods of estates of all sizes in the communities studied. The eventual heirs of such property were almost always offspring; eldest sons figured most importantly in the inheritance of land and capital. Property awarded widows insured further service and attention from remaining children and grandchildren. Arrangements made by men and courts affirm that family patterns in these areas were primarily nuclear; an elderly widow was expected to live in a household headed by one of her children or grandchildren. Men rarely willed two heirs the same farm or dwelling. Rights were granted to particular pastures, buildings, rooms, pieces of clothing, furniture, garden plots, and even, in some cases, to minutely described and named individual horses and cows. There is no indication that several related families shared accommodations granted by wills or courts.

Men and courts preferred to invest eventual ownership of land and capital in male descendents. They protected widows by making that inheritance conditional upon heirs' continued support: sons and grandsons were obligated to live and work in buildings and fields controlled at least in part by their mothers. These patterns suggest a patriarchal structure of inheritance mitigated by men anxious to guarantee security and comfort to women whose domestic functions were dependent upon the interest and effort of male relatives.

Long-term economic control of sons may have been one of many opportunities available to property owners for extended domination of family life in this patriarchal, resource-scarce society. Control of heirs through rights willed their mothers indicated concern for stable family relations, and for the continuous succession of estates. It also suggested a desire to reward the most deserving and most favored of potential heirs by the legacy of land, capital, and obligation. The binding rewards dispensed by many of these men implied a desire to envelop their sons and grandsons in the material structures and achievements of the lives the patriarchs were leaving; to proclaim homage to the lives of the fathers by making them the destiny of sons. The rights of the property owners were sustained and acknowledged in the goods and services willed to their widows.

Notes

1. *The Probate Records of Essex County, Massachusetts,* Vol. II, 1665–1674 (Salem, Mass.: Published by the Essex Institute, 1917), pp. 14–16, 381–382. I am indebted to Barry Levy, Sandra Van Burkleo, John House, and Russell Menard for their generous advice and comments on this essay.
2. Ibid., Vol. I, pp. 293-294.
3. Ibid., Vol. I, pp. 293–294; Vol. II, pp. 14–16.
4. Probates were not used if determination of the age of the husband, age of the widow, value of the estate, or crucial heirs of large amounts of estate property was impossible. If seemingly critical instructions, properties, or valuations of property were absent from the record, the document was not included.
5. William I. Davisson, "Essex County Price Trends: Money and Markets in Seventeenth-Century Massachusetts," *Essex Institute Historical Collections* 103 (April 1967): 163.
6. Ibid., p. 167. William I. Davisson, "Essex County Wealth Trends: Wealth and Economic Growth in Seventeenth-Century Massachusetts," *Essex Institute Historical Collections* 103 (October 1967): 291–342; Linda Auwers Bissell, "From One Generation to Another: Mobility in Seventeenth-Century Windsor, Connecticut," *William and Mary Quarterly* 31 (January 1974): 79–110.
7. *Probate Records of Essex County,* Vol. I, p. 42.
8. Ibid., Vol. II, p. 265.
9. Ibid., Vol. III, pp. 394–395.
10. Ibid., Vol. II, pp. 307–308.
11. Ibid., Vol. I, pp. 185–186.
12. Ibid., Vol. III, p. 399.
13. Alexander Keyssar, "Widowhood in Eighteenth-Century Massachusetts: A Problem in the History of the Family," *Perspectives in American History* 8 (1974): 100–101.
14. *Probate Records of Essex County,* Vol. II, pp. 38–42.
15. Ibid., Vol. I, p. 389.
16. Ibid., Vol. II, pp. 45–46, 52, 225–226; Charles W. Manwearing, *A Digest of*

Early Connecticut Probate Records, Vol. I, Hartford District, 1635–1700 (Hartford, Conn.: R. S. Peck and Co., 1904), pp. 11, 211, 171, 327, 346, 312.

17. *Probate Records of Essex County,* Vol. II, pp. 345–346.
18. John Demos, *A Little Commonwealth: Family Life in Plymouth Colony* (New York: Oxford University Press, 1970), pp. 59-127.
19. *Early Connecticut Probate Records,* Vol. I, p. 290.
20. *Probate Records of Essex County,* Vol. I, p. 373.
21. Ibid., Vol. II, p. 239.
22. Ibid., Vol. II, p. 63.
23. Davisson, "Essex County Wealth Trends," pp. 291–342.
24. *Probate Records of Essex County,* Vol. III, pp. 329, 362; Vol. II, pp. 405, 416-420.
25. Mary Jeanne Anderson Janes, *Congregational Commonwealth: Connecticut, 1636-1662* (Middletown, Conn.: Wesleyan University Press, 1968), pp. 4–35.
26. Bissell, "From One Generation," pp. 79–110.
27. Davisson, "Essex County Wealth Trends," pp. 340–342.
28. *Probate Records of Essex County,* Vol. I, p. 282.
29. *Early Connecticut Probate Records,* Vol. I, p. 127.

Lillian Schlissel

Diaries of Frontier Women: On Learning to Read the Obscured Patterns

Women's participation in the daily life of the westward migration is a subject that has only recently come into the range of historical interest. Historians of an earlier generation, for the most part, were not trained to be interested in the daily lives of ordinary people. The homesteader's wife is "there," but she is rarely noted as a personality with whom history should be concerned. She is like the Indian in the riddle retold by the historian David Potter: a big Indian and a little Indian are sitting on a fence. The little Indian is the big Indian's son, but the big Indian is not the little Indian's father. How, asks the riddle, can this be? To sensibilities sharpened by the last decade of consciousness-raising feminists, the reply is simple: the big Indian is the little Indian's mother. But the riddle for generations hid her identity—from children who were puzzled by the question, and from historians who were the children grown up. Historical writing has never told us very much about the home-steader's wife or the Indian's mother. Historians, however, are beginning to understand the need to know more about the mothers of Indians and the mothers of Americans. We are beginning to recognize that more should be known about the interaction between family roles and social roles, between social dynamics and human dynamics.

One avenue toward gathering that knowledge lies in the diaries, letters, and personal narratives left by the men and women of any given period. These are papers that often have been designated as trivial, relegated to special collections, to family and local histories, and to attics. Nevertheless, they survive in large numbers and offer a new vantage point, a new perspective upon historical events. Personal narratives, however, require that the histori-

[Director of the American Studies Program at Brooklyn College, City University of New York, Lillian Schlissel has written several articles on the lives of women and their families on the frontier. Schlissel's other publications include *The World of Randolph Bourne* and *Conscience in America*. Her current project, *The Women's Journey,* a book on the diaries of women on the Overland Trail, will be published by Schocken Books. Research for this essay was supported by a summer grant awarded by the American Council of Learned Societies.]

an learn additional skills, for as diaries offer new insights, they also present new problems for the writing of history. These documents are accounts of singularities; they record the particular moment and the personal response. The historian must determine whether they are merely idiosyncratic and anomalous, or whether they form part of a larger configuration that contains and explains disparate accounts.

Diaries also conceal information. If one is working on the nineteenth century, one anticipates reticence about subjects such as sex, childbirth, and marital relationships. But personal narratives conceal information in surprising areas. The nineteenth-century diary was often a kind of family history or souvenir meant to be shared much like a family Bible. The men and women who recorded the events of their lives intended that record to be handed down through successive generations like a wedding photograph. And like the wedding photograph, the diary was an account of the family's public life. The internal construction of these narratives is premised upon a conception of the family as upwardly mobile and worthy of note. The historian will search for information about failures and frustrations, the pressure points of daily life, but he or she will need psychological insight and sensitivity to language in order to recognize when significant issues are obscured and omitted.

In the case of the emigrants who followed the Overland Trail to California and Oregon between 1840 and 1870, diaries and journals abound. The westward journey is one of the best chronicled events in all of American history. Even when the focus is narrowed to diary accounts written only by women, the researcher's task is not to locate materials but to keep from being inundated by them.[1] Women may have been unnoticed by historians but they were certainly not silent in their own times. Indeed, frontierswomen were a particularly vigorous and opinionated group. They were literate and observant. Their lives and their conditions differed, but their diaries and journals provide striking information about what the westward migration was like for the women and for the families that ventured to cross the continent.

An exercise in historiography, this essay involves an attempt to make clear some of the difficulties and rewards inherent in using diaries as source materials. Three topics are analyzed: first, the responses of women to the decision to make the overland journey; then, the nature of women's work and women's lives once the journey was begun; and, last, occasions when women were separated from their men, and the omission of these intervals from the diaries.

I.

The decision to make the westward trek was almost always one made by men. The "Oregon fever," or the promise of the gold fields, or the siren call of free land in the new country or just the "itch" to move on—these were the basic lures that drew men west. As heads of households, men bore the responsibility for the family's support, and the determination to go west was usually expressed in terms of a desire for upward mobility. The journey was universally understood by men as a route to economic success and sometimes as an effort to improve the health of one or more family members.[2] The responses of women, on the other hand, seemed to vary from acquiscence to resignation or despair.[3] The different responses suggest the distance between life experiences and expectations in those joined by marriage but separated by gender and role.

The families that migrated to Oregon and to California between 1840 and 1870 were not inexperienced at removing from site to site. Generally speaking, migrating families had moved at least once before and more often several times at frequent intervals. The Oregon Trail, however, meant a major severing of ties, the moving of some 2,000 miles from kin and community. For women, in particular, it meant the loss of a closely woven network of friendships, the loss of access to other women with whom the major part of their daily experiences had been lived.[4]

Many women experienced these leavetakings as cruel separations from other women: from mothers and from sisters and from dear friends. Women's attachment to place was rooted in the relationships that had been formed; men's decisions seemed more determined by the possibilities of tomorrow's "place," and the promise offered for the future. Men also would not lose the company of other men; their lives on the trail would continue much as before. But women knew they faced the possibility of being without the company of other women, and particularly if they had reached child-bearing years, if they had borne and perhaps buried children in the church-yard, if they faced the prospect of giving birth on the trail, the decision to uproot for this particular journey was filled with anguish.

Mary A. Jones wrote: "In the winter of 18 and 46 our neighbor got hold of Fremont's *History of California* and began talking of moving to the New Country & brought the book to my husband to read, & he was carried away with the idea too. I said *'O let us not go!'* Our neighbors, some of them old men & women, with large families, but it made no difference. They must go.... We sold our home and what we could not take with us and what we could not sell... we gave away & on the 7th day of May 1846 we joined the camp for California."[5] Writing almost twenty years later, Abby E. Fulkerth echoed the same feelings: "Agreeable to the wish of my husband, I left all my relatives in Ohio... & started on this long & somewhat perilous journey.... it proved a hard task to leave them but still harder to leave my children buried in... graveyards...."[6] And Margaret Hereford Wilson wrote to her mother in 1850 that "Dr. Wilson has determined to go to California. I am going with him, as there is no other alternative.... Oh, my dear Mother... I thought that I felt bad when I wrote you... from Independence, but it was nothing like this."[7]

Whatever their initial response, women shared acute anxieties about the journey itself. One expression of these anxieties can be found in women's preoccupation with death among the members of the wagon train and in their keeping record of the graves they passed along the way. The diaries of these women show them to have become virtual actuaries, making tallies of the miles traveled and the graves passed. The accounts suggest that for many women, the westward migration was felt to be a time not of new beginnings and hopeful aspirations but of tension and misgivings and backward glances. The journey was felt to be the end of a more secure and familiar past. This mood was exacerbated among the women who emigrated in 1851 and 1852 when cholera, which had begun with the Gold Rush, swept the Prairies. "The route westward was marked with wooden crosses and stone cairns, the crosses often bearing only a name and the word 'cholera.' Nowhere could the disease have been more terrifying than on these trails, where men died without physicians, without ministers, and without friends."[8] The diary of Mrs. Algeline Jackson Ashley, in 1852, contains the following litany of deaths: "June 2... Breedlove [a member of the party] is quite unwell. passed 11 graves. June 3. passed no graves. June 5... passed 5 graves. June 8... passed considerable alkali and 6 graves. June 9... passed 4 graves. June 10... passed 6 graves. June 14... passed 42 graves in all. June 23... It is 800 miles from here to California."[9] The same grim, obsessive recounting occurs in Lodisa Frizzell's diary, describing her travel to California in 1852: "We have passed less than 100 fresh graves... hope [wolves] will not disturb the graves." On the seventy-second day of her journey, she added, "we are hardly half way... the heart has a thousand misgivings and the mind is tortured with anxiety, and often as I passed the fresh-made graves, I have glanced at the side boards of the wagons, not knowing how soon it would serve as a coffin for some one of us."[10]

Ten years later, in 1862, after the epidemic of 1849 had worn itself out and before that of 1866 would begin, the same accounts recur. Jane A. Gould Tourtillot writes, "June 3 in the afternoon we passed a lonely nameless grave.... It had a headboard. It called up a train of thought to my mind. It seems so sad to think of being buried and left alone in so wild a country and no one to plant a flower or shed a tear.... June 5... we passed another grave this afternoon; his name was on the headboard. He was buried in 1861. He was 20 years old. June 6... we see 4 graves in an enclosure... & found they were graves of a father and 3 sons who were murdered by the Indians.... June 12... passed 3 graves in afternoon; one had a silk handkerchief put on the end of a stick."[11]

These accounts are common to the diaries of women and rare in the diaries of men. The doubt men experienced they would not record; their fear they could not express. Women were the keepers of frailities—their own and their men's. Beneath all the exuberance and the energy that characterized life on the Overland Trail, there were agonizing moments of anxiety and fear. So insistent are the notations of death in women's diaries, particularly during the cholera years of 1850–52, that such accounts occur more regularly than do notices of childbirth.[12] The recording of gravesites becomes a veritable hallmark of a certain group of diaries.

Juxtaposed against these records is the determination with which women sought to accommodate their lives to the seemingly anarchic impulses of men. As wives and mothers, women worked to preserve traditional family configurations even when confronted with enormous dislocations. True, life offered women precious few alternatives. Yet if their husbands were determined to go west, the women were just as determined to go west with them and to keep their families together.

The women tried, too, to sustain each other along the way. Diaries reveal the circle of female solicitude and sisterhood that women wove for themselves. They visited with one another in their own wagon trains, and occasionally even exchanged visits with women on different wagon trains. They ministered to each other in times of illness and stress. Responsive to each other's needs, they strove to weave the sort of bonding that preserved the equilibrium of their old lives. Miriam Colt Davis, in her diary, tells of one woman so stricken with rheumatism from the exposure of the journey that she could not care for her own child. "I picked a lovely bouquet of prairie flowers and carried it to her, but she couldn't take it in her hands."[13] The sense that one gleans from these diaries is that women endured the westward migration because of their commitment to maintaining the family, and because life offered them few choices. But their endurance often hid feelings of resentment, anxiety, and pain.

In sharp contrast to these accounts are the diaries of the new brides and young girls for whom the thousand-mile journey was sparked with excitement and bright hope. Young wives who had not yet entered the dangerous childbearing years found the Overland Trail a honeymoon before they took on the heavy burdens of the frontier wife. Unmarried girls found that the journey provided opportunity to share with young men and boys a brief period of free companionship. Young people sang together by the campfires and played mouth organs, guitars, and fiddles. Young girls drove the teams of oxen and even learned to crack the whip as they had seen the men do.[14] Lydia Waters recalled that she climbed hills with young boys: "Sometimes my feet would slip off the [tree limbs] and I would be hanging by my arms. You may be sure my skirts were not where they ought to have been then. . . . There were many things to laugh about."[15] Mary Eliza Warner, who crossed the continent when she was fifteen, wrote, "I drove four horses nearly all day" and then, "Aunt Celia and I played Chess which Mrs. Lord thought was the first step toward gambling."[16] Mrs. Nancy A. Hunt, who traveled with her husband and three children to California in 1854, starkly contrasted the experiences of the young with the older women. "The young people," she recalled, "had a good time, a great deal of fun. They were free from care, and could ride on horseback or in the wagons all they pleased, or could walk along the road together." Hunt, herself, gave her place in the wagon to the children and "walked half way to California. Many times I did not get into the wagon to ride all day." She remembered: "While the young folk were having their good times, some of the mothers were giving birth to their babes; three babies were born in our company that summer.... In every instance, after the birth, we traveled right along the next day, mothers and babes with the rest of us."[17]

In the cases cited, the differences between those diaries that speak of the trail experience as one of unrelieved hardship and those that describe the journey as a pleasant time of fellowship, reflect the stage of the diarist's life cycle as well as her individual condition and circumstances. For women within the child-bearing period, for women caring for young children, for women who were not robust, the Overland Trail was full of hardship. Elizabeth Smith Geer, traveling with seven children, the oldest sixteen and the youngest at the breast, wrote:

> My husband is sick. It rains and snows.... We have 5 miles to go.
> I carry my babe and lead, or rather carry, another through snow,
> mud and water, almost to my knees. It is the worst road.... I went
> ahead with my children and I was afraid to look behind me.... My
> children gave out with the cold and fatigue and could not travel
> and the boys had to unhitch the oxen and bring them and carry
> the children on to camp. I was so cold and numb that I could not
> tell... that I had any feet at all.... We did not get to camp until
> dark and there was not one dry thread on one of us—not even my
> babe.... I have not told you half we suffered. I am not adequate to
> the task.[18]

Young wives without children and unmarried girls, on the other hand, were, for a brief interval in their lives, free of the toils that awaited them in the settlements.

When one reads enough diaries one can see that these accounts are not anomalies; instead, they form a configuration within a larger one. The difference in the attitudes among the women diarists is real; it does not reflect whether or not women possessed the spirit of adventure or enjoyed the excitement of the unknown. The different responses *do* derive from the circumstances of the diarist's life; whether the overland journey came when a woman was most susceptible to the dangers of childbirth and to the heaviest burdens of wifehood, or when she was still on the glad periphery of girlhood. The life cycle of the diarist is the significant configuration.

II.

For the women who came to the frontier from settled and stable communities, the trail brought sharp dislocations in work roles and in social expectations. They had heard the westward journey described as a route toward upward mobility for the family, and yet experience brought them a backward slipping into work that was usually delegated to hired hands. By mid-summer, as cattle and oxen tired, the women and children no longer rode but walked beside the wagons. As firewood disappeared, women were charged with following behind the wagons to collect the indispensable "buffalo chips" or greasewood weeds that would keep the fires going. Elizabeth Geer advised her friends who had remained at home: "Just step out and pull a lot of sage out of your garden and build a fire in the wind and bake, boil and fry by it and then you will guess how we have to do."[19] The women unloaded and repacked the wagons at the countless river crossings. As cattle became crippled or died, they abandoned their possessions leaving ribbons of belongings and keepsakes beside the road. There were few women who did not take their turns driving the ox-teams. They loaded muskets and stood watch at night. And in addition, there were the ordinary tasks, cooking, washing, and baking. Indeed, washing clothes on the Overland Trail could be something of a Herculean labor. Cooking was done under the sun and the wind. Miriam Davis wrote: "Put a blanket over my head, and I would pass well for an Osage squaw."[20] Lucy Rutledge Cooke "made a pie rolling the crust on the wagon seat."[21] The women were also midwives at confinements, herbalists to the sick, and nurses to the dying. They brought all their ingenuity to bear when accidents occurred. Sheer necessity caused them to bear what one historian has called "the double burden of femininity." They did their own work and the work of hired hands and beyond this, they served and supported their men.[22]

The task was not without its price in terms of family dynamics, and diaries suggest that one of the oblique effects of the tension under which women labored emerged in their relations with their daughters. As women found their own work more and more demeaned by the raw life of the trail, they sometimes imposed upon their daughters strict standards of ladylike behavior. Adrietta Applegate Hixon's account of being made to wear her sun-bonnet through all the dusty distance of the Overland Trail is graphic:

> While traveling, mother was particular about Louvina and me wearing our sunbonnets and long mitts in order to protect our complexions, hair and hands. Much of the time I should like to have gone without that long bonnet poking out over my face, but mother pointed out to me some girls who did not wear bonnets and as I did not want to look as they did, I stuck to my bonnet, finally growing used to it. There were cases made for our splint bonnets that were filled with little splints of wood shaved down very thin and smooth, which kept our bonnets from that wilted appearance that many had, where only pasteboard had been used. In the evening our bonnets were hung up to the ridge pole above the wagon, and mother had some sort of cream lotion for our hands and faces that we occasionally used when her eye was upon us.[23]

The question of how to handle oneself as a lady and as a woman on the frontier was an issue of no small complexity. It was an issue as well that caused friction between older and younger women. On the one hand, there were the ideals of propriety established by Victorian society. Against these were the purely physical demands made by the daily exigencies of frontier living. Because conditions were fluid, women might have modified the traditional models and expanded accepted roles of behavior. Indications are, however, that women on the frontier strove to structure their work and their behavior as strictly and as traditionally as their physical environment would permit. Their efforts seem to have been bent on reestablishing the structure, order, and at the very least, a semblance of the life they left behind. However that may be, when younger sisters and daughters on occasion modified standard behavior patterns and sex roles, their efforts strained relationships with their mothers and with the older women in the community.

The same Adrietta Hixon, who learned to accept her poke bonnet, also wrote: "When riding, I always rode aside with my full skirt pulled well down over my ankles. If we had ridden astride as they do now, people would have thought we were not lady-like. Mother was always reminding Louvina and me to be ladies, but sometimes it seemed to me that the requirements were too rigid, for I also like to run, jump and climb...."[24] But others were not so acquiescent, as the diaries of Mollie Dorsey Sanford, Lydia Milner Waters, and Mary Ellen Todd attest. Lydia Waters wrote: "I forgot to say I had learned to drive an ox team on the Platte, and my driving was admired by an officer and his wife who were going with mail to Salt Lake City. I heard them laughing at the thought of a woman driving oxen." Mollie Sanford told how, chasing a runaway cow, she had dressed herself in her father's old suit, but afraid of being discovered, she ran and hid. "When it was all explained, it was very funny to all but Mother, who feared I am losing all dignity I ever possessed. I know I am getting demoralized. . . ."[25]

Harriet Sherril Ward recounted with pride that her daughter Frankie could "go off a half mile and mount a horse without a saddle or bridle"and on one occasion caught a runaway horse as if she were a boy.[26] But in other accounts friction is far more evident. Already established in a frontier settlement in 1870, Jane Jasper wrote to a daughter away at boarding school. The sharp edge of her admonitions betrayed the price that frontier labor had extracted from her own life: "It is no use for me to be thinking and working my life out for you to have the chance for an Education unless you will have sense enough to appreciate what is done for your future."[27] The adults of emigrant families, like those of immigrant families, sought to maintain discipline on the frontier and to recreate something resembling the structured society they had left behind, while the young responded to the "adventure" of the journey and to the primitive quality of life with more casual forms of behavior. The diaries provide us with insights into the dynamics that occurred within families. The new country much like the New World, generated new social responses and these responses, in turn, suggest the dynamics of generational conflict on the frontier. It suggests an important pattern that needs further testing.

III.

The diaries are most tantalizing when they conceal precisely that dimension of life they might most aptly describe. One of the intriguing questions of frontier life is exactly how women and children survived during the periods of time when husbands and fathers were absent. Separations of husbands and wives were commonplace during historic periods of immigration and emigration. Explorations of the New World and of the new country drew husbands, fathers, brothers, and sons distances that sometimes exceeded two thousand miles. Left behind were wives, mothers, sisters, and daughters who were forced to fend for themselves. Separations ranged from weeks to months or years. Chester Warner, for example, traveled from Illinois to California to sell a string of horses. He returned by sailing down the Pacific coast from San Francisco to Panama, traveling by mule across the isthmus to the Atlantic, north by steamship to New York, and by railroad back to Illinois. The next spring, he made the same trip again, but this time he took his brother Alexander with him. When Chester returned to Illinois, he married, brought his bride and his brother's wife and four children back with him to California. For Chester's bride, the Oregon Trail was a wedding trip.

But for Alexander's wife and four children, it was the end of more than a year's separation from husband and father.[28]

According to Mrs. Francis Sawyer, her husband "made 3 trips in all to California. He went overland in '49 and came back in the fall of 1850. He could not content himself to stay in Kentucky, however, and concluded to go back again. So in the Spring of '51 he... went... by way of New Orleans and the Isthmus. He soon got homesick again and came back in the Fall of '51, thinking he would either settle here in Kentucky or move his wife to California. He chose the latter course...."[29]

How did the women fare during the times when they were alone? They were expected to maintain their household as an independent unit; there was no thought that the household would be absorbed or merged with any parental or extended family branch. Indeed, both Chester and Alexander Warner returned after traveling a combined four thousand miles. Alexander's wife had maintained the farm and cared for the children, and on her husband's return, gave back to him the ongoing enterprise of family and homestead. Mrs. Sawyer did the same. But their diaries do not reveal how this was accomplished. We simply do not learn how the women managed alone.

The entries concerning the periods when the women ran the households are ambiguous or missing. Here the historian must venture to hypothesize in the absence of data—almost *because* of the absence of data. The hypothesis is that women maintained the family enterprise whether it was a farm or a business and served as their husbands' surrogates. During these extended periods, the women must have hired the extra "hands," repaired the house, taken charge of buying staples and selling crops, fed and cared for the children, tended to any accidents, and successfully managed the ordinary business of living. Whether the extended family supported these households during the times of female hegemony; whether neighbors and community assisted and how; whether male kin bore any explicit responsibility for such households—all of these questions remain unanswered. There seems a virtual conspiracy to omit such information from the records—even those left by the women.

The only clues come from diaries that record the loneliness of these periods. Margaret Hereford Wilson, left by her husband in Sonora, Mexico, wrote to her mother: "Husband has not yet arrived... will probably get here the first of November. Oh dear Mother, don't that appear like a long time to be separated in a strange country."[30] And Mary Richardson Walker wrote in her diary: "Oh here I am. Far away in this remote wilderness alone with little son and, happen what may, I know not where another human being can be found...."[31] It is both curious and arresting to note that women permitted themselves to record moments of weakness, moments of despair, but not of strength and independence. For manage they did. They evidenced both independence and managerial skills. When the men returned from California, round the Isthmus of Panama and up the Mississippi, or up the Atlantic coast to New York and across by railroad back to a single log cabin in Illinois, Indiana, or Missouri, unfailingly the family unit was still there. The women had sustained the enterprise.

The diaries suggest that transfer of role between husband and wife was a commonplace of the frontier period. There is no indication in any of the hundred or more diaries I have read that the family, when it was composed only of wife and children, was expected to seek shelter from kin or neighbor. Quite the opposite; the expectation was that it would function autonomously. There was matter-of-fact acceptance that the wife would conduct the family's business until such time as her husband returned. One must assume that the community understood and supported these periods of wifely hegemony. One must assume too, that women could take on managerial responsibility because they, as well as their husbands, knew intimately the workings of the family enterprise.

Upon a husband's return, the wife relinquished her managerial prerequisites and resumed the traditional role of helpmate and subordinate. Just how these shifts occurred, how the community participated in these transitions, and how women learned to make these major transitions in roleplaying is not clear. But all of these shifts indicate that family life on the frontier was *not* a time of stability. It was, as Tamara Hareven has written of the nineteenth-century family, "often more complex, more diverse, and less orderly than it is today."[32] Paradoxically, women, who were set amid complex and conflicting role-demands, were duplicitous in recording their means of survival: they set down the ways in which they fulfilled traditional kinds of behavior and left it to historians to piece together the mosaic of their, to us, more radical experience. Their diaries both reveal and conceal the subtleties and the complexities of their lives.

Notes

1. Merrill J. Mattes, in his extensive and careful bibliography to *The Great Platte River Road* (Nebraska State Historical Society, Proceedings 25: 1969), lists almost one hundred diaries of women, both published and manuscript items. Two recent doctoral dissertations, one by John D. Unruh, "The Plains Across: The Overland Emigrants and the Trans-Mississippi West, 1840–1860" (University of Kansas, 1975), and the other by John M. Faragher, "Midwestern Families in Motion: Women and Men on the Overland Trail to Oregon" (Yale University 1977), virtually double this number. Faragher's study has subsequently been published by

Yale University Press. Every major western library and state historical society holds manuscript journals and diaries of women who were part of the overland migration between 1840 and 1880. Mormon diaries are in special collections and one must consider that we have not yet exhausted the survey of these materials. Consult Dale Morgan, *Overland in 1846: Diaries and Letters of California-Oregon Trail* (Georgetown, California: Talisman Press, 1963).

2. See John Unruh, "The Plains Across...," ch. 5; John M. Faragher, "Midwestern Families...," ch. 2.

3. "Denied the chance to participate in the decision to move... failing to accept as their own their husband's reason for undertaking the move, women went, not because they wanted to, but because within the social expectations they accepted they had no choice." Faragher, p. 276. Faragher discusses the anxieties women experienced: pp. 276–283.

4. See William R. Taylor and Christopher Lasch, "Two Kindred Spirits: Sorority and Family in New England 1839–1846," *New England Quarterly* 36 (1963): 25–41; Charles E. Rosenberg, "Sexuality, Class and Role in Nineteenth-Century America," *American Quarterly* 25 (May 1973): 131–53; Barbara Welter, "The Cult of True Womanhood: 1820–1860," *American Quarterly* 18 (Summer 1966): 151–74; Ann Firor Scott, *The Southern Lady: From Pedestal to Politics, 1830–1930* (Chicago: University of Chicago Press, 1970), chs. 1, 2; Aileen Kraditor, ed., *Up From the Pedestal* (Chicago: Quadrangle Books, 1968), ch. 1; Nancy Cott, ed., *Root of Bitterness* (New York: E.P. Dutton, 1972), ch. 3; Kathryn Kish Sklar, *Catherine Beecher: A Study in American Domesticity* (New Haven: Yale University Press, 1973); Carroll Smith-Rosenberg, "The Female World of Love and Ritual: Relations Between Women in Nineteenth-Century America," *Signs* 1 (1975): 1–28; and Joan Kelly Gadol, "The Social Relations of the Sexes: Methodological Implications of Women's History," *Signs* 1 (1976): 809–823.

5. Mary Ann Smith Jones, "Recollections.... 1846," Manuscript Diary, Bancroft Library, University of California, Berkeley.

6. Abby E. Fulkerth, "Iowa to California, April-August 1863," Manuscript Diary, The Bancroft Library, University of California, Berkeley.

7. Margaret Hereford Wilson to Esther Sale Hereford, 1850, Manuscript Letters, The Huntington Library, San Marino, California.

8. Charles E. Rosenberg, *The Cholera Years: The United States in 1832, 1849, and 1866* (Chicago: University of Chicago Press, 1962), p. 115.

9. Mrs. Algeline Jackson Ashley, Manuscript Diary, 1852, The Huntington Library, San Marino, California.

10. Lodisa Frizzell, *Across the Plains to California in 1852* (New York Public Library Pamphlet, 1915), pp. 14–16, 29.

11. Jane A. Gould Tourtillot, Manuscript Diary, 1862, Bancroft Library, University of California, Berkeley.

12. One reads through the entire diary of Mrs. Amelia Stewart Knight, written in

1853, and does not learn until the very last entry that she was pregnant during the course of the journey: "Saturday, Sept. 17. In camp yet. Still raining.... It has cleared off and we are all ready for a start again, for some place we don't know where.... A few days later my eighth child was born. After this we picked up and ferried across the Columbia River, utilizing skiff, canoes and flatboat to get across, taking three days to complete. Here husband traded two yoke of oxen for a half section of land with one-half acre planted to potatoes and a small log cabin and a lean-to with no window. This is the journey's end." Oregon Pioneer Association, *Transactions* 46–56 (1928): 53.

13. Miriam Colt Davis, *Went to Kansas* (Watertown, N.Y., 1862), p. 57.
14. Quoted in John Faragher and Christine Stansell, "Women and Their Families on the Overland Trail to California and Oregon, 1842–67," *Feminist Studies,* 2 (1975): 157.
15. Lydia Milner Waters, "A Trip Across the Plains in 1855," *Quarterly of the Society of California Pioneers* 6 (June 1929): 78.
16. Mary Eliza Warner, Manuscript Diary, 1864, Bancroft Library, University of California, Berkeley.
17. Mrs. Nancy A. Hunt, Manuscript Diary, 1854, Irene Paden Papers, University of the Pacific, Stockton, California.
18. Mrs. Elizabeth Dixon Smith Geer, "Diary, 1848," Oregon Pioneer Association, *Transactions* 26–35 (1907): 171–172.
19. Ibid., 161.
20. Miriam Colt Davis, pp. 53.
21. Lucy Rutledge Cooke, "Crossing the Plains in 1852," Manuscript Diary, Irene Paden Papers, University of the Pacific, Stockton, California.
22. John M. Faragher, "Work and Roles on the Overland Trail," paper read at the American Studies Association biennial convention, Boston, October, 1977.
23. Adrietta Applegate Hixon, *On to Oregon! A True Story of a Young Girl's Journey into the West,* ed. Waldo Taylor (New York Public Library Pamphlet, 1947), p. 12.
24. Ibid., p. 21.
25. Lydia Milner Waters, "A Trip Across the Plains in 1855," p. 77; Mary ELlen Todd, see Faragher and Stansell, "Women and Their Families...," p. 157; also Lillian Schlissel, "Women's Diaries on the Western Frontier," *American Studies* (Spring 1977): 95; Mollie Dorsey Sanford, *Journal in Nebraska and Colorado Territories, 1857–1866* (Lincoln, Nebraska, 1958), p. 53.
26. Harriet Sherril Ward, Manuscript Diary, 1853, Huntington Library, San Marino, California.
27. Jane Jasper, Manuscript Letters to her daughter, October 2 and November 20, 1870, The Huntington Library, San Marino, California.
28. Mary Eliza Warner, Manuscript Diary, 1864, Bancroft Library, University of California, Berkeley.

29. Mrs. Francis Sawyer, "Journey Across the Plains, 1852," Manuscript Diary, Bancroft Library, University of California, Berkeley.
30. Margaret Hereford Wilson to Esther Sale Hereford, March 7, October 13, 1850. Manuscript Letters, Huntington Library, San Marino, California.
31. Mary Richardson Walker, Manuscript Diary, 1842. Huntington Library, San Marino, California.
32. Tamara Hareven, "Family Time and Historical Time," *Daedalus* 106 (Spring 1977): 57–70. Hareven's analysis is very valuable.

Katharine T. Corbett

Louisa Catherine Adams:
The Anguished "Adventures of a Nobody"

"My temper is so harassed and I am I fear so imbued with strange and singular opinions, and surrounded by persons with whom it is decidedly impossible for me to agree...."[1] So Louisa Catherine Adams, the sixty-five-year-old wife of John Quincy Adams, began her autobiography. She chose to call it "The Adventures of a Nobody," and she wrote it in bitter, ironic protest against a life of personal failure and frustration. If her chronicle of despair was merely a self-indulgent plea for recognition as a "somebody," it would hold little historical interest. But Louisa's peculiar background and situation combined with her intelligence, self-awareness, and wit to form a series of perceptions of women's role that transcended her immediate circumstances. Neither a simple victim nor a reformist heroine, Louisa Adams found herself at odds with a world she did not like but could not change. Louisa's personality strained at the constraints of her world, but she accepted its limitations as her own, and her final despair grew out of the denial of expectations.

Early nineteenth-century society had explicitly defined the permissible boundaries within which a woman was to find her purpose. As Alexis de Tocqueville noted, the married American woman remained within a narrow circle of domestic interests and duties, forbidden to step beyond it.[2] Here, as a wife and mother, a woman exerted her influence and received her validation. If, like Louisa Adams, she were an upper-class wife, she might also enjoy the reflected prestige of her husband's position and the social opportunities it provided.[3] Within this narrow definition of female achievement, Louisa Adams considered herself a failure. She had little influence on her husband's attitudes and behavior; three of her four children met tragic ends; she found her social position at best uncomfortable and at worst intolerable. Louisa realized she was caught in a contradiction: her success or failure as a woman depended on her ability to perform her domestic role, but she had neither the

[Katharine T. Corbett is an instructor at the University of Missouri–St. Louis. Presently, she is engaged in research on the use of photographs as historical evidence.]

personality nor the control over her own life necessary for its successful performance.

Louisa Adams was hardly a typical American woman. Born and educated in England, she came to America at the age of twenty-seven, the daughter-in-law of John and Abigail Adams and the wife of a man destined to become a national political and diplomatic figure. Traditional historians have celebrated the personality and accomplishments of Abigail Adams as a model wife, mother, and revolutionary heroine. Louisa, who was less accepting and therefore probably less acceptable, has been largely maligned or ignored.[4] And yet Louisa's ability to analyze and articulate her own alienation and to question its sources and effects makes her a potentially more interesting subject for woman's history than her venerable mother-in-law. Traditional history has been concerned only with "achieving women," but Louisa was by her own definition a failure even in terms of achieving the goals set by most middle-class women of her period. Because she self-consciously identified herself as an alien observer everywhere she lived, she was inclined to measure her expectations against the realities of personal and social situations. She used her memoir to argue for recognition as an individual with her own needs, values, and personal history separate from those of her husband and sons.

By its definition biography deals with the unique individual, but a focus on the way in which an individual interacts with her social environment can contribute to a general understanding of the dynamics between personality, ideology, and historical situation. Louisa's anguished exploration into what she believed to be the causes of a wasted life affords the historian the opportunity to examine not only her experiences but, more importantly, her responses to them. While specific to one woman, such analysis can provide insight into female consciousness and can help to reveal the differences between its perceptions and those of male contemporaries.[5] The principle sources for this essay are "The Adventures of a Nobody" and a shorter memoir, "Record of a Life." "The Adventures" is not a conventional memoir since it was constructed in 1840 from fragments of journals Louisa had kept from the time of her marriage in 1797 until 1812. She analyzed and annotated these diary entries specifically in order to offer an interpretation of her life to her only surviving son. While in many ways Louisa was an atypical Adams, she did acquire the Adams propensity to chronicle events and impressions. In addition to the two memoirs her papers include journal entries meant for other Adamses to read—most notably John Adams with whom she developed a mutually satisfying correspondence—and secret passages meant for no other eyes, least of all those of an Adams.

If one defines autobiography broadly enough to include all these forms of self-history, Louisa's papers represent a rich source from which to elicit the greatest value autobiographical material affords: the revelation of an individual's basic conception of self and personality.[6] The retrospective perspective of the memoir enhances this function because Louisa self-consciously sought "the connecting threads" in the history of her life, while the presence of contemporary diary entries required her to reconcile that assessment with events and attitudes as she had recorded them years before. This material is, of course, extremely subjective since it represents only Louisa's view of herself and her world. Although the papers of other members of the Adams family do not contradict Louisa's own portrait of her external self, they too do not meet any standard of objectivity. The way the world beyond her family perceived Louisa cannot be determined from these sources. However, as Wilhelm Dilthey argued, the autobiographer is the primary historian.[7] By telling us what the meaning of her life was as she understood it, Louisa Adams enables later historians to better understand her and the society in which she lived.

It is difficult to imagine anyone less suited to be the wife of John Quincy Adams of Quincy, Massachusetts—this daughter of an expatriate merchant from Maryland and his English wife. In her autobiography Louisa remembers herself as a delicate, insecure girl with a willful streak and a haughty manner, "accustomed," she wrote, "to live in luxury without display and too much beloved by my family for my own good."[8] Her French and English education provided her with "those accomplishments which properly used are an ornament to female loveliness"[9] and prepared her for a marriage like that of her parents. She believed her parents' marriage was perfect. Her father worshiped her delicate mother, whom Louisa described as a brilliant conversationalist, polished in manners, and fond of reading. If her mother felt unwell, her father would cut her food and warm her fork, wrapping it in a napkin and heating it by the fire. To Louisa, such attention proved that his love for his wife and children was "all that made [his] life desirable."[10] She grew up convinced that marriage would bring her the same affection and indulgence.

Outsiders in English society, the seven Johnson daughters were expected to behave like upper-middle-class English women while upholding the abstract values of American republicanism—values that apparently did not anticipate a different role for women in a republic than in a monarchy. The Johnsons sent their only son to America expressly to learn to live in a republican society. For his daughters, Joshua Johnson wanted marriage to "American men of note and distinction. "[11] Because Johnson served as American Consul in London, such men were often guests in his home. It was there that Louisa met John Quincy Adams.

Years later she described their courtship as a series of misunderstandings between two people who recognized vast differences in their values and personalities, but married anyway. "I had more than one misgiving as to the *fitness* of my *temper* to cope with the difficulties which presented themselves to my imagination," she wrote. "I had already discovered that our views of things were totally different in many essential points, and that there was a severity bordering on injustice in some of the opinions which I heard expressed for want of a more enlarged acquaintance with the customs of my country—and more especially with those peculiar to *my* Sex."[12] And yet Louisa, a young woman reared only for marriage, craving attention and approval, never seriously considered refusing him once he expressed his intentions. Unwilling to set a date for the marriage, John Quincy announced that their engagement might last as long as seven years. Meanwhile, he instructed her to undertake a course of study to improve her mind. To prepare her for marriage, Mr. Johnson rented a separate house for a summer where, with the assistance of two servants, Louisa lived alone, reading and learning English housewifery.[13]

John Quincy, American Minister to the Netherlands, wrote to his fiancée, urging that she understand his patriotic duty and that all interests and feelings inconsistent with that duty "must forever disappear."[14] Although he wrote his parents of his intention to marry, he at first neglected to name his betrothed. A letter from his mother, Abigail Adams, may have prompted his decision to return to England for Louisa within the year. Writing from Quincy, Massachusetts, Abigail suggested that he marry before leaving for his next assignment, since his brother, who had been his traveling companion, was returning home.[15] Abigail's only reservation about Louisa's suitability as a wife was her questionable nationality, and she hoped "for the love I bear my country" that she was "at least half-blood."[16]

Shortly after the wedding in July, 1797, Louisa's father, who planned to bring his family back to the United States, suffered financial ruin and left England hurriedly in embarrassment. Separated for the first time from her family, Louisa became obsessed with the idea that the Adamses believed her father had deliberately palmed her off on the son of the President of the United States. Because she derived her self-esteem from her position as the beloved daughter of an honest, successful businessman, what little confidence she had brought to her marriage disappeared. Well-founded doubts about her husband's priorities, differences in their values and personalities, and the suitability of her upbringing and education for her marital role were overshadowed by the conviction that her father's disgrace had changed her overnight from an asset to a liability. She interpreted John Quincy's cold and austere behavior, so different from that of her father toward her mother, as his mortification over her altered status. A confused and unhappy bride of twenty-two, Louisa Catherine Adams left England for Berlin, where her husband was to serve four years as American Minister to the Prussian

Court.[17]

Looking back on the years in Berlin, Louisa recalled being captivated by the splendor of court life and flattered by the attention she received. But she was also confused by and resented the role she was expected to play. In Berlin she first wrestled with the problem of separating her own personality from the public and private role of Mrs. John Quincy Adams. She willingly rejected involvement in political intrigue. "Mr. Adams had always accustomed me to believe that Women had nothing to do with politicks," she recalled. "And as he was the glass from which my opinions were reflected, I was convinced of its truth and sought no further."[18]

But the social world was hers and she longed to find her place in it. Although she insisted that her loss of dowery and inheritance made her a liability to her husband, it was she who suffered from the effects of her complete financial dependence. Unable to dress competitively with other women she felt awkward and insecure. John Quincy was of little help. He frequently left her alone at parties, failed to introduce her properly, and appeared to be indifferent to social life. His insistence that she not wear rouge to court parties so offended her that she finally refused to appear at court at all.[19] Willful and intelligent, she established patterns of resistance to intrusion on her private self that were to last a lifetime. "Now I like very well to adopt my husband's thoughts and words when I approve them," she wrote to him much later, "but I do not like to repeat them like a parrot, and *prove* myself a nonentity... when my husband married me he made a great mistake if he thought I only intended to play echo.... I like the piquancy of contradiction which calls forth new ideas, and it is fortunate for me that I have a goodly portion to gratify the taste."[20]

Intellectual independence, however, was a cold substitute for a husband's loving approval and companionship. Louisa looked to John Quincy for the same emotional support that she had seen her father lavish on her mother. Instead, she confronted impersonality and his incessant application to his work. Her poor health and a succession of miscarriages only intensified her unhappiness, particularly because she believed that a child was what her husband and the Adams family wanted most from her. Convinced that her husband's anxiety and the concern expressed in letters from Quincy were veiled reproaches for her inability to have a child, she came close to a complete mental and physical breakdown. Only the companionship of John Quincy's brother, Thomas, and her friendship with the family of an English physican prevented it. Many evenings spent with the Browns and their three daughters, while her husband worked or studied, provided a welcome retreat from the responsibilities of marriage and public life.[21]

In 1801, her son, George Washington Adams, was born in Berlin, and later that year her husband was recalled to America. At the age of twenty-seven,

Louisa, who had always insisted that she was an expatriate republican, would see her own country for the first time. "Quincy!" she wrote in her memoir, "What shall I say of my impressions of Quincy! Had I stepped into Noah's Ark I do not think I could have been so utterly astonished.... It was lucky for me that I was so depressed and so ill, or I should certainly have given mortal offence.... Even the Church, its forms, the snuffling through the nose, the Singers, the dressing and the dinner hour, were all novelties to me.... Hitherto I had been the spoiled child of indulgence; could I realize the change? Impossible! And under such circumstances could I appear amiable?"[22]

She immediately perceived that New England attitudes toward women were as far from Europe as Quincy was from Berlin. Her education and experience had prepared her neither to accept nor to be accepted in her husband's culture. "The qualifications necessary to form an accomplished Quincy Lady were in direct opposition to the mode of life which I had led," she later wrote. "I hourly betrayed my incapacity and to a woman like Mrs. Adams, equal to every occasion in life, I appeared like a maudlin hysterical fine Lady...."[23] Not only was Louisa a dependent wife with no property of her own, but now she was an unsuitable one: her education had not prepared her to be useful. Her English boarding school had instructed her in foreign languages, vocal music, dance, drama, and literature—the necessary and proper accomplishments for an upper-class English housewife. From her mother she had learned to supervise the running of a gracious home staffed by eleven servants.[24] She was proud of her talents as an English housewife, but her ability to direct servants scarcely met New England standards of home management. "I tried every means in my power to *work* as they call it; but my strength did not second the effort, and I only made matters worse. Mrs. Adams gave me instructions and advice, but I did not really learn...."[25] Educated to be a social ornament, Louisa found herself in a society that valued only practical accomplishment.

American expectations for women differed from the English not only in their emphasis on usefulness, but also in the insistence on the importance of women to the development and maintenance of republicanism. As in England, woman's sphere was the home, where she was to "sooth and alleviate the the anxious care of man."[26] But for "the nursing mothers of the republic," it was also where she implanted in her children "all the virtues that shall prepare them to shine as statesmen, soldiers, philosophers, and Christians."[27] Although women had no public political role, they were nevertheless responsible for the preservation of the Republic. John Adams argued that rational morality was not possible without pure and chaste women, that without national morality a republican government could not be maintained, and, therefore, that it was woman's job to preserve the Republic.[28]

By the end of the eighteenth century, educational theory included prescriptions that tailored female education to the particular needs of a republican society. American women married young, with little time for French and music, and because American men were so busy, women needed to be trained to manage their husband's property. They were expected to assume responsibility for the education of their children and particularly the education of their sons "in the principles of liberty and government in order to prepare them for public office." Finally, because of the absence of a permanent servant class, women needed good domestic training.[29]

Implicit in this doctrine was the idea that not only was an American woman to be domestic and virtuous, but she should also be flexible enough that, when the occasion demanded, she could enlarge her sphere to fulfill her patriotic duty. Such a demand required a particularly malleable woman, one who could act in an assertive and independent manner and yet not enter the masculine sphere except at the request of men. American patriotic writers and orators, searching for examples of women who willingly subordinated their own desires to patriotic duty, saw the women of the American Revolution as national heroines. They memorialized women's contributions for the same reason they mythologized the personality of George Washington: to provide symbolic models of republican virtue and devotion.[30] Martha Washington, who "followed the foot paths of her beloved hero" and "soothed every care of his wartorn life," was "a bright example of every virtue that adorns the Christian or female character."[31]

Such a heroine was Abigail Adams. She firmly believed that woman's sphere was domesticity and that "every American wife should herself know how to order and regulate her family... and train up her children." For this purpose God had made woman "a help-meet for man, and she who fails in these duties does not answer the end of her creation."[32] Yet during the Revolution she willingly enlarged her sphere in the cause of patriotism to include many of the responsibilities normally assigned to men. In the years that followed she accepted separation from her young sons so that they might learn to serve their country, and both John Quincy and his brother Charles accompanied their father to European diplomatic posts.[33] In 1777 she wrote her husband that she could endure their separation in the belief that he was rendering his "fellow creatures essential benefits" for which she hoped future generations "would rise up and call [him] blessed."[34] "I am willing to do my part,"[35] she said. Thus, the idealized revolutionary woman, as exemplified by Abigail Adams, though capable and resourceful, stepped out of her sphere only at the request of male society. She put patriotic duty before personal desires and never forgot that she was created to be a help-mate for her husband. It is not surprising that on her arrival in Quincy in 1801 Louisa Adams felt as if she were stepping into Noah's Ark.

Fortunately, John Quincy's business affairs enabled her to live in Boston for the next two years, avoiding Quincy and invidious comparisons with her mother-in-law as much as possible. Her husband spent every weekend with his parents. Despite this tension, Louisa always recalled time spent in Boston as the happiest of her life in America. Perhaps it was because Boston, of all the places she lived, was most like London. For the first time since her marriage she was close to living the kind of life she had expected. The women of Boston society entertained her and she felt "surrounded by kind friends... The suppers were delightfully social, and music, dancing and song were called in to enliven and vary the amusements of the passing hours—can you wonder that I disliked the thought of change?"[36]

On July 4, 1803, her second son, John, was born in Boston and the following autumn the family left for Washington, D.C., where John Quincy was to serve as senator from Massachusetts. Travel between Boston and Washington in the early nineteenth century was unpleasant under the best circumstances. Transportation had changed little since colonial times; uncomfortable coaches traveled slowly along bad roads and small boats pitched their passengers over turbulent rivers and seas.[37] For a woman in poor health with two small children, it was a trying journey and Louisa did not take it graciously. They had made arrangements to board with Louisa's family in the home of her married sister, Nancy Hellen. Louisa's first impression of her new home was that "the roads were almost impassable and Mr. Hellen's house lonely and dreary and at least two miles from the capital [sic]."[38] In 1800 there had been only 372 habitable dwellings in all of Washington, and in 1803 it was still a dreary place. Many legislators did not bring their families. Living in boardinghouses clustered around the Capitol, they stayed only for the congressional session. There was no commerce or industry to support any society other than that of government. Much of the population consisted of indigents and "swaggering sycophants" who came seeking their fortunes in this new city built on a swamp. There were no sidewalks or streetlights and the unpaved streets became dust bowls in dry weather and morasses of mud in wet.[39]

Louisa was happy to see her family again, although she was distressed that her widowed mother and sisters were financially dependent upon her brother-in-law. She decided her mother's inability to adjust evoked little sympathy because while "in all countries poverty is an evil, in this it is a crime." Her sisters had grown into "Belles," courted by Washington society, and despite "bridges consisting of mere loose planks and huge stumps of trees, recently cut down, intercepting every path," they participated in the social functions of the governmental elite of the city. As Louisa recalled later: "The general society consisted of charming families who, bred in the school of Washington and Adams, had not yet clothed themselves in the buffoonery of modern democracy." John Quincy's "application to his business was incessant," but she found the society of her sister's house delightful. "Talent, Wit, Good Humour, and an easy and general desire to please prompted freedom without the familiarity of rudeness," and "music, dancing, cards or more frequently, social and brilliant conversation varied the scene."[40]

Living as they did over two miles from the Capitol, the Adamses were isolated from Washington's free-wheeling boardinghouse atmosphere.[41] Louisa, however, was not able to escape the effect of republican politics on social intercourse for long. Washington society confirmed what she had suspected since her arrival in America: republicanism in practice was vastly different from republicanism in theory.[42] A new city with no traditions of its own, no old, established families, no stable middle class, Washington was an empty stage upon which a fledgling republicanism rehearsed. The nineteenth century would see the national scene become but the larger expression of the Capitol's restless society, where status rose or fell according to wealth and political position, and the old constants of family and education counted for little. Included among the players were members of the foreign diplomatic corps, some of whom flaunted their ignorance of American culture. Louisa felt acute embarrassment when the English minister's wife declared with crude vulgarity that Americans were all alike and must have "hog meat" at every meal.[43] Americans were definitely not all alike. Legislators came from increasingly remote parts of the country, which in the early nineteenth century meant they came from diverse cultures with very different educations, customs, and values.[44] Indeed, Louisa observed that "a Republic of Equality is only to be realized... in the impracticed and unsocial brains of needy bookworms."[45]

While she steadfastly denied an interest in politics, Louisa used the metaphor of society to criticize the American political system. She saw, mirrored in democratic social forms, the paradox of democracy. Where all were monarchs, Louisa wrote, there could be no commonly agreed upon rules of etiquette, for all were to be treated equally. But all people were not equal, and where social station was not traditionally defined, individuals would struggle for prestige, developing a loose hierarchy of social conventions with which to validate their positions on the social ladder. To Louisa, a woman who believed that etiquette should reflect character, this ambiguity was tantamount to fraud. Translated into political theory, the attitude "that every man, woman, and child is an incompetent Sovereign who makes or unmakes the *efficient* and *able rulers* of the Land" according to the wisdom of faction, demagoguery, greed, and profligacy could only create institutions that would "pander to the passions of the bad, instead of supporting and sustaining [the good] through the medium of just and efficient Laws...."[46] Unlike Alexis de Tocqueville, who also self-consciously observed American democracy, Louisa did not believe that the mass of people had the intelligence to govern;[47] nor did she think that they would form an electorate capable of choosing men of wisdom and virtue for elective office. Since prestige followed economic class in a democratic society, national leadership would soon devolve upon men whose values reflected the character traits most important for financial success.[48] A land of opportunity inevitably created opportunists and, as Louisa observed, it did not make people any more equal than they were in a traditional society. It only changed the rules. An unabashed elitist, Louisa could find nothing admirable in the kind of society democracy was destined to produce. She kept her promise never to be publicly involved in political intrigue, but privately, her memoir, journals, and letters are filled with incisive, witty, and frequently sarcastic descriptions of Washington politics and political figures.[49]

But what she found most confusing and exasperating about Washington society was the public role expected of a politician's wife. The lack of standard forms of behavior, coupled with a paradoxical insistence upon "rigid etiquette" also distressed her. Because of her husband's position she could not ignore these dictates and spent much of her time making and receiving duty calls. She deeply resented the intrusions of government on her private life. "I am only a secondary object in this," she complained, "being continually told that I cannot by the Constitution have any share in the public honors of my husband... it is certainly very flattering to me that people should insist on becoming acquainted with me and force me even against my will to visit them."[50] Government, by denying women a legitimate public role, had, in her opinion, no right to dictate the circumstances of their private lives. If it was axiomatic that American women be willing to live in the reflected glory of their husbands, it was not so for Louisa Adams. She consented to follow the required procedure only when she was convinced that failure to do so would seriously damage her husband's career.[51]

All her life Louisa tried to create a female model that was intelligent and independent and still had the passive domestic characteristics she admired. She was attracted to strong-willed women who appeared to her "to be what God intended woman to be before she was *cowed* by her master man." Yet she was critical of women who lacked feminine grace, sweetness, and modesty—and she saw an absence of these qualities in women of "masculine mind."[52] She believed women's sphere was domesticity, and yet she struggled to find an outlet for thinking and acting creatively within its confines. This was a continuous personal conflict because she refused to let American male society define the circumstances under which she could legitimately enlarge her role. And while many women of this period found purpose and companionship in church-related activities, Louisa was a public Unitarian and a private Episcopalian, a situation she felt her marital role required, but one which caused her much personal anguish and no social satisfaction.[53]

Louisa did believe with American women that her world centered on her children. During the years between 1803 and 1808 when the Adams family lived intermittently in Washington, Louisa suffered several miscarriages, finally giving birth to her third son, Charles Francis, in 1807. Motherhood became for her, as it did for so many women, both the rationale for her existence and the legitimate outlet for emotional and intellectual energy. When youth, beauty, and the attentions of one's husband are gone, "what can compensate a Wife, but the companionship, the cares, the tender caresses and the fond love of her children," she wrote.[54] However, fulfillment of the maternal role on which she placed so much importance was continually thwarted by circumstances beyond her control. Frequently during these years John Quincy, usually without consulting Louisa, decided that, for financial or educational reasons, mother and children should be separated. Louisa wanted to seize for herself what she understood to be her God-given role in her family, but she was powerless to do so. She had no control over the demands of her husband's profession and, since she would not instill the political calling with that sense of duty and mission which had sustained Abigail Adams during the Revolutionary era, she could not justify its toll on her private life. Because she had no money of her own, she never felt she could oppose the financial arrangements John Quincy made. Moreover, she believed it was her husband's right to make educational decisions for his sons, and his desire to groom them in the Adams tradition required that they receive New England educations. Louisa often disagreed with her husband's rigid expectations for their behavior and educational attainments, yet she was very aware of the problems created by an education that did not realistically prepare one for life. Because she was alien to her children's culture, she doubted her capability to teach them how to live in it. John Quincy had no such doubts.[55]

In 1808, following John Quincy's resignation from the Senate, Louisa hoped she could create the kind of domestic life she craved in a permanent home in Boston. She believed she could accommodate herself adequately if awkwardly to New England society, and even to the proximity of Quincy, if in return she gained the companionship and love of her children.

However, the following year President James Madison appointed John Quincy Adams minister to Russia. Without consulting Louisa, Adams arranged for the two oldest boys, aged nine and seven, to be left behind with his relatives. Thirty years later Louisa reflected on this as the most tragic moment in a lifetime of disappointment, and vowed that "from that hour to the end of time" her life was "a succession of miseries only to cease with existence."[56] Viewed in the perspective of women's sphere, John Quincy's decision was the final denial of a meaningful existence for Louisa. For the rest of her life she wrestled with guilt for denying her maternal role by leaving her young children when she accompanied her husband to St. Petersburg. "If it was to do again nothing on Earth could induce me to make such a sacrifice," she lamented, for it was a mother's duty to "cling... to those innocent and helpless creatures whom God himself has given to your charge—a man can take care of *himself."* At thirty-four Louisa Adams surmised that she had "passed the age when courts were alluring," and experience had taught her years before "the meanness of an American Minister's position at a European Court...."[57] Nevertheless, she felt powerless to change the situation, and despite her genuine distress over leaving her boys, Louisa, a wife totally dependent on her husband, could not consider staying alone with three children in a country that seemed, after eight years, still an alien culture.

On August 12, 1811, Louisa gave birth to her only daughter in St. Petersburg, Russia. The child lived less than a year. Louisa's depression over the baby's death was heightened when war between the United States and England extended John Quincy's tour and also delayed correspondence from her children in Quincy. Although she enjoyed court society more than she cared to admit, she spent long hours reading, writing poetry, and reflecting bitterly on her life: "My body is the only thing in the world over which I may pretend to have a right, and that only conditionally even after death."[58] Her relationship with her husband became even more strained; his uncommunicative self-sufficiency only added to her loneliness.[59] She questioned whether his relentless sense of duty came from patriotism as much as it did from ambition. When he was called to Paris to negotiate the Treaty of Ghent, Louisa stayed behind in Russia with Charles Francis until sent for. The forty-day carriage trip she took alone with her son across Europe in 1815, amidst the social and political confusion of Napoleon's return, was one of the highlights of her life. It was also one of the few times she acted independently, and her ability to master the situation gave her a sense of genuine accomplishment.[60] In England she was reunited with her other sons, now aged twelve and fifteen, whom she had not seen for six years.

"The Adventures of a Nobody" ends with the death of her baby daughter in 1812. In a sense so did Louisa's life, although she lived on for another forty-one years.[61] Measured in relation to her expectations of marriage, mother-hood, and social satisfaction, her life had been a failure—she was a "nobody." Two of her sons had died as young men, one a probable suicide. She believed that it was God's will that He take them because of her neglect.[62] Her husband dedicated his life to politics, spending his last seventeen years in the House of Representatives, although he knew the torment that this caused her.[63] She never felt comfortable in either Washington or Quincy, yet she was destined to spend the rest of her life being shunted between those two inhospitable societies. And underlying the frustration of unrealized expectations was an even greater despair over never being acknowledged as a viable, worthwhile individual in her own right on her own terms.

The irony of the "Adventures of a Nobody," was that Louisa Adams was a somebody, an intelligent, articulate, analytic, but tragic somebody, trapped in a world of contradictory expectations and possibilities. Her specific problems were, of course, unique to her as an individual. Educated in England to believe that if she were a charming and helpful companion, her husband would indulge and appreciate her, she found herself married to a cold, uncommunicative man who did not share her tastes and values. Unwilling to extend her sphere, as had Abigail Adams, to include making sacrifices for the nation, Louisa denied herself the personal satisfactions this might have produced. The nineteenth-century decline of deference politics and the rise of a more democratic social system created ideological questions that Abigail never had to face, and yet the myth of the Founding Mother hung over Louisa's life like a cloud. Her intelligence and keen political insights had no arena for expression except in her private writings.

But Louisa Adams accepted as her own the limitations her society dictated for women of her class, and the anguish that was rooted in questions of power and control over one's life was not merely hers alone. "When Woman, poor feeble, powerless woman, is called upon to act," she exclaimed, "what ought she to do. . .?"[64]

Notes

1. Louisa Catherine Adams (LCA), "The Adventures of a Nobody," *The Adams Papers* III (Massachusetts Historical Society, Microfilm edition at the University of Missouri, Columbia, Missouri), reel 269. This is a handwritten memoir of approximately 300 pages. It consists of intermittent daily journal entries combined with material added in 1840 to form a narrative of Louisa's life until 1812. While some pages are numbered, pagination is often duplicated or missing.
2. Alexis de Tocqueville, *Democracy in America* (New York: Alfred A. Knopf, 1966), Vol. 2, p. 201.
3. For an extensive and insightful study of the female domestic role in this period based on the personal documents of middle-class women, see Nancy Cott, *The Bonds of Womanhood: "Women's Sphere" in New England, 1780-1835* (New Haven: Yale University Press, 1977).
4. Louisa Adams has received very little attention from historians. She has had no biographer and the biographers of John Quincy Adams have treated her only peripherally. Samuel F. Bemis in *John Quincy Adams and the Foundations of American Policy* (New York: Alfred A. Knopf, 1949) discusses her only in relation to her husband's career and concludes that

"from a patriotic point of view the success of their union is attested
abundantly by the survival of the Adams family..." (p. 82). John
Quincy's recent biographer, Marie Hecht in *John Quincy Adams* (New
York: The Macmillan Company, 1972), has used many of Louisa's
papers, but she also does not analyze Louisa's life independently from
that of her husband. The editors of Charles Francis Adams' diary, Aida
and David Donald, attribute Louisa's illness and despair directly to the
decline of John Quincy's political fortunes. Charles Francis Adams,
Diary of Charles Francis Adams, Ed. Aida Di Page Donald and David
Donald (Cambridge, Mass.: Harvard University Press, 1968).

5. For a critique of biography as a useful form of historical writing about
women, see Ann D. Gordon, Mary Jo Buhle, and Nancy Schrom Dye,
"The Problems of Women's History," in *Liberating Women's History,* ed.
Berenice A. Carroll (Urbana: University of Illinois Press, 1976). I am also
indebted to Mary Kelley for her comments on the value of personal
documents to an analysis of the relationship of prescriptions for behavior
to women's actual experience and consciousness.

6. Robert F. Sayre, "The Proper Study—Autobiographies in American Studies,"
American Quarterly 29 (1977): 247–48. Sayre credits Karl J. Weintraub's
essay "Autobiography and Historical Consciousness," *Critical Inquiry* 1
(1975): 821–48, for this evaluation of the value of autobiography. Sayre's
essay argues for the validity of a wide variety of autobiographical
material as sources for historical analysis.

7. Ibid., p. 243.

8. LCA, "Adventures," *Adams Papers* III, reel 269.

9. LCA, "Record of a Life or my Story," *Adams Papers* III, reel 265. This
biographical fragment was written in 1825 and covers the period prior to
Louisa's marriage.

10. Ibid.

11. Ibid.

12. LCA, "Adventures," *Adams Papers* III, reel 269.

13. LCA, "Record," *Adams Papers* III, reel 265.

14. John Quincy Adams to Louisa C. Johnson, February 7, 1797. *Writings of
John Quincy Adams* ed. W.C. Ford (New York: Greenwood Press,
1968), vol. 2, p. 109. For an analysis that evaluates the influence of the
Adams family's image of its political destiny on the personality of John
Quincy, see David F. Musto, "The Youth of John Quincy Adams,"
Proceedings of The American Philosophical Society 113 (August 1969):
269–282.

15. Janet Whitney, *Abigail Adams* (Westport, Connecticut: Greenwood Press,
1970), p. 263.

16. Abigail Adams to John Quincy Adams, May 20, 1776, cited in Bemis, *John
Quincy Adams and the Foundations of American Foreign Policy,* p. 80.
See also Brooks Adams' introduction to his brother Henry's *The
Degradation of the Democratic Dogma* (New York: The Macmillan
Company, 1919), p. 32. Brooks Adams asserts that his grandfather, John

Quincy Adams, "loved his mother as he never loved another human being on earth." Joseph E. Illick in "John Quincy Adams: The Maternal Influence," *Journal of Psychohistory* 4 (Fall 1976): 185–96, concludes that "the emotional tone of John Quincy Adams' life was set not by his father but his mother" (p. 194), and that she "preached the very qualities to her son that her husband is credited with transmitting" (p. 190).

17. LCA, "Adventures," *Adams Papers* III, reel 269.
18. Ibid.
19. Ibid.
20. LCA to John Quincy Adams,Washington, May 14, 1845, *The Adams Papers* IV, reel 515.
21. LCA, "Adventures," *Adams Papers* III, reel 269; Thomas Boylston Adams, *Berlin and the Prussian Court in 1798,* ed. Hugo Pollsits (New York: The New York Public Library, 1916), p. 15.
22. LCA, "Adventures," *Adams Papers* III, reel 269.
23. Ibid.
24. LCA, "Record," *Adams Papers* III, reel 265.
25. LCA, "Adventures," *Adams Papers* III, reel 269.
26. H[annah] Mather Crocker, "Observations on the Real Rights of Women," 1808, reprinted in *Sex and Equality* (New York: Arno Press, 1974), p. 15.
27. N.B. Boileau, "An Oration Delivered on the Fourth of July 1814" as quoted in Lawrence Friedman, *Inventors of the Promised Land* (New York: Alfred A. Knopf, 1975), p. 118n. Crocker, "Observations" in *Sex and Equality,* p. 6.
28. John Adams to Benjamin Rush, 1807, as quoted in Mary Summer Benson, *Women in Eighteenth-Century America* (Port Washington, New York: Kennikat Press, Inc., 1966), p. 248.
29. Benjamin Rush, "Thoughts Upon Female Education," 1787, in *Essays on Education in the Early Republic,* ed. Frederick Rudolph (Cambridge, Mass., 1865), pp. 5–12.
30. For a full discussion of this argument see Linda K. Kerber, "Daughters of Columbia: Educating Women for the Republic, 1787–1805," in *The Hofstadter Aegis,* ed. Stanley Elkins and Eric McKitrick (New York: Alfred A. Knopf, 1974), as well as Kerber, "The Republican Mother: Women and the Enlightenment—An American Perspective," *American Quarterly* 28 (Summer 1976): 187–205; also Friedman, *Inventors of the Promised Land,* pp. 108–44.
31. Crocker, "Observations" in *Sex and Equality,* p. 47.
32. Abigail Adams to F.A. Vanderkemp, February 3, 1814, *Letters of Mrs. Adams,* pp. 415–16; Abigail Adams to Mrs. Shaw, June 5, 1809, *Letters of Mrs. Adams,* p. 401.
33. Whitney, *Abigail Adams,* pp. 137–60.
34. Abigail Adams to John Adams, October 25, 1777, *Letters of Mrs. Adams,* p. 89.
35 Abigail Adams to John Adams, September 29, 1776, *Letters of Mrs. Adams,* p. 82.

36. LCA, "Adventures," *Adams Papers* III, reel 269.

37. Henry Adams, *History of the United States of America during the Administrations of Jefferson and Madison,* ed. Ernest Samuels (Chicago: University of Chicago Press, 1967), p. 9.

38. LCA, "Adventures," *Adams Papers* III, reel 269.

39. James Sterling Young, *The Washington Community 1800–1828* (New York: Columbia University Press, 1963), pp. 26, 41–50.

40. LCA, "Adventures," *Adams Papers* III, reel 269.

41. Young, *The Washington Community 1800–1828,* p. 69.

42. LCA, "Record," *Adams Papers* III, reel 265.

43. Ibid.

44. Young, *The Washington Community 1800–1828,* p. 91.

45. LCA, "Adventures," *Adams Papers* III, reel 269.

46. Ibid.

47. J.P. Mayer, ed., *Alexis de Tocqueville, Journey to America,* trans. George Lawrence (London: Faber and Faber, 1959), pp. 257–58.

48. LCA, "Adventures," *Adams Papers* III, reel 269; LCA, August 29, 1832, *Adams Papers* III, reel 271.

49. LCA, *Adams Papers* III, reel 265. Intermittently from 1819 to 1824 Louisa kept a journal, sending entries to her father-in-law, John Adams. These include many political observations. Her opinions of republican society never wavered: see Louisa C. Adams to John Quincy Adams, November 15, 1840, *Adams Papers,* reel 515.

50. LCA, "Diary 1819–1820," *The Adams Papers* III, reel 265.

51. Despite her aversion to a required social life, Louisa was a charming and accomplished hostess who, in order to fulfill the social obligations of her husband's position, gave fortnightly parties for years. LCA, *Adams Papers* III, reel 265; Mrs. Phoebe Morris to Dolly Madison, January 19, 1824, *Memoirs and Letters of Dolly Madison edited by her Grand niece* (Boston: Houghton, Mifflin and Co., 1888), pp. 169, 170.

52. LCA, "Adventures," *Adams Papers* III, reel 269; LCA, "Records," *Adams Papers* III, reel 265, *passim.*

53. LCA, *The Adams Papers* III, [August 24, 1832, reel 271. See also Nancy Cott, *The Bonds of Womanhood,* pp. 126–159.]

54. LCA, "Adventures," *The Adams Papers* III, reel 269.

55. LCA, December 6, 1821; December 16, 1821, *Adams Papers,* reel 265; John Quincy Adams to Abigail Adams, 1812, *Adams Papers,* reel 412; John Quincy Adams to George Washington Adams, August 15, 1811, *Adams Papers,* reel 412; George Washington Adams, Journal, August, 1825, *Adams Papers,* reel 287.

56. LCA, "Adventures," *Adams Papers* III, reel 269.

57. Ibid.

58. LCA, *Adams Papers,* reel 264.

59. At this time John Quincy made the following assessment of his marriage: "Our union has not been without its trials, nor invariably without dissensions between us. There are many differences of sentiment, of

tastes, and of opinions in regard to domestic economy, and to the
education of children, between us. There are natural frailties of temper in
both of us; both being quick and irascible, and mine being sometimes
harsh. But she has always been a faithful and affectionate wife, and a
careful, tender, and indulgent mother to our children, all of whom she
nursed herself. I have found in this connection from decisive experience
the superior happiness of the marriage state over that of celibacy, and a
full conviction that my lot in marriage has been highly favored." John
Quincy Adams, *Memoirs of John Quincy Adams Comprising Portions of
his Diary from 1795-1848*, ed. C.F. Adams, Vol. II (Philadelphia: J.B.
Lippincott, 1873), July 26, 1811, pp. 282-83.
60. Article attributed to LCA printed in *Mrs. A.S. Colvin's Weekly Messenger*
(Washington, D.C., June 2, 1827), *Adams Papers*, reel 269.
61. The political intrigue and factionalism that surrounded the presidential
campaign of 1824 and the subsequent Adams administration came as no
surprise to Louisa; she had anticipated it as inevitable since her first days
in Washington. Charles Francis Adams, *Diary of Charles Francis
Adams*, ed. Aida Di Page Donald and David Donald (Cambridge,
Mass.: Harvard University Press, 1968), Vol. I, September 19, 1824, p.
328. If the tragedy of John Quincy Adams was, as his grandson Brooks
Adams suggested, that he "fell victim to the fallacy which underlies the
whole theory of modern democracy"—that is, that through education the
selfish instincts of competition can be wedded to the moral principle so
that all should work for the common good—perhaps Louisa's tragedy
was that she never believed it, all the while convinced that her life had
been sacrificed to it. Brooks Adams, introduction to *The Degradation of
the Democratic Dogma*, p. 78; LCA, November 30, 1823, *Adams Papers*
III, reel 265. Most of her years in the White House were spent in semi-
seclusion. She pursued her private literary interests, entertaining only
when absolutely necessary. Ill much of the time she grew increasingly
moody and irritable. "Sublimation to circumstances has been my
doctrine, and as I have nothing to do with the disposal of affairs and
[have] never but once been consulted, I am perfectly indifferent about it,"
she had declared earlier and she was prepared to play it out. LCA, plays
and poetry, *Adams Papers*, reel 274, reel 276; Margaret Bayard Smith,
The First Forty Years of Washington Society (New York: C. Scribners'
Sons, 1906), p. 248; Charles Francis Adams, *Diary*, Vol. II, October 13,
1827; LCA, March 12, 1820, *Adams Papers*, reel 265.
62. LCA, April 12, 1847, *Adams Papers*, reel 270. During the years in
Washington the oldest Adams children were only infrequently at home.
Both attended Harvard as was expected of them, but neither developed
as their parents desired. LCA, December 21, 1820, *Adams Papers*, reel
265. George was an undisciplined, dreamy young man and, despite
unremitting pressure from his father to fit into the Adams mold, he was
more interested in literature and poetry than the law. John Quincy
Adams to George Washington Adams, August 15, 1811, *Adams Papers*,

reel 412. George Washington Adams, Journal, August, 1825, *Adams Papers,* reel 287. Louisa saw in her oldest son many of the characteristics of her own personality that had made it so difficult for her to be an Adams—particularly the tendency to choose the emotional response to a situation, rather than the intellectual one. LCA, 1832, *Adams Papers,* reel 271; LCA, July 1821, *Adams Papers,* reel 266. John also was an indifferent student with no inner drive to succeed. Because of the many years of separation Louisa was not close to her children, and when they were adolescents, she found them difficult to understand. LCA, January 21, 1821, *Adams Papers,* reel 265. Yet she never absolved herself of responsibility for their development; whatever their fates she, as their mother, ultimately deserved either the credit or the blame.

63. LCA to John Adams (son), November 14, 1830, in Charles Francis Adams, *Diary,* Vol. III, p. 349n; LCA to John Adams, October 30, 1830, in Charles Francis Adams, *Diary,* Vol. III, p. 329n.

64. LCA, "Adventures," *Adams Papers* III, reel 269.

Part Two

Identity and Vocation

I. Socialization:
Change and the Illusion of Change

Introduction

The six essays included in this section remind us that socialization is a diverse and subtle phenomenon. Out of socialization come the shades of identity and the paths of vocation. A complex process in which individuals are exposed to cultural values and behavioral patterns are shaped, it is the means by which society maintains continuity or breaks with the past. Individuals can either learn better to control their lives or find themselves being controlled. In transmitting its culture, through nurturing and educating its citizens, society can fulfill or deny the expectations of individuals, forge new identities, invite different behavior or retrench the old, and solidify its traditions.

For women at least, especially white, middle- and upper-class women, identity and vocation have tended to merge in wifehood and motherhood. The following essays consider both informal and formal aspects of socialization and examine the process itself, the individuals involved, and the interaction between the two. Two significant issues are addressed in this regard. Whatever the facet of socialization chosen for analysis, the authors agree that the values prescribed for women cannot be equated with behavior. Indeed, those authors dealing most explicitly with prescription point to the disjunction between the image of women presented and the realities of their experience. The conclusion is twofold. Women neither totally fulfilled the stereotype nor remained completely immune from its dictates. Instead, the relationship between prescription and behavior was an extraordinarily complex one which varied with individual and historical circumstances. Equally important, all of the essays are characterized by the basic premise that women were not only affected by the process of socialization, but they affected that process as well. In short, women were active participants as well as passive recipients in the elaboration of culture.

The first two essays, both of which consider socialization of an informal variety as found in the mediums of painting and film, locate visual imagery concerning women in a particular historical context. The result is a counterpoint between image and social realities. Ann Uhry Abrams analyzes in the iconography of late-nineteenth-century America the emergence of the passive, aloof, elegant woman as an ideal counterposed to an unwanted reality. The ornamental symbol of femininity stood in contrast to the experiences of growing numbers of white, middle- and upper-class women. The equation made between beauty and dependence was more representative of the traditional stereotype than reflective of the lives of educated, independent women actively and increasingly engaged in the world beyond the home. Abrams' essay explores this counterpoint between ideals and realities in the paintings of Abbott Thayer and Thomas Dewing. Noting that both offered idealized images of the woman as a being set apart from a fragmented, transitory world, Abrams argues that the imagery indicated the painters' allegiance to older values which were being challenged in their own time. The fact that Thayer and Dewing were warmly welcomed into the academy and their paintings were popular among collectors also tells us that a genteel, wealthy segment of society shared their convictions.

The same counterpart between image and reality is explored in Sumiko Higashi's essay on the working girl as heroine on the silent screen of the 1920's. The medium and the audience addressed are different, the woman presented decidedly less elegant and aloof, and the period later, but image still stood in contrast to reality. Granted that the film industry's depiction of the working girl accorded with particular trends in female employment during the early twentieth century, nevertheless, the disparity between her image on the silver screen and her actual experience in the marketplace suggests that another sector of society, Hollywood, was resisting the emergence of a "new woman," by enveloping a new image in old shadows. For example, Higashi notes that the primary motivation for employment, material sustenance, was generally ignored, and employment, as well as the film, was terminated by marriage, frequently and happily. Even in Hollywood fantasy woman's ultimate destiny remained the traditional one of wife and mother within the home.

With the essays by Nancy Green and William Jenkins, the focus shifts to socialization of a more formal and basic variety. Educational theories and systems represent the attempt to prepare the younger generation for the assumption of adult roles and reflect the interaction of traditional perceptions and practices with planned and unplanned change in society. Focusing upon early-nineteenth-century criticism of emulation, Green's essay explores the impact of the presence of females in primary and secondary education upon a common educational practice promoting competitiveness and rewarding those successful in classroom rivalry. Competition among students, or emulation as antebellum America termed it, had been encouraged as a stimulus to achievement in school since the eighteenth century. But by the 1820's, however, the composition of the student body began to change with the extension of schooling to adolescent girls. Shortly thereafter, the attitude

toward emulation changed as well. The connection was more than coinciden-
tal. Educators, Green notes, were caught in a dilemma. Schooling was
justified as the means by which girls might prepare themselves for their adult
role as wives and mothers and yet it was feared that practices such as
emulation, perceived as appropriate in the teaching of males, might distort
the "natural" purity and benevolence of females and affect adversely the
future performance of their moral role. Although girls in the classroom
forced educators to confront the question of whether emulation was a proper
educational technique to be employed with those on the brink of womanhood, tradition for a variety of reasons delineated by Green, finally prevailed
and competition in schools remained. This study of the practice of emulation
also sheds light upon a broader issue in antebellum America, namely, the
roles to be played by both women and education in a rapidly changing
America.

Just as the presence of females in the antebellum classroom stimulted
controversy and reflection in the educational community, so new developments in educational curricula continued to affect women in old ways. Seen
from the perspective of William Jenkins' essay, the emergence of home
economics as a formal discipline not only developed from the Progressive
movement generally, it also was promoted by already acknowledged trends
within Progressivism as varied as the child study movement, John Dewey's
"New Education," the settlement house movement, and vocationalism. The
introduction of home economics into secondary and collegiate curricula
along with the appearance of professional associations and journals gave
added recognition to the supposed science of domesticity and elevated it to
the status of a discipline. It meant as well that traditional values concerning
woman's role and place were reinforced. Progressivism may have contributed
to suffrage for women, but its support of home economics indicated that, the
ballot box aside, woman's primary function in society was wifehood and
motherhood and her place was still at home. Most Progressives would have
acknowledged only the first part of the current slogan, "A Woman's Place is
in the House—and the Senate."

Examining the same period as Jenkins, essays by Lynn Gordon and Joan
Zimmerman move from methods and curricula to the experiences of women
at colleges and universities. The focus is twofold: the response of both women
and institutions to co-education. Beginning with the assumption that co-
education might have prompted a significant challenge to gender-role desig-
nation, Gordon and Zimmerman find that such was not the case. Instead,
women in the face of a collegiate ideal that was male in orientation,
established subcultures that reflected and reinforced conventional attitudes
about women and their place in society. These subcultures, however, did not
develop in a vacuum. Indeed, administrators and faculty fostered segregated

activities and housing for the women on their campuses. Not surprisingly, their motivations were influenced by their gender. Men, for example, were especially concerned that supposedly innate distinctions between the sexes might dissolve were women and men to be treated without regard to gender. Women would be "masculinized," men "feminized." Women who constituted only a small minority within the administrations and faculties either accepted societal definitions of sex roles or believed themselves too vulnerable to challenge those definitions. Whatever their gender, students, faculty, and administrators cooperated in the accommodation of the collegiate ideal to women, and, in the process, women were defined, absorbed, and circumscribed along traditional lines. In many respects, co-education was a misnomer, separate education the reality.

Ann Uhry Abrams

Frozen Goddess:
The Image of Woman in
Turn-of-the-Century American Art

"The American girl is placed upon a pedestal," Samuel Isham wrote in 1905, "and each offers worship according to his abilities, the artist among the rest." In his discussion of contemporary female iconography, Isham observed that although Americans "have no goddesses or saints... something of what goddess, saint, or heroine represented to other races they find in the idealization of their womankind. They will have such idealization decorous," he continued, "there is no room for the note of unrestrained passion, still less for sensuality. It is the grace of children, the tenderness of motherhood, the beauty and purity of young girls which they demand, but especially the last."[1]

Isham's statement echoed an iconographic theme which appeared at the close of the nineteenth century. During those years a remote goddess drifted into American art, filling private parlors and public halls with her image of aloof dignity. Although these elegant beauties symbolized the ideal woman to scores of Americans during the late Victorian era, the concept of passive femininity did not apply to the increasing numbers of independent and educated women who were emerging in urban, middle-class white neighborhoods. As several colleges opened their doors to women in the 1860's and 70's, many new career opportunities arose. Therefore, pioneers like Elizabeth Blackwell in medicine, Anna Howard Shaw in theology, and Maria Mitchell in astronomy could enter fields which were once exclusively male.

Tensions between the small but vocal women's movement and the larger population of traditional sympathizers produced reactions among artists, most notably in their rendering of the ethereal female. This essay will examine that iconographic phenomenon in the works of two popular academic painters of the late nineteenth century: Abbott Handerson Thayer and Thomas Wilmer Dewing. Although the images of women presented by these two artists differed in concept and interpretation, both were reflecting a

[Ann Uhry Abrams is an Assistant Professor of art history at Spelman College. Abrams' present research concerns the image of women as well as blacks in American and European art.]

counterpoint between contemporary realities and traditional ideals. Both were responding to uncertainties of a changing industrial society by removing their women from worldly environments and by revising an older image of feminine subservience. Clearly, the paintings of Dewing and Thayer were products of the transitional social conditions of late-nineteenth-century America.

In earlier years when women's place in the social structure was relatively secure, a simpler, more direct female image prevailed. But with growing sophistication and accelerated social change of the 1880's and 90's, artists began to romanticize the female and exaggerate those characteristics taken for granted by earlier generations. The difference between the worldly and aloof goddess of the late nineteenth century and the demure, naive, and immediate maidens of mid-century would be best understood if we were to compare Dewing's *Girl with a Lute* of the 1890's and Charles Ingham's *The Flower Girl* of 1846. Dewing used an assymetrical composition and subdued tones to create a bizarre and mysterious atmosphere; Ingham, on the other hand, placed his figure squarely in the foreground surrounded by brilliant colors. Dewing's woman is withdrawn and introspective, Ingham's friendly and responsive, offering flowers to the viewer as a metaphor for her blossoming femininity. While Dewing's subject exemplifies the late-nineteenth-century image of subtlety and sophistication, Ingham's represents an earlier vision of innocence and willing obedience. The mid-century ideal is described in a poem from *Godey's Magazine and Lady's Book* of 1846 entitled "Female Charms." The perfect female is defined in the following terms:

> I would have her as pure as the snow on the mount—
> As true as the smile that to infamy's given—
> As pure as the wave of the crystalline fount,
> Yet as warm in the heart as the sunlight of heaven.
> With a mind cultivated, not boastingly wise,
> I could gaze on such beauty, with exquisite bliss;
> With her heart on her lips and her soul in her eyes—
> What more could I wish in dear woman than this.[2]

Nostalgic idealization of pure, unworldly, and submissive womanhood increased as traditional patterns were shattered. Recent explorations into social relationships among American women reveal that in the early nineteenth century, women constituted a distinct subculture within the confines of close family and neighborhood clusters. Female friendships and familial ties created a comfortable atmostphere of emotional stability. Mothers, daughters, cousins, and girl friends shared household responsibilities and social rituals in an isolated environment which men rarely entered. As these communities were disrupted by growing urbanization and industrialization, the social patterns of women changed.[3]

Rhetoric utilized by both sides of the suffragist movement further emphasized woman's social alienation. Suffragist publications and speeches explained that women were deliberately kept apart from the decision-making processes of a democratic society. Opponents of women's suffrage extended the idea of female isolation by exaggerating sexual differences which prevented women from competing with men. The stereotype of the idolized goddess further separated women from the male world. A New York politician employed a popular cliche when he declared that a woman should remain "as a queen in the eyes of all mankind, unrivaled and unsurpassed, as will enshrine her forever in the hearts of the father, the husband, and the son"[4] Set apart from social and political intercourse with men, women were alone. Elevated onto the pedestal, they were removed physically and emotionally from worldly contact. The idealized images in the paintings of Thayer and Dewing reflect and foster these prevailing concepts of woman's isolation.

To the opponents of women's rights, beauty and female independence were mutually exclusive. No woman could possess both. This notion pervaded the iconography of women throughout the nineteenth century. As one antisuffragist proclaimed: "When a woman is beautiful, she is generally satisfied with playing a woman's part."[5] Equation of beauty with woman's traditional role was basic to the artistic interpretation of the "frozen goddess." The artist's vision extolled passivity, delicacy, and helplessness in opposition to strength, determination, and assertiveness. Thus as the women's movement accelerated its publicity and increased its momentum, the painter's counter-image gained in popularity.

By creating an illusion of female divinity, artists of the late nineteenth century appealed to the nostalgic tenor of the times. Pristine beauty, harmonious colors, and classical motifs were equated with feminine delicacy, domestic tranquility, and Olympian virtues. Not surprisingly, patronage and academic acceptance came to artists who evoked images of mythical womanhood. Such was the case with Abbott Handerson Thayer (1849–1921), a distinguished member of the National Academy of Design, the Society of American Artists, and the American Academy of Arts and Letters. From 1880 until 1910, Thayer was considered one of America's leading painters, noted for his portrayals of women which were said to embody "the highest of universal truths."[6]

Apparently, Thayer expected the real women in his life to live up to his painted ideal. His first wife, Kate, whom he met in classes at the National Academy of Design, had aspirations to become a professional artist. But, once married, she failed to realize her goal. Her friend, Maria Dewing, recalled that Kate attempted to be Thayer's personification of the nineteenth-century paragon. "She was in all ways his ideal of womanhood," Mrs. Dewing recalled, "innocent, poetic, graceful, maternal."[7] Thayer's father wrote that Kate "had unlimited patience, nothing ruffled her temper," even though her husband was "often hard, pushing his personal views to the extreme and sometimes criticising her unmercifully."[8] After twelve years of being the "perfect" wife and mother, Kate began to display signs of "melancholia." When her bouts of depression grew more severe, Thayer's father, a physician, helped his son admit her to a mental institution where she subsequently died.[9] Only months after her death, Thayer married her closest friend, Emma Beach, who had been caring for the children while Kate was in the sanitarium. In his letter of proposal, Thayer told Emma that he needed a woman to care for him, to love his children, and to bring "noble comfort" into his home.[10]

Thayer's relationship to the women in his life followed a familiar nineteenth-century standard in his expectation that the wife serve as loving nursemaid, conscientious housekeeper, and cheerful companion. Kate's inability to continue meeting such expectations might well have contributed to her mental collapse. Undoubtedly, similar frustrations caused frequent breakdowns of women during that period.[11] "Nobility," "miraculous love," and "worship" were terms Thayer often used when writing about women, just as in his paintings he portrayed females as angels and madonnas. By placing them on the proverbial pedestal he separated them from the male world and isolated them from the realities of life. His younger daughter, Gladys, recalled that many types of women displeased her father. "On the whole," she confided, "I can sincerely say that I think he preferred the company of men as a general rule" even though he believed women to be "'touchstones' in aesthetic matters."[12] As aesthetic touchstones, women were thus mythologized into Platonic ideals devoid of human failings.

Although Thayer vehemently denied any affiliation with formal religion, he often employed Christian iconography in his depiction of females. *The Virgin* of 1893 and *The Virgin Enthroned* of 1891 (Figure I) are two of his better known renditions. The latter shows his elder daughter "enthroned" in an outdoor setting with her younger brother and sister on either side. The title, "Virgin," not only established the purity of his daughter (aptly named Mary) but also emphasized Thayer's intention to ally himself with Renaissance masters who painted the Holy Family in pastoral settings. The balanced composition, clarity of line and excessive drapery are imitative of Renaissance techniques, but the central figure is unmistakably a creation of the late nineteenth century. Compared to the tender madonnas of Raphael or the sensuous beauties of Titian, she appears sensitive and withdrawn, dignified and pensive. Thayer began *The Virgin Enthroned* shortly after his first

Figure I. Virgin Enthroned, *Abbot H. Thayer, 1891*
(Courtesy National Collection of Fine Arts, Smithsonian Institution)

wife was confined to the mental institution and finished it during the summer she died. The "Virgin" might thus be interpreted as a symbol of both daughter and wife, and by virtue of the pose and title, a representative of the archetypical virgin. The pathos of the seated madonna, the sentimental adoration of the kneeling children, the delicate blossoms in each of their hands all contribute to the enigmatic combination of familiarity and distance which distinguishes Thayer's work.

By endowing modern individuals with classical attributes, Thayer was employing the same mixture of reality and fantasy which characterized the close of the nineteenth century. His paintings held special meaning for a generation that engineered a mechanized extravaganza to celebrate the anniversary of Columbus' voyage, and built Doric mausoleums to house exhibitions of modern technology. Thayer's paintings combined the present with the past. By evoking an image of classical purity, he recalled bygone virtues; by placing modern women in Arcadian settings, he rejected contemporary reality. Mount Olympus superseded the National American Woman's Suffrage Association; Ariadne triumphed over Susan B. Anthony.

Several of Thayer's contemporaries mused about his use of wings on ordinary individuals. Royal Cortissoz commented:

> There are women on Thayer's canvases who with their maidenly bloom have also the heroic dignity of the Roman matron of legend. Their charm is drawn, as I have indicated, from Olympian sources. Yet it is one of their finest traits that they stand with their feet unmistakably on the solid earth. They are profoundly human presences. It is by character, by qualities of the soul that they triumph, not through any dramatic or other significance derived from a specificially pictorial ingenuity.[13]

Others, like Homer Saint-Gaudens, believed that Thayer rejected earthly realities in his desire to capture only the ideal. His use of wings, Saint-Gaudens explained, "indicates simply that his figure presents no claim to be regarded as realistic, but rather stands as one neither Greek, heathen nor Christian, which unfolds its own intangible, unthought message."[14] Thayer admitted that his winged women suggested "an exalted atmosphere (above the realm of genre painting) where one need not explain the action of his figures."[15] In other words, Thayer painted immobile angels who epitomized beauty, distance, and inaction. Goddesses not only made lovely displays, they never attempted to compete in the marketplace. Both Thayer and his critics were pitting the traditional myth against contemporary reality and strongly rejecting the latter.

In *Winged Figure* Thayer depicted a disgruntled young girl whose haunting stare and pleading gestures are poignantly human. How misplaced she appears in a gilded wreath and angel's costume. Again we feel the tension between modern reality and traditional ideals. Similarly, the *Stevenson Memorial* angel (Figure II), perched on the grave of Robert Louis Stevenson, conveys an enigmatic combination of human attributes and traditional religious symbols. With her casual, impish pose she appears uncomfortable in her role as an angel. This may well have been the case, for Thayer often persuaded members of his family and their friends to don the white robes, wings, and haloes which he stocked in his studio, and serve as his models. In fact, his daughter Mary posed for the painting entitled *Angel*. Her flushed young face contrasts dramatically with the stark whiteness of the wings and robe; her slightly tilted head and wisps of hair act as the only deviations from the monotony of a perfectly balanced canvas.

Symmetrical composition was symbolically significant for Thayer because innate balance represented stability and classical rationality. The contemporary journalist, Henry Turner Bailey, commented that Thayer's paintings were balanced "according to impartial laws" the highest of which was love. "No other artist," Bailey continued, "has so perfectly realized in a single vision the universal ideal of Love benevolent."[16] Bailey was referring to Thayer's large painting, *Caritas,* in which a standing woman draped in the familiar Greek-styled robe was sheltering two small cherubs with her outstretched arms. As the title implies, the woman represented "Charity," a virtue which Bailey praised as

> love in its purest form.... Such is the love incarnate in this young
> woman in white, manifesting itself as the love of the strong for the
> weak... the *noblesse oblige* of a regal spirit.... What a superb
> creature Caritas is! Tall, athletic, intellectual, refined, calm, acting
> from conviction, she is the embodiment of 'Love without weakness.'
> She stands with bowed head and outstretched arms, a beautiful
> echo of the figure upon a cross, man's supreme symbol of sacrificial
> love.[17]

This passage explains the rationale of Thayer's females, for in *Caritas* and in his other allegorical paintings, a similar theme is repeated: the female figure embodies ideals of universal truth, virtue, and "sacrificial love." As a regal, intellectual, and athletic figure she seems to defy the stereotypical image. Yet the strength of *Caritas* is not that of aggressive dominance, rather she is the personification of maternal protection, a pillar of unbending love and staunch faithfulness. Surrounded by symbols of antiquity and Christianity, she is sacrosanct, rejecting human passions for the betterment of mankind. As the epitome of perfected womanhood, she is above earthly transgressions and petty vexations of daily existence. Indeed, she has sacrificed her life to the care and protection of her family. With head bowed she performs her

Figure II. Stevenson Memorial, *Abbot H. Thayer, 1903*
(Courtesy National Collection of Fine Arts, Smithsonian Institution)

charitable mission.

It is extremely significant that Thayer's paintings had tremendous appeal among late-nineteenth-century collectors, especially Charles Freer and John Gellatly. Could the popularity of these ethereal goddesses have been due to Thayer's skill in capturing contemporary ideals? In a society haunted by nostalgic yearnings for a past world where women were unquestionably secondary to their mates, Thayer's works represented the cherished ideal, elevated above contemporary pressures. Samuel Isham evoked these sentiments when he observed that Thayer's women could "not make Welsh rabbits [sic] or go skating.... They are set up frankly," he wrote, "for our adoration, and it goes to them at once without reserve, they are so strong and beautiful and pure. It is a noble ideal, a sort of revivifying of the figures of Phidias with modern spirituality, and the execution corresponds with it."[18]

Thayer's colleague, Thomas Wilmer Dewing (1851–1938), shared his friend's reverence for past values and, like Thayer, he gained national prominence in the 1890's for his ethereal renditions of women. Dewing's associate described him as a warm, zealous man whose heart was as large as his rather cumbersome frame. In an obituary of 1939, Royal Cortissoz recalled: "In my youth when I first visited him in his studio,... I used to be charmed by the harp on the door which gave forth delicate music. And he, like his art, was endearing."[19]

Dewing's interpretation of and experience with women was quite different from Thayer's. Whereas the latter's painted women were angels, his real women were subservient. Dewing's subjects, on the other hand, were aloof and delicate, removed from reality not by wings and haloes but by compositional devices and stylistic maneuverings. His real women, however, were remarkably independent for the late nineteenth century. His wife, the former Maria Oakey, received extensive artistic training at home and abroad, including studies with the noted French master, Thomas Couture. Husband and wife often painted side by side. In fact, several of Dewing's early canvases bear both of their signatures. Best known for her flower paintings, Maria Dewing held exhibitions in Philadelphia and New York during the early years of the twentieth century.[20]

Maria Dewing's ideas on art and aesthetics apparently influenced her husband's approach to painting. In 1881, she published a book entitled *Beauty in Dress,* in which she outlined her concepts of feminine beauty. "Nothing is more elegant than simplicity," she wrote, "nor in worse taste than over elaboration." She emphasized harmony, subtlety of line, and application of the "fixed laws" of form and color. Her description of the beautiful woman was often repeated by her husband in his paintings. Restrained elegance and natural beauty were the hallmarks of her conception of womanliness:

Let us see our women gracefully poised upon comfortably shod feet, with erect head, moving easily forward with the free, unconscious motion.... A dress perfectly fresh, light in color... beautifully cut, and almost entirely untrimmed, cannot be improved upon for a young girl. It is the sweet, rounded forms, the dewy bloom of the cheek, the clear, young eyes, the soft, tender lips that we want to see.[21]

The women of Dewing's paintings are visual manifestations of his wife's writings, for he created a type of ideal beauty which was simple, delicate and elegant. He told Freer in 1901: "My decorations belong to the poetic and imaginative world where a few choice spirits lie."[22] In *The Necklace* and *The Garland* (Figure III) we note several of his iconographic and compositional devices. In each, a single woman sits alone in the center of a sparsely funished room. She appears to be frozen in an airless world, her actions halted, her emotions subdued. The composition of these works (as in Dewing's many interior settings) places the woman in middleground surrounded by vacant space. In the subtle coloration and soft diffused lighting, we can detect Dewing's debt to his artistic antecedents, Vermeer and Whistler. As in Vermeer's meticulous interiors, Dewing has displayed an interest in the object. But unlike his Dutch predecessor, Dewing does not distinguish between his human subject and the objects which surround her, treating the woman just like the book, the pearls, the vase, the bowl—a lifeless object to be collected and admired. As in a Whistler "arrangement," Dewing has viewed the interior setting in terms of surface pattern and mood; the subdued tones and muted colors evoke the ambiance of a Japanese print. The women are, indeed, part of the total decoration, little more than patterns and designs.

Unlike Thayer, Dewing followed certain contemporaneous stylistic trends, using female subjects to answer formal and compositional problems. His impressionistic technique diffused color and lighting; his artistic allegiance was to the present, not the past. But like Thayer, he resorted to classical aesthetics by equating harmony, balance, and decorum to exalted feminine beauty. In *A Reading,* he presented two women seated at a table, their eyes closed as if communicating with spirits from beyond. The solemn stillness of the muted pastel colors and large areas of empty space heighten the mood of transcendental mysticism. Similar symbols appear in *The Letter* where two women occupy opposite corners of a vacant room, one posed before an empty table, dreamily gazing into space, the other sitting at an open desk presumably writing the letter mentioned in the title. Familiar accessories in *A Reading* and *The Letter* reemphasize the ethereal and fragile quality of these women who seem alienated from each other and from the world. Flowers traditionally symbolize blossoming femininity; the ubiquitous straightbacked

Figure III. The Garland, *Thomas Wilmer Dewing*
(Courtesy the Freer Gallery, Smithsonian Institution)

chair connotes propriety; and the nonreflecting mirror creates an air of insular remoteness. Spatial arrangements have been carefully planned to isolate each woman in dramatic solitude.

From Whistler, Dewing borrowed ideas of harmony and tonality by combining the ethereal women with a musical motif. Playing musical instruments was a respectable outlet for nineteenth-century ladies and was thus a familiar theme for American painters. But Dewing has incorporated erotic symbolism into the popular woman-in-music theme. In *Girl with a Lute* and *The Piano* he portrayed women in isolated corners of vacant rooms caressing their musical instruments. They appear strangely aroused as they drift into a passionate state evoked by the mysteries of exotic music. The space which surrounds them becomes intensely suggestive, symbolizing an open corridor between the waiting woman and the admiring viewer.

Four of Dewing's most provocative women are found on a pair of screens painted for Freer between 1895 and 1898 entitled *The Four Sylvan Sounds*. As they lounge in flower-laden meadows, these women epitomize Dewing's use of subtle eroticism. Their knees and feet are projected forward while their averted faces recede. These positions make them appear relaxed and dreamy, lying among the leaves and flowers, each holding a musical instrument—a xylophone, a flute, a drum, a lyre. Yet none of the women are actually playing the instruments they hold. Instead they drift in a state of motionless tranquility, while muted colors and subdued tones suggest the paradoxical combination of pristine innocence and seductive expectation.

In other paintings, Dewing expanded his use of provocative sexual allusions. *After Sunset, Spring Moonlight* and *Summer* (Figure IV) are typical examples of women drifting through pale meadows with no visable relationship to anything worldly. They are simultaneously accessible and remote, passionate and frigid, reflecting that peculiar combination of desire and restraint which characterized the transitional state of late Victorian morality. On close examination, we see that the women in Dewing's paintings were not the innocent maidens of earlier years. These goddesses possessed an air of tragic awareness and sultry sophistication. The disparity between real sexual fulfillment and the prudish ideal which frustrated Victorian women also pervades Dewing's works. In their vacant rooms or deserted meadows, Dewing's females symbolize the physical and emotional loneliness of late-nineteenth-century womanhood. Restrained by social custom they remain lonely and remote, sadly awaiting contact with others.

Contemporary appraisal of Dewing substantiates implications of eroticism in his paintings. Charles Caffin commented that Dewing's women were "intellectually sensuous" because they expressed "the condition of pure abstract enjoyment through the senses,... not passion," Caffin explained, "but its essence."[23] Thus these works, which seem so innocent and demure to

*Figure IV. Summer, Thomas Wilmer Dewing, ca. 1890
(Courtesy National Collection of Fine Arts, Smithsonian Institution)*

twentieth-century viewers, undoubtedly titillated refined Victorian sensibilities by suggesting passion for the unpossessable. Indeed they represent a type of female perfection which contains the paradoxical elements of purity and sensuality, qualities equated with sublime beauty in the language of the period.

When analyzing Dewing's approach to painting, Caffin commented: "Out of the sense-impressions received and their stimulus to his mind he projects a scheme of form and color that shall give expression to a conception of abstract beauty."[24] Cortissoz also observed that Dewing's paintings were "freighted with suggestion," because of their "power to charm without the aid of any adventitious appeals to either poetry or incident, without any reliance upon eccentricity or even marked originality of subject." He went on to explain that Dewing had the "ability to achieve beauty just through the imaginative impulse which animates and guides his brush" and through such imagery he conveys "the truths of nature, deep in the beauty of a finely artistic spirit."[25] Thus in the sublimated imagery of the 1890's Dewing was expressing the Victorian sexual mystique. His remote and refined women, lost in pensive contemplation, epitomized dignity and propriety coupled with subtle eroticism and compliance.

From differing perspectives, Thayer and Dewing painted remote goddesses to satisfy personal and public concepts of morality and aesthetics. Thayer turned his female models into angels and madonnas, elevating them above the problems of everyday life. Dewing, on the other hand, removed his women from earthly contact by isolating them in empty rooms and distant landscapes. These ethereal beauties were the antithesis of Elizabeth Cady Stanton and Lucy Stone Blackwell. Instead of signifying the newly independent female, these delicate maidens represented a nostalgic ideal. With different techniques, each artist provided traditionalists with what they wanted—beautiful women beyond the reach of the world. These were not sensuous nudes that would evoke the scorn of "proper" society, rather they were dignified, respectable ladies who inspired intellectual passions.

Yet these women seem alienated from contact with other humans. They appear to be unable to move of their own volition. On Thayer's pedestal, women exist in a mythical kingdom where relationships with peers seem remote and indeed impossible. In Dewing's airless chambers or desolate fields, women appear to be awaiting male presence for their motivation and direction. In both artists' conceptions, they were the women imagined by Henry James when he wrote that American women of the late nineteenth century "did with themselves nothing at all; they waited, in attitudes more or less gracefully passive, for a man to come that way and furnish their destiny."[26]

Notes

1. Samuel Isham, *The History of American Painting* (New York: The Macmillan Co., 1936), pp. 468–471.
2. Quoted in Barbara Welter, "The Cult of True Womanhood: 1820–1860," *American Quarterly* 18 (Summer 1966): 128.
3. See Carroll Smith-Rosenberg, "The Female World of Love and Ritual: Relations between Women in Nineteenth-Century America," *Signs* 1 (Autumn 1975): 1–29; Jill Conway, "Women Reformers and American Culture, 1870–1930," *Journal of Social History* 5 (Winter 1971–72): 164–77; Eleanor Flexner, *Century of Struggle: The Woman's Rights Movement in the United States* (Cambridge, Mass.: Harvard University Press, The Belknap Press, 1975); Page Smith, *Daughters of the Promised Land, Women in American History* (Boston: Little, Brown and Co., 1970); Aileen Kraditor, *The Ideas of the Woman Suffrage Movement, 1890–1920* (New York: Columbia University Press, 1965); and Ernest Earnest, *The American Eve in Fact and Fiction* (Urbana: University of Illinois Press, 1974).
4. Quoted in Aileen S. Kraditor, ed., *Up From the Pedestal: Selected Writings in the History of American Feminism* (Chicago: Quadrangle Books, 1968), p. 197; Also see Ellen DuBois, *Feminism and Suffrage* (Ithaca: Cornell University Press, 1978).
5. Max O'Rell, *Her Royal Highness Woman and His Majesty-Cupid* (New York: Abbey Press, 1901).
6. Column from *Smith's Magazine* 6 (March 1908), in Abbott Handerson Thayer Papers, Archives of American Art, Washington, D.C.
7. Maria Oakey Dewing, "Abbott Thayer—A Portrait and an Appreciation," *International Studio* 46 (August 1921): xi–xii.
8. Quoted in Nelson C.White, *Abbott H. Thayer, Painter and Naturalist* (Hartford: Printers Inc., 1951), p. 57.
9. Ibid. These events are described in detail in an autobiography written by William Henry Thayer, Thayer Paper.
10. Quoted in Ibid., p. 58.
11. See Carroll Smith-Rosenberg, "The Hysterical Woman: Sex Roles and Role Conflict in Nineteenth-Century America," *Social Research* 39 (Winter 1972): 652–678; and Charlotte Perkins Gilman, *The Yellow Wallpaper* (Old Westbury, N.Y.: Feminist Press, 1973).
12. Letter from Gladys Thayer Reasoner to Nelson White, Thayer Papers.
13. Quoted in White, *Abbott H. Thayer...*, p. 211.
14. Homer Saint-Gaudens, "Abbott H. Thayer," *International Studio* 33 (January 1908): lxxiv.
15. A.H. Thayer to the Director of the Hillyer Art Gallery, Smith College, 1912, quoted in White, *Abbott H. Thayer...*, p. 219.
16. Henry Turner Bailey, newspaper column, no date or publication, Thayer Papers.

17. Ibid.
18. Isham, *History. . .,* p. 472.
19. "Player's Bulletin," (March 1, 1939), Thomas Dewing Papers, Archives of American Art, Washington, D.C.
20. For information on Maria Dewing, see Jennifer A. Martin, "The Rediscovery of Maria Oakey Dewing," *The Feminist Art Journal* 5 (Summer 1976): 24-27, 44; and the catalogue of her exhibition at the Pennsylvania Academy of Fine Arts, March, 1907. Copy in the New York Public Library.
21. Maria Oakey Dewing, *Beauty in Dress* (New York: Harper & Bros., 1881), pp. 161, 164, 167.
22. Dewing to Freer, February 16, 1901, Charles Freer Papers, Archives of American Art, Washington, D.C.
23. Charles H. Caffin, "The Art of Thomas W. Dewing," *Harper's,* 116 (April 1908): 711.
24. Ibid., p. 723.
25. Royal Cortissoz, "Some Imaginative Types in American Art," *Harper's,* 91 (July 1895): 168.
26. Henry James, *The Portrait of a Lady* (New York: Signet, 1963), p. 59.

Sumiko Higashi

Cinderella vs Statistics: The Silent Movie Heroine as a Jazz-Age Working Girl

The role of popular culture in reflecting or influencing the American woman's changing socioeconomic status and society's consequent image of her has been a subject of increasing study in interdisciplinary approaches to women's history.[1] Any consideration of twentieth-century prescriptions of femininity must of necessity include a focus upon the movies.[2] Underlying such an approach is the premise that a circular relationship, however difficult and complex to gauge, exists between film and society. Just as movie production itself is tied precariously to the economics of the profit motive, so the content of film both shapes and reflects the social and cultural milieu. As part of a mass communication system, the movies have recorded, interpreted, and distorted female behavioral norms and expectations for a wide audience of passive spectators. Without doubt, movies have had an immense impact upon women's self-image, the nature of their relationship to men, and generally their status and function in society.

A fruitful period of investigation both in terms of cultural images of women and the growth of the motion picture industry is the twenties. By coincidence the Jazz Age, a decade characterized by a revolution in manners and morals, was also the era of silent film. And it was during the twenties that movie production became the country's fourth largest business with an investment totaling $1,500,000,000, an output yielding 90 percent of the world's film, and a weekly audience numbering between ninety and one hundred million spectators.[3] Social observers have often speculated about the role of the movies in the so-called Jazz-Age revolt in manners and morals and in influencing consumption habits, two not unrelated phenomena in a decade labeled hedonistic.[4] On screen a partial reflection of these develop-

[Director of Women's Studies and Assistant Professor of History at State University of New York, College at Brockport, Sumiko Higashi is the author of *Virgins, Vamps, and Flappers: The American Silent Movie Heroine.* Her recent article, "Charlie's Angels: Gumshoes in Drag," published in *Film Criticism* is part of a project on the image of women in television action series.]

ments was the emergence of the silent movie heroine as working girl, a female who achieved some degree of independence because her labor was in demand in a postwar economy. Significantly, the working-girl heroine became popular during a period when the United States entered an economic phase of high mass consumption and embraced what Malcolm Cowley described as "the consumption ethic."

The characterization of the movie heroine as working girl did reflect certain employment trends for women in the teens and twenties. Statistics indicate that increasing numbers of women were crowding the job market: between 1910 and 1930 their working numbers doubled and by the end of the twenties they comprised 21.9 percent of the labor force. Since employment figures for women have steadily risen despite the Depression and massive layoffs following World War II, a more important phenomenon may have been the pattern of female employment which emerged during the teens and twenties. Figures show a decline for women employed in agriculture and remain relatively constant for those in manufacturing. But statistics for women working in areas such as transportation (usually as telephone operators), trade (generally as sales clerks), domestic and personal services (especially as laundresses and servants), and the professions (mostly as teachers and nurses) show an increase. The most dramatic increase was in the clerical field where figures more than tripled.[5] Women workers in a consumer economy were increasingly drawn and locked into job categories today labeled pink collar. Equally significant is the fact that this pattern of employment for women has persisted to the present day despite the emergency requirements of World War II, which resulted in a temporary "Rosie-the-riveter" ideal, and contemporary efforts at affirmative action.

Although the pin-money hypothesis about working wives is still voiced, the fact that married women outnumbered single women as recruits to the labor force between 1910 and 1930 suggests that women's earnings, though roughly 45 percent less than men's, were necessary in achieving the standard of living maintained by their families. But despite the concern that social observers voiced about the problem of child care, married women who worked outside the home received little if any institutional support to cope with domestic responsibilities.[6] The working wife and mother was—and is still—penalized by a form of double duty which also prevented her from competing in the job market on an equal basis. As for single women, they too contributed to the maintenance of households. According to the Women's Bureau, 90.7 percent of unmarried women contributed all or a significant portion of their income to the support of their families.[7] During the early decades of the twentieth century, then, growing numbers of women, both married and single, were employed outside the home. Economic necessity was a basic motivation, the job pink collar, and the setting an increasingly urban and consumer-oriented

Laura La Plante, Pauline Frederick, and Malcolm McGregor in Smoldering Fires.

economy.

The portrayal of the working girl in silent films usually ignored the fact that single women contributed to the support of their families as well as the exigencies that dictated continued employment after marriage. Predictably, the daily routine of women who worked out of economic necessity was relegated to yet another world beyond the silver screen. The depiction of the work experience of the silent movie heroine—not to mention the length of the film—lasted only until her wedding day. And her employment served a purpose secondary to earning a living, for she usually met her future husband while on the job. Should Prince Charming chance to be the son of a millionaire, that fortuitous circumstance obviated the necessity for clerking at Macy's once the honeymoon was over. Usually the silent screen working girl married and stepped into a cozy, rose-covered cottage or better still, a palatial mansion.

Silent movie stars cast as working girls found themselves in an assortment of jobs, most of them rendered true to life. Gloria Swanson portrays a bargain basement salesgirl in *Manhandled* (1924), a waitress in *Stage Struck* (1925), and a chorus girl in *Fine Manners* (1926). Evelyn Brent and Louise Brooks as sisters are employed in a department store in *Love 'em and Leave 'em* (1926). As *Irene* (1926), Colleen Moore demonstrates beds in a display window, delivers merchandise, and enters a modeling career through the intervention of a suitor. In another feature, *Orchids and Ermine* (1926), she operates the switchboard of a Fifth Avenue hotel. Attempting to escape her popular little girl roles, Mary Pickford plays a five-and-dime stock clerk in *My Best Girl* (1927). Clara Bow in a film which would dub her the "It Girl" (1927), sells lingerie, while in an earlier picture, *Mantrap* (1926), she is a barbershop manicurist. A Frank Capra silent titled *That Certain Thing* (1928) features Viola Dana as a cigar counter salesgirl who later runs a successful boxlunch business. And in a series of Hollywood movies about Hollywood, working women aspired to that most spectacular success of all, stardom. Beauty contestant Mabel Normand arrives starry-eyed at a movie studio in *The Extra Girl* (1923) and is put to work in wardrobe before she wins a screen test. Another contest winner, Colleen Moore, arrives in movieland to crash the studio gates and become a star in *Ella Cinders* (1926). And Marion Davies graduates from custard pie slapstick to movie stardom in a film called *Show People* (1928).

Although few women were launched into movie careers, this inventory of jobs as depicted by silent films accurately reflected the growth of a mass consumption economy. But this was as far as movie realism tread and in fact it served to perpetuate fantasy despite the element of satire in several films. By identifying with a heroine in a realistic work situation, moviegoers found themselves proceeding from a plausible starting point to implausible wish-

Colleen Moore in Irene.

Mary Pickford in My Best Girl.

fulfillment. Not too subtly, one of the films was titled *Ella Cinders*. An updated version of the fairy tale dictated that the heroine be rescued from continued employment rather than domestic drudgery.

The number of millionaires and rich men's sons floating on the movie marriage market was enough to turn the head of any young shop girl. Although scarcely knowledgeable about upper-class amenities, she was able to bound up the social ladder in a single marriage. The appearance of an elegant, sophisticated, well-bred rival only served to highlight her basic, homespun charm and virtues. Irene O'Dare, daughter of an Irish washer-woman, marries Don Marsh, son of a socialite and head of an electrical company. Pink Watson, a PBX operator who covets orchids and ermine, wins the affection of an Oklahoma oil tycoon. Maggie Johnson becomes the best girl of Joe Merrill, son of a millionaire who owns a chain of five-and-dimes. Betty Lou Spence, saucy "It Girl," attracts Cyrus Waltham, head of the world's largest department store. Tessie McGuire, wiser for having been manhandled by playboys, becomes engaged to an old sweetheart who has invented an automotive gadget and promises to support her in style. Chorus girl Orchid Murphy lacks fine manners but appeals to a debonair lover who divides his time between Park Avenue and South America. And Molly Kelly in *That Certain Thing* marries an heir who, temporarily estranged from his father, puts her culinary and his capitalistic talents to use.

Films in which the heroine achieved stardom ironically tended to denigrate the pursuit of fame and fortune in lieu of woman's true destiny. Ella Cinders exits from a motion picture career to marry a former boyfriend who is really a rich man's son in disguise. Sue Graham, the extra girl, finally obtains a screen test but gives up any prospects to marry a childhood sweetheart. Later she tells her husband as they screen her test for their son: "Dearest, to hear him call me mama means more than the greatest career I could ever have had." Peggy Pepper, the successful movie queen of *Show People,* walks out on an extravaganza marriage to her leading man and instead gives a fillip to the career of an ex-boyfriend with whom she is still in love. A woman's responsibility to encourage the employment prospects of her man is also dramatized in *Love 'em and Leave 'em. Stage Struck,* and *That Certain Thing.* The heroines in these films possess skills useful in joint ventures with their men but certainly do not upstage them. For instance, Mame encourages the aspirations of her fiance Bill to become a window decorator in *Love 'em and Leave 'em,* although clearly she is the one who displays the talent for such a career. For the silent screen working girl, then, employment was simply a detour en route to the altar. And to the extent that being on the job enhanced her marital prospects, an independent life style reinforced tradition.

The so-called "new woman" or flapper could be discerned with respect to personality and style in a few of these films, but she was in the minority compared to the sweetness-and-light heroine typified by Pickford in *My Best Girl.* Despite her appearance in some flapper roles, Colleen Moore cast as a working girl is a comic ingenue and often a bungling one at that. The Swanson heroines in *Manhandled, Stage Struck,* and *Fine Manners* are more modern in temperament but incompetent in coping with their personal or professional problems. A new breed of woman is observable, however, in characters portrayed by Clara Bow and Louise Brooks, actresses with different personalities but similar in exhibiting a more overt and unabashed form of sexual appeal. But despite some displacement of the Victorian notion that women were asexual creatures, the much touted sexual revolution of the twenties did have a conservative dimension. Shop girls may have defied convention but did so only to achieve the conventional end of marriage. Put another way, women became more sexually available to men but in the process acquired more leverage to manipulate them into matrimony. And, in general, there was an objectification of women as bodies associated with commodities available for pleasurable use in a consumer economy.

The flapper in F. Scott Fitzgerald's world was a leisure-class phenomenon but her aggressive pattern of behavior was evident in a few of the working-girl films.[8] Clara Bow as sexual predator has been described as vivacious, pert, saucy, madcap, restless, rebellious, mischievous, and flirtatious. Vincent Canby rightly labeled her as the *auteur* of Paramount's famed film, *It*. A dichotomy between work and play is set up in the opening sequence which takes place in the office of Cyrus Waltham, Jr. (Antonio Moreno). The lettering on the office door reveals the fact that Junior has only recently

Clara Bow and Antonio Moreno in It.

supplanted Senior as head of the world's largest department store. Inside, his effeminate friend Monty, who is impervious to work and chatters about the quality of "It" (later defined by Elinor Glyn as that "quality... which draws all others with its magnetic force") is positioned so that he intermittently obscures a patriarchal bust to the right of the desk. Later as the two men walk about the main floor of the department store, Monty inspects a row of salesgirls, each standing next to a single, plastic, female leg thrust upside down into the air—a mise-en-scene that would provoke any Freudian analyst. According to Monty, the only salesgirl present who possesses "It" is Betty Lou Spence (Bow), but she has already set her sights on her wealthy and handsome boss. ("Sweet Santa Claus, give me him!") As the film progresses, she plots and schemes, utilizing "It" to full advantage, and finally extracts a proposal. The characteristic Bow heroine, whether a flapper or not, is in perpetual motion in pursuit of her man—almost any man.[9]

Although Bow was spunky and spirited, she was basically good-natured, whereas Louise Brooks had a touch of the stereotyped vampire in her rather unique sensual appeal. In *Love 'em and Leave 'em,* she plays Janie Walsh, a spoiled brat who takes advantage of her older sister Mame's better nature and acquires everything she has, including her boyfriend Bill. When Janie loses the funds collected for a Welfare Dance, she has no compunction about shifting the blame and disgrace to Mame. In the end, she discards Bill, flirts with a middle-aged department store manager, and drives off in a Rolls with the store owner himself. No doubt she is beginning a promising career. If Mame has been too indulgent in rearing her younger sister, she is in other respects competent and mature and proves to be no long-suffering martyr. As Janie becomes increasingly thoughtless, Mame reacts angrily and is probably relieved to be rid of her sibling burden in the end. As for the man between the two sisters, he is overshadowed by the unscrupulousness of the one and competence of the other. In a symbolic scene, Bill arrives to rescue Mame in her confrontation with a disreputable bookie concerning the Welfare Dance money lost by Janie. Not only do his pants fall to the floor as he stumbles into the room, his presence is rendered superfluous by Mame who has successfully trussed up the villain in a hide-a-bed. The subsequent reconciliation of the former lovers as they head for the altar at the conclusion of the film thus appears to be a mismatch. Why does Mame need a vascillating and inept male except for the convention that all women should be marriage bound?

Despite the fact that the silent screen working girl earned her own living for a time, she was conventional in that she usually married and became economically dependent upon a male. A film titled *The Eyes of Youth* (1919) made a blunt if rare observation in a scene in which a discarded wife exclaimed: "I came here to laugh at all these fool women who never stop to think that all they have depends on the whim of some man." Since women in these working-girl films had little economic choice besides marriage, obviously the style and object of courtship assumed importance. And when it came to catching a husband, especially a well-heeled one, tactics changed with the heroine. A few "new women" were not the decorous types admired during the Victorian era but were instead aggressively in pursuit of rich husbands. At times, plot devices such as the momentary reversal of a suitor's fortunes intruded to mitigate the heroine's predatory character and to prove that romance triumphs over money. Significantly, the male leads on screen were overshadowed by the persona of well-known actresses as well as by their respective characterizations. A number of actors in these films were quite anemic in comparison to the swashbuckling Fairbankses, Valentinos, and Barrymores. During a decade in which "the little man" became a cog in the wheel of an economy which was standardized well beyond his comprehension or control, the male image on screen became schizophrenic. As opposed to period pieces in exotic locales where superheroes rescued damsels in distress, men in contemporary settings often paled vis-à-vis sexually frank or aggressive women. The very fact that vibrant women were paired with such uninspiring lovers is a statement about their destiny: rebelliousness led to marriage with a lackluster and conventional companion and the maintenance of the status quo. In short, it led nowhere.

Were there any movies which portrayed successful women in the professions who remained in control of their own purse strings? Such an alternative was anathema as it meant not conflict between marriage and a career, but no marriage at all. The lesson of a film titled *Smouldering Fires* (1924) was not to be taken lightly. Unlike most working-girl films which are rendered as comedies, *Smouldering Fires* is a melodrama. Jane Vale, the female lead played by Pauline Frederick, is a middle-aged career woman who has become president and general manager of a clothing factory built by her father. In the opening sequence of the film, Jane is presiding over a business meeting. She has short, unwaved hair, dresses in a mannish suit with white shirt and tie, and makes emphatic gestures by pounding the table and jabbing her finger in the air. Jane's mottoes are "Be Necessary to Others" and "Let No Man Be Necessary to You." She reproves a flirtatious, blond secretary by inquiring: "Do you girls ever think of anything but clothes and a man to lean on?" And she dominates the men of her staff who ridicule her in private but dare not contravene her in public.

Vale's portrait is drawn in a heavy-handed manner but it gets worse. Enter Robert Elliott, a young factory inspector whose direct and outspoken conduct impresses her. She promotes him to assistant general manager. Nothing is wrong with her usual business acumen, but Jane falls in love with her employee like any adoring, young girl and Bob is chivalrous enough to propose. The situation develops into a triangle when Jane's much younger

Mary Pickford and Charles Rogers in My Best Girl.

sister Dorothy, played by Laura La Plante, arrives from Bryn Mawr. A vivacious blond, Dorothy is almost immediately drawn to Bobby but is self-sacrificing and alludes to "the first real happiness Jane has ever known."

Smouldering Fires is a deadly film. According to the plot, a woman cannot successfully pursue a business career without becoming mannish and to be mannish means in effect to be unloved. The film further implies that a forty-year-old woman already has one foot in the grave. When Jane and Bobby entertain guests one evening, some young couples engage in frenetic steps on the dance floor. Jane watches from the sidelines and exclaims in despair to her sister: "Oh darling! You're all so young—so young!" The original print of *Smouldering Fires* was tinted in various symbolic colors to evoke the mood and this scene was dyed a deep red, as was the final scene in which Jane relinquishes her youthful husband to her sister.[10] As stressed by these scenes in red tint, Jane's predicament is shameful and embarassing. She ruins her life by succeeding as a businesswoman and then makes a fool of herself over a younger man. Essentially, she fails as a woman. Vale's name is meaningful in more ways than one.

Although women's work was mostly devalued on celluloid, a few exceptional films such as *Miss Lulu Bett* (1920) and *The Homemaker* (1924) dealt with themes stressing the heroine's struggle towards economic independence or self-expression as a legitimate act. *Miss Lulu Bett* is the simple and moving narrative of a small-town spinster who revolts against family tyranny. *The*

Marion Davies in Show People.

Homemaker features an unusual plot about a role reversal. Significantly, both films were adapted for the screen by women from works written by women: Zona Gale's novel, *Miss Lulu Bett,* was adapted by Clara Beranger and Dorothy Canfield's novel, *The Homemaker,* by Mary O'Hara. Also a stage play, *Miss Lulu Bett* was a minor work directed by William deMille for Famous Players-Lasky which distributed through Paramount.[11] *The Homemaker* was a production of Universal, a lesser studio of the twenties. Although prints of both films have managed to survive to the present day, neither was a box-office smash in its time. A New York reviewer described *The Homemaker* as "a serious attempt at domestic naturalism," and correctly observed that "a certain number of people will think it splendid.... they do not promise, however, to be numerous...."[12]

Miss Lulu Bett, realistically portrayed by Lois Wilson, is a stereotyped spinster living on sufferance in the tyrannical household of her brother-in-law, Dwight. Earning her keep more as an abused servant than a relation, she is made painfully aware of her dependent status. A bogus marriage which she is forced to abandon provides but a temporary refuge and the realization that marital life in itself is no automatic solution to personal unhappiness. After a series of incidents during which she is further mistreated, Lulu finally erupts in anger, leaves the household, and goes to work in the village bakery. She is then assured of "Life... Liberty... and Pursuit of Happiness" (a relevant quotation in the film's last title)—happiness in the person of a local school-teacher named Neil, with whom she has developed a sympathetic understanding.[13]

Miss Lulu Bett was an atypical film because it depicted family life—at least in Dwight's household—as particularly oppressive, marriage as no guarantee of personal fulfillment (after her own aborted marriage, Lulu prevents the elopement of a headstrong and immature niece), and employment as a woman's means of achieving self-reliance. Another heroine who escapes from an unhappy domestic life is Eva Knapp portrayed by Alice Joyce in *The Homemaker*. Married for thirteen years and the mother of three children, Eva continues to be an efficient housewife: she maintains her modest home in apple pie order, is a superb cook, and artfully sews her children's clothing. Unfortunately, her husband Lester is a bumbling clerk whose $1,800 a year salary obligates her to an endless round of "sewing, scrimping, and scrubbing." Far from receiving an anticipated promotion, Lester is dismissed by a new manager who values efficiency, not seniority. In despair, he even fails at a suicide attempt and the resulting injury confines him to a wheelchair. This mishap leads to a rare role reversal in which Eva becomes an adept saleswoman and earns $3,000 a year plus a bonus at Lester's former firm.[14] And Lester proves to be a better parent since his fanciful and dreamy nature endears him to his sons and daughter, previously constrained by Eva's qualities as a martinet. If Lester's childlike personality unsuits him for the business world, it enables him to relate to the children whereas Eva's perfectionism proves more advantageous in the sales department than at home.

The uniqueness of the role reversal in *The Homemaker* is underscored by the film's melodramatic and ridiculous ending. Lester's sudden recovery, prompted by a desperate action to save his daughter during a fire, promises to undo a satisfactory arrangement and disturb the contentment of the entire family. Against the protests of his incredulous doctor, Lester decides to spend the rest of his life as an invalid in a wheelchair so that the role reversal can be sustained. This implausible film ends with the title, "Who is the homemaker? Is it the one who stays home, or the one who goes forth to battle?" Although a

Lois Wilson in Miss Lulu Bett.

more provocative title would have redefined these roles or questioned their assumption on the basis of gender alone, the film was unorthodox in questioning traditional marital relationships and in underlining the importance of work in a woman's life.[15]

Films such as *Miss Lulu Bett* and *The Homemaker* were isolated instances in their realistic depiction of the woman's domestic role and their treatment of the subject of work with respect to self-realization. Usually, working-girl movies were modernized versions of the Cinderella tale whose moral dictated that the heroine be rescued from work and ensconced in a romantic marriage. The impact of these conventions and their variations repeated ad infinitum for the audience relates to the complex phenomenon of stars as role models.[16] The rise of the star system, a development associated with the spectacular career of Mary Pickford as America's sweetheart, was based upon the blurring of the line between screen image and everyday life. Movie magazines early capitalized upon the public's curiosity and hunger for details about the lives of the stars. The delicacy magazines served was a taste of voyeurism, or another course of the film-viewing experience itself. Since the viewer was led to identify with an actor or actress, stars provided powerful role models of a type and on a scale which never before existed. Ironically, the female stars who played shopgirls intent on being rescued from work were successful and highly paid career women, but the merging of screen persona and a glamorized private life may have served to obscure this fact.

Among the facts publicized about movie stars were the astronomical figures of their salaries. For example, Pickford's legendary financial coups were repeatedly noted by the press. Although Pickford was an exceptionally astute businesswoman who had a cash-register brain and was the driving force behind United Artists, other screen actresses also commanded sizeable salaries. When Gloria Swanson left Paramount, her last contract negotiations involved figures quoted as high as $20,000 a week. Colleen Moore collected $12,500 a week under the terms of her contract with First National while her rival, Clara Bow, earned $7,500 a week at Paramount. Comedienne Mabel Normand reportedly drew a salary of $10,000 a week at the height of her popularity. Laura La Plante, Universal's leading female star, was grossing $3,500 a week when she decided to abandon her film career. Viola Dana stated in an interview in the early twenties that she spent $50,000 on clothes alone one year. And the story goes that Marion Davies was able to hand William Randolph Hearst a million dollars when his empire suffered a setback in the thirties.[17]

For the movie stars featured in these working-girl films, being successful and well-paid women did not preclude their marrying, and often more than once. Gloria Swanson and Pauline Frederick married five times. Mary Pickford, Colleen Moore, Evelyn Brent, and Viola Dana married three times. Laura La Plante married twice. Mabel Normand, Louise Brooks, and

Gloria Swanson in Manhandled.

Clara Bow married only once. Marion Davies did not marry until her famous thirty-year liaison with Hearst ended with the publisher's death.[18] Admittedly, marriages made in tinsel town were hardly conventional, but actresses did repeatedly play out in their personal as well as screen lives the destiny appointed for women.

Film historian Iris Barry wrote rather haltingly during the twenties: "We are beginning to realize that a woman who isn't well—I mean who doesn't feel she is doing the best that's in her—inside marriage, is best out of it. But it's hard to get people to admit this, even if they believe it, for 'popular opinion' is against them...."[19] Certainly during the twenties when more and more women were working out of economic necessity if not by choice, movies portrayed them either being rescued from employment by millionaires or giving up careers in favor of marriage. Women's ideal state was matrimony unencumbered by the rigors of remunerative employment. Films thus contradicted the economic realities of urban living in a mass consumption economy and, by doing so, helped to perpetuate less than positive attitudes about women working, especially married women. Despite an increase in the number of women employed outside the home, the significance of work in women's lives remained unexplored in film. Although the material base of women's existence might have served as a pre-condition for attitudinal or even institutional changes in sex roles, the prevailing cultural ideology proved resistant to change. Unfortunately, the women's movement which today articulates a counter ideology had gone into eclipse in the twenties. And the movie industry, which in that decade became streamlined in production, distribution, and exhibition, became less open to innovation and increasingly reliant upon formularized plots and characters. Standardization was an effort to ensure box office receipts but it also perpetuated in the audience an acceptance of movie types which discouraged novelty. And types could always be rationalized on the basis that the industry was only giving the public what it demanded as entertainment.

It has been suggested that as dishwashers and vocational enticements threaten to free women from traditional conjugal chores and roles, men need romance more than ever to distract and entangle them.[20] The convention of romantic love continues to bind women to gender-based roles in opposition to the liberation offered by technology and the possibilities of economic independence. Characterizing romance as a fantasy that renders women playthings, Germaine Greer has observed that, "sexual religion is the opiate of supermenial."[21] Dreams about a romantic Prince Charming still exist in drugstore novels, movies, and television programs as part of a mass communications system geared for a female market. And it is in this respect that the media is retrograde. For if the uses of advanced technology can liberate women, in the form of mass communications it has greater capacity to provide them with ready-made interpretations of their existence and thus distance them from it. During the twenties, working-girl movies alienated women from work experience by perpetuating Cinderella fantasies. It remains to be seen whether in our technological future, women themselves can devise a new cinema which will enrich and liberate women rather than falsify and rigidify their lives.

Notes

1. Portions of this article are based on research which appears in *Virgins, Vamps, and Flappers: The American Silent Movie Heroine* by Sumiko Higashi (Copyright, Eden Press Women's Publications, Inc., Canada, 1978). Used with permission.
2. A significant theoretical problem which should be addressed is the question of whether or not there is an interface between historical methods of research, which are empirical, and structuralist film theory, which is ahistorical and applicable to any filmic text regardless of social context.
3. Hunter, Dulin and Co., *The Golden Harvest of the Silver Screen* (Los Angeles: Hunter, Dulin and Co., 1927), pp. 7, 24.
4. See standard works on the twenties such as William E. Leuchtenburg, *Perils of Prosperity* (Chicago: University of Chicago Press, 1958); Frederick Lewis Allen, *Only Yesterday* (New York: Bantam Books, 1959; originally published 1931); Mark Sullivan, *Our Times* (New York: Charles Scribner's Sons, 1933), Vol. V; and Malcolm Cowley, *Exiles Return* (New York: Viking Press, 1951). For a reevaluation of the twenties, see Roderick Nash, *The Nervous Generation* (Chicago: Rand McNally and Co., 1970).
5. Report of the President's Research Committee on Social Trends, *Recent Social Trends in the United States* (New York: McGraw Hill Co., 1933), pp. 711–735; United States Department of Commerce, *Statistical Abstract of the United States* (1916), pp. 243–254; *Statistical Abstract* (1924), p. 57; *Statistical Abstract* (1933) p. 67; Mary Ross, "Shall We Join the Gentlemen?" *Survey* (December 1, 1926): 265–66; William H. Chafe, *The American Woman: Her Changing Social, Economic and Political Roles; 1920-1970* (New York: Oxford University Press, 1972), Chs. 2, 3, 4; W. Elliott Brownlee and Mary M. Brownlee, *Women in the American Economy* (New Haven: Yale University Press, 1976), Introduction.
6. For contemporary literature about the domestic problems of the working woman, see the issue of *Survey* published in December, 1925. The entire issue was devoted to the subject of women and work. Also see *Recent Social Trends* and Robert S. Lynd's and Helen Merrell Lynd's *Middletown* (New York: Harcourt, Brace and World, 1929).
7. Robert L. Dickinson and Laura Beam, *The Single Woman: A Medical Study*

in Sex Education (New York: Reynal and Hitchcook, Inc., 1934), p. 351.

8. The movie flapper, unlike Fitzgerald's models, was for reasons of censorship if nothing else, quite spirited in behavior but very conventional in her moral standards. See *The Plastic Age, Our Dancing Daughters, Our Modern Maidens, Wine of Youth.*

9. Despite her being dubbed the "It Girl" after *It*, Bow played flapper roles in films such as *Black Oxen, The Plastic Age,* and *Dancing Mothers,* all dated prior to *It.*

10. Keven Browlow, *The Parades Gone By* (New York: Ballantine Books, 1968), p. 330.

11. Unlike his more famous brother Cecil B., who discovered that biblical spectaculars meant big business, William made a series of simple pictures stressing human interest. Also interesting to note is that deMille was married to Clara Beranger. (Interview with Lois Wilson, New York City, November 24, 1972. Telephone conversation with Agnes deMille, New York City, October 19, 1972.)

12. *The Homemaker,* clipping file, Academy of Motion Picture Arts and Sciences, Los Angeles (hereafter cited as AMPAS).

13. The plot resolution of the novel is not as forceful as that of the film since Neil, a musician with poor prospects rather than a respected schoolteacher, proposes to Lulu as she is about to leave town in search of employment. The film version is less subtle in detailing Lulu's character but stronger in outlining her rebellion and quest for independence.

14. These salary figures were realistic. According to the Lynd's study of Middletown, "the minimum cost of living for a 'standard family of five' in Middletown in 1924 was $1,920.87" (pp. 84–85). A study of the American Association of Business and Professional Women disclosed that one-fourth of the women in clerical and publicity work and in teaching positions in 1927 earned less than $1,213 annually; one-half less than $1,548; and three-fourths less than $2,004. (*Recent Social Trends in the United States,* p. 736.)

15. A recent article about role reversal in *Time* queried, "how many men have actually agreed to swap the daily commuter train for domesticity? Report *Time* correspondents nationwide: a very scant, very hardy few." Sheldon Schacter, one of the few, related: "At first I just lolled around the house, doing chores, watching soap operas, and growing lonesome. I found myself waiting for Sandy to come home as the highlight of the day. There was a dependency starting to build up in me." ("Men of the House," *Time,* February 18, 1974, p. 76.) Apparently separate functions are not necessarily equal and this may account for the scarcity of role reversal today.

16. James Monaco, *How to Read a Film* (New York: Oxford University Press, 1977), pp. 217–227.

17. Clipping files and scrapbooks, noncatalogued, listed under names of the stars, Library for the Performing Arts, Lincoln Center, New York City, and AMPAS.

18. Ibid.

19. Iris Barry, *Let's Go to the Movies* (New York: Payson and Clarke, 1926), p. 65.

20. See *The Dialectic of Sex* (New York: Bantam Books, 1971), pp. 146–147. Also see Germaine Greer's discussion of romance in *The Female Eunuch* (New York: Bantam Books, 1972), pp. 179–199. Stendhal remarked in his inimitable style that woman would become man's rival instead of companion "as soon as you have abolished love by law" (*On Love,* trans. H.B.V. under the direction of C.K. Scott-Moncrieff [New York: Grosset and Dunlap, 1967], pp. 228–30). See Simone de Beauvoir's study of Stendhal, "Stendhal or the Romantic of Reality," in *The Second Sex,* trans. and ed. H.M. Parshley (New York: Bantam Books, 1961), pp. 223–237.

21. Germaine Greer, *The Female Eunuch* (New York: Bantam Books, 1972), p. 197.

Nancy Green

Female Education and School Competition: 1820–1850

In October, 1832, William C. Woodbridge noted with alarm a phenomenon that was "producing in our own country, at this moment, a scene of contest, and slander, and falsehood, and violence, which should make the patriot tremble, and the Christian weep."[1] The source of this catalogue of evils was the encouragement of competition—or "emulation," as it was then termed—in American schools. The most dangerous form this encouragement took was the awarding of prizes for scholarship. Woodbridge, though more alarmed than most, was not alone in his denunciation of emulation; the effects of competition were discussed in the new journals of education, in manuals for teachers, at teachers' institutes, and finally in normal schools throughout the 1830's and 1840's.[2]

An examination of this forgotten episode in American school history reveals hitherto unremarked connections between what actually went on in classrooms and the ideas of social and educational reformers. The timing, the arguments, and the cast of characters in the attack on emulation suggest a close relationship between this phenomenon and the growing presence of females in schools. Its study allows us to see how a fact (girls in schools) prompted reconsideration of a school practice (competition for prizes) which had been taken for granted, and how rejection of the practice in turn was integrated into educational theory. At the same time, it illuminates the relationships between two larger themes in the intellectual history of ante-bellum America. The first of these is the image of woman as a source of stability in a period of aggressive expansion and growing economic competition. The second is the belief that the character of individuals shapes the character of society, a view which necessarily placed education at the center

[Nancy Green is an Assistant Professor in the Educational Foundations Department at Northeastern Illinois University. Her article, "Women in United States College Texts," appeared in *The Maryland Historian*, and her present research concerns teaching methods at Hampton Institute in the late nineteenth century. The following essay was published originally in the *History of Education Quarterly*, and is reprinted with permission.]

of reform and committed educators to shaping educational processes in accordance with grand goals.

Educational reformers of the second quarter of the nineteenth century supported the extension and improvement of education for females. Their reasons for this support went beyond a belief in the enlightenment schooling might bring to the populace in general; they were convinced that woman's ability to fulfill the role society prescribed for her would be enhanced by proper education.

The image of women was being redefined in this period in response to the increasingly impersonal character of economic life and the decline of the family as a productive unit. At the same time that men were exposed more and more to competitive pressures without the constraints—or supports—of traditional relationships, women (at least in the middle class) lost much of their former economic function of producing the family's consumable goods.[3] In this situation, the need of men for an embodiment of the old values of community and stability united with the need of women for a sense of purpose: women would be the moral guardians of the family and the nation. Protected from the harsh realities of commercial life by the safe confines of the home, they could maintain there a purity and serenity so sorely lacking in the lives of men. Still more important, as mothers they could mold the character of future generations in such a way as to counter the excessive competition of the present. Thus their influence on society through the formation of their sons' character was described in extravagant terms: "In the helplessness of infancy, woman is to him as Providence, awakening in him those feelings which afterwards rise and expand to philanthropy and devotion.... All that is good in him, all that is true, all that is immortal... is owing to her watchful and tireless nurture of his instincts."[4]

With such a responsibility resting upon them, it was vital that women be equipped for the task. While they were believed to be naturally more pure than men, it seemed that nature could be improved upon by exhortation and discipline, and many reformers felt that these benefits could best be bestowed in schools. At first the argument for the education of females centered on its importance for their effectiveness as mothers, but thanks to the influence of Catharine Beecher, Sarah Josepha Hale, and others it was broadened to include their potential as teachers, an extension which its advocates carefully maintained was entirely consonant with the moral guardian role.[5]

The years between 1820 and 1850 saw the beginning of schooling beyond bare literacy, and continuance in school beyond the age of about twelve, for large numbers of girls. New "female seminaries," many operated by women, appeared in the Northeast and provided in their graduates teachers and principals for similar schools in the South and West.[6] There was a wide range in the curricula and ages of students in these schools, but the most ambitious of them (Hartford, Troy, Mt. Holyoke) were the forerunners of college education for women. The first public high schools to admit girls appeared in the 1820's, and the first normal schools (which were either solely for women or were co-educational) were founded in the late 1830's. Not only did the proportion of girls both in common and higher schools increase, but the trend began which was to replace men with women as teachers in elementary schools. [7]

Extension of schooling to new groups in society is not accomplished without challenge to existing social and educational theory and practice. Extending schooling to adolescent girls, so clearly on the point of assuming adult female roles in society, forced teachers to become conscious of classroom procedures which they had previously accepted without question. When confronted with girls in the classroom, educators realized that the traditional stress on competition as a means of motivating students was in conflict with their ideal of womanhood, and further, educators were prompted to question its implications for the formation of the character of men.

There were a number of ways of stimulating competition in early nineteenth-century classrooms; some of these were regarded as innocuous while others attracted varying degrees of criticism. The very popular, and often public, contest of the spelling bee focused the attention not just of the school but of the community on academic competition, yet critics of emulation seem to have found it unobjectionable. Nor was the teacher's praise regarded as apt to stimulate unhealthy competition; on the contrary, it was often mentioned as a salutary alternative to more tangible rewards. More suspect were the common practices of assigning scholars numbered seats based on academic standing and of making each recitation a contest, with the correct answer moving the student towards the "head" and an error sending him towards the "foot" of the class. [8] Most universally condemned by critics of emulation was the awarding of prizes of money, medals, or books to the best students in each term or year. [9]

The use of prizes was a standard part of late-eighteenth and early-nineteenth century school practice. Franklin, in his "Idea of the English School," proposed giving prizes once a year at a public ceremony to "such boys as distinguish themselves and excel the others in any branch of learning."[10] So persuaded was he of the usefulness of prizes that he left a bequest of £100 sterling to the free schools of Boston, the interest from which was to be used for silver medals for "the encouragement of scholars in the free schools."[11]

Until the mid-1820's, even teachers of girls apparently did not consider that school competition and public rewards might be inappropriate for creatures who were destined to live quiet, domestic lives. Perhaps this can be explained by the fact that very few girls attended school for more than the rudiments, and these were the daughters of gentlemen, most of whom learned the "accomplishments" of French, painting, and music. The few more serious schools for girls were modeled on academies for boys and adopted their methods. The Young Ladies Academy of Philadelphia, the first girls' school to be incorporated in America (1792), held public competitions each year, with prizes going to the best students in reading, spelling, arithmetic, writing, English grammar, and geography.[12] Albert and John Pickett note in their short-lived journal, *The Academician,* that on August 1, 1818, members of the Senior class of young ladies of their Manhattan School were examined by the mayor "and other worthies" and awarded gold medals;[13] and the Franklin awards were extended to Boston school girls beginning in 1821.[14]

The offering of rewards to students, particularly young students, received an additional impetus through the influence of Joseph Lancaster, who recommended using small rewards and honorific titles not only for academic achievement but for good behavior in monitorial schools. There was, for example, in the New York Free Schools, a complete system of payment and fines for conduct as well as scholarship, with tickets being issued for good behavior and withdrawn for bad (four tickets for talking), the tickets being redeemable for balls, books, combs, mittens, and money.[15] Lancaster associated material rewards with every action of his pupils; to a more limited degree the use of awards, usually given annually, was part of a common-sense approach to the stimulation of study, and as such was not seriously questioned until the middle 1820's. Then rather suddenly the practice became the object of a vigorous published attack, led by teachers of girls.

Critics of emulation shared with other reformers a newly optimistic view of child nature and of its susceptibility to kindly influence, derived in some cases from Pestalozzi and Fellenberg,[16] but also part of a general trend away from an older view of children as naturally slothful and recalcitrant. They believed that children were born with "generous affections,"[17] had a natural desire to please adults, and could be led by gentle methods to value knowledge for its own sake. Thus both sexes were capable of learning without the "deep-driven spur" of emulation,[18] though the amount of competition that was desirable for each sex remained a matter of disagreement among those generally opposed to emulation. Emulation was criticized from two slightly different perspectives—that of practicing teachers concerned with its effects in the classroom and that of educational theorists concerned with its long-range consequences.

On the practical side, stimulating emulation by giving prizes or ranking students was rejected by a number of prominent figures in female education. Catharine Beecher outlined her reasons for opposing such stimuli in articles in the *American Annals of Education.* Authors of teachers' manuals who advised instructors not to use emulation included Jacob Abbott and George

B. Emerson, both well-known heads of girls' schools, and Samuel Hall, an early supporter of female education.[19] With the exception of Emerson, these authors drew no distinctions between the sexes with regard to emulation, but rejected it as inappropriate and ineffective in any classroom. While there were differences of emphasis among them, they agreed that (1) emulation reached only a small proportion of the scholars—those who felt they had a good chance of winning; (2) it produced envy and ill-will among students; (3) it focused attention on winning rather than on learning; (4) it rewarded natural ability rather than effort, with the result that "those often obtained the prize, who were least deserving of it."[20]

One of the opponents of ranking students has left a vivid account of the experiences that led him to reject this practice. R. Putnam, a master in the English High School in Salem, wrote:

> While in the East Female School, for the first few years, in obedience to custom, I had a head to each class, the scholars exchanged places in the class, at every recitation, if any were more successful than others; they took rank quarterly, —those who ranked highest taking the highest seats for the next term, etc. The result was, that scarcely a recitation was heard from which some scholar did not return to her seat shedding tears, sobbing, pouting, or giving other indications that all was not peaceful within. After hesitating and deliberating for months, I one morning announced to the school my determination to give up the entire system,—that in future, each scholar must aim to do her duty,—that they must be arranged in classes, and seated *alphabetically.*

Though a few of the students who had been near the head of the class were unhappy with the new arrangement, after a short time "the happy results of the change very far exceeded all that I had dared to hope for," and "I see not why similar results may not be expected in any school." Putnam acknowledged that students accustomed to competition might be less inclined to work hard when it was first removed, but he believed that with more "healthful aliment" they would recover, and "a more healthy and rigorous action ensue, than under the present system."[21]

The new experience of teaching girls prompted re-evaluation of a classroom technique in terms of its application to both boys and girls. Projecting its effects into the future, a number of educational theorists, many of them supporters of female education, concluded that school competition would have destructive long-range consequences for both sexes.[22]

George B. Emerson, in a two-part article in the *Common School Journal* for 1839, examined in detail the "motives to be addressed in the instruction of children," noting that those motives ordinarily employed in schools were fear of pain, fear of shame, and emulation. As principal of the Boston English Classical School (for boys) from 1821 to 1823, Emerson had substituted emulation for corporal punishment, believing it to be more humane and more effective; however, he found that giving medals also had some harmful results and questioned "whether the habits formed by emulation, were the most likely to lead to the regular, quiet, and conscientious discharge of the daily duties of life."[23] In 1823 he became principal of a private school for girls; this move led him to pursue his inquiry into the results of emulation still more vigorously, because, "distrusting... its influence on the character of boys, I suspected, still more strongly, its effects on the gentler sex."[24] His investigations confirmed his worst fears as to the tendency of emulation to unfit females for the duties of their sex, encouraging boldness, vanity, and selfishness at the expense of humility, devotion to duty, and the desire to do right for its own sake. Having built an elaborate case for its destructive effects on the virtue of females, he was led to wonder whether it was appropriate to distinguish between the sexes in terms of morality, and asked, without supplying an answer: "But are there higher virtues of any sex? Can those motives which are obviously wrong for children of one sex, be the best possible for those of the other?"[25]

Emerson was raising an issue that was difficult for educators in this period to resolve. Much of nineteenth-century morality was indeed based on the assumption that certain motives were wrong for one sex yet right for the other;[26] in the case of emulation, those who supported it appeared to be thinking of its application to boys and men,[27] while many of those who opposed it were thinking of its effects on girls and women—*or* on both sexes. (It is easier, apparently, for men thinking about males to be unaware of females than for men thinking about females to be unaware of males.)

At the heart of this difficulty lay the nineteenth-century stress on the dichotomy between head and heart, and the association of this split with differences between the sexes. Throughout the theoretical criticism of emulation ran the theme that, while it *may* encourage intellectual achievement, it is necessarily destructive of morality. For example, Catharine Beecher said that "the great object of education is *to form the disposition, habits, and conscience*, and the mere acquisition of knowledge is but a minor consideration. All the *benefits* I have ever discovered in employing [emulation] have been in reference to intellectual improvement. The *evils* have had a much more important and extensive range...."[28] Horace Mann maintained that an instructor's views on the usefulness of emulation would obviously be determined by the relative importance to him of "mental, as distinguished from moral qualities." Hence if a teacher wishes that his pupil "should be a great man rather than a good one; or that he should acquire wealth rather than esteem... then he will goad him on by the deep-driven spur of emulation...

until he outstrips his fellows, at whatever peril to his moral nature. But if. . .
the teacher. . . would see his pupil dispensing blessings along the lowliest
walks of life, rather than blazing athwart the sky with a useless splendor, then
he will forego [emulation]."[29]

While Beecher and Mann were referring to the education of both sexes, the
moral/intellectual dichotomy worked neatly into the commonplace view of
the roles of the sexes, and this sex differentiation strengthened the feeling that
some motives were acceptable in one sex but not in the other. Some critics of
emulation for girls thought perhaps it would be impossible to eradicate
competition between boys and that therefore it should be turned to the best
advantage—in stimulating intellectual effort. Not quite so prepared as
Beecher and Mann to stress moral over intellectual development, at least in
the education of boys, they expressed uncertainty about the role emulation
should play in boys' schools. But they hastily added that, even though the
question had not been settled so far as boys were concerned, for girls the
matter was perfectly clear. "Whether any proper substitute can be found, in
our sex, for competition and rivalry," one such educator wrote, "I must leave
to others to decide. . . . The application of the system of rivalry to the softer
sex. . . appears to me fraught with mischief."[30]

Since their function in society was supposed by everyone to be preeminent-
ly moral, it was agreed that females should be exposed to nothing in their
education that could distort their moral growth. Indeed "dispensing blessings
along the lowliest walks of life"—or at least in the privacy of the home—was
precisely the task of women. Intellectual eminence, the one possibly desirable
result of emulation, was far from appropriate to their role. As a speaker
before the American Institute of Instruction said in 1830: "Since the very
highest grade of literary acquirement is not essential to the duties of the sex,
[rivalry] seems as unnecessary as it is pernicious."[31]

The pernicious effects of emulation on the character of women were
assumed to be similar to those it produced in men—restlessness, excessive
ambition, attachment to material marks of success. Reformers had advocated the extension of schooling to females in order that their moral role in
society might be enhanced; yet schools, reflecting the competitive aspects of
male society, might inadvertently destroy those very qualities men most
valued in women. Women were, at least according to the men who wrote
about them, "naturally" submissive, forbearing, quiet and self-sacrificing; but
this inborn character was surprisingly susceptible to corruption by the wrong
influences. Feelings of selfishness, envy, and aggressiveness were said to be
"unnatural, but easily acquired"; competition, it was feared, would stimulate
such feelings, leading the girl to deny "the gentle promptings of her sex." Thus
nature, it seemed, must be rather heavily backed by nurture in order for what
is truly natural to be preserved. Submissiveness was all too easily subverted,

especially by a "discipline which has taught her to regard a station of inferiority as one of disgrace."[32]

George B. Emerson, in his inquiry into the effects of the use of emulation in girls' schools, found that prizes usually went to the bold, rather than to "talent, united with a delicacy which shrank instinctively from exhibition." The system "tended to repress the gentle and retiring qualities, which are the most beautiful in the female character, and to foster those which we should least wish a wife or sister to possess." Motherhood, too, came into Emerson's argument, but he seemed to speak most from the heart when he asked: "Would the desire of distinction, of surpassing her friends, be the most sure to suggest to a wife the numberless little kindnesses and attentions so essential to the happiness of a husband?"[33]

The link between methods used in school and the future character of students was the formation of habits. Opponents of emulation pointed out that the subject matter of their lessons was not all that children learned in school; they were also acquiring a body of principles regarding how they should behave which would guide them throughout their lives. According to Horace Mann, the moral, like the intellectual faculties grow or diminish according to their exercise; for this reason, "in the education of children, MOTIVES ARE EVERY THING.... There was profound philosophy in the old theological notion, that whoever made a league with the devil, in order to gratify a passion through his help, became the devil's property afterward. And so, when a teacher stimulates a child to the performance of actions, externally right, by appealing to motives intrinsically wrong, he sells that child into bondage to the wrong motive."[34]

J. Henshaw Belcher, in a lecture before the American Institute of Instruction in 1836, suggested that being rewarded by prizes in school would lead students into a sort of addiction to material rewards—a "morbid hankering... which cannot easily be eradicated."[35] Once addicted, the individual was likely to carry into his life after school an excessive ambition, an inclination to drive ahead without regard to moral obligations or religious precepts.[36] A writer in the *American Journal of Education* said in 1827 that motives appealed to habitually would become part of the character of the individual, and that consequently it is "of vast consequence to the happiness of female life" that "incentives to study be pure and unquestionable in their influence."[37]

Thus the consequences of the use of emulation went beyond the mere well-being of the individual, for the character of individuals would shape the character of society as a whole. Looking around them, educational reformers saw faults in their world which seemed to be the adult embodiment of schoolroom rivalry. Party spirit and its attendant corruption, speculation in the mercantile community, ostentation in private life, and restlessness among the masses all appeared to be the result of the faulty character of individuals as formed through education: "To what cause, more than this, acting universally in schools... can be attributed the insane desire, so prevailing amongst us, of outstripping each other in wealth, in houses, in dress, in every thing which admits of external comparison?... Why else is it that so few are willing, for themselves or their children, to avail themselves of the means of good and happiness so bountifully placed within their reach, and to remain, happy, in their own condition?"[38] The solution to these problems lay in the proper education of the young, since education formed the character of individuals and individuals shaped society. Women in particular should be raised to abhor competition and be happy in their own condition.

Along with all this rhetoric there is evidence of some action taken to minimize competition in schools for girls, particularly older girls, and in a few cases even in male institutions.[39] Catharine Beecher began by giving rewards at her Hartford Female Seminary, but gave them up after observing their effects; Ebenezer Bailey, head of the early, short-lived Boston High School for Girls, gave no medals; Zilpah Grant and Mary Lyon at Ipswich discouraged "all display of attainments... all direct comparisons of one with another";[40] Dr. Webber in his Female Seminary in Nashville, Tennessee, was so concerned to prevent any feeling of superiority among his pupils that he did not even number the classes;[41] Cyrus Peirce in the first Massachusetts Normal School at Lexington (a female institution) lectured to his charges about the ills of emulation;[42] Emma Willard at Troy, Alma Phelps at Patapsco, and George Emerson in Boston never gave medals or rewards. Emerson, indeed, took the matter so much to heart that, as a member of the Boston School Committee in 1848–49, he made "strenuous efforts" to have the Franklin medals for girls in the Boston public schools discontinued.[43] Interestingly enough, he failed.

In fact, the detractors of emulation, though they prevailed in a number of schools, and vastly outproduced their opponents in ink spilt, seemed throughout to be on the defensive. While it is impossible to arrive at a precise estimate of the number of schools in which competition was encouraged, the testimony of its critics suggests that before, during, and after the controversy, prizes were given in a majority of common schools and institutions of higher education for males. Over and over critics prefaced attacks on emulation with such remarks as: "In the present modes of education, great pains are taken to excite the imagination by competition."[44] "In most modern systems it is the *factotum*. Nothing can be done without it."[45] "Constant appeals are made to the spirit of emulation."[46] "The universal practice and almost universal sentiment of mankind are against me."[47] "Such is the system that has prevailed almost universally, and continued almost as universally as ever."[48]

Emulation had tradition and popular opinion on its side. As in many another battle for educational reform in America since this early one, the reformers would appear to have won if we look at the educational journals, the most forward-looking schools, and what was taught at normal school; but in the long run ancient practices die hard, and emulation lives on, though under a different name and with different prizes. In fact, by the 1850's emulation had ceased to be an issue. While a few articles appeared in the educational journals criticizing prizes or advocating competitive examinations, the fire had gone out of the argument and even the word "emulation" dropped out of use. Schools went on giving prizes, but it no longer seemed important to anyone to inveigh against them or to claim that the evils of the age could be traced to their use.

An explanation for the slackening—like the earlier quickening—of concern about school competition may be found in the context of the two themes mentioned at the beginning of this essay—the relationship of education to social reform, and the popular image of women.

By 1850 the nation had passed through an era of reform and into a period less confident that schools for either sex could perfect individuals and that the perfection of individuals would create a good society. The goal of antebellum school reformers had been to build an institution which could act as a stabilizing agent, forming character and preserving morality at a time when older sources of stability—the community, the church, and the family— seemed to be losing their authority. Through schools, the poor were to be brought within the reach of the values of the larger society; through schools, women were to be prepared to impart to succeeding generations those attributes of their nature (selflessness, piety, kindness, etc.) that reformers felt were threatened by the competitive spirit of the age. While the goals of schooling had a conservative tone, and many school reformers were politically conservative, the means reformers proposed implied a fervent belief in progress. G. B. Emerson, for example, believed that educating women would mean that each generation of males could begin its "public" education at a higher level than that of the last. "Educate all the females," he said, "and you will give a permanent impulse to the onward movement of the race."[49]

As the evangelical spirit waned, however, and reform energies were absorbed into the antislavery crisis, human perfectibility and its correlate, educational solutions to social problems, began to seem naive and impractical. Within the world of educators, there was a shift in emphasis away from concern with the long-range moral implications of school practice to problems of organization and professionalism. In making this shift, educators were responding not only to the general mood of the country, but to developments specific to education. The findings of Mattingly about the changing origins of educational leaders and of Tyack about the staggering demands for schools in the growing cities suggest some specific reasons why educators turned from grand goals to practical ones.[50]

By about 1850 females were in one small way—their ability to handle competition for school honors—being accepted as no different from males.[51] This acceptance had come, however, only after a period of uncertainty. As adolescent girls appeared in their schools, teachers responded by trying new methods, methods sometimes consciously and explicitly tailored to an all-female clientele, but often apparently suggested for both sexes by the presence of girls. At the same time, educational theorists, many of them also teachers of older girls, considered the long-range implications of using the same methods for girls that were traditional for boys, and in the process were forced to look with new eyes on these methods even as applied to boys. Finally, tradition prevailed, but with the significant difference that girls had been assimilated into the picture.

The assimilation of girls as secondary school students on the one hand lent force to the movement for full-scale women's colleges, and on the other was inseparable from the acceptance women were gaining as teachers. Already in the fifties the idea was current that there should be colleges for women just like those for men, and many such colleges had been established, though according to Woody, "the fact that their fame was chiefly local" meant that "institutions arising much later regarded themselves as pathfinders of the new movement."[52] At the same time, by 1860 schoolmarms outnumbered schoolmasters in most states, and parents were encouraging their daughters to stay in school longer in order to qualify as teachers.[53] Schooling for adolescent girls was no longer a matter of the luxury of accomplishments for the daughters of the rich, but the avenue into a productive role for middle-class women outside the home, a role which as Beecher and Hale so tirelessly maintained did not conflict with traditional ideas of the character of women.

It is likely that the prospect of this productive role, based on a certain level of intellectual competence, made it seem more fitting to encourage girls to do well in school in the same ways that had stood the test of time with boys. The lonely voice of a female teacher had been raised as early as 1828 in the *American Journal of Education* in defense of honors for school girls: "There is a great want of object or *motive* to lead young ladies into intellectual pursuits, because they get no honour by them: if these could be rendered more honourable, their pursuit would, it might be hoped, induce genuine taste."[54] Leaving aside the question of "genuine taste," twenty-five years later the prospect of a career in teaching supplied a motive for study, a motive perhaps so nearly sufficient in itself that the more fleeting rewards of medals and gilt books lost their capacity to alarm defenders of the female character.

Notes

1. *American Annals of Education* 2(1832): 550. Woodbridge edited this journal from 1831 to 1837, using it as a forum for the most advanced educational ideas of the time.
2. Emulation is mentioned briefly by Merle Curti, *Social Ideas of American Educators* (originally published 1935: Totowa, N.J.: Littlefield, Adams, 1971 Mass.:), p. 59; Michael Katz, *Irony of Early School Reform* (Cambridge, Massachusetts, Harvard University Press, 1968), p. 137–144; and Robert Church, *Education in the United States* (New York: The Free Press, 1976), pp. 100–102.
3. See Ann D. Gordon and Mary Jo Buhle, "Sex and Class in Colonial and Nineteenth-Century America," in *Liberating Women's History*, ed. Berenice A. Carroll (Urbana: University of Illinois Press, 1976) and Gerda Lerner, "The Lady and the Mill Girl: Changes in the Status of Women in the Age of Jackson," *Midcontinent American Studies Journal* 10 (1969): 5–15. For a view of related trends in Europe, see Joan W. Scott and Louise A. Tilly, "Women's Work and the Family in Nineteenth-Century Europe," in *The Family in History*, ed. Charles E. Rosenberg (Philadelphia: University of Pennsylvania Press, 1975) and Louise A. Tilly, Joan W. Scott, and Miriam Cohen, "Women's Work and European Fertility Patterns," *Journal of Interdisciplinary History* 6 (1976): 447–476.
4. "Woman's Influence over Man," *Common School Journal* 13 (1851): 312.
5. See Glenda Riley, "Origins of the Argument for Improved Female Education," *History of Education Quarterly* 9 (Winter: 1969): 455–470.
6. Thomas Woody, *A History of Women's Education in the United States* (New York: The Science Press, 1929), Vol. I, p. 341.
7. Richard M. Bernard and Maris A. Vinovskis, "The Female School Teacher in Ante-Bellum Massachusetts," *Journal of Social History* 10 (Spring 1977): 332–345.
8. Ebenezer Bailey, "Regulations of the High School for Girls (Boston)," 1827, in *Education in the United States: A Documentary History*, ed. Sol Cohen (New York: Random House, 1974), Vol. II, p. 1249; John F. Reigart, *The Lancasterian System of Instruction in the Schools of New York City* (New York: Teachers College, Columbia University, 1916), p. 83; R. Putnam, "Prizes in Schools," *Common School Journal* 7 (1845): 37–38.
9. Some teachers rejected the use of prizes while retaining systems of ranking students. Ebenezer Bailey, for example, employed an elaborate system of merits and forfeits to arrange the graded seating of students, but rejected the use of rewards or medals. At his High School for Girls (Boston), he used no means "for promoting punctuality or exciting emulation, but such as are congenial to the legitimate objects of a school. If such means are sufficient to produce the desired effect, it would seem worse than useless to appeal to mercenary motives."

10. *Educational Views of Benjamin Franklin,* ed. Thomas Woody (New York: McGraw Hill, 1931), pp. 128–129.

11. James Robinson, "Boston Public Schools,"*Massachusetts Teacher* 7 (1854): 350.

12. Ann D. Gordon, "The Young Ladies Academy of Philadelphia: Teaching 'Modest Merit'" (unpublished paper, Conference on Women in the Era of the American Revolution, George Washington University, July 24–26, 1975); Woody,Vol. I, p. 334.

13. "Academical Honors," *The Academician* 1 (1819): 143–144.

14. Robinson, *Massachusetts Teacher* 7 (1854): 351.

15. Reigart, *Lancasterian System,* p. 83.

16. William Woodbridge wrote a number of articles for his *American Annals of Education* on Fellenberg's school at Hofwyl; Horace Mann of course was an exponent of the ideas of Pestalozzi.

17. Horace Mann, "A Lecture on Special Preparation, a Prerequisite to Teaching" (1838), in Henry Barnard, *Normal Schools* (Hartford: Case, Tiffany & Co., 1851), Vol. I, p. 175.

18. Mann, "Ninth Annual Report of the Board of Education," *Common School Journal* 8 (1846): p. 205.

19. Jacob Abbott, a leading popularizer of evangelical beliefs, spent some time as principal of Mt. Vernon Female School, Boston; he used many illustrations from his experience as a teacher of girls in his manual, *The Teacher, or Moral Influences Employed in the Instruction and Government of the Young* (Boston: William Pierce, 1834). George B. Emerson headed a girls' school in Boston from 1823 to 1855, was a member of the Boston School Committee (1847–48), and was a close associate of Horace Mann. His manual, *The Schoolmaster,* was published in 1843. Samuel R. Hall, whose *Lectures on Schoolkeeping* (Boston, 1829. Reprinted 1929 by the Dartmouth Press, Hanover, N.H.) was the earliest and most widely-circulated of antebellum books of advice for teachers, was also the founder of the first teacher-training school in America, Concord Academy (1823).

20. Samuel R. Hall, "Emulation," *American Annals of Education* 2(1832): 206.

21. Putnam, *Common School Journal* 7 (1845): 38.

22. In the 1830's the dominant forum for their views was the *American Journal of Education,* edited by William Russell, and its successor the *American Annals of Education,* edited by William Woodbridge. Both of these men were prominent in the education of girls, Russell as a teacher and Woodbridge (whose father had called himself "the Columbus of Female Education"—Woody, I, 154) as a publicist. During the 1840's, while a number of other journals published articles attacking emulation, the most vociferous was the *Common School Journal* under the editorship of Horace Mann. Mann's dislike for emulation may be traced to his acceptance of the ideas of Pestalozzi, but was undoubtedly strengthened through his long and close association with George B. Emerson.

23. "On Motives to be Addressed in the Instruction of Children," Part II.

Common School Journal 1 (1839): 373.

24. Ibid.

25. Ibid., p. 374

26. See Kathryn Kish Sklar, *Catharine Beecher: A Study in American Domesticity* (New Haven: Yale University Press, 1973), p. 83.

27. Most published supporters of emulation addressed themselves to its usefulness in men's colleges. See, for example, "The Principle of Emulation," *North American Review* 43(1836): 476–515; and Francis Wayland, *Thoughts on the Present Collegiate System in the United States* (Boston: Gould, Kendall & Lincoln, 1842).

28. "On the Best Motives in Education," *American Annals of Education* 3 (1833): 30.

29. "Ninth Annual Report of the Board of Education," in *Common School Journal* 8 (1846): 205.

30. J. C. Warren, "On the Importance of Physical Education," *American Institute of Instruction* 1 (1830): 39.

31. Ibid.

32. Professor Anderson, "Address before the Institute of North Carolina," *American Annals of Education* 4 (1834): 353.

33. "On Motives," p. 374.

34. "A Lecture on Special Preparation, a Prerequisite to Teaching," pp. 172–3.

35. "On the Incitements to Moral and Intellectual Well-Doing," *American Institute of Instruction* 7 (1836): 85.

36. See Also Rev. S. W. Lynd, "The Moral Influence of Rewards, in a System of Education, Founded upon the Doctrine of the Word of God," *Western Academician and Journal of Education* (1837): 522; Catharine Beecher, "On the Best Motives in Education," *American Annals of Education* 3 (1833): 29; Joseph A. Hill, "Address before the Institute of North Carolina," *American Annals of Education* 4 (1834): 350.

37. "Education of Females," *American Journal of Education* 2 (1827): 549.

38. "On Motives," p. 374.

39. Rev. Nathan Lord, who became president of Dartmouth in 1828, decided in 1835 that there should be no prizes or prize commencement orations (Ralph N. Hill, *The College on the Hill: A Dartmouth Chronicle* [Hanover, Dartmouth Publications, 1964], p. 75). Philip Lindsley, President of the University of Nashville, allowed no student honors (*American Annals of Education* [1835]: 444 and Barnard's *American Journal of Education* [1859]: 33). See also an address by the President of Middlebury College, Joshua Bates, "Intellectual Education in Harmony with Moral and Physical," *American Institute of Instruction* 9 (1840): 1–27.

40. "Motives to Study in the Ipswich Female Seminary," *American Annals of Education* 3 (1833): 75.

41. *American Annals of Education* 6 (1836): 235.

42. *The Journals of Cyrus Peirce and Mary Swift* (Cambridge, Massachusetts: Harvard University Press, 1926), pp. 99–100.

43. Barnard's *American Journal of Education* 5 (1858): 424. Others had objected to the Boston system. With regard to its institution by Benjamin Franklin, Cyrus Peirce said: "Great men are not always wise. I consider that the cause of education, *real* education, has suffered rather than gained by every donation of this sort." "The Substitute for Premiums and the Rod," *Common School Journal* 6 (1844): 268.

44. Warren, "On the Importance of Physical Education," p. 39.

45. "The Nature and Effects of Emulation," *American Quarterly Register* 5 (1832): 68.

46. Rev. S. J. May, "An address delivered at the opening of a... schoolhouse," *Common School Journal* 2 (1840): 224.

47. Joshua Bates, "Intellectual Education in Harmony with Moral and Physical," *American Institute of Instruction* 11 (1840): 25.

48. Warren Burton, "On the Best Mode of Fixing the Attention of the Young," *American Institute of Instruction* 5 (1834): 44.

49. "The Education of Females," *American Institute of Instruction* 3 (1832): 40.

50. Mattingly finds that as the century progressed the social class origins of teachers declined and concern with academic training for teachers gave way to the inculcation of mechanical methods. Tyack identified the problem of educating unprecedented concentrations of children as a crucial factor in the rise of rigidly bureaucratic school systems. See Paul Mattingly, *The Classless Profession: American Schoolmen in the Nineteenth Century* (New York: New York University Press, 1975); and David B. Tyack, *The One Best System* (Cambridge, Massachusetts: Harvard University Press, 1974).

51. It remained for a later generation to become aware that girls could learn to compete in situations, and to the degree that social expectations allowed, without betraying to the world the conflicts this caused for them.

52. Vol. II, p. 148.

53. Bernard and Vinovskis, "The Female Schoolteacher."

54. Vol. III, p. 525.

William D. Jenkins

Housewifery and Motherhood: The Question of Role Change in the Progressive Era

As the suffrage movement gathered momentum after 1910, the most radical suffragists looked hopefully to the coming abandonment of traditional role expectations for women. Despite passage of the suffrage amendment in 1920, however, their expectations remained unfulfilled. Until the 1960's popular and historical interpretations mistakenly claimed that the 1920's marked the arrival of the "new woman," totally emancipated and economically independent.[1] More recent studies have demonstrated the inaccuracy of such an interpretation and raised the question of why the suffrage amendment had so little impact upon society's restricted conception of woman as housewife and mother.[2] A facile answer might be found in the emergence of conservative and substantial roadblocks during the 1920's. But on closer analysis a more convincing explanation of the limited changes wrought by suffrage can be found within the Progressive era.

Recent monographs and articles suggest that Progressivism was not a cohesive movement endowed with a comprehensive philosophy, but a coalition of diverse and often competing interest groups, which produced a hodgepodge of reform measures varying greatly in their effect.[3] Despite its diversity, Progressivism produced an atmosphere conducive to the expansion of women's political role. Freed from some of their duties in the home by technology and wealth, many middle- and upper-class women joined clubs and established organizations to promote reform in a society they looked upon as often corrupt, immoral, and unjust. The acceptance of these women within reform circles—even as organizers of the Progressive Party in 1912—indicated society's willingness to accept women in the political sphere and made suffrage appear as the logical development of that acceptance. Suffrage, then, was achieved within the context of political reform and not as

[An Associate Professor of History at Youngstown State University, William D. Jenkins has published other articles on Progressivism. Research for this essay was begun in a National Endowment for the Humanities Seminar on the History of Childhood in America.]

part of a drive toward total equality. It did mark the inclusion of women within a formerly all-male sphere, but the franchise did not diminish the expectation that women would continue to fulfill their roles as housewives and mothers. Indeed, suffragists themselves argued that women should have the vote primarily as an extension of these traditional roles. Although Aileen Kraditor in *The Ideas of the Woman Suffrage Movement, 1890-1920* has labeled such an argument as "expedient," it appears more likely that the majority of suffragists argued from conviction and perceived politics as an area to which women, different in nature from men and practised in different roles, could make a unique contribution.[4] The fact that, after passage of the suffrage amendment, reform, not role change, continued as the major goal of the suffragists was an important indication of this point.

The Progressive era began, however, with a challenge to woman's traditional roles from Charlotte Perkins Gilman, a leading feminist philosopher. Observing the transformation brought about by industrialization, Gilman argued that the increasing organization of women's work outside the home and orientation toward specialization in some line of work would eventually free the wife to pursue a career, while workers trained in cleaning, cooking, and the care of children handled her home duties. Gilman attacked the notion that mothering was an intuitive skill inherent in each woman; rather, it was something to be learned, as indeed were the principles of cleaning and cooking. In Gilman's mind there existed neither "born" mothers, nor natural housekeepers.[5] Gilman's conclusions about the future directions of American society were an extrapolation of trends generated by industrialization, advances in scientific knowledge, and increasing leisure afforded by new found wealth. Inevitably, these changes produced much speculation about their potential impact upon society and its institutions. A society can accept change, or it can modify and adapt its institutions in the face of change in order to assure their survival. In the Progressive era society rejected the changes suggested by Gilman and sought instead to adapt the institution of domesticity—along with woman's traditional role—without fundamentally altering either the institution or the role. Significantly, the process of adaptation took place within Progressivisism, especially within the social-welfare wing, in which a large number of women participated.

The major adaptation occuring at this time was the development of home economics programs in both secondary and collegiate curriculums.[6] Although the trend in women's education before 1900 was toward equality, the Progressive era reversed that trend by rejecting Gilman's notion of training workers for labor irrespective of gender and by attempting instead to formally train each young woman for her traditional role. The demand for more training came from many sources, including the child study movement of this period, which had grown rapidly in the 1890's and early 1900's under the guidance of G. Stanley Hall, founder of the Child Study Institute at Clark University.[7] Hall contributed directly to the adaptation of woman's roles in the chapter on the education of girls in his book *Adolescence*, a major work on the final stage of childhood. While Hall was willing to admit that woman's intellect "was not inferior to that of man," he condemned the increasing emphasis on similar education for both sexes through high school and college. According to Hall, since the course of evolution proceeded from sameness of function for the sexes to greater differentiation in the more advanced stages of civilization, society should reinforce sex differentiation as the children matured. Accordingly, Hall advocated that adolescent girls and young women be formally educated for motherhood. As evidence of the failure of equal education, Hall cited statistics proving that young women who attended college married later and less frequently than those not attending college, and also produced fewer children.[8]

While Hall was considered the father of the child study movement, the movement spread beyond the discipline of psychology into the fields of medicine and social work. In each of these areas the investigation of problems concerning children reinforced belief in the need to prepare and train the woman in a more systematic way for her duties as wife and mother.

The high rate of infant mortality received special attention as both the National Conference of Charities and Corrections and the American Medical Association undertook special studies of the phenomenon. At least one student of the problem, George Mangold of the St. Louis School of Social Economy, believed that the rate could be reduced by 40 percent and cited improper feeding, parental ignorance, and unsanitary conditions as major controllable causes of infant deaths. While he considered public regulation of the preparation, storage, and delivery of milk as the single most important step in the prevention of childhood diseases, Mangold advocated the following corrective as well: the education of mothers about breastfeeding, dietary habits, and the "value of good food, fresh air, sunlight, clean water, ventilation, and ourdoor exercise." Mangold advised that "domestic science, the art of housekeeping, proper uses of food, the importance of cleanliness, hygiene, and sanitation, and other items of value should become part of the instruction of every young woman."[9] Formed under the auspices of the American Medical Association in 1909, the American Association for the Study and Prevention of Infant Mortality echoed Mangold's convictions. In its conventions from 1910 through 1913 it recommended the establishment through state departments of education of continuation schools for homemakers.[10]

As those involved in the child study movement began to turn to the field of education, they found a fertile ground for their ideas prepared by John Dewey and advocates of vocational education. By 1900 John Dewey's "New Education" with its emphasis on preparing the student for life was beginning to replace the older psychological view that the mind was composed of separate faculties. The result was a change in the focus of education from rote memorization and discipline of each faculty to a more functional approach based on the child's anticipated adult occupation. Although Dewey did not contribute directly to the changes in education of young women, his thought provided an important impetus toward a reexamination of such education. His vision of the school as a part of life was similar to that of the newly emergent vocationalists, who were espousing education for life and a career. Never a devotee of narrow vocationalism, Dewey believed in the development of critical intelligence, but his famous dictum, "learning by doing," seemed to provide justification for a curriculum based on job training.[11]

The interest in such a curriculum stemmed from changes wrought by industrialization. The replacement of the craftsman by the factory system and the decline of apprenticeship as a means of preparing young men for work in the factories, particularly in what might be described as semiskilled positions, led both industrialists and workers to demand that public education provide the desired courses.[12] This movement toward vocational education gained momentum with the creation in 1905 of the Massachusetts Committee on Industrial Education and the formation of the National Society for the Promotion of Industrial Education, an industry-backed organization.[13] By 1911 the United States Commissioner of Education could report the establishment of 142 industrial schools.[14]

The combination of Dewey's philosophy and the movement toward industrial education had an important impact on the education of young females. Whereas much of the older education emphasized cultural and humanistic courses, the new education followed a philosophy of preparation for life's work. Since most young women, even those at work in the factory, eventually became homemakers and mothers, it was deemed necessary to offer them courses in home economics. Not surprisingly, in 1913 the National Society for the Promotion of Industrial Education described housekeeping "as a big, vital progressive enterprise, requiring as much skill in the administration of its affirs as a manufacturing plant or a business undertaking," and duly recommended proper training for its management.[15] As thirty-five states followed Massachusetts' lead in passing laws for the support of industrial education, thirty-three saw fit to include home economics as part of industrial education, and twenty-nine states provided additional aid.[16] In 1917 the federal government offered matching grants to states for the development of vocational education, including home economics, through the Smith-Hughes Act.[17]

While the "New Education" and vocationalism were providing a rationale for the introduction of home economics within collegiate and secondary curriculums, pressure for the expansion of such courses was coming from

advocates within the discipline. The founder of the home economics movement for the Progressive era was Ellen H. Richards (1842–1911). An 1870
graduate of Vassar, Richards entered the Massachusetts Institute of Technology in 1871 as its first female student, and took her degree in sanitary
chemistry. Her efforts to apply scientific knowledge to the household resulted
in a number of books, including the *Chemistry of Cooking and Cleaning*.[18]
Almost as important as Richards was Helen Campbell, who gave the first
series of lectures at the University of Wisconsin on home economics under the
auspices of Richard Ely and the School of Economics in the 1890's.[19]

Both Richards and Campbell considered women in general poorly prepared for their roles of housewife and mother. Claiming that the skills of
housewifery had received little study because they were thought to be
acquired through woman's intuition and because the tasks of the household
were demeaned as "woman's work," Campbell called for rigorous scientific
analysis of cooking and cleaning.[20] As a professional chemist, Richards
deplored the failure to introduce the science of chemistry into the home and
blamed those schools that taught the principles of chemistry for not applying
them to the domestic sphere. According to Richards, such an application
would promote health among family members, save labor, reduce wear, and
achieve a more economical operation.[21] At the World's Fair in Chicago in
1893, Richards created the Rumsford Kitchen, which she viewed as "the first
attempt to demonstrate by simple methods to the people in general. . . the fact
that there are scientific principles underlying nutrition."[22] Thus, the growing
passion for scientific management so evident throughout the Progressive era
buttressed the movement toward inclusion of home economics in secondary
and collegiate curriculums.

Along with increased knowledge came the desire to establish home
economics as a profession. In 1899 Ellen Richards helped to found the Lake
Placid Conference on Home Economics, and served as its only president
until its demise in 1908. Never very large—it had only 202 members in 1908—
the Lake Placid Conference was the first professional organization in the
field of home economics. Its major goals were the establishment by state
universities of departments of home economics, better preparation of teachers, the organization of courses of study, and the introduction of training for
the home into all public schools.[23]

To confront a task that was national in scope, the Lake Placid Conference
disbanded in 1909 and formed the American Home Economics Association
with Ellen Richards as its first president and with a membership of seven
hundred. National conventions and the establishment of the *Journal of
Home Economics* marked the arrival of home economics as a profession.[24]
By 1913 the Association was issuing a "Syllabus of Home Economics," and a
definition of home economics as "the study of the economic, sanitary, and

aesthetic aspect of food, clothing and shelter as connected with their selection, preparation, and use by the family in the home or by other groups of people."[25]

The creation of advocacy groups was an important adjunct to the formation of professional organizations. At the Chicago Exposition of 1893 the Woman's Congress, upset with the lack of progress in education for the home, decided to organize the National Household Economics Association (NHEA), whose main function was convincing the General Federation of Women's Clubs to take some action. Having finally convinced the General Federation to place the topic on its convention program in 1903, the NHEA assumed a new identity as the Committee on Home Economics of the General Federation.[26] By 1910 the United States Commissioner of Education could report that over 250 of the women's clubs had "helped materially" in their push for acceptance of home economics in the public schools.[27]

Settlement workers joined the women's clubs in pressuring the public schools. From a survey conducted by the National Federation of Settlements among 2000 settlement workers, Robert A. Woods and Albert Kennedy concluded that schools had to broaden their program to include domestic science. According to Woods and Kennedy, although the typical young woman from a lower-class neighborhood worked, she found "it hard to free her mind from the thoughts of marriage...." Since her thoughts did not extend to the necessity of preparation for marriage, Woods and Kennedy suggested that "model apartments and cottages should be furnished in connection with every settlement, and ought to be developed as a part of the public system of education as quickly as possible."[28]

The example of Lillian Wald and the Henry Street Settlement in New York was typical. Wald rented a flat in which to teach housekeeping, a tactic that was emulated in other "Housekeeping Centers" set up around the city. Eventually, Dr. Maxwell, superintendent of schools, permitted each principal to include instructors from these centers as part of the school system. Reflecting on the success of these centers, Wald commented that "perhaps we may one day see one attached to every public school; and I am inclined to believe that, when institutions of higher learning fully realize that education is preparation for life, they too will wonder if the young women graduates of their colleges should not, like our little girl neighbors, be fitted to meet their great home-making responsibilities."[29] The fact that Wald, other settlement workers, and the General Federation of Women's Clubs advocated a home economics curriculum for young women was a definite indication that for many women, and particularly for those who belonged to the social-welfare wing of the Progressive coalition, role reinforcement and training was a predominant value.

The introduction of home economics into high schools and colleges was important not only to settlement workers concerned about young, immigrant women and their adaptation to American society, but also to upper-class, old-stock Americans who were beginning to realize that the new immigrants were outproducing them. Wary of the declining birth rate, Theodore Roosevelt challenged women to increase their rate of reproduction, thus saving the race and preserving America.[30] A partial explanation for the decline came from G. Stanley Hall, who blamed the college curriculum. Since a woman's body and soul were "made for maternity, and she can never find true repose for either without it," Hall argued that woman's education had to focus on motherhood and wifehood, or else result in the creation of "functionally castrated" graduates and "parturition phobiacs."[31] Seen from this perspective, domestic science became a necessary reform. The introduction of home economics as part of the secondary curriculum meant that high schools which were beginning to serve all classes after 1900 might train every woman in her proper role, while the subject as taught in colleges which remained a preserve of the upper classes might influence the woman from old stock to pursue her traditional role, the begetting and rearing of children. The eugenicist's fear was thereby allayed and home economics promoted.

Home economics was not the only area in which reformers were trying to adapt the role of motherhood to a changing society. After the Civil War, workers in charge of dependent children had concluded that it was best to care for such children within an institution, but by 1909 at the White House Conference on the Care of Dependent Children they determined that, wherever possible, the child should remain with the original parents, or be placed in a foster home. An institution, it was argued, inevitably suppressed the individuality and creativity of its inmates, and where it was the only alternative, the cottage system was recommended as the closest approximation to familial surroundings.[32] Ellen Key, a Swedish suffragist and a liberal regarding the rights of women in marriage, reached similar conclusions in her books, *The Century of the Child* and *The Renaissance of Motherhood*, both of which sold well in the United States. Challenging Gilman's claim concerning the superiority of professional mothers, Key contended that the professionals were not succeeding in providing proper care for dependent and delinquent children in institutions. They, too, were stressing the importance of the family in child development, and thus indirectly of the mother since her role made her the focal point of family life. The mother in short provided the emotional support and individual attention necessary for the child's development.[33]

Such ideas contributed to the mother's pension movement, an attempt to have the state support mothers deprived of a husband through death or divorce. The delegates at the White House Conference had indicated a preference for "private charity rather than public relief," but had also recommended that "children of parents of worthy character, suffering from temporary misfortune, and children of reasonably efficient and deserving mothers who are without the support of the normal breadwinner, should as a rule be kept with their parents, such aid being given as may be necessary to maintain suitable homes for the rearing of the children."[34] The state of Illinois enacted the first mother's pension in 1911, followed by nineteen states within two years.[35] Although the money offered was minimal in order to discourage dependency, the adoption of public relief was remarkable considering attitudes toward relief, and a definite indication that reformers considered motherhood a strong enough value to risk the provisions of public aid.

Public concern about the child's need for mothering produced not only mother's pensions, but also protective legislation for working women. Statistical studies undertaken by social-welfare advocates, Sophonisba P. Breckenridge and Josephine Goldmark, were used by Louis Brandeis in his famous defense before the Supreme Court of an Oregon statute limiting the hours of working women. In the Brandeis brief, the Breckenridge data were used to argue not only that long hours adversely affected the efficiency of working women, but also that "the deterioration is handed down to succeeding generations. Infant mortality rises, while the children of married working women, who survive, are injured by inevitable neglect. The overwork of future mothers thus directly attacks the welfare of the nation."[36] Justice Brewer, in writing the majority opinion, concurred with Breckenridge's concern about the deleterious effects of long hours on future mothers and their offspring, and agreed that "the physical well-being of woman becomes an object of public interest and care in order to preserve the strength and vigor of the race."[37] Once again, public concern about the proper functioning of motherhood had led to the passage of reform legislation in an area heretofore considered out of the realm of public policy, and in this instance to approval of the legislation by the Supreme Court.

In the spring of 1914 Congress unanimously passed a resolution establishing Mother's Day, another piece of public legislation indicating that, while Gilman had accurately read the trend of society toward increasing organization of women's work outside the home and specialization of function, she had overlooked the emotional attachment to home and motherhood. Advancing technology and the training of specialists could have been utilized in relieving wives and mothers of many domestic tasks as was done by the upper class, but society did not consider the emotional functions replaceable. Ellen Key reflected prevailing social norms in her statement that "each young soul needs to be enveloped in its own mother's womb to grow in and the baby the mother's breast to be nourished by."[38] Questioning the consistency in quality of trained experts in homemaking and child care, Key contended that they could not replace the love and individual attention afforded by a mother. In Key's mind, the solution lay, not in communal child raising, but in "a training for the inherently womanly vocations" for each female.[39]

There was more acceptance of Gilman's contention that mothers were deficient in their knowledge and expertise. The child study movement had generated much evidence for the fact that mothers did not possess adequate knowledge and information concerning the health of the child, dietary and nutritional needs, and sanitation within the home. With creation of the discipline of home economics based on advances in science and medicine, society could have followed Gilman's direction of training specialists in child nurture, but instead it attempted to make a specialist of each potential mother through training in domestic science.

Thus, at a time when Gilman foresaw the evolution of a society in which women were freed from their traditional tasks, Progressive reformers were examining those tasks within the context of an industrialized, technological society, and concluding that each woman needed a more systematic education in order to perform them effectively. In addition, reformers attempted to keep mothers at home via state pensions for fatherless homes, and to protect future mothers from the deleterious effects of factory work through protective legislation. This emphasis on the protection and enhancement of motherhood colored the entire Progressive era, and made especially strong the suffragists' argument that women deserved the vote because of their contributions as wives and mothers to a modernizing America. Ultimately, such an emphasis, coming as it did from within the Progressive coalition, also meant that suffrage would not produce significant role changes for American women.

Notes

1. William H. Chafe, *The American Woman: Her Changing Social, Economic and Political Roles, 1920–1970* (Chicago: Quadrangle Books, 1971), pp. 49–50. Chafe cites George Mowry, Arthur Link, Henry Steele Commager, Samuel Eliot Morrison, and William Leuchtenberg as prime examples.
2. Ibid., J. Stanley Lemons, *The Woman Citizen: Social Feminism in the 1920's* (Urbana: University of Illinois Press, 1975), pp. 228–244. Lemons does contend that social feminism, which put reform above emancipation or equality as a goal, survived in the twenties and served as a bridge between Progressivism and the New Deal. William L. O'Neill in *Everyone Was Brave: A History of Feminism in America* (Chicago: Quadrangle Books, 1971) is very present-minded in blaming the suffragists for failing to develop a more radical critique. Ellen DuBois in

her *Feminism and Suffrage: the Emergence of an Independent Women's Movement in America, 1848-69* (Ithaca: Cornell University Press, 1978) argues that suffrage did possess value in and of itself and without reference to other woman's issues because it enabled a woman to undertake part of a man's role. In DuBois's words, "it was a particularly feminist demand, because it exposed and challenged the assumption of a male authority over women. To women fighting to extend their sphere beyond its traditional domestic limitations, political rights involved a radical change in woman's status, their emergence in public life." This paper does not challenge DuBois' perspective, but rather seeks to explain why the roles of housewife and mother continued to dominate as the major lifestyles of most American women.

3. Peter G. Filene, "An Obituary for the 'Progressive Movement,'" *American Quarterly* 22 (Spring 1970): 20-34.

4. Aileen S. Kraditor, *The Ideas of the Woman Suffrage Movement, 1890-1920* (New York: Columbia University Press, 1965), pp. 38-64.

5. Charlotte Perkins Gilman Stetson, *Women and Economics*, (Boston: Small, Maynard and Co., 1899), Chapters X-XV.

6. For general coverage of this development see Eleanor Flexner, *Century of Struggle: The Women's Rights Movement in the United States,* revised edition (Cambridge, Massachusetts: Harvard University Press, 1975); Mabel Newcomer, *A Century of Higher Education for American Women* (New York: Harper and Brothers, 1959); S. Alexander Rippa, *Education in a Free Society: An American History*, 2nd ed. (New York: David McKay Company, 1971); Thomas Woody, *A History of Women's Education in the United States,* Vol. II (New York: Science Press, 1929; reprint ed., New York: Octagon Books, 1966), Chapter II. Linda Marie Fritschner has conducted a fascinating doctoral study entitled "The Rise and Fall of Home Economics: A Study with Implications for Women, Education and Change" (Ph.D. dissertation, University of California, Davis, 1973), which investigates specific schools and builds a regional interpretation of the beginnings of home economics.

7. Lawrence A. Cremin, *The Transformation of the School: Progressivism in American Education, 1876-1957* (New York: Alfred A. Knopf, 1961), pp. 100-105.

8. G. Stanley Hall, *Adolescence*, Vol. II (New York: D. Appleton, 1904), pp. 561-647.

9. George Mangold, *Child Problems*, (New York: The Macmillan Co., 1910), pp. 80-94.

10. U.S. Office of Education, *Education for the Home,* Bulletin No. 37 (Washington, D.C., 1914), p. 190.

11. Cremin, *Transformation*, pp. 100-105.

12. Ibid., pp. 34-36.

13. U.S. Office of Education, *Report of the Commissioner of Education, 1911,* Vol. I (Washington, D.C., 1911), p. 147.

14. Ibid., p. 146.

15. U.S. Office of Education, *Report of the Commissioner of Education, 1913,* Vol. I (Washington, D.C., 1913); William T. Bawden, "Progress in Vocational Education," pp. 253–263.
16. *Education for the Home,* Bulletin No. 37, p. 190.
17. Cremin, *Transformation,* pp. 56–57.
18. Caroline L. Hunt, *The Life of Ellen Richards* (Boston: Whitcomb and Barrow, 1912); U. S. Office of Education, *Education for the Home,* Bulletin No. 36 (Washington, D. C., 1914, pp. 10–13.
19. Helen Campbell, *Household Economics: A Course of Lectures in the University of Wisconsin* (New York: G. P. Putnam's Sons, 1897), p. xv.
20. Ibid., pp. 9–12 and 140–148. Although Richards emphasized training of each young woman, Campbell, who at one time roomed with Gilman, was more interested in training specialists. According to Campbell, "the woman need have no lack of occupation, for she can find it in genuinely caring for her family, teaching and training as today she cannot" (p. 243). Richards' role as founder of the AHEA indicated which position was considered more acceptable.
21. Hunt, *Life of Richards,* pp. 180–185.
22. Ibid., pp. 220–226.
23. "Announcement: The American Home Economics Association and the *Journal of Home Economics,*" *Journal of Home Economics* 1 (1909): 1–6; Emma Seifrit Weigley, "It Might Have Been Euthenics: the Lake Placid Conferences and the Home Economics Movement," *American Quarterly* 26 (March 1974): 78–96.
24. "Announcement," *Journal of Home Economics,* pp. 1–6.
25. *Education for the Home,* Bulletin No. 36, pp. 22–23.
26. Linda Hull Larned, "The National Household Economics Association, 1893–1903," *Journal of Home Economics* 1 (1909): 185–187.
27. U.S. Office of Education, *Report of the Commissioner of Education, 1910,* Vol. I (Washington, D.C., 1910), pp. 62–63.
28. Robert A. Woods and Albert J. Kennedy, *Young Working Girls* (Cambridge, Massachusetts: Riverside Press, 1913), pp. 15, 31–33, 154–159.
29. Lillian Wald, *The House on Henry Street* (New York: Henry Holt and Co., 1915), pp. 107–109.
30. Elting Morison, ed., *The Letters of Theodore Roosevelt,* Vol. III (Cambridge, Massachusetts: Harvard University Press, 1951), pp. 355–356 and 86.
31. Hall, *Adolescence,* II, pp. 590–610 and 631–634.
32. "Letter to the President of the United States Embodying the Conclusions on the Care of Dependent Children," in *Children and Youth in America: A Documentary History,* Vol. II, ed. Robert H. Bremner (Cambridge, Massachusetts: Harvard University Press, 1971), pp. 364–69.
33. Ellen Key, *The Renaissance of Motherhood* (New York: G. P. Putnam's Sons, 1914), pp. 137–145.
34. "Letter to the President," *Children and Youth,"* p. 365.
35. Grace Abbott, ed., *The Child and the State,* Vol. II (Chicago: University of Chicago Press, 1938), p. 229.

36. Louis D. Brandeis, *Women in Industry* (New York: National Consumers League, 1908), p. 47.
37. Ibid., II, p. 6.
38. Key, *Renaissance,* p. 136–137.
39. Ibid., pp. 137–138, 156–157.

Joan G. Zimmerman

Daughters of Main Street: Culture and the Female Community at Grinnel, 1884–1917

Women's education in the midwest entered a new stage beginning in the 1890's. An increasing number of women from middle-class backgrounds came to assume that college would be a logical step after graduation from high school. The establishment of opportunities for the higher education of women in single-sex colleges had taken place earlier in the east. What was new for women in the Midwest in the late nineteenth century was participating in the institutionalization of co-education at liberal arts colleges. However, as the example of Grinnell College demonstrates, rather than a broadening of opportunity for women or providing a vehicle for women significantly to alter their status in American society, the institutionalization of co-education instead reinforced and perpetuated into the twentieth century the careful segregation of the sexes which had characterized Victorian America.

Historians of education have documented disruptions to the collegiate ideal occasioned by the rapid influx of students with a variety of backgrounds.[1] The increased enrollment of women at Grinnell College in the late nineteenth and early twentieth centuries posed a new problem. (See Table I.) Nevertheless, potential conflict did not materialize as both the administration and women students continued to subscribe to Victorian notions regarding woman's role and place. The larger presence of women prompted the administration to attempt to create a collegiate ideal that accommodated women by defining and circumscribing their place along traditional lines. For women, entrance into the collegiate realm appeared to offer the same opportunity as men to explore all the curricular offerings of higher education and seemed to represent a culmination of women's efforts to equal educational advancement. Even so, the opportunity went unrealized to a great extent as women at Grinnell became involved in the process of creating a

[Joan G. Zimmerman is a member of the Department of History at the University of California, Los Angeles. She is currently engaged in a study of college culture in the Midwest which concerns the experience of midwestern college students, the dissemination of high academic culture, and changing attitudes toward liberal culture.]

distinctive female collegiate subculture that in effect duplicated their society's separate and "special" female world of mutual support.[2]

While it is true that opportunities were offered in the curriculum for women and men to explore regardless of gender, women rarely opted for majors in such fields as business administration or pre-med training. And as the curriculum expanded, women's roles and place, due to the actions of both the administration and women themselves, were increasingly circumscribed and remained largely traditional. An examination of changes in the curriculum, the administration's attitude toward women, and the female community at Grinnell will illuminate how the heightened emphasis upon roles desig-

Table I. Percentage of Women at Grinnell*

Year	Men	Women	Percent of Women
1892	142	80	36.0
1893	147	73	33.2
1894	139	75	35.0
1895	128	92	41.8
1896	106	87	45.1
1897	132	117	47.0
1898	145	116	44.4
1899	142	119	45.6
1900	142	134	48.6
1901	124	146	54.1
1902	122	162	57.0
1903	127	174	57.8
1904	133	188	58.6
1905	126	180	58.8
1906	169	219	56.4
1907	210	240	53.3
1908	191	272	58.7
1909	202	271	57.3
1910	225	261	53.7
1911	212	263	55.4
1912	221	258	53.9
1913	208	277	57.1
1914	210	292	58.2
1915	245	319	56.6
1916	249	327	56.8
1917	329	367	52.7

*The figures in this table refer only to those taking the four-year college course.

Source: *Grinnell College Catalogue.*

nated by gender and the strict separation of relations between the sexes facilitated the process of the institutionalization of co-education at one liberal arts college in the Midwest.

When the college opened its doors at Grinnell, Iowa, in 1861, women were admitted along with men. The administration initially provided for the education of women by creating a "Ladies Course" which culminated in a diploma, rather than a degree. This watered-down version of the classical course had less rigorous requirements than a regular college course. From 1862 to 1892, when the Ladies Course was discontinued, the faculty slowly moved to lengthen the Course from three to four years and make it more demanding. A major change had come in 1884 when the Ladies Course was transformed into the Literary Course with a B. Litt. degree. The Literary Course, offered until 1891, emphasized modern languages and literature, but it never achieved the status of a "College Course."[3]

Martha Foote Crowe, Lady Principal of Grinnell College from 1884 to 1891, reviewed these changes with a critical but hopeful eye in her resignation in 1891. She pointed out that women had been in an anomalous position in the college because in actuality "the principle of co-education [had not been] adopted when the women were admitted." The result, she said, was that women had been denied the same opportunities and challenges as the young men, and when enrolled in the same classes with men had been less prepared and less disciplined. The conclusion was inescapable that "this could only lead to their disadvantage and detriment." In Crowe's opinion, from the outset the administration's reluctance to admit and educate women on an equal basis with men had been substantial. As for changes in the curriculum over the years, she noted that:

> This process has been made little by little and every step of the way has been hotly contested. But as experience showed that the young women did not suffer from the advances made, the opponents one by one ground their arms and turned in to help in the development of a course that should be distinctive in its character and choice of subjects rather than in its adaptation to inferior intellects!

Crowe claimed there had been rapid progress in the four years between 1884 and 1888 as more and more women had taken the full-degree Literary Course. Responding perhaps to the popular argument of the time that higher education for women was damaging to their health and reproductive capacity, Crowe noted that the number of women who dropped out was not greater than that of the young men. Moreover, the women had demonstrated superior scholarship. In Crowe's view, the admission of women on an equal basis in 1884 had been probably the greatest development of the previous six years. It, like other advances, had "taken place, too, in the face of opposition from many sources." Crowe modestly disclaimed any credit for herself. Instead, she insisted: "It is in the air. It is the woman's era, and the young women will enter every door that is left ajar." In 1892, the faculty abolished the Literary Course, and it became known thereafter as the Philosophical Course, with a Ph.B. degree. Even so, all of these courses, which were taken primarily by women, were notable for their lack of a requirement in Greek, the hallmark of a nineteenth-century liberal arts education. Education of the sexes at Grinnell was still unequal.[4]

When the Grinnell curriculum was finally changed in 1895 to the Group System, all of the new majors—in the sciences, Greek, Modern Languages, English, Latin, History, Philosophy, Mathematics, Economics, Education, and Political Science—were open to women. The Group System was a major innovation in the late-nineteenth-century curriculum of the liberal arts college because it recognized finally that a study of Greek and the Classics was no longer the sole criterion of liberal culture.

These changes in the curriculum had apparently opened up a wide horizon of opportunities at the disposal of both women and men on an equal basis. On the face of it, it appeared as though women had been invited into the collegiate life as equal participants with men. Judged by their increased enrollment, women responded to this opportunity with enthusiasm. And yet women did not explore all of the new offerings. In the years from 1896 to 1914, 203 (34 percent) of the women chose majors in the Modern Languages, 112 (19 percent) chose English, 106 (18 percent) chose Greek, 68 (11 percent) chose History, and only 39 (6 percent) took majors in the sciences. Taken as a whole, of the 602 women who graduated from Grinnell between 1896 and 1914, a total of 81 percent took degrees in the standard cultural areas: Modern Languages, English, Greek, and History. By contrast, 41 percent of the men chose these fields in the years 1896 to 1904 and 1909 to 1914. In the period 1916 to 1930, the percentage of women choosing majors in the standard cultural areas dropped only from 81 percent to 74 percent indicating that most women were still not exploiting all of the curricular offerings of the college as late as 1930.[5]

Not surprisingly, despite the fact that more and more women were entering college during the late nineteenth and early twentieth centuries, once out they did not tend to pursue careers other than the traditional female occupations such as teaching or library work. Most Grinnell women taught for a few years and then married. Of all the women graduates from Grinnell between 1884 and 1915 who had an occupation, almost 80 percent were teachers at some point. Moreover, even though more women than men had taken new offerings in the fields of sociology and psychology, they tended to apply their expertise in the areas of social service and schoolteaching, rather than in pursuit of research-oriented careers. Of further interest is the fact that most

Table II. Geographic Destinations after Graduation of Grinnell Women: Classes of 1904–1905; 1909–1917

Class	Moved to Larger Town		Moved to Smaller Town		Returned Home		Unknown*		Total
	N	%	N	%	N	%	N	%	
1904	8	28.6	9	32.1	4	14.3	7	25.0	28
1905	7	26.9	11	42.3	7	26.9	1	3.8	26
1909	11	18.6	23	40.0	24	40.7	1	1.7	59
1910	5	12.5	11	27.5	4	10.0	20	50.0	40
1911	5	10.9	12	26.1	8	17.4	21	45.7	46
1912	6	17.1	12	34.3	2	5.7	15	42.9	35
1913	12	24.0	23	46.0	11	22.0	4	8.0	50
1914	7	13.5	19	36.5	11	21.2	15	28.8	52
1915	10	22.2	8	17.8	19	42.2	8	17.8	45
1916	15	30.6	19	38.8	10	20.4	5	10.2	49
1917	12	21.8	23	41.8	14	25.5	6	10.9	55
TOTAL	98	20.2	170	35.1	114	23.5	103	21.2	485

*Most of the unknowns went to towns not listed in the 1910 census suggesting that they were probably under 1000 in population. For 1904–1905 the 1900 census was used; all other years were calculated from the 1910 census.

Source: Alumni Section of *Grinnell Review*.

women graduates did not go to urban areas after graduation. Most of them migrated either to smaller towns than the ones they had come from, or they returned home. Going to college, it appeared, did not introduce change into their lives. Apparently it had been an act of conformity and not an act of independence.[6] (See Tables II and III.)

Two basic factors conditioned the college experience for women at Grinnell. The first involved the attitudes and actions of the administration, particularly those of John Hanson Thomas Main, president of Grinnell from 1906 to 1931. Main was forced to react to pressures which made the liberal arts college seem increasingly fragile, particularly the prevailing notion that the classic liberal arts education was becoming obsolete in the face of vocational training. His primary objective was the establishment of the independent or "detached" college as a distinctive institution in the Midwest. In both respects, Main's sense of the college's mission, and thus its needs, interacted with his attitude toward women to produce college policies that had special effects upon the women themselves. Main's perspective concerning women and co-education was one which regarded the presence of women as a disruptive intrusion into a male-defined collegiate world. The second factor involved the female students' own "Main-Street" background which was dominated by Chautauqua literary circles and women's clubs which supported and reinforced intimacy among women. While these groups

Table III. Occupations of Grinnell Women (Graduates), 1884–1915

Total	Teacher		Librarian		School Administrator		College Professor		Other	
468	369	78.8%	19	4.1%	16	3.4%	14	3.0%	50	10.7%

Note: Between 1884 and 1915 a total of 804 women graduated from Grinnell. Of these 58.2% listed an occupation. Other occupations included college administration, physician, nurse, literary work, missionary work, clerk, social welfare and YWCA, etc.

Sources: Alumni Address Book (Grinnell) 1913 and alumni sections of *Grinnell Review*.

expressed a firm commitment to women's education, they did not express an equal commitment to professional careers for women.

Generally, Main shaped and implemented policies at Grinnell that led to a continuation and intensification of Victorian society's practice of according separate roles in separate spheres to men and women. He moved in the direction of a more practical and vocational curriculum for the men in part because of the increased importance and appeal of state universities which were drawing students and faculty away from the supposedly stagnating liberal arts colleges by offering practical training for students and higher salaries for faculty.[7] The decision to offer practical training, however, was due not only to the challenge of the state universities but also to Main's efforts to maintain a sexual balance in the four-year college course. As more women began to attend college beginning in the 1890's, and as men students appeared to be drifting to the state universities where they could obtain more practical training, the ratio between men and women in liberal arts colleges was drastically altered. For example, from 1893 to 1905—a period of twelve years—the percentage of women in the four college classes rose from 33 percent to almost 60 percent. Not surprisingly, Main considered this development "unfortunate in itself" and argued that if co-education were to continue, it would have to be accomplished through a suitable balance of men and women, that is, at least an equal proportion of both sexes. Ironically, then, the larger percentage of women at Grinnell helped push Main to the conclusion that liberal culture had to suffer in favor of more technical training. Since women flocked to the courses which were the backbone of liberal culture, Main sought to introduce courses in business and engineering to attract more men. By 1909, Main had introduced mechanical drawing and the idea of a department of public affairs, and he was trying to offer science courses that would be acceptable for credit in medical schools. By 1915, Grinnell was prepared to offer a complete course in business administration. In the end, then, Main chose to compromise the standards of liberal culture, which distinguished the liberal arts college from the university, in large part because of the presence of women.[8]

Just as he had responded to male demands for a more practical curriculum, so Main addressed himself to what he considered to be women's proper needs. The context for his definition of women's needs combined his overall goal of making Grinnell a unique and distinctive institution in the Midwest and his traditional view of women's place in society. In conjunction with his efforts to maintain a sexual balance, Main sought to establish an orderly, close-knit community whereby he could define and direct the affairs of the students, meet their needs as he saw them, and control their lives completely, while providing a heightened sense of community. Imitating the eastern pattern of separate but affiliated schools for men and women, Main established what he called a "co-educational college for men, and a co-educational college for women." He wanted to organize the social life of the entire institution and revive the collegiate idea of community, but he wanted to accomplish that along the lines of separate spheres. Housing men and women in separated, college-owned buildings was a key part of his plan. As he was to state in blunt terms at a later date:

> For one thing the organization of the men's life can be kept
> separate from the organization of the women's life. If either is to
> succeed they must shut themselves entirely away from any
> influences, whether direct or indirect, on the part of each other.[9]

The physical manifestation of the closely-knit community for women was the Women's Quadrangle, a series of dormitories built on the Oxford model and completed in 1915. Boasting that the Quad for women was "a real innovation in the West," Main revealed that his attitude toward co-education had changed, but his perspective on women remained the same.[10]

So far as Main was concerned, the separate Quad answered a definite need precisely because it provided a home, albeit a temporary one, for women and thus an appropriate collegiate setting for the development of their skills as homemakers, spiritual leaders, and guides of the rising generation. As female as well as male students had lived in town before the Quad was built, women experienced diminished freedom of movement once they entered the supposed home Main had created for them. By locating women in one place, Main in effect more closely circumscribed the female sphere of activity. And as women were housed, so they were taught. Main's definition of educated womanhood did not differ essentially from classic "True Womanhood," and his expressed policy throughout his years in the presidency was to instill the concept of ideal womanhood in the college girl. As he remarked near the end of his career:

> In spite of the franchise recently given to them, in spite of the new
> avenues of service open to them out in the world, *women will*

continue to exercise their influence in the home and from the home as a creative center. [11]

On the whole, female students at Grinnell before 1917 appeared to duplicate at the college, attitudes and behavior that reflected their home environments and did not significantly challenge traditional views of women's role and sphere. These women came from rural and "Main-Street" backgrounds where a primary cultural influence was generated by Chautauqua circles or women's clubs, both of which emphasized self-improvement along with genteel literary culture. Yet the firm commitment to women's education did not result in the same commitment to careers beyond the home. Women's introduction to academic culture through alternative sources such as Chautauqua and women's clubs provided an avenue to high culture, but these organizations did not essentially challenge the conventional perspective on gender roles. An educated woman, it was believed, would make a better wife and mother who would in turn be an asset to her community. [12]

Both women's clubs and Chautauqua circles reflected adult women's desires to enhance their educational experience, and they provided a cultural background for younger, college-bound women. Women's interest in self-improvement was one reason why they dominated the assemblies held in Chautauqua, New York, and the Literary and Scientific Circles, hundreds of which dotted the midwestern landscape. Chautauqua home reading circles offered those who were unable to obtain a college education the opportunity to follow an outline of readings with a group of fellow readers. The purpose of CLSC (Chautauqua Literary and Scientific Circles) was stated in the opening number of *The Chautauquan* in 1880:

> The new organization aims to promote habits of reading and study in nature, art, science and in secular and sacred literature, in connection with the routine of daily life (especially among those whose educational advantages have been limited) so as to secure to them the college student's general outlook upon the world and life, and to develop the habit of close, connected, persistent thinking.

The course outlines included readings in History, Physical Science, Literature, and Theology. Chautauqua book titles appeared to resemble the types of books read by college students, and indeed, Chautauqua initially seemed to offer an exposure to culture that was more than superficial entertainment. Yet there were differences between what a college course offered and what Chautauqua offered. For example, discussing a variety of readings with hometown friends was likely to be less directed than reading supervised by a college professor. Moreover, reading the many books and articles suggested by Chautauqua outlines would constitute an episodic exposure to "knowledge" that may not have instilled a coherent way of thinking. Episodic reading more likely resulted in the retention of scattered bits of information. Without a disciplined, intellectual focus, Chautauquans may have found the potential conflict between a sustained exploration of difficult questions and Bible readings no conflict at all. While they were exposed to high culture, Chautauquans were exposed simultaneously to a sustained religious message. As one "class motto" put it: "We study the word and the works of God." The cultural background provided by Chautauqua may have offered midwestern women a taste of academic learning, but it was a safe exposure since Chautauqua teachings made no effort to introduce controversial or radical ideas. If anything, Chautauqua offered a bland type of culture that would accommodate a variety of groups without threatening the values of any of them. [13]

While women's clubs more specifically emphasized the education of women, these groups never intended to provide a basis for professional training. Nor did they confront the explosive potential for frustration inherent in the juxtaposition of education for women with emphasis on traditional roles. Many women's groups grew out of Chautauqua Home Reading Circles. The number of clubs in Iowa grew from 99 in 1895 to 668 clubs in 1919 with a total of 20,000 members. Grinnell alone had three clubs in 1907. The organization and work of these clubs resembled that of small college classes. One of the largest clubs in Iowa, The Dubuque Ladies' Literary Association, boasted 250 members. This group divided itself into twelve classes which included Art, English Literature, Classic Literature, Historical Art, Current Events, and Biblical History. Women from these groups presented papers on such topics as "Women of the Orient," "Shakespearean Essays," "Work of Women as Founders of Civilization," and "American Schools." The President of the Women's Federation in Iowa who suggested that these papers should be shared with other groups revealed a significant ordering of priorities. Such sharing, she said, would serve as a means of "establishing a stimulating interchange of courtesies and extending fellowship, as well as giving direct benefit by the dissemination of knowledge and the introduction of new elements into club life." Included as yet another priority was the promotion of sisterhood. Not surprisingly, these impulses dominated the women's organizations in midwestern colleges. [14]

Chautauqua circles and women's clubs provided a cultural milieu for midwestern middle-class women that gave them an introduction to academic culture. While women's clubs in particular provided a firm commitment to the education of women and to intellectual life, neither of these two alternative sources of culture threatened ideas about women's traditional roles. Both not only reinforced a genteel culture which was designed to avoid conflict but also reinforced traditional notions of women's sphere. Avenues of self-improvement for women through alternative sources of culture diffused the inherent tension produced by a stress on domesticity and exclusion from institutional forms of educational training.

The educational policies of President Main represented an attempt to adapt to the increasing flow of college-bound women without in effect altering women's traditional patterns, intellectually and socially. By building the Quad, Main had strengthened the female community at Grinnell and increased the likelihood that female students upon entering college would duplicate a familiar social and cultural environment. The Quadrangle not only brought the women onto the campus and out of the town, it also closed off women from the rest of the campus. As one alumna from the class of 1911 commented: "I think it took a little while for the men to get adjusted to the new women's dorms. It took courage to go into a house full of girls and ask for your date and then wait for her to appear." Males may have experienced a greater sense of distance from their female cohorts, but strong, intimate friendships among women were encouraged. When asked what features of their college experience had a lasting significance, many women mentioned their longstanding friendships.

Female friendships had long been encouraged at Grinnell by the several groups on campus which were run by and for women. The earliest literary society for women, the Calocagathian Society, was founded in 1863. Literary societies had been formed by the students as alternatives to the curricular offerings of the college. They were mainly discussion groups where students met to debate or talk about literature or politics. For example, the Calocagathian Society was primarily interested in modern literature. Other literary societies for women were created as the female population on the campus grew. Calocagathian was followed by the Ellis Society, founded in 1882, Philadelphica (1907), and Aegis (1913). The women themselves eventually voted to abolish literary societies in the mid-1920's. The literary societies offered a supplement to the standard classical curriculum and provided an alternate source of high culture. But when the literary societies lost their primary educational focus, they tended to degenerate into social cliques.[15]

The meetings of the literary societies resembled the format of other noncollegiate women's organizations of the day. Literary societies patterned themselves after women's clubs in many cases. A typical meeting of one of these literary societies might consist of a brief musical performance and a short talk given by one or more members. In fact, *Scarlet & Black,* the student newspaper otherwise known as *S & B,* noted in 1899 that the afternoon subject at one meeting was "women's clubs." One girl spoke on "Club Work as an Aid to Higher Education." At another meeting in 1900 the theme was "College Life in Other Institutions" in which a Miss Currie "brought out the contrast between the Bohemian life of a large university and the close fellowship of a small college." The societies usually stated their aims in terms of raising the tone of social and cultural life of the women.[16]

In addition to literary societies, the other major organization for women was the YWCA, which was established at Grinnell in 1884. Both the literary societies and the YWCA served a dual function. Those in the administration who were concerned with the education of women wanted to develop poise and a strong religious commitment on the part of female undergraduates. On the one hand, then, women's organizations helped to achieve the goals of administrators who were concerned with educated womanhood as the embodiment of liberal culture. Women themselves enjoyed these extracurricular activities for reasons in addition to those offered by administrators. Women's literary organizations and the YWCA not only gave women experience in speaking in front of groups and organizing social activities but also gave women an opportunity to enjoy the fellowship the female undergraduate community offered. For most women, the enduring qualities of these two organizations were the personal friendships they engendered.

While the literary societies performed a useful function for the administration in attempting to instill the proper goals and exposing women to cultural activity, women's organizations on campus served a useful function in bringing students together in groups other than those based on living situations. When asked to state the significance of women's organizations such as literary societies or YWCA, one alumna from 1913 said: "We enjoyed the opportunity to meet girls of all ages. The older ones we looked up to as Freshmen and Sophomores, and enjoyed being looked up to as Juniors and Seniors." Another woman wrote, the YWCA was important for the fellowship it offered, a fellowship that was not only Christian fellowship, but also the fellowship of young women. "I think that was the outstanding feature of the college," said an alumna of 1911. "We all knew each other and had so many opportunities to see one another, we naturally made friendships which were lasting." And from the class of 1908 came the sentiments that, "I have enjoyed many fine friends, but I believe the College friends have been generally more special, as we lived in rather close contact, and did things together." Of organizations like the YWCA it could always be said that, "it is an association which strives to develop in us those things which make for true noble womanhood."[17]

The Grinnell College experience brought women together, not only in terms of day-to-day contact, but also in the context of an entire living situation. For most young women this was the first major adjustment to living away from home. One of the main functions of YWCA was to provide each incoming freshman girl with a "big sister" to make her feel welcome. These circumstances were bound to sustain the feeling of female community. The college experience was unique for young women in that the college was the only institution in late-nineteenth and early-twentieth-century America, aside from convents and working-class boarding houses perhaps, where adolescent girls lived together for long periods of time. As might be expected, the bonds they formed with one another were strong and long-lasting. Many alumnae maintained these college friendships for over sixty years, often through round-robin letters. When asked if she had formed special friendships at college, one alumna from the class of 1914 replied:

> Definitely—After two years in 'The Shack' (the only dormitory at that time) I was invited to join seven friends to live on the 2nd floor of Pottle House. At the end of two years we were very close. Thru the years we have kept a circle letter going, had many houseparties and the five of us left have traveled together and we still spend a month together in LaJolla, Cal. every other year.

The comment was typical, and again it pointed to a fairly strong female network of friendships among college-educated women. Women's clubs and organizations were manifestations of women's needs to share common experience, but college life brought women together on a sustained institutional basis which contributed to the formation of deeper and more lasting friendships.[18]

The segregation of the sexes in midwestern colleges reinforced the tendency of women not to assume positions of authority in college-wide organizations. Although a few women had held positions on editorial boards of campus publications, avenues of participation in college-wide activities were essentially limited for women. Limitation on the student newspaper was evidenced by the fact that at Grinnell a special women's edition was published, sometimes annually, beginning in 1905. As stated in the *S & B*: "Although Grinnell women have always had a prominent share in things literary, journalistic work had not been open to them so it seems only right that, once a year, opportunity should be given to them to publish a women's number...." This was a small concession indeed for the editors of the *S & B* to make. Women did well in leading their own organizations but did not consistently hold leadership positions when they were competing with men. When asked whether women received encouragement to participate in college-wide organizations, one alumna commented, "not particularly so. Men hold most offices in organizations and we said little about sharing." Another woman agreed: "It was somewhat conventional that men were the presidents and women secretaries, perhaps treasurers, except in purely women's organizations."[19]

This general theme of female complacency and contentment also showed in alumnae responses to a question on whether or not men students resented women in class or favored co-education. The alumnae answered overwhelmingly that they felt no resentment. There were only two qualifications. Margaret McCandless observed: "Co-education was so taken for granted in the Middle West. I never thought so [that men resented women] —perhaps in physics or chemistry classes where they outnumbered the girls." Rosamond Rule was more specific, saying: "Only in laboratories did I feel that some men felt we were an *inferior* species—a nuisance." It was no doubt a feeling that made more women choose English and language as majors, rather than science.[20]

On the whole, however, men and women apparently got along well as long as women did not rock the boat. Certainly one reason why relations between men and women were congenial was that women had their own organizations which performed important functions for them. In many ways the female community was very comfortable for Grinnell women. Nevertheless, while providing a medium through which women were exposed to high culture and helping to promote female friendships, the community women created for themselves did not encourage them to become intellectuals and did not promote their leaving a feminine sphere. By fostering what today's feminists would consider a false consciousness, the female community at Grinnell reinforced the women's acceptance of a traditional passive role.

From the administration's point of view, the Quadrangle and women's organizations contributed to the desired goal of producing female college graduates who would embody the ideals of educated womanhood. For women, on the other hand, the Quad and women's organizations strengthened an already existing female network and did not promote dissent.[21] Domesticity had triumphed in this first stage of the institutionalization of co-education at Grinnell. To consider only the administration's actions would be to regard college women solely as passive victims of a male-defined educational experience. Women were complicit in their own domestication.

Main's plan for a sex-segregated collegiate environment worked better for women than for men. Main had conceived of the Quad as a means of providing a college home for the women while at the same time making Grinnell unique in the Midwest. In addition, the Quad would fulfill other functions: it would prevent the women from imitating the social life of the men, and it would also dispel the notion that college unfitted women for their domestic duties. The women had treated Mears (their first dorm) as a club and had also gone so far as to participate in the class scrap. In order to complement the Quad, Main conceived of the idea of housing the men in a fortress-like series of dorms at the opposite end of the campus from women. As he sought to organize the men's living situation as he had the women's, he found himself under attack by more independent-minded men. While the women seemed to find life in the Quad congenial, the men objected to the resulting alienation engendered between men and women. On September 22,

1915, the *S & B* bemoaned the fact that the men and women would no longer eat together. Another editorial on December 13, 1916, entitled "Keep the Family, Or Not!," complained: "Lately, with the rapid growth of the institution, there has come a change in which the men and women have become more alienated from each other.... The natural social relations between men and women, always somewhat warped in the college atmosphere, has been almost completely thwarted by the establishment of artificial barriers." The editors also described the resulting decline in table manners and the inability to form a wide circle of friends of both sexes.[22]

The men not only objected to the building of the Quad, they also objected to being housed on campus. Over two-thirds of the men held some kind of outside job, which no doubt gave them a sense of independence. In fact, the objections of the men delayed the construction of the men's dorms. Nevertheless, Main pushed ahead with his project, and the men's dorms were completed in 1917. The argument continued, however, as the men still refused to eat in the dining hall provided for them. This issue reached a crisis in 1920 when it appeared that the college dining facility for men might have to close since the men preferred to eat downtown. Rather than yielding, Main decided to coerce the men into eating on campus by charging them for room and board in one lump sum.[23]

Obviously, Main ran into opposition in attempting to fulfill his goals. The argument over student housing triggered a heated exchange over several other features of student life including the subject of mixed dancing, an issue that had surfaced even before Main's tenure when Grinnell students protested an 1898 rule which stated that mixed dancing would result in expulsion. By 1921, students had gained control over most of their affairs. But, Main continued to stand his ground. As early as 1909 in a chapel talk on dancing as reported by *S & B*, Main indicated what the nature of his rule would be:

> In answer to the question 'Why should the college control the
> personal life of the student?' Main stated,... the *college* life must be
> maintained; that no person anywhere can be a law unto himself....
> In being faithful to our traditions we should find—and have
> found—the greatest unity and harmony.[24]

For women, the most significant of those traditions was a strict separation of the sexes. In a 1926 editorial, entitled "Sons of Old Grinnell," Main reiterated a theme which had been implicit in his presidency from the beginning:

> The advantages of a men's college for men, a women's college for
> women, and the social advantages of co-education are established
> as distinctive features of Grinnell's development. Just now its
> development as a men's college for men is receiving particular

emphasis. Although the number of men at Grinnell has increased forty percent in the last few years, and is now a larger percent of the total enrollment than most co-educational colleges can show, we are not satisfied and we should not be. There are colleges— Grinnell is not one of them, and never will be—which are drifting toward the status of women's colleges with an annex for men.[25]

While the presence of women at Grinnell College led to controversy over the arrangement of student life, the women themselves never upset their traditional role in the college "family." The irony was that in spite of the fact that women created a strong network and amounted to a majority of the undergraduate population, the cultural impact they had on the college was to heighten sex roles, which in turn more closely circumscribed their sphere of activity. It was clear that access to higher education alone was not enough to produce dramatic changes in the status or attitudes of women. While a college education might have served as the starting point of a professional career, instead it offered women a good set of friends and a taste for high culture. In short, the presence of women at Grinnell between 1884 and 1917 changed college policy more than the college experience changed women.

Notes

1. Two recent discussions of the causes of student riots in nineteenth-century New England colleges are David Allmendinger, *Paupers and Scholars* (New York: St. Martin's Press, 1975) and Steven Novak, *The Rights of Youth: American Colleges and Student Revolt, 1798-1815* (Cambridge, Mass.: Harvard University Press, 1977). See Table I.
2. For an insightful analysis of this phenomenon among nineteenth-century women see Carroll Smith-Rosenberg, "The Female World of Love and Ritual: Relations between Women in Nineteenth-Century America," *Signs* 1 (Autumn 1975): 1-29.
3. Shelton Beatty, "A Curricular History of Grinnell College, 1848-1931" (Ph.D. dissertation, Stanford University, 1955): pp. 158-185.
4. Martha Foote Crowe to President George A. Gates, Chairman of the Board of Trustees of Iowa College, folder "Faculty Report to the Trustees, 1890-1895," pp. 15-19, Grinnell College Archives (hereafter GCA). Crowe had also written a resignation in 1888.
5. Information on majors was compiled from the *Grinnell College Catalogue* for the years 1896 to 1930.
6. *Alumni Address Book* (Grinnell) 1913; alumni sections of *The Grinnell Review*; William Chafe, *American Woman: Her Changing Social, Economic and Political Roles, 1920-1970* (New York: Oxford University Press, 1972), pp. 89-111. While some men also taught after graduation,

they tended to use teaching as a temporary measure until they entered business or another profession. See Tables II & III.

7. John H. T. Main, *President's Report*, 1907–1908, p. 17, GCA.

8. Main, *President's Report*, 1907–1908, pp. 8–9; *Grinnell College Catalogue*, 1909–1916. Commenting on the rapid influx of women, Main wrote, "this need not cause any especial fear; but in view of the general tendency, it must be taken into account as emphasizing the trend in education at the present time and given the most serious consideration.... This condition of things insistently brings up... questions: How can the college of liberal arts renew and enlarge its appeal to men.... Briefly, the only way to do it is to put the college into touch with modern practical life." (p. 11).

9. *Scarlet and Black* (Grinnell student newspaper, May 5, 1920) (hereafter *S&B*).

10. *The Grinnell Review* (January 1914): 51–52. Main also commented that "Grinnell is a man's college—a co-educational college for men." Commenting on predormitory student life, Earl Strong observed: "Scattered alone or in little groups in a hundred spots around town, often with the scantiest of the amenities of life, with no places to come together for even the elements of youthful association, there was little sense of community, for there was no community." "Builders of Grinnell," March 24, 1954, Grinnell College Chapel Speech, verticle file, GCA. J.H.T. Main to H.A. Wilder, September 15, 1910, folder "H.A. Wilder," Nollen Box, GCA. Gerard Nollen to J.H.T. Main, August 28, 1925, folder "Trustees," GCA.

11. Main, *President's Report*, 1908–1909, p. 16; Main, "Education for Women," October 15, 1927, vertical file GCA.

12. That Chautauqua teachings reinforced conformity was illustrated in this excerpt from *The Chautauquan* in 1880: "An 'odd' person. How often one hears the word, and generally in a tone of depreciation, as if it implied a misfortune or a disgrace, or both. Which it does, when the oddity or eccentricity is not natural but artificially assumed, as is frequently the case. Of all forms of egotism, that of being intentionally peculiar is the most pitiful. The man who is always putting himself in an attitude, physical or moral, in order that the world may stare at him; striving to make himself different from other folks under the delusion that difference constitutes superiority—such a man merits, and generally gets, only contempt." November, 1880, p. 90.

13. *The Chautauquan*, (October 1880): 45.

14. *Official Register and Directory of Women's Clubs in America*, Vol. XXI, 1919 (Shirley, Mass.: Helen Winslow Publisher, 1919) and *Official Register and Directory of the Women's Clubs in America 1907–1919*, Vol. 9–12 (Boston: Helen Winslow Publisher, 1907); Ella Hamilton Durley, "Club Federations in Iowa," *Midland Monthly* 3 (June 1895): 581–589.

15. Margaret McCandless '11 Grinnell, questionnaire. A questionnaire was sent to

alumnae of Grinnell, Carleton, Beloit, and Knox who graduated before World War I (1894–1917). A total of 276 questionnaires was sent as follows: 140 to Carleton women; 100 to Grinnell women; 20 to Beloit women; and 16 to Knox women. I received about a 50 percent return.

16. *S&B*, January 7, 1899; September 29, 1900.

17. Ruth Compton '13 Grinnell, questionnaire; Margaret McCandless '11 Grinnell, questionnaire; Alice Whitney '08 Grinnell, questionnaire; *S&B*, October 14, 1911.

18. Pearl Fellows '14, Grinnell, questionnaire.

19. *S&B*, October 4, 1911; Rosamond Rule '09 Grinnell, questionnaire.

20. Margaret McCandless, '11 Grinnell, questionnaire; Rosamond Rule '09 Grinnell, questionnaire.

21. In her report for 1904, Principal of Women Louise Berry pointed out that college women treated the Mears cottage more like a club than a college home: "Time and vital energies have been wasted in foolish dissipation, such as too frequent 'spreads,' late hours, and untimely visiting. Cottage girls are too prone to consider the Cottage not a *home* provided to secure their best interests but as a college club or fraternity designed primarily for 'social enjoyment and a good time.'" GCA.

22. *S&B*, September 22, 1915; December 13, 1916.

23. *S&B*, May 20, 1920; November 18, 1916; October 20, 1920; May 14, 1921.

24. *S&B*, April 16, 1898; April 24, 1909; December 11, 1909; January 26, 1910; January 21, 1911; February 14, 21, 1917; February 16, 1921.

25. *S&B*, March 24, 1926.

Lynn D. Gordon

Co-Education on Two Campuses: Berkeley and Chicago, 1890–1912

Controversies surrounding women in higher education in the immediate post-Civil-War era dealt mostly with their mental and physical capacities. Could they keep up with the work? Would their health, and most importantly, their reproductive systems, collapse under the strain of higher education? Should colleges and universities admit them as students? Since the issue of women's admission to college had not yet been settled in the public mind, fewer arguments focused upon the desirability of co-education.[1] Furthermore, among the very small group of women in college in 1870 (0.7 percent of the female population aged 18–21), less than half attended co-educational institutions.[2].

The generation educated between 1870 and 1890 proved that women could withstand the rigors of college and perform creditably. And in the 1890's, on many campuses, they served as teachers, deans, and mentors for young women students. As secondary school teachers they often inspired young girls to go to college. Women philanthropists and social reformers— some college graduates and some not—also took a friendly interest in women students in the 1890's. They donated money for dormitories, club houses, and scholarships, and frequently appeared on campus as speakers. By 1890, too, a whole range of institutions admitted female students. While the total number of college women remained small (2.2 percent of the eligible population), they represented 35.9 percent of the student body, and fully 70.1 percent attended co-educational schools.[3]

Between 1890 and 1912 the two generations of college women, aided by other prominent women, made a bid for recognition and status on co-educational campuses. Their activities, along with the increased percentage of female students, led to the great turn-of-the-century debate on the social

[Lynn D. Gordon is a doctoral candidate in the Department of History at the University of Chicago. Her dissertation, "Women on Campus in the Progressive Era," concerns the relationship of higher education, feminism, and popular images of women.]

implications of co-education. Co-education caused concern largely because of nineteenth-century beliefs about the sexes. Scientists and doctors of that time offered evidence that physical distinctions led to emotional and intellectual differences between the sexes. Analyses of physical characteristics such as skull capacity, brain weight, facial angle, body dimension, and the percentage of muscle in the body, established males and females as almost separate species.[4]

The experts claimed that the differences meant that each sex should live according to its own separate nature. Occupations, dress, language, thoughts, pleasures, and feelings appropriate for one sex were not so for the other. Each sex had a sphere of influence, each was important to the maintenance of society, but lines separating sex-role behavior must not be crossed. Middle-class men and women in the Victorian era lived largely separate lives, surrounded by support networks of same-sex associations. Particularly after puberty, the sexes were expected to have little informal contact. And they were never to compete, for to do so would have challenged the whole notion of complementary spheres of influence and competence. Men's and women's worlds touched mostly in courtship and marriage. Even within the intimacy of marriage, however, the social distance between the sexes often prevailed.

> If men and women grew up as they did in relatively homogeneous and segregated social groups, then marriage represented a major problem in adjustment. From this perspective we could interpret much of the emotional stiffness and distance that we associate with Victorian marriage as a structural consequence of contemporary sex-role differentiation and gender-role socialization. With marriage, both men and women had to adjust to life with a person who was, in essence, a member of an alien group.[5]

Co-education, post-puberty, then, represented a major departure from the attitudes and experiences of the conventional middle class. What would happen when the sexes shared the same life style, competed for the same prizes, and were in constant association with one another? Would co-education "effeminize" men, make them less aggressive, less able and willing to function in the world? Would it coarsen or "masculinize" young women, obliterating the pure, benevolent, morally superior natures they alone possessed? Would it, by lessening the distance and mystery between the sexes, make them less attractive to each other?[6] These fears cannot be dismissed solely as the self-serving rantings of males anxious about women as competitors, because women, too, worried about the consequences of exercising new options.

By examining two universities with different styles and experiences of co-education, we can perhaps better understand how these attitudes affected the

experiences of women college students in the Progressive era. Their generation came to maturity at a time when traditional sex roles were being
challenged not only by co-education, but in the business and political worlds.
Their female mentors were often active in reform movements, feminist
causes, and the fight for suffrage. Thus, the impact of higher education for
women of the Progressive era had truly revolutionary potential. They had the
tools, the opportunities, and the visibility to challenge conventional sex roles
had they wished to do so.

Berkeley[7]

Women had been students at the University of California since 1870, after the
all-male College of California became the state university in 1869. Although
they increased their representation in the student body from 9 percent in 1870
to 25 percent in 1880 and 31 percent by 1892, they continued to play an
insignificant part in campus life.[8]

Between 1870 and 1890 college traditions and activities centered around
class loyalties and rituals—with gender distinctions. Class officers, with rare
exceptions, were male. Occasionally a vice-presidency was set aside for a
woman, but men and women never competed for the same positions. The
men of each class wore distinctive headgear: soft blue "pork pies" for
freshmen; grey-checked caps for sophomores; "plugs" or top hats for upperclassmen with the juniors wearing grey plugs and the seniors black. Social
custom decreed that women wear hats in public, but they did not adopt any
form of distinctive class apparel. Other traditions reveal the same dichotomy
for men and women. When the yearbooks began using photographs in the
1890's, men's pictures appeared by class, women's pictures from all four
classes appeared together in a separate section. On campus, men of each class
had special benches and stairs reserved for their exclusive use. Women of
whatever class were supposed to avoid using those places. Men were thus
encouraged to identify themselves strongly by class, while women had only
the sense of being an undifferentiated group of "co-eds." Yearly rituals reinforced these patterns of identification. Each year the freshmen and sophomore classes "rushed" each other, competing to see which class could wrestle
and tie up all the members of the other class. The spring burial of Bourdon
and Minto, the freshman algebra and composition texts, called for another
fight as sophomores sought to prevent the freshmen from burying the books
and symbolically ending their new-comer status on campus. Upperclassmen
acted as referees during rushes, with juniors looking out for the freshmen,
and the seniors taking the sophomores' side. Needless to say, "rushing" was
restricted to males. Silly as they sound, these traditions represented oppor-

tunities for men to get to know each other, display leadership, plan strategy and develop an "old-boy" network of good fellowship. In short, they conferred status and recognition, and developed a sense of community.

Women also did not participate in other areas of college life. Most college clubs had no women members, and even the academic organizations, such as the Philosophical Union, listed only a few female participants in the yearbook. Musical groups, debating societies, camera clubs, and honorary societies had only male members. Even physical education classes and athletic activities for women were sharply curtailed because they had access to the gymnasium only after 5 P.M. each day. Housing arrangements exacerbated an already difficult situation. Berkeley had no student dormitories until after World War I. Most students in the early years commuted from San Francisco or Oakland, although some families moved to Berkeley to make it easier for their children to attend the university. More men than women lived on campus—50 percent of the women students still lived at home in 1914, while after 1900 71.9 percent of the student body lived on campus.[9] Men lived in boarding houses, formed residence clubs, and organized fraternities. Kappa Alpha Theta, Berkeley's first sorority, did not appear until 1890. Naturally, since many more male students lived on campus, they had greater access to activities and were more involved in university life.

Women of this early generation at Berkeley left no organizational record and few memoirs. A few, like Milicent Shinn, '80, became famous. Shinn edited for some years the *Overland Monthly*, an important regional literary magazine, before becoming Berkeley's first female Ph.D. in 1890. As an authority on child psychology, her books were translated into several languages. About the other alumnae we know very little. Why did they attend college? Did they see themselves as pioneers? Did their exclusion from campus life concern them? What became of them, and how did their experiences at Berkeley affect the remainder of their lives? Beginning in the 1890's, a far more self-conscious generation of female students made a place for themselves at Berkeley, aided by the philanthropy of Phoebe Apperson Hearst. Hearst's influence and support led to the organization of a social life for women students, and the appointment of Berkeley's first female faculty members. Hearst herself served as the first woman Regent of the university from 1897 through 1919. The wife of wealthy Senator George Hearst, Phoebe Hearst inaugurated her philanthropy in 1891 with a gift of eight, three-hundred dollar scholarships for women. Hearst's support had a great impact on the lives of women students. While not a college graduate, she had been a teacher before her marriage, and was active in many educational causes including the kindergarten movement, and secondary schools for girls.[10] She donated a building, Hearst Hall, to the women students in 1900. The top floor became a gymnasium, finally making physical education classes possible. Athletic clubs for tennis, boating, and fencing followed, as the women now had a place to meet and store equipment. In 1901 Hearst gave money for a women's outdoor basketball court (surrounded by a twelve-foot fence with no knotholes to discourage observers). Some years later she donated a swimming pool. She set up a fund to hire Dr. Mary Bennett Ritter, the first female faculty member, who gave lectures in hygiene, and served as the women's medical examiner. In a new lunchroom at Hearst Hall, Hearst supplied free tea for all women students, encouraging them to gather there at lunchtime. The Hall became the meeting place for women's clubs, and the site of parties. She also founded the Hearst Domestic Industries to teach cooking and sewing so that women students could learn these skills and use them to find part-time jobs to finance their education. Hearst's bounty encouraged women to help themselves, and it also set an interesting pattern for their social lives. Women students gradually gained recognition, but as a separate group. Rather than share men's social and organizational life, they created their own, using Hearst Hall as a focus.

In 1894 the Associated Women Students of the University of California (AWS) called its first meeting. AWS paralleled the functions of the Associated Students of the University of California (ASUC), the male-controlled student organization. Women continued to join the ASUC, but they did so by paying dues to AWS, which turned over a portion of the money to ASUC. AWS became the umbrella organization for women's clubs and committees. It sponsored, for example, the Sports and Pastimes Association to supervise women's athletic clubs and competition with Stanford, Mills, and local high schools. Other groups under the AWS aegis included all-female debating societies, musical organizations, and a dramatics club. The university yearbook, *The Blue and Gold*, began devoting an entire section to women's organizations, including the growing number of sororities and residence clubs.[11] Some segregated academic clubs also appeared: the XYZ Club for women interested in higher mathematics, and the Chemistry Fiends. The Chemistry Fiends had a revealing practice—to make themselves feel more comfortable in the chemistry building, an all-male preserve, women practiced traditional female activities: they held evening parties there, making fudge and coffee over the Bunsen burners. AWS also issued a special handbook for incoming women students, listing all the clubs available for them, and urging them to participate in campus activities. Additionally, women active in YWCA work spent time at the West Berkeley Settlement League helping working-class and poor children.

The men students had formed all-campus honor societies for service to the university—the Skull and Keys and the Golden Bear. Membership in these societies was a highly coveted honor, awarded only to prominent upperclassmen. In 1901, students Adele Lewis and Agnes Frisius, with the help of Dr.

Ritter, formed their own honor society—the Prytaneans. Junior and senior women who had served the university in some way—through work in AWS, for example—could be asked to join. The Prytaneans held festivals and masques to raise money for a student infirmary. When the infirmary opened in 1907, they continued to work for a women's dormitory, a senior women's building, and the establishment of home economics courses.

With the appointment in 1906 of young Lucy Sprague, a Radcliffe graduate, as Berkeley's first Dean of Women, female students gained another advocate. Almost immediately Sprague expressed concern about the housing situation, social life, and career choices of women students. She pointed out that many women still took no part in campus life (one-third belonged to no organizations at all); that most noncommuting women lived in boarding houses over which the university exercised no control; and that 90 percent of women students planned to be elementary and secondary school teachers in a rapidly shrinking market. Sprague complained that women took narrowly specialized and technical courses, with much work in education and thereby ignored the benefits and the broadening effects of liberal arts courses. [12] Sprague attacked these practices by promoting an expansion of social life for women. She held poetry readings for women students at her own home, and took them into the community to study industries and social institutions. She started "Critics on the Hearth," a club for women to learn parliamentary procedure. Most importantly, she proposed and helped found the Partheneia, an annual pageant written, produced, and acted by women students.

Sprague also attended meetings of sororities, AWS, the YWCA, the Prytaneans, and other women's groups, assisting them in setting social standards for women students. Neither Sprague nor the students in the early twentieth century wished to flout rules or set new standards of behavior. Together they made lists of approved boarding houses for women students, set curfews for university functions, and recommended that women students attend no more than two social functions per week. [13]. Sprague did not like functioning as a "warden of women," [14] and could not have done so anyway considering how many students lived off campus. What social control she had came from her cooperation with the women's organizations.

When Sprague married economist Wesley Clair Mitchell and moved to New York City in 1913, Lucy Ward Stebbins became Dean. Stebbins agreed with Sprague that too many women went into teaching without investigating other careers. She also expressed concern that the university failed to provide formal training for alumnae who never worked outside their homes. [15] To promote greater awareness of possible careers for women, Stebbins sent questionnaires to the thirty-seven undergraduate academic departments asking: "To what fields of paid work for women other than teaching does training in your department lead?" "What course should be pursued by the student who wishes to equip herself for any one of these fields?" "How many years of graduate or professional work is required in each case?" "What are the opportunities for advancement and the salaries paid?"[16] Stebbins also addressed herself to the needs of those who would remain in the home. With the help of the Prytaneans and political economy professor Jessica Peixotto, she took the lead in setting up a department of home economics between 1912 and 1916.

The new interest in appropriate education and expanding career choices for women, the wealth of social activities and organizations, the athletic program, the presence of supportive female faculty, and the active philanthropy of Phoebe Hearst, had greatly improved the lives of the growing numbers of Berkeley women. Representing 37 percent of the student body, 1333 undergraduate women were enrolled in 1911–1912,[17] and *The Blue and Gold* recognized their new status in an editorial aptly titled "How the Other Half lives":

> It has taken many, many years for the University of California co-ed to "find herself." When Berkeley was first on the map, the co-ed was not. The small classes of the early days struggled along without her. Today the large classes struggle with her. The co-ed has come to stay and the classes are largely lasses. In spite of the phenomenal growth of the numbers of women students in recent years, it has been only in comparatively recent times that any unification and independence has developed among them. Today, while a part of the whole college community, the women students find it profitable to carry on a distinct line of activity.... The co-ed traditions... may be properly said to be still in the making.[18]

Women had created a separate power structure, but separate was not equal on their campus. The women students and faculty at Berkeley remained marginal in some significant ways.

Intercollegiate athletics with Stanford began to replace the class traditions of the 1890's as the focus for campus activities. In 1905 freshmen and sophomore men ended the rushes, cooperating to build a "Big C" on campus for anti-Stanford rallies. Women took as small a part in the new campus atmosphere as they had in the old. They did not participate in the pregame demonstrations, parades, and "sings" except as spectators. They sat in a separate section at the games, while the men cheered alone in theirs.[19] The campus newspaper, *The Daily Californian*, devoted most of its space to discussion of athletic events. The paper's "women's editor" contributed little more than notices about club meetings. Once a year, on Women's Day, a special female staff put out the *Daily Californian*, underscoring the fact that their participation in campus journalism was an unusual event. Class officers continued to be male. And as late as 1900 Lillian Moller Gilbreth, 1900, complained:

> There was no prejudice against women students. Consequently it was a surprise, and a painful one, to aim for a Phi Beta Kappa key, only to learn that there would be no girls on the list because when it came to finding a good job, men needed the help of this honor more than women did.[20]

Career counseling and options for women remained limited. Respondents to Stebbins' questionnaire included the following occupations in their suggestions: dietitian, physician's helper, designer of costumes, designer of decorative needlework, professional shopper, food analyst, art librarian, executive secretary, caseworker, institutional worker, or buyer for a department store.[21] Just as home economics prepared women for a traditional role, the careers cited reflected equally traditional conceptions of women as nurturing and supportive.

Female faculty at Berkeley were as effectively isolated as their student counterparts. They had little influence on the tone of campus social life and did not even attend faculty meetings. As Sprague said: "Certainly we could have gone, but I knew that it would have prejudiced the men against us, and we already had enough prejudice to live down."[22] Sprague's comment suggests a partial explanation for the cooperation of Berkeley women in maintaining a limiting separate but equal policy. Clearly, they were reacting to the hostility toward co-education exhibited by many Berkeley males. Evidence of this hostility could also be found in the college yearbook where the stereotyping of women masked prejudicial attitudes and fears at the prospect of women leaving their traditional sphere to compete with men. *The Blue and Gold* poked fun at male students stereotyping "the grind" and "the fraternity man," but all women students were still "co-eds" and all alike. An ode to "Tender Dolores" in the 1893 yearbook warned that however pretty a newly arrived female student, if she studied too hard she would make "her pretty little nose very red," her "rosy cheeks" would become jaundiced, and her hair thinned. After graduation, she would become an ugly, bespectacled schoolmarm.[23] Also in 1893 *The Blue and Gold* contained a "Farewell Address of the Seniors to the Coeds of '92":

> In your future careers as schoolmistresses, when, after a wearisome day, you push your spectacles upon your brow and dream of the past, think on us, your admirers and brothers. You never will forget us, we know full well, and believe fully that indeed, indeed we will be brothers to you. In fact we desire nothing more.

The college humor magazine, *The Pelican*, took its name from the slang term for older women students attending the university while on leave from their teaching careers. Supposedly they looked like pelicans—skinny, ugly, with long noses and (at least in cartoons) spectacles. *The Pelican* featured antisuffrage cartoons showing cigar chomping female ward bosses, women drilling as soldiers, females proposing marriage to males, and generally making social institutions ridiculous by aping men's roles. *The Pelican* promoted separate but equal practices by offering support for the activities of female students if conducted within their own sphere. For example, it encouraged women to cheer at football games as long as they stayed in their own section and did not use the same yells the men did.[24] Although it is harder to find public records of their sentiments, some male faculty and administrators shared the students' views. Responding to complaints from his faculty that women students "effeminized" liberal arts courses by driving the men students away, President Benjamin Ide Wheeler ascribed declining male enrollments in such courses to increasing interest in vocational training.[25] Yet Wheeler himself warned women students not to stray from approved feminine roles. His 1904 speech to Berkeley women is indicative:

> You are not like men and you must recognize the fact....You may
> have the same studies as the men, but you put them to different
> use. You are not here with the ambition to be school teachers or
> old maids; but you are here for the preparation of marriage and
> motherhood. This education should tend to make you more
> serviceable as wives and mothers.[26]

Women faculty and students seemed to share the view that male-female social separation was natural and desirable. Phoebe Hearst never suggested that men and women students share the lunchroom and other facilities she provided. Lucy Sprague recognized the problems, but tried to give Berkeley women a positive self-image by encouraging them to reach out to each other, rather than by challenging the men. Lucy Stebbins phrased her career questions in terms of what was "appropriate" for women. Female students themselves made no efforts and expressed no wishes to share control over the campus, or to take dramatically feminist positions. Between 1968 and 1970, Prytanean alumnae from 1901 to 1920 were interviewed about their college days. Inverviewees happily described the number and range of women's activities, stressing their good times and enjoyment of college life. Even allowing for poor memories and sentimentalization, the lack of feminist consciousness is astonishing.[27] Not one woman mentioned the Berkeley chapter of the College Equal Suffrage League. In fact, at the time, its activities rated only an occasional paragraph in *The Daily Californian*, and it seemed to be of more interest to townswomen than to college students.[28]

At Berkeley, then, between 1890 and 1912, advanced education and close contacts between young men and young women had not broken down old ideas about appropriate sex roles and the supposed natural, innate differences between the sexes. Berkeley alumnae seeking to challenge conventional ideas about women had to look elsewhere for their inspiration.

Chicago

John D. Rockefeller and the American Baptist Education Society wanted a "magnet college" in Chicago to draw young Baptists from the Midwest for a superior undergraduate education, but Chicago's first president, William Rainey Harper, had other ideas. Envisioning the university as a major American graduate school, he conditioned his acceptance of the presidency upon Rockefeller's endorsement of his dream. Harper hoped that the first two years of undergraduate instruction would eventually move off campus, and that only upper level students would come to the University of Chicago, after proving themselves elsewhere. Recruited in the two frantic years before the University opened in 1892, Harper's faculty reflected his view of Chicago as primarily a graduate school. Scholars with German doctorates, men from Yale, Cornell, Clark, and other important eastern and midwestern institutions agreed to come to the new university. Harper's persuasiveness was legendary, and he offered top salaries to those in the upper professorial ranks. These men very consciously modelled Chicago on the Eastern universities, and it early became known as the "western Yale."[29]

The old Baptist college at Chicago had been co-educational and the university's charter explicitly stated that women were to be admitted on the same terms as men. Later, during the 1902 "segregation" controversy, trustees, president, faculty, and students claimed they had all along doubted the wisdom of co-education, but these doubts did not surface during the first ten years. In fact, Chicago's women students enjoyed a far more respected and advantageous position than Berkeley women ever achieved.

It is not, of course, appropriate to compare the Berkeley of 1870–1890 with the Chicago of 1892. By the time Chicago opened, the first generation of college-educated women could serve as supporters and mentors for women students. Off campus, the role of women in social settlement work and other Progressive era reform movements, the revival of the suffrage cause, and endless discussions of the "new woman" gave women's needs and concerns far more prominence than in the 1870's and 1880's. But even after 1890, Berkeley failed to match women's achievements at Chicago, mostly because of Chicago's strong, active women faculty. While Berkeley's Phoebe Hearst did a great deal for the women students, no female faculty appeared until the first decade of the twentieth century. Even then, the young and inexperienced

Lucy Sprague had to cope with a strongly male-oriented campus virtually on her own. And, she herself had few theories about women's education and social life.[30]

In keeping with his policy of hiring established, prominent faculty, Harper asked former Wellesley College president Alice Freeman Palmer to be Chicago's Dean of Women. Palmer could only be at Chicago twelve weeks out of the year, as her marriage to Harvard philosophy professor George Herbert Palmer, and her many educational activities necessitated her presence in the East. She chose as her assistant and successor, Marion Talbot, instructor in sanitary science at Wellesley. Both women belonged to the earlier generation of college women—Palmer graduated from the University of Michigan in 1876, and Talbot from Boston University in 1880. Both had long been involved in women's higher education at Wellesley and as founders of the Association of Collegiate Alumnae (later the American Association of University Women). Talbot in particular had a strong consciousness of Eastern traditions for women's education, as the Chicago men did for Yale. When she left Boston for Chicago in 1892 a friend gave her a small piece of Plymouth Rock to take along. "I felt the gift was rather symbolical. . . . I must be reminded that the United States, at least my part of it, was founded on a rock; I might forget that four of my ancestors landed from the little ship 'Mayflower' and be tempted to follow strange gods unless I had some. . . reminder close at hand." If Chicago would be a western Yale, Talbot and Palmer determined to make it also a western Wellesley.[31]

Palmer resigned in 1897, and Talbot became dean, remaining at Chicago in that position until her retirement in 1925. Since she was perhaps the largest single influence on Chicago women, it is important to take note of her position on women's education.

Talbot firmly believed in the intellectual capacities of young women. Women, she said

> have proved their ability to enter every realm of knowledge. They
> must have the right to do it. No province of the mind should be
> peculiarly man's. Unhampered by traditions of sex, women will
> naturally and without comment seek the intellectual goal which
> they think good and fit. The logical outcome of the present status
> of women's education will be intellectual freedom on an individual
> basis.[32]

Yet she also advocated "special education" for women. Her own field of home economics taught women to run their homes and raise their children scientifically. She urged college women to understand good chemistry, proper ventilation, textiles, wise shopping, and economics so they would have efficient, modern homes. She did not question the desirability of most college women becoming full-time homemakers and mothers. Indeed, she assured parents that college attendance need not lead to the schoolroom and spinsterhood, but to an enhanced life in the home. In 1909–1910 her correspondence with Walter De La Mater of Pecatonica, Illinois, she urged him to keep his daughter Mabel in college, promising to take a personal interest in the young woman, and assuring the anxious father:

> [M]y experience leads me to believe that if you are able to give your daughter a collegiate training, it will not of necessity result in her devoting herself to the calling of teacher. There are many women who have the intellectual satisfaction of education who find their happiness in family life and render efficient and noble service in the home.[33]

Talbot supported women's intellectual equality and yet expected them to fulfill traditional roles because she felt those roles to be crucial. Healthy families produced a healthy nation. Like other feminists of her day, Talbot thought women uniquely qualified as homemakers because of their "special" sensitivities and innately superior morality. College-trained women in particular could use these womanly attributes along with their educations to reform their communities along more humane and democratic lines. In fact, many feminists supported women's suffrage because they felt women would use their political power to make badly-needed social changes.[34] This view of women's potential power included separatism, as a technique for bringing women together, reinforcing their virtues, and influencing men. Graduates of the Eastern women's colleges had already demonstrated the power of education, feminism, and separatism in the social settlement movement.[35] Thus when Marion Talbot promoted social separatism on the Chicago campus, she did so to make women more powerful, and increase their influence over the University community. Her separatist ideals had little in common with the separatism practiced at Berkeley. The social arrangements she made as Dean of Women successfully imitated the Eastern women's colleges and created a strong women's community at Chicago.

Unlike Lucy Sprague, Talbot did not merely cooperate with existing organizations to set social policy. Instead she framed the women's social life at Chicago to fit her ideals. She and Palmer lived with the women students at the Hotel Beatrice during the year 1892–1893 before the women's dormitories opened. Freshman Demia Butler's diary recorded her arrival in Chicago on September 21, 1892, entrance examinations on September 22, and sitting on a mattress in the Hotel Beatrice while Talbot and Palmer explained what the women's halls would be like when they opened in May.[36]

The residence halls represented the heart of Talbot's plans for a coherent and strong social life for Chicago women, similar to that experienced by the students at eastern women's colleges. She wanted as many women as possible to live on campus, to consider the residence halls their home, and the other residents as family. Incoming students were assigned to a hall, but could only stay for six months. At the end of that time, other residents had the option of asking them to become full members or to leave. Each hall elected officers, held house meetings, gave its own parties, set its own rules, and ran its own social life. Women faculty frequently lived in the halls, presiding over the dining tables. Talbot herself became head first of Green Hall, then of Kelly, and lived in the halls until her retirement. Important visitors, male and female, were entertained in the women's halls at teas, dinners, and receptions.

Because the halls provided a focus for women's social life, the deans opposed the forming of national sororities at Chicago. Most eastern women's colleges did not have sororities, and boasted of their democratic style of life. By 1910 Barnard, Wellesley, and Mt. Holyoke had banned their secret societies.[37] Many felt that sororities divided women, fragmenting what should have been a close female community. As Talbot said:

> [T]he University of Chicago was to provide both these essential factors (housing and social life) in the life of its students, and in addition the city provided cultural and social opportunities usually not within the reach of students in a small town. It seemed to us important that the situation should not be complicated by the introduction of policies directed by persons outside of the University and not familiar with its aims.[38]

Between 1894 and 1896 Talbot and Palmer struggled to keep the sororities off campus. A compromise was reached with Chicago women permitting the existence of local "clubs" with no national affiliations. While the clubs— Quadranglers, Mortarboard, Esoteric, Sigma, and Kailailu—had many of the trappings of sororities, including rushing, pledging, and the wearing of ribbons and pins, Talbot kept a close watch on them. Each year she checked membership lists for failing students, and urged them to make pledging practices more democratic. Chicago's clubs were not as important as Berkeley's sororities—they did not own their own buildings, and never replaced the women's halls as the focus for social life.[39]

In addition to running the halls and supervising the social clubs, Talbot's duties included: the formation of general policies concerning women, both graduate and undergraduate; the registration and approval of all social functions; direction of the social calendar; conferences with social committees and officers of organizations; assisting fraternities in maintaining good social standards; advising the Board of Student Organizations which approved or disapproved all student clubs; supervising publicity and hospitality for women's guests and speakers; setting standards of dress, dancing, conduct, and manners; organizing women's occupational conferences; and exercising "charge of the conduct of men in the Women's Quadrangle."[40] Thus, while her duties included some that Lucy Sprague would not have performed, considering them to be those of a "warden of women," she exercised control over male students and their relations with women, which Sprague did not. Her influence spread far beyond the women's halls.

Like Sprague, Talbot encountered little resistance to the social standards she set. In one case, male students invited the women to a dance they were giving at a neighborhood public hall. Talbot was dubious, but said: "Let us find out how parties are given and invitations issued by the people who are showing interest in the University. I have no inclination to force on the community the standards to which I have been accustomed, but I do not think we are compelled to adopt the standards of Podunk."[41] After some discussion it was decided that women graduate students could go if they liked, but undergraduates would be forbidden to attend. Talbot's claim that the women students supported her decision is borne out by student Demia Butler. Butler noted in her diary that the women were disappointed, but felt better when Dean Talbot wrote notes to all their escorts, explaining the situation. Butler's escort, Mr. Stone, "took it beautifully. He talked with Miss Talbot, and then understood." Talbot suggested that the men come to the Hotel Beatrice in the evening and "dance a little" instead.[42] Social regulations at Chicago limited male callers at the halls to Friday and Saturday evenings until 10:15 P.M. Dances could not be held more often than once a week, had to take place on campus, and ended at midnight. The only complaints students voiced came from those who wanted a 1 A.M. curfew for the big dances of the year—the Washington Promenade and the Settlement Dance.[43]

Talbot took the lead in founding the Women's Union in 1901. While 20 percent of Chicago's students lived in university halls, and another 40 percent in rooms close to the campus, fully 40 percent commuted from their parents' homes in the city.[44] Because of this, Talbot wanted to provide women day students with a place where they could feel more involved with campus life. The Union took over some rooms in a neighborhood church, turning them into rest rooms, reading rooms, and lunch rooms for women students. It held regular Wednesday afternoon receptions and provided women's clubs with meeting places. Undergraduate, graduate, and faculty women all joined the Union, and Talbot herself served as its president.

Her concern for the academic achievements of women students showed in her annual statement "The Women of the University," included in the *President's Report*. She listed the home states, curricular choices, and grades of undergraduates, comparing their honors to those received by male students. Women graduate students, particularly those holding fellowships or taking their degrees, received recognition in her report. She also discussed the appointments, promotions, and resignations of women faculty, and commented extensively on all aspects of women's lives at the university.

Not only the times and the female faculty, but conditions at the university favored the development of a strong women's presence. Because of Chicago's emphasis on graduate work, undergraduate pranks and games held far less importance there than they did at other schools. Since such traditions of athletics, politics, and roughhousing commonly led, as at Berkeley, to a male-oriented campus, their lesser importance at Chicago contributed to a more favorable position for women. And since campus newspapers were not dominated by discussions of the big game or class elections, they featured articles on the scholarly work of professors, the meaning of student religion, the activities of social settlements, and literary work by students. Discussions of events on the Women's Quadrangle and the parties at the halls also became important news.

Furthermore, Chicago's large arts and sciences graduate school contained a significant number of women studying for their master's and doctoral degrees. Reformers Sophonisba Breckinridge, Grace and Edith Abbott, Katherine Bement Davis, and scholars Helen Bradford Thompson, Myra Reynolds, Elizabeth Wallace, and Madeleine Wallin all did their graduate work at Chicago. Not only did Talbot publicize their efforts in her annual report, but campus newspapers proudly reported their progress.[45] These women joined academic and social clubs with undergraduate women, and often lived in the residence halls, presiding over the dinner tables. In addition to her many other achievements, Breckinridge became the assistant dean of women, serving as a link between academic women, students, and the Hull House reformers.

Particularly during the first ten years of Chicago's existence, male students reacted to their female colleagues in proud and positive ways. In addition to devoting space to women's activities and articles in campus publications, they made many supportive statements about co-education and female achievement. In contrast to Berkeley, one does not find in Chicago publications any of the degrading comments about the supposedly negative effects of co-education on femininity. Instead, the *University Weekly* asserted that "we students at Chicago shall all our lives be better for constant association with those who may be now our sweethearts, someday our wives."[46] Chicago men reiterated this position in smug comparisons of their own attitude about co-education relative to that prevailing at less enlightened institutions.[47]

In the absence of any student or faculty poll it is difficult to assess opinion on a specific feminist issue like suffrage. Nevertheless, the student newspaper gave detailed coverage to the College Equal Suffrage League's activities and proposals. The Chicago chapter was founded in 1908 by student Harriet Grim and Dean Breckinridge upon their return from the convention of the

National Equal Suffrage Association of College Women. The newspaper gave front-page coverage to their plan to enroll every woman student at the university as a member of the League. The paper also featured stories on prominent prosuffrage speakers such as Charlotte Perkins Gilman.[48]

Unquestionably, Chicago's brand of separation did not lead to equality or to the breaking down of sex roles any more than Berkeley's did. Male students ran the publications, class politics, and the debating contests. They had more options for living on or near the campus than did women students. While Harper disapproved of undergraduate fraternities, he did not forbid them, and by 1902 twelve chapters of national fraternities owned houses on or near the campus.[49] Female faculty made up only a small fraction of the instructional staff, and generally served at the lowest levels of instruction.[50] Despite the achievements ot its graduate students, Chicago's undergraduate women had very conventional career aspirations. When Talbot and Breckinridge polled ninety-six freshmen and sophomore women in 1909, fifty-six of the women wished to become teachers, while fifteen listed no choice at all. The deans followed their poll with a vocational conference, attended by three hundred thirty-six Chicago women. One hundred eighty women attended the teaching sessions, while forty heard speakers on "household management." Talbot noted that "while only 2 out of 96 women specified homekeeping as their vocation, the conference on household management drew the largest attendance but one."[51] Quite possibly some of the women who expressed interest in "art" or "writing" or "general culture" also had homemaking interests at heart.

Nevertheless, during its first ten years, the University of Chicago developed a distinctive style of co-education far more respectful of and advantageous to women than was the case at Berkeley. In fact, the very success of co-education at Chicago alarmed some faculty and students and led to the "segregation" controversy.

Between 1900 and 1902 administrators discussed the possibility of separate instruction of the sexes in the Junior College, that is, during the freshman and sophomore years. Harper proposed a Men's Quadrangle and a Women's Quadrangle, each with its own residence halls, classrooms, and gymnasium. He noted that the Junior College was increasing in numbers anyway, necessitating new buildings. Why not use the opportunity to remove undergraduates from the center of campus, and to separate them by sex? Harper believed that co-education could destroy sex-role distinctions, harming everyone. He compared "trying to conform the college life of men and women to a common standard" to attempting "to train all their voices to a common pitch." "Is there not," he asked, "a serious loss to both men and women if the university places too much emphasis upon what they have in common and gives too much emphasis to the fact that in many respects these essential common interests may be best promoted separately?"[52]

As might be expected, Marion Talbot led the vigorous opposition to the plan. She based her objections on the grounds of the intellectual equality of the sexes.

> The atmosphere of intellectual freedom enjoyed by our students, through which they have exercised their mental powers as human beings without reference to the fact that they are either men or women, has been appreciated by them and admired by the world. Separate instruction... would affect this condition unfavorably. If the trustees could know how eager girls and women are to study as thinking beings and not as females, they would hesitate in justice to women to adopt this measure.[53]

Talbot also feared that the quality of instruction offered to women would inevitably suffer from the expense of maintaining dual classes. She protested to Harper that the public would not understand separate instruction, and might suspect it had been initiated because women students were immoral, or because they could not keep academic pace with the men.[54] Those joining Talbot's protest included John Dewey; James Weber Linn, associate in English and a nephew of Jane Addams; classicists William G. Hale and Charles Chandler; James Tufts, Dean of the Senior College; geologists Thomas Chamberlin and Rollin Salisbury; and virtually all the female faculty. In addition, the university's Alumnae Association took up the "antisegregation" cause.

Why, after ten years, did fears arise concerning co-education? In part, we can attribute the controversy to the successes of Chicago women and resulting male fears about their domination of campus life. In her 1902 report Marion Talbot pointed out that the Junior and Senior Colleges now had more female than male students. Furthermore, between 1892 and 1902 women took 46 percent of all bachelor's degrees awarded by the university, and represented 56.3 percent of the Phi Beta Kappa membership.

Educators believed that men would not attend schools or classes where women predominated. Because the sexes differed so greatly, what attracted one would repel the other. Berkeley President Wheeler's view that men left the liberal arts due to a lack of job opportunities, not because of a surplus of women, was ignored. Instead of offering courses, as the state universities did, in agriculture, mining, and engineering, in order to attract men, private liberal arts colleges made plans to limit the numbers and influence of their women students.[56] Harper's reply to a Chicago clubwoman who wrote to him protesting segregation showed this concern about attracting male students: "The University of Chicago... has never taken any step to discourage the attendance of women. It may fairly be criticized, on the other hand, for having done much more for women than for men."[57]

Harper's view prevailed, at least for a time. Segregation took effect at Chicago in the fall quarter, 1902. But by 1907–08 it became clear that the plan was too expensive and cumbersome. Gradually, separate sections for courses were dropped. At best, however, Chicago women won the battle and lost the war. By 1910, they represented much less of a threat to conventional sex-role definitions. Between 1902 and 1912 the enrollment of men went up, the law school opened, and the Reynolds Club was established as a focus for men students' social life. The student newspaper, the *University Weekly* folded, giving way to the *Daily Maroon*. The *Maroon* dropped literary contributions, scholarly articles, and detailed news of women's activities. Instead the paper featured exhaustive accounts of athletic events and articles on the need for "spirit." Editorials addressed themselves to "Chicago men," ignoring the existence of women students.

As the position of men improved at the expense of women, and the campus atmosphere became more traditionally collegiate, women continued to develop their separate social life. Talbot considered the dedication of Ida Noyes Hall, a women's clubhouse and gymnasium, in 1915, the pinnacle of her achievement at Chicago.[58] Since she never sought the abandonment of conventional sex roles by women, she did not consider the Chicago experience a failure when that did not happen. Even on Talbot's own terms, however, women continued to lose ground at Chicago. In 1908–1909, for example, the female faculty consisted of one professor, one associate professor, two assistant professors, five instructors, one associate, one assistant, and twenty-one women associated with the newly-affiliated College of Education.[59] By 1912 women held only 15 percent of the graduate fellowships, compared to 26 percent in 1895.[60] Talbot's reports to the president grew shorter, her analyses less numerous and pointed. One of her last actions before her retirement was to complain officially to the administration about the low numbers, pay, and status of faculty women.[61] When she retired in 1925, the reports were discontinued, and her duties divided among various committees.

Conclusion

During the Progressive era, college women, with the help of their female mentors, established themselves on co-educational campuses, building good academic records and strong social lives, but for the most part acting separately from male students. Those who had feared a challenge to the social order from co-education need not have worried. Women's higher education, and co-education in particular, did not break down the barriers between the sexes, causing each to lose its "natural" distinctiveness. Instead, higher education served more conservative ends by training young women for traditional jobs, mostly in teaching or household management, and encouraging them to think of themselves in conventional ways. The results were similar whether separation was a reaction to male domination at Berkeley or a way of expanding women's roles and influence as at Chicago.

Events at Chicago, Berkeley, and other universities reflected the ideals and experience of the off-campus feminist movement. Social feminists stressed women's specialness and separateness. They asked for rights and privileges not on the basis of equality, but because women were morally superior beings. It would be beneficial, they argued, if women attended colleges and voted. Unfortunately the separate but equal theory could function like a double-edged sword. Doubtless President Harper wondered why Marion Talbot objected so strongly to separate instruction since she actively sought separation in all other areas of university life. And sadly, feminists' hopes for a new social order incorporating womanly ideals failed to materialize.

Furthermore, even when women could attend universities freely, exercise more legal rights, and vote, their ideology prevented them from entering the mainstream of American educational and political life. As separate, special, even morally superior beings, they were thought to exercise their most important influence from the sidelines. If women wanted to challenge the conventional definitions of sex roles they would first need to develop a new ideology, find ways of making their education serve those ends, and persuade men of the need for change.

Notes

1. Thomas Woody, *A History of Women's Education in the United States* (New York and Lancaster, Pennsylvania: The Science Press, 1929), Vol. II. See also Edward Clarke, *Sex and Education* (Boston: Osgood, 1874). I should like to thank Professors Steven Schlossman and Harold Wechsler of the University of Chicago for their help in preparing this essay. Archivists J.R.K. Kantor and Marie Thornton at Berkeley and Albert Tannler at Chicago were also most generous with their time and assistance.
2. Mabel Newcomer, *A Century of Higher Education for American Women* (New York: Harper and Brothers, 1959), pp. 46, 49.
3. Ibid.
4. John S. Haller, Jr., and Robin M. Haller, *The Physician and Sexuality in Victorian America* (Urbana, Illinois: University of Illinois Press, 1974). The chapter entitled "The Lesser Man," pp. 47ff., discusses how the experts designed the tests to show what the testers already believed:

woman was a separate and inferior species.

5. Carroll Smith-Rosenberg, "The Female World of Love and Ritual: Relations between Women in Nineteenth-Century America," *Signs* 1 (Autumn 1975): 28.

6. Woody, Vol. 2, p. 208, and Newcomer, p. 212, discuss lower marriage rates among college women. I found little evidence that during the Progressive era the opposite was feared—that is, that co-education would lead to sexual immorality.

7. The University of California had only one campus—at Berkeley—until 1919 when UCLA was founded. Most sources of the Progressive era refer to the school as "the University of California." To avoid confusing the modern reader I have used the term "Berkeley" in this essay.

8. Verne A. Stadtman, ed., *The Centennial Record of the University of California* (Berkeley: University of California Press, 1967), pp. 212–219.

9. *President's Report*, University of California, 1900–1902, p. 23; 1913–1914, p. 14.

10. Rodman Wilson Paul, "Phoebe Apperson Hearst," in *Notable American Women* (Cambridge, Mass.: Belknap Press of Harvard University Press), Vol. 2, pp. 171–173.

11. By 1915, one-third of the student body belonged to Greek letter societies. Eight hundred thirty male students belonged to thirty-two fraternities, while thirteen sororities had three hundred ninety-seven members. Additionally there were fifteen residential clubs for men and nine for women. Thus, while opportunities to live on campus had increased for both sexes, men still had more "places" available than did the women. Then too, some fraternity and sorority members did not live at the houses. Each year the *Blue and Gold* listed the members of Greek letter societies.

12. "Report of the Dean of Women," in *President's Report*, 1906–1908, pp. 105–109. See also "Pioneering in Education," interview with Lucy Sprague Mitchell by Irene Prescott, Menlo Park, California, 1962, available in Bancroft Library, University of California at Berkeley, p. 41 of transcript.

13. References to Lucy Sprague's work with women students appear in "Reports of the Dean of Women," contained in the *President's Reports*, 1906–1912. See also the Associated Women Students' *Handbooks* (1915–1920). The University of California Archives, The Bancroft Library, Berkeley, California.

14. Lucy Sprague Mitchell, *Two Lives: The Story of Wesley Clair Mitchell and Myself* (New York: Simon and Schuster, 1953), pp. 194–195.

15. "Report of the Dean of Women," in *President's Report*, 1913–1914, p. 197.

16. Files of the Office of the President, The University of California Archives, The Bancroft Library, Berkeley, California.

17. Stadtman, *Centernnial Record,* pp. 212–219.

18. *Blue and Gold*, 1905.

19. See Stadtman, *Centennial Record*, pp. 113–117, for a list and description of

student customs.

20. Lillian Moller Gilbreth, in Irving Stone, ed. *There Was Light: Autobiography of a University, Berkeley 1868–1968* (Garden City, New York: Doubleday and Company, 1970), pp. 84–85.

21. Files of the Office of the President, The University of California Archives, The Bancroft Library, Berkeley, California.

22. "Pioneering *in* Education," p. 42.

23. Since *The Blue and Gold* rarely used page numbers, more specific references are not possible. The type of comment referred to usually appeared in a joke section at the back.

24. *Pelican*, November 1910, editorial page.

25. *President's Report*, University of California, 1902–1904, p. 9.

26. *The Daily Californian*, September 1, 1904.

27. *The Prytaneans: An Oral History of the Prytanean Society, Its Members and Their University* (Berkeley, California: The Prytanean Alumnae, Inc., 1970).

28. *The Daily Californian*, March 16, 1909; October 6, 1909; December 11, 1911; Frequently townswomen organized the meeting, urging college women to attend. Meeting notices often reassured the college community that the club was not necessarily prosuffrage, and would be sure to consider the other side of the question. Apparently, suffrage aroused only antipathy or indifference at Berkeley.

29. See Richard J. Storr, *Harper's University: The Beginnings* (Chicago: University of Chicago Press, 1966), for a discussion of "the eastern question" and Harper's faculty-building between 1890 and 1892. Robert Herrick's roman à clef, *Chimes* (1926), about the early years at Chicago also deals with the preeminence of "eastern" ideas.

30. Sprague was not the first female faculty member at Berkeley: Dr. Ritter and associates in physical education preceded her. She, and her successor Lucy Ward Stebbins were Radcliffe alumnae. At the time they attended Radcliffe (around 1900) it was still very much "the Harvard Annex," and had little social life for women students. Radcliffe also lacked a female faculty to provide role models for its students. The Chicago women came from eastern women's colleges with stronger traditions concerning women's academic and social life, most notably Wellesley. Part of the reason for their stronger showing on behalf of women students might have been their participation in the Wellesley tradition. I am indebted to Sally Schwager and Patricia Palmieri of the Harvard Graduate School of Education for discussing with me their research on Radcliffe and Wellesley Colleges.

31. Marion Talbot, *More Than Lore: Reminiscences of Marion Talbot, Dean of Women, the University of Chicago 1892–1925* (Chicago: University of Chicago Press, 1936), p. 6. The memoirs contain numerous references to eastern ties, and attempts to make social life for Chicago women similar to the life at the women's colleges. When Talbot visited other colleges to study their residence systems and social activities she went to Barnard,

Bryn Mawr, Smith, Vassar, and Wellesley.

32. Marion Talbot, *The Education of Women* (Chicago: The University of Chicago Press, 1910), p. 22.

33. Marion Talbot to Walter De La Mater, November 25, 1910. Talbot papers, Special Collections, University of Chicago, Box IV, folder 1.

34. See William L. O'Neill, *Everyone Was Brave: A History of Feminism in America* (Chicago: Quadrangle Books, 1969).

35. Ibid. See also John P. Rousmaniere, "Cultural Hybrid in the Slums: The College Woman and the Settlement House, 1889–1894," in Michael Katz, ed., *Education in American History* (New York: Praeger Publishers, 1973).

36. Diary of Demia Butler, Special Collections, University of Chicago (no page numbers used). Many entries also undated.

37. See Anna Mary Wells, *Miss Marks and Miss Woolley* (Boston: Houghton Mifflin Company, 1978), for a discussion of the secret societies, and administrative attempts to ban them.

38. Talbot, *More Than Lore*, p. 88.

39. See Talbot's annual reports in *The President's Report*, University of Chicago, 1898–1920. She commented extensively on social life at the university, and almost always said something about the secret societies—usually something critical. See, for example, "The Women of the University," *President's Report*, 1909–1910, p. 95.

42. Talbot papers, Box IV, folder 1.

41. Talbot, *More Than Lore*, p. 62.

42. Diary of Demia Butler, February 19, 1893.

43. "The Women of the University," in *President's Report*, University of Chicago, 1897–1898, p. 133.

44. *President's Report,* 1892–1902. This report, published in honor of the decennial, summarized the university's first ten years. The figures cited come from the section called "The Student Social Life." They are not broken down into male/female students. I suspect that, as at Berkeley, more women were commuters than men.

45. Chicago had 354 graduate women in 1899–1900, while Berkeley had only 83. The difference is even greater, if we take into account that the Chicago figures do not include Education students. At Berkeley many women took a fifth year of graduate study to be eligible to teach in a secondary school; such students probably represent most of the 83. See "The Women of the University," *President's Report*, 1892–1902, p. 125, and Stadtman, *Centennial Record*, pp. 212–219. See also *University Weekly*, December 12, 1895.

46. *University Weekly*, December 7, 1893.

47. The student newspaper at Chicago usually carried stories about events at other colleges and universities. When these stories concerned discrimination against women students, the Chicago paper was quite critical. See, for example, *Daily Maroon*, April 30, 1908; May 1, 1908.

48. *Daily Maroon*, October 15, 1909; May 13, 1908; October 23, 1908.
49. President's Papers 1889–1925, Special Collections, University of Chicago, Box 26, folder 2. Also, *President's Report*, 1892–1902, p. 391.
50. "The Women of the University," *President's Report*, 1897–1898, p. 112, lists twelve women besides Talbot and Palmer who had been on the faculty at various times between 1892 and 1898. In 1897–1898 seven women were teaching in the departments of Greek and Latin, English, Romance Languages, Physical Culture, and History. None ranked above assistant professor. Figures for 1908–1909 are given in the text.
51. "The Women of the University," *President's Report,* 1909–1910, pp. 94–95.
52. *The President's Report*, 1892–1902, preface.
53. Marion Talbot to William Rainey Harper, January 16, 1902, President's Papers, 1889–1925, Box 60, folder 11.
54. Ibid.
55. "The Women of the University," 1892–1902, p. 139. Thomas Woody discusses the "turn of the century reaction against co-education" in volume two of his *History of Women's Education in the United States,* pp. 267–297. Stanford and other schools restricted their women students in some way.
56. See note 29, above.
57. William Rainey Harper to Miss Mary B. Harris, Chicago ACA, May 13, 1902, President's Papers 1889–1925, Box 60, folder 11.
58. See "A Dream Come True," in *More Than Lore*.
59. "The Women of the University" in the *President's Report*, 1908–1909, p. 96.
60. President's Papers, 1889–1925, Box 33, Folder 3. See also, *Daily Maroon*, April 30, 1909; April 20, 1910; May 9, 1912.
61. "The Weaker Sex" in *More Than Lore*.

II. A Woman's Place:
The Halls of Domesticity

Introduction

In the nineteenth century a woman's place was in the home, but exactly where and what that place was historians are still seeking to determine. The four essays in this section represent a contribution to that ongoing search. Having left undisturbed for such a long time the banner proclaiming the glory of domesticity, we have been a while in dislodging from our collective historical consciousness the image of the placid and pampered ornamental middle- and upper-middle class woman perched upon her pedestal of leisure and comfort. For not as long a period, we have been preoccupied with recounting the exploits of those women of the same class who joined the women's rights movement and other reform efforts, and looking at those efforts outside the home we have neglected the fact that those women, too, had domestic experiences.

Increasingly, historians have made the effort to examine women's lives and relationships within the context of wifehood and motherhood, and more and more it has been recognized that stereotypes of either inevitable victimization or triumphant autonomy bear little relation to the reality of women's lives. In the process of dismantling monolithic images, subtle but important distinctions have had to be made in studying such issues as the relationship between an ideology developed and actual experience. In studying the individuals, themselves, the question has been posed as to what the expectations were and what the realities became. And no more important questions can be asked, nor answers found, in this regard than to such questions as how did women perceive themselves and what was their response to their mandated role of wife and mother within the home? What was the interaction between prescription and behavior?

My essay on Harriet Beecher Stowe presents the first of four glimpses of a powerful spiritual and moral ambition grounded in the bedrock of mundane domesticity. Stowe, along with other literary women of the nineteenth century, was part of a major fictional force that propounded as preeminent the spiritual and social value of service to others with the middle-class woman, recruited and depicted in her role as wife and mother, in the vanguard as the inspirer of man and his society and the educator of her children as the future leaders of the nation. As the essay shows, the evidence of Stowe's personal life reveals that her allegiance to the ethic of selflessness for the benefit of others was more than merely public. Stowe brought the same expectations to her marriage and tried to fulfill the ideal within her own life. And yet, just as Stowe's fiction is riddled with tension and ambiguity, so was the distance between the ideal and reality in her life striking.

The reasons were manifold. Stowe's correspondence with her husband and other members of her family dramatizes, perhaps more graphically than her fiction, as much a struggle for survival as for perfection. She was critical of man and his society in her fiction and she anguished that her own husband was not an ideal partner. Their marriage was marred by strain and discord. The physical demands of her husband Calvin were overwhelming. And Stowe, who sought to control the number and spacing of her children, was forced to curb his sexual demands through abstinence and absence. Her success in this regard was only partial. Nor was she able to offer the emotional support her husband demanded. Motherhood, regarded by Stowe as the glory of woman, was just as debilitating. Her efforts to control and shape human development were often unsuccessful. In time, she recognized that the fault lay to a great extent with her expectations. Nevertheless, chastened and wiser, Stowe's identity remained with wifehood and motherhood and her total commitment to her family continued to the end of her life.

Mary Grant questions another apparent paradox between Julia Ward Howe's unhappy, character-crossed marriage and her glorification of woman's role within the home. Despite her marital experiences with a husband who refused to allow her the married woman's traditional domestic prerogatives, and who withheld even affection and companionship, Howe emerged a surprising champion of domesticity. Thwarted in her own attempts to function as a wife and mother, she remained convinced that the *competent* wife and mother could not only preside successfully over her home, but more importantly she could transform the home into a base for the exercise of power beyond the home.

For Howe, at least, marriage was more significant as a vehicle than as an end in itself. Motherhood, Grant argues, was the key. Rather than a burden and restriction, motherhood symbolized woman's supreme opportunity and legitimacy. Howe insisted that if women were fitted to assume the responsibility for the moral training of children and thus determined to a large extent the nation's future, then they were certainly morally and mentally equipped to participate in the world beyond the home. And if woman presumed to be mentor to the child, it was her obligation as well to assume a leading role in building a future society for that child.

Given the direction of Howe's feminism, a feminism that looked beyond the home as much as within, it is not surprising that Howe's fame and achievement as a public figure were greatest once she was widowed and freed from patriarchal demands. With motherhood as the linchpin of her feminism, Howe pursued a variety of reforms for women, not the least of which was to persuade and demand that her society allow women to assume their unique and critical role in spheres within and without the home.

The relationship between ideology and experience also provides the general theme for Elisabeth Griffith's study of Elizabeth Cady Stanton. A woman who became the principal philosopher of the nineteenth-century women's movement, Stanton's ambitions did not loom as large at the outset of her marriage. Nevertheless, Griffith indicates that even before her marriage Stanton was already beginning to develop a strong sense of her own independence as a human being and looking toward total autonomy. Anticipating a marriage of equals, expecting neither hardships or restraints, Stanton instead found herself locked into a marriage that entailed more burdens than benefits.

In contrast to many of the feminists cited in Blanche Hersh's essay, Stanton did not enjoy an egalitarian marriage in which both partners were actively and freely involved in private and public endeavors. And unlike Julia Ward Howe's predicament, Stanton's problem was a husband who refused to help her with familial obligations and resented her growing public activities. Tracing the initially subtle but burgeoning elements of Stanton's domestic discord and discontent, Griffith illustrates how Stanton's feminism developed into a wholesale indictment of traditional marriage. Differing again from Howe's perspective, Stanton's judgment was that patriarchal marriage was the primary obstacle to female emancipation. Ahead of her time, Stanton pushed vigorously for reform of divorce laws. Stanton did not forget that most women's lives were domestic bound, but in her efforts to improve women's overall economic, legal, and social status she sought foremost to gain for women full recognition as human beings, first, and wives and mothers, second.

Employing a model made famous by Erik Erikson, Charles Strickland's essay records in the life of Juliette Low a convergence of personal and historical crises. Prepared to assume the role of companion, hostess, and mother of his children, Low instead faced loneliness, confronted a motherless existence, and ran headlong into her husband's affair with a widow. The result was a marriage that not only brought anguish but ended in a humiliating divorce. Alone and unable to find an alternative role, Low considered her life devoid of meaning.

Strickland proceeds to demonstrate how Low's opportunity to resolve her crisis of identity came only when she found in the Girl Scout movement a cause to which she could dedicate herself. Scouting, itself, was given impetus by the crisis of World War I. And, as Strickland argues, scouting under Low's leadership came to be directed toward unforeseen and unfeminine ends. As a Southern lady, Low had not been tutored to develop the personal virtues of strength, self-reliance, and independence. But just as she had been in need of those very qualities during her own crisis, so she sought to make them hallmark principles of scouting. Scouting might not have challenged all conventional definitions of women's role and sphere, but under Low's tutelage it did demand that women become more than delicate, helpless ornaments.

Mary Kelley

At War with Herself:
Harriet Beecher Stowe as Woman in
Conflict within the Home

Like other nineteenth-century sentimentalists, Harriet Beecher Stowe sought a place and purpose for woman in an America being transformed by modernization. The place was the home, the family the unit for the dissemination of values, and woman the spiritual and moral overseer.[1] Likening the home to the church in *The Minister's Wooing,* Stowe compared woman's role to the minister's. Home, she stated, was the "appointed sphere for woman, more holy than cloister, more saintly and pure than church and altar.... Priestess, wife, and mother there she ministers daily in holy works of household peace."[2] The wife and mother was portrayed as the exemplar and inculcator of the pre-eminent value of service to others, the inspirer and reformer of man, and the educator of children, all within the confines of domesticity. The home was assigned a dual function. Not only was it rhapsodized as a peaceful, joyful retreat, but it was christened as the hallowed ground for the dissemination of a selflessness that would purify the larger society.[3]

Concurrent with their attempt to idealize woman's role as wife and mother, the sentimentalists sought to glorify the marital relationship. Addressing themselves to the bonds uniting wife and husband, they alternately presented frothy, beribboned, love letters and sacred intonements. Stowe assured the readers of *We and Our Neighbors* that the true tale of a wife's and husband's union was an intense, egalitarian devotion. "Intimate friendship—what the French call *camaraderie,*" she proclaimed, was "the healthiest and best cement."[4] At the same time, the bond, as a sacred responsibility, implied more than earthly intimacy and delight. Writing in the introduction to *My Wife and I,* Stowe described marriage as "the oldest and most venerable

[An Assistant Professor in the Department of History at Dartmouth College, Mary Kelley is completing a study on Stowe and eleven other women writers in nineteenth-century America. Her articles on this subject have appeared in the *New England Quarterly* and *Signs: Journal of Women in Culture and Society.* The essay reprinted here was originally published in *American Studies.*]

form of Christian union on record." Her chosen title, "My Wife and I," Stowe stressed, was to be construed as the "sign and symbol of more than any earthly partnership," as, instead, "something sacred as religion, indissoluble as the soul, endless as eternity—the symbol chosen by Almighty Love to represent his redeeming eternal union with the soul of man."[5] Underlying these sentiments was the anticipation that wife and husband would perform in perfect harmony their respective duties within designated spheres. The superior, selfless woman set an example for her husband and nurtured her children, while the strong, reliable male absented himself from the family on a daily basis in order to provide for its support.[6]

Seeking to promote the image of women as superior beings and wedded to their domestic dreams, Stowe and the other sentimentalists openly presented models of correct behavior along with instances of idyllic family life. Stowe's preface to *Pink and White Tyranny* is typical of a group of writers who were anxious to instruct as well as entertain a readership that numbered in the hundreds of thousands and was largely female. Stowe did not hesitate to inform her audience that hers was "a story with a moral." Concerned that her message might elude obtuse readers, she took them by the hand and explained her none too subtle approach. Her readers were told that she had decided upon "the plan of the painter who wrote under his pictures 'this is a bear,' and 'this is a turtledove.'" For those who needed additional guidance there was yet her assurance that "We shall tell you in the proper time succinctly just what the moral is, and send you off edified as if you had been hearing a sermon."[7] At other times, Stowe and her literary coherts were less obvious, but there was no doubting their presence. Maneuvering behind the scenes, manipulating characters, and concocting incongruous endings, their presence was plain and their intent obvious.

The sentimentalists were directing their novels and stories to women not only because there was a vast, commercial, female market waiting for their fiction, but also because they had a message. As moralists they sought to prescribe standards of behavior for an entire society. Their demand for selfless behavior extended to everyone regardless of gender. But they present-ed and promoted woman as a distinct being, and charged her with the mission to reform society, both because they believed in her superiority and felt the need for a reformation of society's values, and because they found man inferior and wanting, just as wanting as the values they sought to change.

The heroine's self-discipline, her self-denial for the benefit of others, is proclaimed the behavior necessary to redeem society. Self-sacrifice and service to others was the dominant value. Man is the central, predatory villain in the fiction because he is perceived as the primary transgressor of this value. That all men in the novels and short stories are not evil incarnate tells us that the writers were not motivated by a vengeful hatred of men. Quite often it is the male who dispenses accolades to the sterling character of the heroine. In *Poganuc People,* Stowe's Dolly Cushing receives just such an accolade from her suitor, Alfred Dunbar: "'She impresses me as having, behind an air of softness and timidity, a very positive and decided character.'" That character, that "'sort of reserved force,'" is apparent in Dolly's defense of "'everything high and noble.'"[8] Nor did the sentimentalists think that every erring, sinning man was hopeless. The great encampment of reformed men confirms that conclusion; male tributes to women point to the source of reformation. Stowe's Mary Scudder is offered the typical paean by her fiance, James Marvyn, who proclaims, "'It is only in your presence, Mary, that I feel that I am bad and low and shallow and mean, because you represent to me a sphere higher and holier than any in which I have moved, and stir up a sort of sighing and longing in my heart to come toward it.'"[9] Reformed or not, however, man can never be woman's equal. Lest inferior man forget that fact, superior woman reminds him of it, as Stowe's Mara Lincoln in *The Pearl of Orr's Island* reminds her repentant lover, Moses Pennel, on her death bed, saying, "'I have felt in all that was deepest and dearest to me, I was alone. You do not come near to me nor touch me where I feel most deeply.'"[10]

Although the sentimentalists wanted to glorify woman's role as wife and mother, wanted to idealize marriage, indeed, sanctify the bond between husband and wife, they were conflicted about woman's place in the home and her relationship with her mate. Their conflict stemmed from what they observed and what they experienced concerning woman's situation in nineteenth-century America. Note, for example, Stowe's bewailing in *We and Our Neighbors* "that a large proportion of marriages have been contracted without any advised or rational effort." She was even more dismayed at the "wail, and woe, and struggle to undo marriage bonds, in our day. . . ."[11] And, elsewhere, she alluded to man's shortcomings and his failure to fulfill the husband's responsibilities in the marital relationship. In querulous tones, she commented in *My Wife and I* that "In our days we have heard much said of the importance of training women to be wives. Is there not something to be said on the importance of training men to be husbands?"[12] Her most despairing and poignant observation was a private one. "Women," she said in a letter to her brother, Henry Ward Beecher, "hold the faith in the world. [It is] the wives and mothers who suffer and must suffer to the end of time to bear the sins of the beloved in their own bodies."[13]

In the case of the sentimentalists, it is possible to go beyond an exploration of the perceptions of reality in the fiction, if not to the lives of the readers, to the lives of the writers, themselves.[14] Fortunately, several of the writers left a substantial body of personal papers. By examining their papers, further insight can be gained into the crucial and complex relationship between socially accepted prescription and social behavior. The sentimentalists' per-

sonal opinions and ideas as well as moments of recorded behavior reveal the
extent to which they internalized their own prescriptions and how they
managed, if at all, to resolve the discrepancies and contradictions apparent in
the fiction. Such an examination also provides additional means for investi
gation and analysis of women's consciousness. Women can thereby be
presented as they actually were: active, involved human beings coping,
sometimes successfully, sometimes less so, with a rapidly changing nineteenth-century world; human beings struggling to find a sense of identity
within roles deemed appropriate for them and a familial institution increasingly isolated from the world beyond the four walls of the home.

Like other sentimentalists, Harriet Beecher Stowe differed from most of
her peers in that she achieved great success in a profession traditionally
dominated by men—and achieved that success while publicizing women as
superior to men. Involved in a demanding and lucrative career that required
stepping beyond the doors of her home, Stowe provided a receptive audience
with a seemingly endless stream of prose glorifying woman and the family.
Nevertheless, as a woman, as a wife and mother, her own life frequently
diverged from the ideal presented in her fiction. There was alternately
ambivalence and tentativeness, confusion and conflict in her life, as there is in
the lives of the heroines she paraded before her adoring public. Stowe's life
symbolized the tension between an ideal to which the sentimentalists subscribed and a reality which they as women experienced. Stowe's own
experiences were fraught with anxiety and uncertainty. At times, she maintained a relatively satisfying marriage, but signs of discord and friction are
apparent in her relationship with her husband, and in her open admission
concerning the heavy burden associated with the rearing of her children.

Harriet's relationship with her husband, Calvin, was marred by strain and
doubt. In part, the difficulties stemmed from the frequent and lengthy
separations that characterized the early years of a marriage that spanned
more than half a century. From time to time, Harriet herself left the family for
visits with various brothers and sisters. Much more frequently, Calvin, a
teacher at Lyman Beecher's Lane Theological Seminary for half of his career,
left Stowe and the children in order to recruit students, raise funds, and
purchase books for the seminary. At different times, each of them spent at
least a year at a water cure in Brattleboro, Vermont. Yet, the friction between
them was rooted to a greater extent in disparate needs and conceptions of
their relationship. Their correspondence tells a tale of longing in a double
sense of the word. There, of course, was the longing for each other during the
separations, but, just as significantly, there was the longing for an unattain-
able relationship during their times together.

Just as Harriet was unable to sustain an ideal relationship with Calvin, so her attempt to create an idealized home met with frustration. The transfer of the Edenic, the perfect, home from the pages of her fiction to the reality of her life in the nineteenth century proved to be impossible. Try as she might Stowe could not create the idyllic home in which the serene and contented wife and mother presided over a refuge from a restless, transitory society. Ironically, she found such a home only as a visitor. Writing to Calvin during a short visit to her brother, Henry Ward Beecher, she described the Beecher's home as the "calm, placid quiet retreat I have been longing for...."[16] (Of course, she probably found their home ideal simply because someone else was meeting the demands of wifehood and motherhood.) Her own home mirrored the more unsettled, disrupted outside world; control of her own sphere remained elusive. To Calvin she fretted: "You have no idea of the commotion that I have lived in since you left."[17] The endless litany of household duties to be performed and children to be cared for echoed through her letters. Always there was "the cleaning—the children's clothes, and the baby." The burdens on her, the tensions and apprehensions that tortured her, were equally apparent in Stowe's anguished dirge that everything in her home "often seemed to press on my mind all at once. Sometimes it [seemed] as if anxious thought [had] become a disease with me from which I could not be free."[18]

Certainly as much as any of the sentimentalists, Stowe's life approximated the stereotype of the domestic dream as set forth in the fiction. She married, bore seven children, and considered her duties as a wife and mother more important than the demands imposed upon her as a writer. Invariably, Stowe gave a higher priority to guiding and restraining a husband who was a self-admitted "creature of impulse,"[19] and to rearing and supporting children who received "all [her] life and strength and almost [her] separate consciousness."[20] Considered a means to an end rather than an end in itself, she envisaged her literary activity as yet another opportunity to serve her family and contribute to its welfare. In a letter written to one of her sisters at the beginning of her career as a writer, she expressed convictions that were to govern the rest of her life. Noting that she had received forty dollars for a "piece," she related that, "Mr. Stowe says he shall leave me to use [it] for my personal gratification." That she should do so she thought ludicrous—"as if a wife and mother had any gratification apart from her family interests."[21]

Before she wrote *Uncle Tom's Cabin*, Stowe's literary endeavors were restricted to occasional short stories submitted to newspapers and magazines. So peripheral was her writing to her major involvement with wifehood and motherhood that she was surprised by Sarah Josepha Hale's request for biographical material to be used in *Woman's Record* and actually doubted that she ought "to rank among 'distinguished women.'" Appropriately, Stowe read Hale's letter "to my tribe of little folks assembled around the evening table to let them know what an unexpected honour had befallen their Mama." Her reply to Hale's request indicates the choices made and the proportionate energies expended. Reminding Hale of the "retired and domestic" life she had chosen, she told her that she was devoted to her family rather than to her writing: "I have been a mother to seven children—six of whom are now living—and... the greater portion of my time and strength has been spent in the necessary but unpoetic duties of my family."[22]

Stowe's career as a writer changed radically with the publication of *Uncle Tom's Cabin*. Abraham Lincoln's witticism that she was "the little lady who made this big war" was a fitting characterization in the eyes of many. She quickly became a prominent figure. Her literary production increased and included nine additional novels along with innumerable essays. But her perspective on the importance of being a wife and mother remained the same. Despite her newly acquired prominence, the demands of her family still came first—sometimes to the extent that she was forced to curtail her writing. At one point she wrote to her publisher's wife, Annie Adams Fields, that she had temporarily ceased writing; in fact, she had "not been able to write a word, except to my own children." Writing metaphorically, she stressed that the varying needs of her children required that she "write chapters which would otherwise go into my novel."[23] Yet another time her writing was restricted by the care given her husband during the long illnesses that preceded his death. That she considered his need legitimate and did not resent its impact upon her literary activities is revealed in a letter to their doctor: "I have him in my room nights and watch over him as one time in our life he used to watch over me. 'Turn about is fair play' you know."[24]

Whatever earnings Stowe derived from her writings were used to meet the monetary demands of her family, and, as familial circumstances changed, those earnings became more crucial. Only a supplement prior to the early 1850's, her royalties provided major support for the family after the publication of *Uncle Tom's Cabin*. As early as 1853, Stowe's husband, Calvin, informed her that "money matters are entirely in your hands, and no money is spent except in accordance with your judgment and that saves me a great deal of torment and anxiety."[25] Having relieved himself of the obligation to manage the family's resources, Calvin had no qualms about transferring the duty to support the family. Throughout the 1850's, he reminded his wife to "think of your responsibilities—an old man and six children."[26] Although it would have been equally superfluous, he could have added that she was also obliged to contribute to the support of her father and his third wife. Harriet's earnings became even more critical from the mid-1860's onward. Calvin retired from teaching in 1864 and became completely dependent upon his wife. With the exception of Georgiana, all of their children who survived to adulthood continued to rely upon their mother for support. The twins, Hattie and Eliza, who remained unmarried, lived at home; Fred who became an alcoholic required institutionalization and then support during his unsuccessful attempts at rehabilitation; and Charley who entered the ministry needed substantial aid after beginning his career.

Stowe's correspondence with various members of her family reveals her continuing need to juggle the private and public, the domestic and literary, to accommodate the needs of her family. Never questioning the legitimacy of their demands, her letters indicate her unwavering commitment to serve them—and they indicate, as well, the cost of that commitment. Harriet's letters to Calvin are replete with allusions to her dual responsibilities and with admonitions to him: "You must not expect very much writing of me for it drinks up all my strength to care for and provide for all this family—to try to cure the faults of all—harmonize all."£ She also pleaded with him "to *try* to be considerate and consider how great a burden I stagger under."[28]

Alternating between sentimental effusions of affection and graphic descriptions of her financial difficulties, Stowe's letters to her children document her attempt to fulfill both roles simultaneously. Beginning one letter with the comment, "let me tell you first how heavy is the weight which lies upon me," she hastened to inform Hattie and Eliza that she was providing daily income from her writing and also attempting to arrange the family's finances in order to secure "a higher income from our property so that we may have a solid and certain basis of two *thousand* a year to go on." That these were wearying challenges was obvious, but they seemed insignificant before the threatening prospect that "if my health fails all will fail."[29] A later letter to the twins bemoans the fact that illness had interfered with her attempts to provide needed income from writing. Fully recognizing that "*all* the income that supports the family comes from my ability to labor at my pen," she found it particularly frustrating to be suffering from poor health when she was "beset with offers" for her fiction: "Mr. Ford who has sent me 300 for two stories in the South's Companion wants me to promise him another for the same sum. The Western Home sent a cheque for 100 and begs for an article—In short you see that my health just now is gold for my family."[30] Just as Stowe dedicated herself to her daughters, she expected and received whatever aid they could offer. Together Hattie and Eliza became her housekeeper, secretary, and amanuensis.

Stowe's obligations extended beyond those children who continued to share a home with her. Hoping that Fred's stay in an institution would end his alcoholism, she willingly bore the expense. That failed attempt notwithstanding, she then proceeded to arrange various positions for her son. Investing $10,000 in Florida's Laurel Grove Plantation, she insured that Fred would be made overseer of the thousand acres devoted to the production of cotton. But she could not guarantee the cure of a son whose drunkenness remained habitual. Her final and equally unsuccessful effort involved an arrangement in which Fred helped in the management of her own orange groves in Mandarin, Florida. Stowe's unswerving commitment to her son, her continuing attempts to aid him were testimony to her devotion; her son's failure to rehabilitate himself was the most enduring sorrow of her life. Stowe also helped her son, Charley, and his wife, Susy, establish themselves in Charley's first parsonage in Presque Isle, Maine. When Charley considered moving for financial reasons, she offered to send them "$500, rather than have you make any change—or try any other place—I will back you up."[31] Even after Charley had taken another position in Saco, Maine, Stowe advised them that "you may count on $300 a year from me a sum I calculate equal to houserent and fuel."[32] At a later date, she gave them the $7,000 necessary for the purchase of a parsonage after they had settled permanently near Stowe's own home in Hartford, Connecticut. In contrast to Fred, Stowe's other son, Charley, was able not only to return her devotion but also to fulfill her desire that at least one son enter the same profession as her father, husband, and seven brothers.

Through prescription and protest, Stowe, as a writer, performed in the service of improving woman's self- and social-image, and yet, as an individual, she was less a professional writer than she was a woman in the nineteenth century. Stowe did come to provide the primary financial support for her family, but her career as a writer remained secondary to her role as a wife and mother. Her family always came first, her fiction second. In fact, her struggle to succeed as a writer became part of a larger struggle to succeed with a marriage that brought alternating suffering and satisfaction. Unlike the majority of her female contemporaries, she assisted her husband in his prescribed obligation to support the family. Her success in this endeavor was obvious. But Stowe's needs and expectations made her less successful in meeting the responsibilities of her role as a wife and mother. Calvin's demands came into conflict with her own desire to protect her sexual and emotional autonomy, and she found it necessary to deny her husband physically and emotionally. Her attempt to provide a model for her seven children, to mold and control human development, met with equally mixed success. Her efforts acquainted her as much with failure as with achievement, with grief as with joy. This is not to say that Stowe lacked sincerity and conviction in her attempt to promote the role of wife and mother as the ideal for woman. The zealous tone and didactic thrust of her prescriptions speak to that. It is to say that Stowe internalized her prescriptions, only too well.

Separated during nearly a third of the first fifteen years of marriage, Harriet's and Calvin's correspondence tells a story of a relationship continually beset by crisis. The separations themselves were a relatively minor part of the crisis—and at times proved to be beneficial. More important was the fact that each brought differing expectations to the marriage. Stowe was not content merely to achieve a satisfactory relationship with a husband. What she sought was an idyllic one in which both husband and wife shared intimately but acted autonomously. Unfortunately, she achieved far less. In contrast, Calvin, who had been left a childless widower little more than a year before his marriage to Harriet, sought to fulfill much more specific, more pragmatic needs. Initially drawn to Harriet because she had been the closest friend of his first wife, Calvin hoped that she would provide an end to his desperate loneliness, satisfy his sexual and emotional needs, and give him the children denied him in his first marriage. Rooted in disparate needs and desires, exacerbated by differing temperaments, their conflicts were inevitable. Harriet wanted to actualize the ideal relationships protrayed in the pages of her fiction, but Calvin's sexual and emotional demands were so intense and unremitting that her own autonomy was continually threatened. Again and again, she found herself hoping that the end of each separation would find him "indeed renewed in spirit," yet she wrote that she feared "that may not be so, and that we may again draw each other earthward."[33] Letter after letter of Calvin's points to the impossible demands that would dash Harriet's hopes. Writing to her prior to their marriage, he foretold the immensity of his demands: "I will react upon all you have given me thus far, I will keep asking for more as long as I live (the fountain of that which I want is in you inexhaustible)."[34]

The problem, of course, was that Harriet's reserves were *not* inexhaustible. To try to meet Calvin's physical demands meant not only disregarding the need to protect her health but also yielding her desire to control her reproductive function. To attempt to fulfill Calvin's emotional demands involved the risk of setting her own self adrift in the turbulence of Calvin's continually vacillating, volatile temperament. The problem, too, was that Calvin found it practically impossible to curb his demands. His loud and angry complaints reverberated through their correspondence, his emotional demands continued unabated. Faced off as if soldiers in combat they struggled to maintain both their own positions *and* their marriage.

Calvin's letters harp upon his sexual needs. An extremely sensual person, Calvin repeatedly lamented: "my arms and bosom are hungry, hungry even to starvation."[35] He recalled the times that he had "lain on the same pillow with you, your face pressed to mine, and our bare bosoms together," and practically cursed the celibacy enforced by their separations. His desire to "just step into your bedroom... and take that place in your arms to which I alone of all men in the world ever had a right or ever received admission," nearly drove him into a frenzy.[36] A devoted but markedly more restrained Stowe did not respond with the same passion. Determined to control the number and spacing of her children, Stowe saw their separations from a different perspective. Certainly she was sincere in writing: "I have thought of you with much love lately—a deep tender love—and I long to see you again."[37] But she was also aware that the most effective method for controlling fertility, abstinence, was inherent in separation.

Harriet's and Calvin's differing perspectives, their conflicting needs and desires, were brought into sharpest relief during their times together. Calvin was not willing to deny himself in his own bedroom, while Stowe remained bent upon serving her own interest through restriction of their sexual involvement. Their sexual relationship provides a means for the examination of various hypotheses concerning the decline in fertility during the nineteenth century. These hypotheses have pointed to either the female or the male as the primary determinants. Daniel Scott Smith has argued that the female tended to be the controlling party. Women, as Smith has termed it, were practicing "domestic feminism" and thereby exercising significant power and autonomy within the family.[38] In contrast, Gerda Lerner has noted that the lowered birth rates can be attributed just as easily to the male's desire, motivated by economic considerations, to limit the number of children in his family.[39]

The evidence from Harriet's and Calvin's correspondence suggests not only the complexity of sexual relationships but the tenuousness of broad generalizations about the most intimate of human experiences. In their unabating sexual tug-of-war, neither Harriet nor Calvin emerged unscathed, or victorious. Clearly, Stowe wanted to engage in domestic feminism. But just as clearly her struggle to control her fertility was only partially successful: she gave birth to seven children and suffered at least two miscarriages. The cost was great for both of them. Theirs was an irresolvable conflict in an age in which sexual relations were always shadowed by the threat of pregnancy. Sexual denial limited intimacy; sexual gratification led to child after child. For them at least the conflict heightened the tensions between them—and not only fueled Calvin's resentment and anger but was also an important factor in Stowe's decision to escape from him (and the hostility) by spending an entire year away from her family.

Stowe's decision to try the water cure in Brattleboro, Vermont, in the mid-1840's, was determined by a growing invalidism. Her sickliness was hardly unique. The high incidence and variety of female invalidism in the nineteenth century has led a number of historians, Kathryn Kish Sklar and Carroll Smith-Rosenberg in particular, to interpret sickliness as a response, albeit a negative one, to the role of wife and mother.[40] The woman who became an invalid effectively shed a role that demanded unremitting concern for others. In turn, she became the center of attention. Her individual needs became dominant. Simultaneously, she made herself unavailable sexually. She no longer had to act to restrict her sexual relationship or bear the responsibility for that act.

Stowe's invalidism was fed from manifold sources, physical and psychological. She no doubt sought to rest a body battered by at least two miscarriages, drained and worn by the demands of family chores. Her journey away also promised a retreat from the tension engendered by psychological as well as sexual conflict, and by the demands associated with bearing and rearing children. And it offered the opportunity to contemplate in relative repose unfulfilled ideals. Most certainly, Stowe would have agreed with her husband that their conflicting needs were "bringing us both to the grave by the most lingering and painful process."[41] Recalling that Stowe had been "so feeble, and the prospect of permanent paralysis [had been] so threatening" during the winter prior to her departure for Vermont, Calvin admitted that he was resigned to their separation. Nevertheless, he informed her that he himself had fallen into a species of invalidism, had been in "a sad state physically and mentally" that winter, but the cure he proposed for himself meant the end of their separation and promised a recurrence of Stowe's invalidism: "If your health were so far restored that you could take me again to your *bed and board*, that would be the surest and safest, and indeed the only infallible way."[42] In the end, they could not help each other: one's needs clashed with the other's; one's cure brought the other's illness.

Inevitably, the separation had a different effect upon each of them. Stowe had sought the water cure only after her condition had worsened. She could therefore envision absence from husband and children not as abandonment but as separation necessary for her eventual restoration to them. She could rationalize that she was continuing to serve them rather than herself. Her psychological conflicts resolved, the water cure brought relief from the burdens of domesticity, a supportive environment that was predominantly female, and physicians sympathetic to her maladies. It also brought a welcome respite from Calvin's demands.[43] The separation intensified rather than assuaged Calvin's sexual longings, and it reintroduced loneliness.[44] Letter after letter written by Calvin refers to their sexual relationship and his desire for her. Brimming with anger and frustration, he recounted the one week that he had joined her in Vermont. Their separation had made him all the more eager to see her, yet he still had to deny himself during this interlude. He had enjoyed their visit, had been satisfied to "see that you do love me after all." But that satisfaction had been severely limited by the "mean business of sleeping in another bed, another room, and even another house, and being with you as if you were a withered up old maid sister instead of the wife of my bosom." He concluded that "of all contemptible things the most unutterably intolerable is *having the love of marriage and denying the power thereof.*"[45]

Other letters indicate that Calvin almost preferred separation to the practice of abstinence when with his wife. In one letter written after Harriet had been away for ten months, he told her "much as I suffer from your absence, I should suffer still more from your presence, unless you can be in a better condition than you have been for a year past." Why? Why would the presence of someone to whom he was devoted bring pain and frustration? Calvin bluntly reminded his wife: "It is now a full year since your last miscarriage, and you well know what has been the state of things both in regard to yourself and me ever since."[46] A few months later he had changed his mind and stated emphatically "I want you to come home." Why the reversal? What would he expect with her return? A sentence or two later he revealed his hope that her return would bring an end to his celibacy: "it is almost in fact eighteen months since I have had a wife to sleep with me. It is enough to kill any man, especially such a man as I am."[47]

Stowe did return shortly. She would write to Calvin that she was "better but not well." She would compare herself to "a broken pitcher that has been boiled in milk, that needs very careful handling, or it will come to pieces again."[48] Inevitably, the conflict between them would continue. Calvin no doubt continued to lament any restrictions on their sexual relationship. And Harriet, her devotion to her sons and daughters notwithstanding, must have had some misgivings about the two children that crowded the end of her childbearing years.

Forced to curb his sexual demands, Calvin openly advanced others. Freely admitting that "my good feelings are quiet and silent and my ill ones urgent and obstrusive,"[49] Calvin's temperament alternated between an irritating excitability and an equally trying despondency. He relied upon Stowe to help him achieve a more stable, calmer state. Her absences made him "go bamboosing about like a hen with her head cut off, because you are not here to be a balance wheel to my emotions."[50] That Harriet found it difficult to cope with Calvin's mercurial temperament is obvious from her letters to him. Pointing to his "hypochondriac morbid instability" in letter after letter, she anguished about the unhappiness he caused her and begged him to try to relieve this source of strain in their marriage.[51] Calvin might not be able to control either his moodiness or its toll upon his wife but his absences did provide at least temporary relief. Unlike Calvin, Stowe admitted to a certain ambivalence about the end of their separations. Her description of the typical reconciliation made that ambivalence understandable: "You will love me very much at first when you come home and then, will it be as before all passed off into months of cold indifference[?]"[52]

Stowe was also very conscious of the pain, suffering, and burdens entailed in the rearing of children. She freely gave of herself and suffered much as a consequence of her attachments. Her approach to Hattie and Eliza, was both affectionate—and efficient. Perceiving herself as a model, she did not hesitate to advise and instruct them in a self-confident manner exuding strength and expecting the same from them. They would never know, she wrote, how much she loved them "*till* you love someone as I do you—you have educated me quite as much as I you—you have taught me the love of God—by awakening such in me."[53] The devotion of parents was "all giving—the child can neither understand nor return it—but the parent is learning by it to understand God."[54] Yet she was also conscious of the trials of parenthood. Writing to Calvin, she noted that Hattie's and Eliza's "tempers are very trying to me." She and Calvin "must bear with all the impatiences, excrescences and disproportions."[55] Of course, Calvin's frequent, lengthy absences while engaged in professional activities meant that Stowe bore most of the burden herself.

There was as much love and pain involved in the raising of her sons. Despite her distaste for liquor inherited from a father who had been a prominent agitator for temperance, Fred's alcoholism elicited a deep and tolerant sympathy in his mother. Replying to their criticisms of Fred, Stowe wrote to Hattie and Eliza: "If God had not meant us to pass through exactly this form of trial there were many ways for him to prevent it—but *just this and no other is our cross.*" Instead, she urged her daughters to adopt the more heroic, demanding posture, prescribed in the pages of her novels and short stories: Hattie and Eliza "should remember how young men are tempted and tried [and] feel that instead of casting them off you who lead pure and sheltered lives ought to try to rouse their noble natures and influence them to good."[56] Henry Ellis' death at the age of nineteen led her to write that "between him and me there was a sympathy of nature a perfect union of mutual understanding." He was "the *lamb of my flock* [*and she*] *rested* on him as on no other."[57] His death also reminded her that she loved her children "with such an *overwhelming* love."[58]

Written a few days before their eleventh wedding anniversary, a letter of Harriet's to Calvin is indicative of her marital experiences, symbolic of her hopes and disappointments. Recognizing that she was "a very different being" at the outset of their marriage, she recalled her total desire "to live in love, absorbing passionate devotion to one person." The first time she and Calvin were separated was her "first trial." Comfort came with the prospect of motherhood: "No creature ever so longed to see the face of a little one or had such a heart full of love to bestow." That experience, however, proved to be agonizing: "Here came in trial again sickness, pain, constant discouragement—wearing wasting days and nights...." In all of Harriet's marital experiences there was much disappointment, much agony. She noted retrospectively that hers and Calvin's very different characters made "painful friction inevitable." After eleven years, the damage had been done and the cost counted in Stowe's admission that, "I do not love and never can love with the blind and unwise love with which I married." Stowe's love had been blind because it had known little of human inadequacy; unwise because it had asked too much. Had she the choice of a mate to make again she would choose the same, but she would love "far more wisely." Hers was the comment of a matured, chastened individual who had come to recognize the disparate needs and expectations brought to the marriage by each of them. Stowe's attitude toward motherhood suggested greater regret. She had wished for much, but felt she had received little: "Ah, how little comfort I had in being a mother—how all that I proposed met and crossed and my way ever hedged up!" In despair, she was even brought to thank God for teaching her "that I should make no family be my chief good and portion."[59] Nevertheless, for the remaining half century of her life her family remained her primary and fundamental concern.

Not only does Stowe herself serve as a case study of the tension engendered between an ideal and a less felicitous reality, but her experience sheds light upon important questions concerning women in the nineteenth century. For example, in addressing themselves to the implications of the nineteenth century's glorification of woman's nature and role, historians have sought to determine not only the benefits women might have derived from being considered different from men in more than a biological sense, but also what difficulties they might have encountered in striving to fulfill the role as the creator of a family utopia.

Stowe located the idea of female distinctiveness in the context of self-sacrifice. In a woman's selflessness was her superiority and means for her fulfillment. In *Pink and White Tyranny,* Stowe told her female readers: "Love, my dear ladies, is self-sacrifice; it is a life out of self and in another. Its very essence is the preferring of the comfort, the ease, the wishes of another to one's own for the love we bear them. Love is giving, not receiving."[60] The efficacy of such a doctrine was obvious. As the major practitioner of self-sacrifice, woman was the logical candidate for spiritual and moral leadership. The embodiment of selflessness, she should be its primary teacher. In one sense, the doctrine served Stowe well. It rationalized her denial of self for husband and children and gave her a sense of purpose. That she perceived her role as a writer as an extension of woman's role as a wife and mother is thoroughly documented in her writings and reflected in her own life. She firmly believed that it was the duty of woman to devote herself to her husband and children, and she was gratified that she could meet their monetary as well as emotional demands. Simply, the role of wife and mother provided the focus for her life. Envisioning herself as a model, she strove to actualize the selflessness preached in the pages of her fiction. The members of her family were the primary beneficiaries.

But while Stowe subscribed to the ideal set forth in the sentimentalists' fiction, and to a certain extent fulfilled that ideal in her life, her personal papers indicate that her own experience as a wife and mother was riddled with the same tensions, ambiguities, and conflicts that characterize the negative strains in the novels and stories. Her commitment to wifehood and motherhood made her captive to an ideal that in many respects she was unable to realize in her own life. Her hopes that Calvin would become an ideal partner were doomed to disappointment. Her children were as much a burden as a source of satisfaction. Neither Calvin nor the children were transformed into models of selflessness. And the family together struggled not so much for perfection as survival. Stowe also confronted the limitations inherent in her doctrine of self-sacrifice. If she wished to stand as a model of selflessness, she simultaneously wanted to act as an autonomous individual. But frequently she had to place the needs and desires of her husband and children first, rather than her own. Rather than develop an autonomous identity she had to merge hers with theirs. In this dilemma, too, she symbolized the plight of nineteenth-century womanhood.

Notes

1. This essay stems from a manuscript, tentatively entitled, "The Crisis of Domesticity: Women Writing of Women in Nineteenth-Century America." The manuscript focuses upon the twelve most prominent sentimentalists of the century and delineates their perspective on woman's role and status. It is based upon the novels and short stories and the letters, diaries, and journals of the following sentimentalists: Maria Cummins, Caroline Howard Gilman, Caroline Lee Hentz, Mary J. Holmes, Maria McIntosh, Sara Parton, Catharine Maria Sedgwick, E.D.E.N. Southworth, Harriet Beecher Stowe, Mary Virginia Terhune, Susan Warner, and Augusta Evans Wilson.
2. Harriet Beecher Stowe, *The Minister's Wooing* (Cambridge, Mass.: Houghton Mifflin Company, 1896/1859), pp. 567–568. The original publication date of the novel or collection of short stories is noted following the virgule.
3. For an elaboration of my analysis of the fiction, see along with my manuscript already cited, Mary Kelley, "The Sentimentalists: Promise and Betrayal in the Home," *Signs: Journal of Women in Culture and Society* 4 (Spring 1979): 434–446.
4. Harriet Beecher Stowe, *We and Our Neighbors, or the Records of an Unfashionable Street* (Cambridge, Mass.: Houghton Mifflin Company, 1896/1873), p. 399.
5. Harriet Beecher Stowe, *My Wife and I or, Harry Henderson's History* (Cambridge, Mass.: Houghton Mifflin Company, b1896/1871), p. xi.
6. For particularly insightful analyses of attitudes toward roles and family structure, see William E. Bridges, "Family Patterns and Social Values in Victorian America," *American Quarterly* 17 (Spring 1965): 3–11; Kirk

Jeffrey, "The Family as Utopian Retreat from the City," *Soundings* 55 (Spring 1972): 21–41; Rowland Berthoff, *An Unsettled People: Social Order and Disorder in American History* (New York: Harper and Row, 1971), esp. pp. 204–217.

7. Harriet Beecher Stowe, *Pink and White Tyranny: A Society Novel* (Cambridge, Mass.: Houghton Mifflin Company, 1896/1871), pp. ix–x.
8. Harriet Beecher Stowe, *Poganuc People: Their Loves and Lives* (Cambridge, Mass.: Houghton Mifflin Company, 1896/1878), p. 262.
9. Harriet Beecher Stowe, *The Minister's Wooing* (Cambridge, Mass.: Houghton Mifflin Company, 1896/1859), p. 53.
10. Harriet Beecher Stowe, *The Pearl of Orr's Island* (Cambridge, Mass.: Houghton Mifflin Company, 1896/1862), p. 391.
11. Harriet Beecher Stowe, *We and Our Neighbors,* p. 870.
12. Harriet Beecher Stowe, *My Wife and I*, p. 40.
13. Harriet Beecher Stowe to Henry Ward Beecher, undated, Beecher Family Papers, Manuscripts and Archives, Sterling Memorial Library, Yale University, New Haven, Connecticut.
14. I do not mean to imply that the fiction of the sentimentalists has little value in an attempt to assess the personal perceptions of reality of the writers. On the contrary, I believe it to be a primary and significant source for this purpose, but that is not the focus of this essay.
15. The following collections have been consulted in the preparation of this essay. Most of Harriet Beecher Stowe's letters to members of her family are deposited with either the Beecher-Stowe collection, Arthur and Elizabeth Schlesinger Library on the History of Women in America, Radcliffe College, Cambridge, Massachusetts, or the Joseph K. Hooker Collection and Katherine S. Day Collection, Stowe-Day Memorial Library and Historical Foundation, Hartford, Connecticut. Other letters are found in Miscellany, Massachusetts Historical Society, Boston, Massachusetts; Clifton Waller Barrett Collection, Manuscripts Department, Alderman Library, University of Virginia, Charlottesville, Virginia; Beecher Family Papers, Manuscripts and Archives, Sterling Memorial Library, Yale University, New Haven, Connecticut; Miscellany, Manuscript Department, New York Historical Society, New York, New York; James T. Fields Papers, Manuscript Collection, Henry E. Huntington Library, San Marino, California. A few of Calvin Stowe's letters to his wife are deposited in the Beecher-Stowe Collection, Arthur and Elizabeth Schlesinger Library on the History of Women in America, but the major body of Calvin's correspondence has only recently been found and made available by the Stowe-Day Memorial Library and Historical Foundation. Particular gratitude for their aid is extended to two of Stowe-Day's librarians, Diana Royce and Ellice A. Schofield. The letters of the Stowe children are deposited in the Beecher-Stowe Collection, Arthur and Elizabeth Schlesinger Library on the History of Women in America. For a perceptive discussion of the opportunities (and the

pitfalls) involved in analysis of the interaction between prescription and behavior, see Carroll Smith-Rosenberg, "The New Woman and the New History," *Feminist Studies* 3 (Fall 1975): 185–198. See also my analysis of the private correspondence of another of the sentimentalists, entitled, "A Woman Alone: Catharine Maria Sedgwick's Spinsterhood in Nineteenth-Century America," *New England Quarterly* 51 (June 1978): 209–225.

16. Harriet Beecher Stowe to Calvin Stowe, July 1844, Beecher-Stowe Collection, Arthur and Elizabeth Schlesinger Library on the History of Women in America, Radcliffe College, Cambridge, Massachusetts (hereafter referred to as SCH).

17. Harriet Beecher Stowe to Calvin Stowe, [July 1844], Beecher-Stowe Collection, SCH.

18. Harriet Beecher Stowe to Calvin Stowe, [May 1844], Beecher-Stowe Collection, SCH.

19. Calvin Stowe to Harriet Beecher Stowe, 16 October 1836, Acquisitions, The Stowe-Day Memorial Library and Historical Foundation, Hartford, Connecticut (hereafter referred to as S-DF).

20. Harriet Beecher Stowe, Undated Memorandum, Beecher-Stowe Collection, SCH. Quoted in Edward Wagenknecht, *Harriet Beecher Stowe: The Known and the Unknown* (New York: Oxford University Press, 1965), p. 63.

21. Harriet Beecher Stowe to one of her sisters, [1838], Beecher Family Papers, Manuscripts and Archives, Sterling Memorial Library, Yale University, New Haven, Connecticut.

22. Harriet Beecher Stowe to Sarah Josepha Hale, 10 November [1850], Miscellany, Manuscripts Collection, Henry E. Huntington Library, San Marino, California.

23. Harriet Beecher Stowe to Annie Adams Fields, 27 July 1868, James T. Fields Papers, Manuscripts Collection, Henry E. Huntington Library, San Marino, California.

24. Harriet Beecher Stowe to family physician, 22 December 1882, Joseph K. Hooker Collection, S-DF.

25. Calvin Stowe to Harriet Beecher Stowe, 11 July 1853, Acquisitions, S-DF.

26. Calvin Stowe to Harriet Beecher Stowe, 22 July 1853, Acquisitions, S-DF.

27. Harriet Beecher Stowe to Calvin Stowe, 6 November 1850, Acquisitions, S-DF.

28. Harriet Beecher Stowe to Calvin Stowe, 4 April [1860], Beecher-Stowe Collection, SCH.

29. Harriet Beecher Stowe to Hattie and Eliza Stowe, 5 October 1863, Beecher-Stowe Collection, SCH.

30. Harriet Beecher Stowe to Hattie and Eliza Stowe, 1 August 1869, Beecher-Stowe Collection, SCH.

31. Harriet Beecher Stowe to Charley and Susy Stowe, 10 September 1879, Beecher-Stowe Collection, SCH.

32. Harriet Beecher Stowe to Charley and Susy Stowe, 8 March 1882, Beecher-Stowe Collection, SCH.

33. Harriet Beecher Stowe to Calvin Stowe, September 1844, Beecher-Stowe Collection, SCH.

34. Calvin Stowe to Harriet Beecher Stowe, 24 May [1835], Acquisitions, S-DF.

35. Calvin Stowe to Harriet Beecher Stowe, 7 August 1836, Acquisitions, S-DF.

36. Calvin Stowe to Harriet Beecher Stowe, 20 June 1836, Acquisitions, S-DF.

37. Harriet Beecher Stowe to Calvin Stowe, 4 September 1842, Beecher-Stowe Collection, SCH.

38. See Daniel Scott Smith, "Family Limitation, Sexual Control and Domestic Feminism in Victorian America," *Feminist Studies* 1 (Winter-Spring 1973): 40–57.

39. See Gerda Lerner, "Placing Women in History," in Berenice A. Carroll, ed., *Liberating Women's History: Theoretical and Critical Essays* (Urbana, Illinois: University of Illinois Press, 1976), pp. 357–367.

40. See Kathryn Kish Sklar, *Catharine Beecher: A Study in American Domesticity* (New Haven, Connecticut: Yale University Press, 1973); Carroll Smith-Rosenberg, "The Hysterical Woman: Sex Roles and Role Conflict in Nineteenth-Century America," *Social Research* 32 (Winter 1972): 652–678.

41. Calvin Stowe to Harriet Beecher Stowe, 1 November 1846, Acquisitions, S-DF.

42. Calvin Stowe to Harriet Beecher Stowe, 30 June 1846, Acquisitions, S-DF.

43. For interesting speculations about the importance of water cure establishments to women, see Sklar, *Catharine Beecher*. Stowe's experience provides evidence for some of Sklar's hypotheses. Sklar, however, speaks only of the benefits to women. It should be noted that Calvin's sickliness rivaled Stowe's, and he spent as much time at the water cure as his wife. Perhaps differing needs were served, but for both the water cure provided freedom from familial responsibilities.

44. Calvin found it nearly intolerable to deny himself sexually. Reminding Stowe that she knew "how exceedingly excitable and irritable is my temperament in all respects," he asked her: "What but the most deep-seated love could ever, in such a temperament as mine, have curbed the sexual instinct, as it has been curbed in me to spare you?" He was convinced that Stowe appreciated neither his devotion nor his denial: "You have not, and cannot, have the least idea of the sacrifice it has been to me." Calvin Stowe to Harriet Beecher Stowe, 19 May 1842, Acquisitions, S-DF.

45. Calvin Stowe to Harriet Beecher Stowe, 20 August 1846, Acquisitions, S-DF.

46. Calvin Stowe to Harriet Beecher Stowe, 22 November 1846, Acquisitions, S-DF.

47. Calvin Stowe to Harriet Beecher Stowe, [1847], Acquisitions, S-DF.

48. Calvin Stowe to his mother, Hepzibah Stowe, 7 February 1847, Acquisitions, S-DF.

49. Calvin Stowe to Harriet Beecher Stowe, 22 December 1837, Acquisitions, S-DF.
50. Calvin Stowe to Harriet Beecher Stowe, 10 June 1837, Acquisitions, S-DF.
51. Harriet Beecher Stowe to Calvin Stowe, 1 January 1847, Beecher-Stowe Collection, SCH.
52. Harriet Beecher Stowe to Calvin Stowe, 31 August-3 September 1844, Beecher-Stowe Collection, SCH.
53. Harriet Beecher Stowe to Hattie and Eliza Stowe, 10 April 1859, Beecher-Stowe Collection, SCH.
54. Harriet Beecher Stowe to Hattie and Eliza Stowe, 8 March 1859, Beecher-Stowe Collection, SCH.
55. Harriet Beecher Stowe to Calvin Stowe, 14 February 1851, Acquisitions, S-DF.
56. Harriet Beecher Stowe to Hattie and Eliza Stowe, November 1867, Beecher-Stowe Collection, SCH.
57. Harriet Beecher Stowe to Eunice Beecher, 26 July [1857], Beecher Family Papers, Manuscripts and Archives, Sterling Memorial Library, Yale University, New Haven, Connecticut.
58. Harriet Beecher Stowe to Hattie and Eliza Stowe, 27 July 1857, Beecher-Stowe Collection, SCH.
59. Harriet Beecher Stowe to Calvin Stowe, 1 January 1847, Beecher-Stowe Collection, SCH.
60. Harriet Beecher Stowe, *Pink and White Tyranny*, p. 366.

Mary H. Grant

Domestic Experience and Feminist Theory: The Case of Julia Ward Howe

Born in New York City in 1819, Julia Ward Howe lived a secluded life there until her marriage, in 1843, to Samuel Gridley Howe, the Boston reformer famous for his work with blind and handicapped children at the Perkins Institute for the Blind. Julia later became a founding member of the American Women Suffrage Association, a vigorous proponent of higher education for women, a supporter of the female ministry, an early advocate of world peace, and one of the more influential club women of the nineteenth century. She founded the New England Woman's Club, and she presided for decades over the Association for the Advancement of Women.

Along with the demands of a busy public life, Julia Ward Howe had to balance the requirements of a large family. Her household consisted of her husband, six children, and several servants. Samuel, or Chev, as Julia called him, complicated her domestic life with severe demands, and Julia's marriage was frequently unhappy.

Her ability to combine domestic and public life fluctuated over time. Like many women of the nineteenth century, she enjoyed her greatest success once she was widowed and freed from patriarchal demands. Nevertheless, throughout her extensive writings on women's rights and status, she maintained that domestic life was woman's noblest endeavor. The apparent paradox between her difficult marriage and her glorification of domesticity invites analysis.

I

From the late 1860's until her death in 1910, Julia Ward Howe wrote hundreds of lectures, speeches, letters, and journal articles concerning women's place in society. She sought a variety of reforms for women: higher

[A doctoral candidate and teaching fellow at George Washington University, Mary Grant is writing a dissertation titled "'A Woman's Woman': A Life of Julia Ward Howe." She also teaches Women's Studies at the National Cathedral School.]

education, opportunities in the professions, reform of divorce and child custody laws, protection of women's property, and suffrage.

Julia drew upon several different sources in the process of crystallizing her feminist thinking. Her religious convictions provided an underlying basis. Julia's father had been profoundly affected by the Second Great Awakening in the third decade of the nineteen century. (Family legend has it that as soon as he became converted to temperance, old Sam Ward poured all his excellent wine down the open streets of New York City, lest his father or brothers be tempted to drink the treacherous alcohol in his stead.) Julia took the tenets of her father's creed seriously, and despite her eventual conversion to liberal Christianity, she clung to much of her early training. Most importantly, she genuinely believed in the return of Christ to earth and that an era of peace and general well-being would precede this event. In this she resembled many reformers of her generation who believed that the perfection of man was possible and that the United States would lead the way to this achievement.

For Julia at least the inequitable treatment of women was one of the imperfections which obstructed the establishment of the ideal Christian state.[1] As a consequence, she contended that responsible people ought to commit themselves to righting this wrong, just as they earlier had committed themselves to the eradication of slavery. Her belief in the imminence of a perfect society bolstered Julia's feminism in another way. If America were to progress towards the establishment of Christ's kingdom on earth, the efforts of women, as well as of men, would be required. No longer could anyone justify the exclusion of women from public life as long as so much work remained to be done.[2]

Her Calvinist background fed another stream of Julia's thinking. The great evangelical reformers, Lyman Beecher and Charles Grandison Finney, had argued that each individual carried responsibility for salvation in his or her own hands. Julia clung to this philosophy and even carried it a step further. Not only did each individual have to take responsibility for herself, each woman was also required to heed her own conscience, no matter what the dictates of society might decree. Social conventions could be ignored in favor of one's inner direction.[3] This gave Julia the philosophical and ethical basis for challenging the patriarchal notions of her husband and of her class, and it reassured her that ultimately only she could decide what to believe and how to act on her beliefs.

Julia was also influenced by the ideology of the early women's rights movement. Blanche Hersh has shown that antebellum advocates combined conventional ideas with arguments premised on the concept of justice to explain why women should enjoy greater rights and opportunities.[4] Julia borrowed from both lines of thinking, but she developed her ideas concerning domesticity more extensively than most of her contemporaries in the late nineteenth century. Woman's superior moral sense was one widely accepted idea which Julia turned to feminist uses. In speaking of prostitution reform as the kind of work women were fitted for, Julia alluded to woman's special moral virtue. "There are some vices," she said, "which women have less temptation towards than men. This fact gives women the power to oppose these vices from which society suffers so unduly."[5]

The sentimental view of woman's powerful emotional ties to home and family provided a similar rationale for woman's wider participation in public life. According to Julia, women were able to recognize their "extended relations to humanity" as a result of their experience with "the sure footing of family affections."

> The slave, the barbarian, the criminal, the outcast, claim our compassionate care and regard. And the very intensity of our feeling for home, husband, and children gives us a power of loving and working outside of our homes, to redeem the world as only love and work can.[6]

Julia was adept at turning the ideal of the domestic woman back on itself. If women were especially gifted to help society, society was especially responsible for helping women. New rights and broader opportunities were women's due, if only to strengthen their abilities to be good wives and mothers. Political power was necessary if women were to protect themselves. Julia, for example, told Charles Sumner that the ballot was as essential to the destiny of motherhood as it was to the destiny of the black man.[7] Education, too, was important because "if a woman had more knowledge, she would have more wisdom, more womanly power to fill her woman's sphere, to do her womanly duties."[8] As a result, the educated and politically aware woman could rear children properly fitted for "intelligent service to the State."[9]

Lucy Stone offered more specific inspiration. In her memoirs, Julia recalled her first public commitment to suffrage, in which Stone figured prominently. At the request of Thomas Wentworth Higginson, Julia had agreed to sit on the platform while he and Lucy Stone conducted a woman suffrage meeting in Boston. It was a rainy night in November, 1867, and Julia's spirits were as dismal as the weather. As she listened to Lucy Stone, however, she felt a sudden conviction that the suffragists had found the key to a better life for women. When called upon to comment, she said simply, "I am with you."[10] On that occasion, Lucy Stone had, most likely, advanced a defense of woman suffrage based upon what Aileen Kraditor has called "justice arguments." This type of suffragist argument maintained that women had the same "inalienable right to political liberty as men." Not only did women have the same natural rights as men but they had the same potential for responsible participation in a democratic government. If women were not yet in fact the equals of men, this was only because they had been systematically denied the opportunities with which to develop their potential.[11] Although other feminists tended to slight these arguments after the 1890's, Julia persisted in using them as the fundamental basis for demanding an extension of woman's sphere.[12]

The interesting aspect of these opinions is certainly not their originality. What is significant is the relationship of these opinions to Julia's actual experience with marriage. The language she used to express her ideas conveyed not only acceptance, but enthusiasm, for the conventional domestic role. Yet her actual experience with marriage was hardly so positive.

II

Theoretically, at least, Victorian women could claim a limited degree of status and respect by creating a home which provided a moral refuge from a threatening society. In Julia's case, however, her husband never allowed her to claim her home as her sphere. Without this conventional source of power and dignity, Julia was on weak ground as she sought to establish her identity as a woman in the nineteenth century.

To a certain extent, Julia's difficulties stemmed from her own predilictions. As a girl and young woman, Julia had avoided housekeeping chores, preferring books on philosophy to books about cooking. With minor exceptions, Julia left household management to her aunt and younger sister, Louisa. When she married at the age of twenty-three, Julia was ill-fitted as a housekeeper, and her inadequacies irked Chev. He *used* her "lack of system" and "disorderliness" to claim increasing control of a sphere which ought to have been Julia's. Whatever her limitations, Julia did attempt to improve. But her efforts to master Catherine Beecher's cookbook, to manage without the accustomed servants, and to adopt Chev's theories of domestic scheduling did not impress a husband who continued to exert control in a variety of ways over the Howe household.

Chev's control over their living arrangements did not produce the order and stability which might have helped Julia prosper as a housekeeper. Chev deliberately ignored her opinions about where they should live. He bought and sold houses in South Boston, Newport, and Beacon Hill without regard to convenience, economy, comfort, or even his own professional needs. As their daughter, Laura Elizabeth Richards, later described it, Chev was unaccountably restless, and he moved his family at will, "plucking them up from one comfortable house to another."[13]

At different times, the family was put down at the Perkins Institute, a dismal structure smelling of waterclosets. Laura recalled the events this way:

> We were whisked about from place to place, often from motives
> that we never knew.... Between moves we were apt to spend weeks
> or months at the Perkins Institute for the Blind... here we children
> lived from time to time, a rather breathless sort of life... never
> exactly taking root, floating rather, like joyous little sea
> creatures....[14]

If the children loved such a life, Julia did not. She more than once grieved at the loss of a beloved house. Moving furniture was not always a problem, for the Institute was furnished, but food, linens, wardrobes, books, toys, carriages, and horses (to say nothing of a grand piano) all had to be packed, moved, unpacked, repacked, and moved again. It is hard to imagine Julia's relishing the rootless life of a "joyous sea creature," especially when she shared the conventional expectations about family life. But she was never allowed to derive pleasure from helping to choose, arrange, and organize a house for her family's comfort and welfare. Yet another aspect of Chev's control over Julia's sphere resulted in her spending a substantial part of her married life in isolated South Boston. She was cut off from the center of the city, and her only access to company was by the inconvenient omnibus which ran only once every two hours. There she was forced to rear her children with no female friends to share her work, leisure, or feelings.

Chev further whittled down Julia's domestic responsibility by his determination to select the servants in the household. Because of his concern for the training of blind, deaf-mute, and handicapped children, he placed a number of them in his home as helpers, a source of frequent confusion. He insisted as well that Julia retain housekeepers whom she detested.[15] The extent of Chev's control in the hiring of servants went to bizarre lengths. Prospective servant girls had to remove their bonnets and submit their heads to inspection in order to be hired. As an enthusiastic phrenologist, Chev was convinced that he could predict the honesty of his servants by examining the contours of their craniums.[16] In addition to the hiring, Chev also did the firing. Indeed, he thought nothing of dismissing the whole staff, from nursery to kitchen, when Julia was out of town and unable to offer any opposition.[17] The result of Chev's interference was that Julia never settled down with a competent, reliable staff of her own choosing.

Given her vision of the domestic role as woman's noblest work, Julia felt thwarted by Chev in even more significant ways. For example, he was determined to direct as much of the process of child-rearing as he could. He instructed Julia about the nursing of their newborns, advocating a six-month nursing period for their third child when Julia would have preferred to nurse longer.[18] He controlled the education not only of his son, but also of his daughters. He sent them to one school after another and finally decided that Julia should devote her spare time to teaching the fundamentals of reading and arithmetic in the nursery.[19]

Julia found that she could get her way on occasion simply by persevering in her chosen path. She could not, however, avoid Chev's control when it came to visits to and from her family. He prevented her on several occasions from visiting her sisters, and he refused to allow Sam Ward, Julia's brother, in his house. When Julia did succeed in arranging a trip to visit her family, Chev decided which children would accompany her. He even went so far as to select the nurse who would care for the children while she visited a sister in Bordentown, New Jersey. Commented Julia wryly, "Chev's will be done in Bordentown, as it is in Boston."[20]

Not only did Chev deny Julia comfort, satisfaction, and autonomy in the sphere supposedly her own, Chev also sought systematically to thwart his wife's attempts at a public career. Julia's literary aspirations were rejected as unseemly. Because Chev opposed publication of Julia's poetry, she felt it necessary to issue her first volume of poetry, *Passion Flowers* (1853), anonymously in order to avoid his wrath. When he realized that his wife was the author of the much-celebrated volume, he refused to speak to Julia for several days.[21] So far as Chev was concerned, she was making a public spectacle of herself, something he would not tolerate. He also tried to prevent her lecturing in public on ethics and philosophy in the 1850's and 1860's. Chev made no distinction between parlor lectures and platform lectures or between lectures to women only and lectures to mixed audiences. He opposed them all. Even at the end of his life, when Chev was losing the physical stamina to quarrel with his energetic wife, he criticized her suffrage campaigning. It was not the principle of suffrage to which he objected, but the mobility Julia acquired as she became involved in the suffrage movement. Chev complained to his old colleague Charles Sumner that Julia spent entirely too much time traveling and not enough at home.[22]

When Julia pointed to the contradiction between his support of Florence Nightingale, whom Chev had encouraged to go into nursing, and his implacable opposition to her attempts to a career, Chev replied that he would not have permitted Nightingale to embark on her career, either, had she married him.[23] Chev's rigid patriarchal view of husbandly control and wifely subordination led Julia to write in her journal: "I have never known my husband to approve of any act of mine which I myself valued."[24]

The constant disapproval and quarreling led to periods of severe emotional strain for Julia. Chev's cold looks withered Julia's spirits; his rebukes left her nervous and debilitated; and his silence—whole long winter evenings of wordlessness—drove her nearly to despair.[25] Julia suffered periods of depression bordering on madness. "When I last wrote," she confided in a letter to her sister Annie, "I was suffering from recent illness and horrible depression.... I had at that time one fit of raving hysterics. I was perfectly mad, and rushed from room to room like a wild creature."[26]

Commonly, Chev denied Julia even the simplest expressions of affection. He seemed to regard her need for kisses as a vexation and as a form of sensuality inappropriate for a woman.[27] Besides withholding affection from Julia, Chev entered into adulterous relationships with another woman—her identity is unknown—in the 1850's and 1860's. Julia received confirmation of this when Chev, on his deathbed, confessed to the affair. Julia had no evidence of this at the time of its occurrence, but she sensed the alienation of affection, and it made her miserable.

> Chev is as cold and indifferent to me as a man can be.
> I sometimes suspect him of having relations with other women,
> and regret more bitterly than ever the sacrifice which
> entails upon me....[28]

The "sacrifice" referred to was her fifth pregnancy which produced her fourth daughter, Maud, born in November, 1854.

It is likely that Julia had tried to limit Chev's sexual attentions in hopes of preventing another pregnancy and that Chev turned to other women partly for that reason. Julia ultimately yielded to his insistence that she renew their physical relationship. The results were her last two pregnancies in 1854 and 1859. The quandry they faced is evident. Chev desired a woman who would, in Julia's words, "love him utterly," and Julia craved affection without the danger of increased household responsibilities. Neither of them fully understood the other's needs, and their sexual conflicts drove them further apart.

In fairness, it should be noted that the Howe marriage did have happy moments. There were brief periods of renewed affection and tenderness, and their relationships with their children were close and loving. Yet Chev's control of living arrangements and servants, his interference with childrearing and with his wife's relationships to her own family, and his unwelcome sexual demands meant that Julia's domestic role was largely unsatisfactory and unfulfilling. Deprived of power and displaced in her husband's affections, she was denied the basic identity and vocation available to nineteenth-century women. In consequence, Julia turned her thoughts and energies to two different, yet related, subjects—the glorification of motherhood and the elevation of woman's status in American society.

III

Against the background of her own painful experience, Julia spent the last thirty years of her life exalting domesticity. In part, the paradox can be explained by the fact that it was a useful strategy. Julia recognized that the promotion of domesticity was a convenient way to promote various reforms for women. The use of acceptable and familiar images enabled her to capture her audiences' approval as she developed her feminist arguments. She fully recognized, too, that her role as wife and mother gave the suffrage movement credibility in its early days.[29] As long as Julia Ward Howe was on the platform, the charge that suffragists were unwomanly, deviant, and radical was preposterous.

But Julia was not merely opportunistic when she dwelt on the virtues of marital life. She exalted home and family for several substantive reasons. Julia, for example, firmly believed that association with a husband, whose role allowed him extensive contact with the world outside the home, could be broadening for the wife. It was an access that the lowly-regarded spinster would be less likely to obtain. This conviction was based on her own experience with Chev, whose reform-minded friends introduced her to a world of ideas and action she had never known in New York City.[30] In particular, Julia believed that she owed to Chev her introduction to abolitionism. Like Lucretia Mott, Elizabeth Cady Stanton, Mary Livermore, and Lucy Stone before her, Julia's involvement with abolitionism led directly to an increased awareness of women's rights. In her journal entry for Sunday, February 25, 1866, she revealed her new perspective: "Our slaves had no rights. Women have few."[31] As she recalled in her old age:

> There seemed a special incongruity in putting this great mass of ignorant men into a position of political superiority to all women.... Should they, simply on account of sex, be invested with a power and dignity withheld from women...? Here were ignorance and low life commissioned to lord it over the august company of mothers....[32]

Another reason for Julia's exaltation of domesticity was her conviction that the home could be more than a duty or responsibility for women; it could serve as a power base for her sex. If women took full advantage of the theoretical power and dignity vested in them as wives and mothers, they could claim respect and influence in their own households. Julia emphasized the importance of the domestic role in lectures and articles addressed to young women. She urged them to become practiced in the arts of house-keeping. "Learn to make a home," she advised, "and learn this in the days in which learning is easy. Cultivate a habit of vigilance and forethought."[33] According to Julia, this tutelage would not only prevent the sorrows which she had suffered in her married life, but would also guarantee the position of power which she had lost.

> [N]o love of intellectual pursuits should lead any of us to disparage
> and neglect the household gifts and graces. A house is a kingdom
> in little, and its queen, if she is faithful, gentle, and wise, is a
> sovereign indeed.[34]

Such skill would insure a good grasp of the domestic sphere from the start,
and the young bride would embark on married life from a position of
strength.

But most important was the fact that marriage itself was the prerequisite
for motherhood. *That* was the real reward of domestic life. Sometimes the
company of her children had provided Julia with her only pleasant moments.
"My babies are all the poetry and beauty that I can see in life," she wrote in
1846.[35] Her four daughters, as they grew older, pleased her with their
affectionate company, and she enjoyed the "variety of character" which her
family demonstrated.[36]

She believed, too, that children expanded the *potential* for happiness in a
woman's life. "A new life will come to you with that of which you are the
giver.... In giving life, [the mother] has found a manifold extension of her
own life."[37] Even in an unhappy marriage, then, motherhood alone made
domesticity worthwhile. In fact, as time passed and her arguments became
more polished, Julia identified marriage *not* with wifehood, with its abun-
dant sources of conflict, but with *motherhood,* with its greater potential
rewards.

In stressing motherhood, Julia believed she had found the critical link
between domesticity and feminism. Women who were charged with the
responsibility for children—and thus for the nation's future—could certainly
argue that they were morally and mentally suited to a sphere wider than that
of the home.[38] Women, in fact, had a duty to their children to contribute to
the uplift and progress of the society around them.[39] And, as noted earlier,
Julia believed that the duties and privileges of a broader sphere would make
women better mothers. In short, woman's claim to legal and political rights,
to property, to educational opportunity, and to recognition in the professions
all hinged on her status as mother or potential mother.

In January of 1876, Chev died. Although Julia had formulated virtually all
of the feminist arguments she would ever use before his death, this event freed
her in a number of ways. Psychologically, a source of strain and conflict was
removed from her life. There was as well much more free time once she no
longer had to attend to her husband's needs and wishes. Chev's death, then,
inaugurated the period when Julia began to travel widely, honing her
arguments and polishing her speaking abilities.

By the mid-1880's, Julia had gained widespread recognition for her
activities as a "woman's woman." She received requests for articles, for

appearances, for lectures, and she was asked to head the Woman's Department of two large fairs. Her success made her memories of Chev less painful; it took the sting out of her past mistakes. Her friend, Thomas Wentworth Higginson, noted the happy effect of Julia's new public role, particularly her new role as an outspoken suffragist: "[T]here was a visible change; it gave a new brightness to her face, a new cordiality in her manner, made her calmer, firmer; she found herself among new friends and could disregard old critics."[40] Julia herself recognized this, commenting in her memoirs that participation in the suffrage movement relieved her from feelings of "isolation and eccentricity."[41]

The recognition accorded Julia as a reformer enabled her to see herself as a successful person. The autonomy and identity which she had never found in her own marriage became available to her as she gained public stature. Nevertheless, this sense of self had deep roots in the private sphere. A part of Julia's identity remained a domesticity that she exploited for public ends. The legitimacy denied her by Chev was conferred by an American public which began to enshrine her as the ideal wife and mother. Indeed, unexpected personal power devolved upon Julia as a result of her association with conventional marriage, fueling her efforts to link domesticity and women's rights. The fame and recognition which she enjoyed came in unique form— the cult of Julia Ward Howe as Great American Mother. In 1885, the Des Moines Woman's Club described her as the "Mother of the Club."[42] Julia referred to herself as the "mother of the new woman."[43] Articles about Julia stressed her home-centered role. One enthusiastic, if ungrammatical, reporter wrote: "She brought up a charming family, her children, now grown up and living in homes of their own, cherishing delightful memories of the hours spent by their beautiful mother in reading to them, playing with them, and telling them charming stories."[44] Even her appearance was motherly; journalists described her as a "maternal figure attired in rich black silk."[45] Total strangers rushed up to Julia after her lectures and speeches to kiss and embrace her as they would their own mothers.[46] This sort of reception confirmed Julia's belief that she argued most persuasively for women when she built upon the role of motherhood.

In this light, the paradox between Julia's married life and her feminist theory is more apparent than real. By treating marriage as a means of broadening women's horizons, by identifying the home as the first source of woman's power, and by stressing the fulfillment of motherhood, Julia had constructed a theory of feminism both personally satisfying and politically useful. Having successfully linked facets of domestic life to the demand for a wider sphere for women, she could earnestly and honestly embrace domesticity as a beneficial role for herself and for all women. "Every true woman," she claimed, "has the mother in her and this grand spiritual motherhood, exerting its desired influence and watchfulness in all walks of life will give every woman a noble part to perform in the great drama of the world."[47]

Notes

1. Sermon, Julia Ward Howe (hereafter JWH), no title (n.d.), JWH Collection, Folder 53, Library of Congress, Washington, D.C. (hereafter DLC).
2. Sermon, JWH, no title (n. d.), JWH Collection, Folder 57, DLC. See also the address written by JWH in JWH Collection, Folder 60, DLC.
3. JWH Journal; 17 January 1864 and 11 May 1864, Howe Collection, Houghton Library, Harvard University, Cambridge, Massachusetts (hereafter HL).
4. See Blanche Glassman Hersh, "A Partnership of Equals: Feminist Marriages in Nineteenth-Century America," Paper delivered at the Conference of Women, Historians of the Midwest, October, 1975. Also see Hersh's essay in this volume.
5. Sermon, JWH, no title (n.d.), JWH Collection, Folder 38, DLC.
6. Clipping, JWH, "Address to the Fourteenth Woman's Congress," JWH Collection, Vol. 1, Schlesinger Library, Radcliffe College, Cambridge, Massachusetts (hereafter SL).
7. Lecture, JWH, "Education," JWH Collection, Folder 28, DLC; Clipping, JWH, "Debt to Pioneers," (23 March 1907), JWH Collection, Vol. 4, SL.
8. Sermon, JWH, no title (n.d.), JWH Collection, Folder 39, DLC.
9. Sermon, JWH, "The Wise Woman Buildeth Her House" (n.d.), JWH Collection, Folder 10, DLC.
10. Julia Ward Howe, *Reminiscences* (New York: New American Library, 1968; facsimile ed.), p. 375.
11. Aileen Kraditor, *Ideas of the Woman Suffrage Movement, 1890-1920* (Garden City, N.Y.: Doubleday and Company, 1971), pp. 38-43.
12. An excellent example of this, written well after the "expedient arguments" are said to have taken hold, is found in Julia Ward Howe, "Woman and the Suffrage," *Outlook,* 3 April 1909, p. 781.
13. Laura Elizabeth Richards, *Samuel Gridley Howe* (New York: D. Appleton-Century Company, 1935), p. 179.
14. Laura Elizabeth Richards, *Stepping Westward* (New York: D. Appleton and Company, 1931), pp. 12-13.
15. JWH to Anne Eliza Ward Mailliard (hereafter AWM), 13 August [1854], Howe Collection, HL.
16. JWH, *Reminiscences,* p. 133.
17. JWH to AWM, Saturday [1849?], Howe Collection, HL.
18. JWH to AWM, Friday 8 [1850], Howe Collection, HL.
19. JWH to AWM, Sunday 26 [1852], Howe Collection, HL.
20. JWH to AWM, March 1850, Howe Collection, HL.
21. JWH to AWM, Monday, December [1853], Howe Collection, HL. JWH

Journal, 25 September 1864; 5 November 1864; 18 March 1865; 23 April 1865, Howe Collection, HL.

22. Samuel Gridley Howe to George Finley, 13 August 1874, Howe Collection, HL.

23. JWH, Journal, 24 April 1865, Howe Collection, HL.

24. JWH Journal, 23 April 1865, Howe Collection, HL.

25. JWH Journal, 29 May 1864, Howe Collection, HL. Julia wrote: "His face has the power of emptying my brain of vitality so that I hardly know what I am about." See also JWH Journal, 24 April 1865, Howe Collection, HL; and JWH to AWM, 25 November [1851], Howe Collection, HL.

26. JWH to AWM, 19 June [1854?], Howe Collection, HL.

27. JWH to Samuel Gridley Howe, Thursday [1846], Howe Collection, HL.

28. JWH to AWM, 19 July [1854?], Howe Collection, HL.

29. Laura Elizabeth Richards and Maud Howe Elliott, *Julia Ward Howe,* Vol. I (Boston: Houghton Mifflin Company, 1916), p. 369.

30. JWH, *Reminiscences,* pp. 147-151.

31. JWH Journal, 25 February 1866, Howe Collection, HL.

32. Clipping, JWH, "What Life Means to Me," *Cosmospolitan,* July 1906, JWH Collection, SL.

33. JWH, *Reminiscences,* p. 216.

34. Ibid., p. 217.

35. JWH to Louisa Ward Crawford, 15 February 1846, Howe Collection, HL.

36. JWH Journal, 9 July 1865, Howe Collection, HL.

37. Clipping, JWH, "The Joys of Motherhood" (n.d.), JWH Collection, Vol. 4, SL.

38. As Aileen Kraditor has noted, these sorts of arguments, which she labels "expedient," were widely used by suffragists after 1890. Julia, however, used this line of argument as early as 1871 in her efforts to organize a woman's campaign for peace. It was part and parcel of her vision of women as complex people who could combine domestic life with public service throughout their adult lives. See Aileen Kradetor, *Ideas of the Woman's Suffrage Movement, 1890-1920* (Garden City, N.Y.: Doubleday and Company, 1971).

39. Linda Kerber, in her article, "The Republican Mother: Women and the Enlightenment—An American Perspective," demonstrates that this argument was an old one, dating back to the early years of nationhood. Here again, Julia's contribution was not that she invented the line of reasoning which she used, but that she clothed it in the language of her century, using the religious, political, and domestic images with which Victorian Americans were familiar. See *American Quarterly* 28 (Summer 1976): 187-205.

40. Thomas Wentworth Higginson, "Col. Higginson on Mrs. Howe" *Outlook,* 26 January 1907, p. 167.

41. JWH, *Reminiscences,* p. 376.

42. Clipping, no title, (n.d.), JWH Collection, Vol. 5, SL.

43. Clipping, no title, (n.d.), JWH Collection, Vol. 8, SL.

44. Clipping from the *Home Journal* (n.d.), JWH Collection, Vol. 4, SL.

45. Clipping, no title (January 1890), JWH Collection, Vol. 2, SL.
46. JWH Journal, May 1900 and 1 September 1901, Howe Collection, HL.
47. Sermon, JWH, no title (n.d.), JWH Collection, Folder 38, DLC.

Elisabeth Griffith

Elizabeth Cady Stanton on Marriage and Divorce: Feminist Theory and Domestic Experience

Although Elizabeth Cady Stanton is usually identified as either Susan B. Anthony's sidekick or the author of the 1848 Seneca Falls suffrage resolution, she is less well known as the principal philosopher of the nineteenth-century women's movement. Her critique of the inferior status of American women in a male-dominated society, and her catalogue of remedies, ranging from birth control and property rights to girls' sports and vocational training, has become the unacknowledged agenda for the second women's movement. At the center of her analysis of "woman's portion" was a indictment of the patriarchal institution of marriage, a defense of divorce, and a description of an ideal or "equitable marriage relation," which depended in part on improving women's overall economic, legal and social status, and in part on innovations within domesticity.

Stanton claimed that traditional partriarchal marriages were degrading for women as human beings and wrongly beneficial for men. Her criticism became the core of her feminism, from which she never retreated and which she reiterated until the month she died, in October 1902.[1] She built her argument against "man-made marriage" between 1840 and 1863, the first half of her own forty-seven year marriage, and used as evidence from "my own life, observation, thought, feeling and reason."[2] In a cumulative and complex manner, Stanton's theory about marriage and divorce was the product of her entire life.

Before her own marriage in 1840, Stanton was already aware that marriage, for some women, resulted in hardship and heartache. There were the vivid recollections of deserted wives and disinherited widows who had appealed to her father for legal assistance.[3] There was as well recognition of women's inferior status before the law. New York statutes, like those of every other state, offered little protection to married women and took away what

[The recipient in 1978 of a Woodrow Wilson Research Grant in Women's Studies, Elisabeth Griffith is a doctoral candidate in the Department of History at The American University. Her dissertation is a biography of Elizabeth Cady Stanton.]

limited rights they had enjoyed while single. Women lost their legal individuality in marriage and became wholly subordinate to their husbands. Wives had no rights to sign contracts, initiate suits, establish credit, inherit property of their own, or claim more than one-third of their husbands' estates. Mothers had no rights to control or custody of their children.[4]

Against women's more abstract vulnerability before the law were juxtaposed personal examples of strong, commanding women. Stanton's mother, Margaret Livingston Cady, was an unusually independent wife and a strong individual. Married at sixteen, she gave birth to ten children in twenty-four years, managed a large house with many servants, and became a leader in community and charitable affairs. Her own family's wealth and connections had assured her husband's fortune. That and her towering, nearly six-foot height, military attitude, and athletic prowess made her a commanding figure. Margaret Cady's personality matched her physical appearance. Evidence that she asserted herself within the sphere accorded women ranges from her refusal to yield to her husband's wish that the family move to an isolated estate to her sixty-year defiance of his ban on rocking chairs. Her assertiveness extended to the public sphere as well: she once schemed to gain female parishioners the vote in a church election.[5] Similarly, Stanton's oldest sister, Tryphena Cady Bayard, was a forceful woman.[6] She made all the financial decisions in her own household, and later, as executor of her father's estate, became the family's financial manager and investment counselor.[7]

Prior to her own marriage, the most unusual, and perhaps the most appealing union Stanton had as a model was that of her cousin Gerrit Smith and his second wife Nancy Fitzhugh. The son of John Jacob Astor's business partner, Peter Smith, and Elizabeth Livingston, Stanton's aunt, Gerrit Smith was the largest landowner in New York and a nationally known philanthropist and reformer.[8] Daniel Cady was Gerrit Smith's attorney and Elizabeth Cady was his daughter's closest friend for seventy years. Smith and his wife had dedicated themselves and their immense fortune to abolition, temperance, and other reforms with evangelistic zeal. Visits to their estate at Peterboro in the 1830's provided Stanton with her first exposure not only to radical politics but also to a marriage conceived as a "partnership of equals" and rooted in affection and shared objectives. Just as she found the Smiths' commitments to reform attractive, so she was drawn to the example of their marriage. At Peterboro she also found in the abolitionist Henry Brewster Stanton a man who endorsed marriage as a partnership.

When Elizabeth and Henry met in October of 1839, their lives contrasted completely. Henry, the executive secretary for William Lloyd Garrison's American Anti-Slavery Society, was an abolitionist agent famous for his compelling oratory and his courage when confronted with mobs.[9] Elizabeth's primary occupation was paying and receiving calls. Since graduating from

Emma Willard's Seminary in 1833, she had whiled away her girlhood in the manner of upper-class daughters. In a household staffed by six servants, Elizabeth's most onerous chore was sitting on her underwear (rather than ironing it) while reading French novels.[10] Once a serious student, encouraged by several male mentors, she found as she grew older that logical argument and Greek prizes were no longer rewarded by her politically conservative and sternly Presbyterian family.[11]

Having dedicated himself to abolition with the ardor of an evangelist, Henry was understandably critical of a life wasted "in a giddy whirl of fashionable follies." Elizabeth's potential made the condemnation more serious. "It pains me," Henry wrote to Gerrit Smith, "to see a person of so superior a mind and enlarged heart doing nothing for the wicked world's salvation."[12] With typical fervor, Henry offered Elizabeth the means to fulfill her potential in an alliance comparable to that of the Smiths and Theodore and Angelina Grimké Weld.[13] Influenced by the currents of revival, reform and romanticism that characterized the 1830's, Elizabeth had been quietly questioning her own life and was cautiously searching for an alternative to her circumscribed role as Daniel Cady's daughter.[14] In Henry she thought she had found a brave and handsome "knight" committed to a righteous cause who would share his work with her.[15] His proposal was accepted immediately. In deciding to marry Henry, Elizabeth anticipated neither the hardships of her father's clients nor the restraints of a traditional marriage. Indeed, she expected the model of partnership that made reformers' marriages distinctive.

Unimpressed by his Mayflower credentials and alarmed by his radical views and impecunious position, the Cady family pressured Elizabeth into ending the engagement in March 1840. She saw it only as a temporary postponement.[16] When Henry announced plans to be in Europe from May until December, she insisted that they wed at once, rather than allow "an ocean to roll between the lovers."[17] The couple were married in a small family ceremony in Johnstown, New York, on May 1, 1840. The word "obey" was omitted from the ceremony. It is unclear whose decision it was as Henry may have been following the example of the Welds for whom he had served as best man. But Elizabeth claimed it was hers.[18] The bride was twenty-four years old, the third of the Cadys' five daughters. The groom was thirty-five, and, having split with the Garrisonians, unemployed.[19]

Henry had badgered colleagues for weeks to raise the price of their ocean passages to England, where he was to be a delegate to the World Anti-Slavery Convention.[20] London was the first stop of an eight-month honeymoon of abolition lectures and newspaper correspondence which paid their expenses. Henry's chronically insecure financial position, in comparison to her family's substantial wealth, would become a source of discord later, but it caused no friction at this time. Rather unexpectedly, however, the convention in London generated their first political dispute. Delegates to the meeting were immediately embroiled in the debate over Wendell Phillips' motion to seat the eight American women delegates, including Lucretia Mott, the Philadelphia Quaker.[21] Proponents argued that it was only fair to allow women to participate in a forum whose purpose was to end slavery. Opponents answered that it was unseemly, not to say ungodly, for women to speak and vote in public. In a gathering of the most liberal leaders of the most radical movement of the era, the opponents prevailed in a voice vote.

How Henry Stanton voted remains a matter of debate among witnesses, but he had earlier objected to women voting in the meetings of the American Anti-Slavery Society, whose leader, William Lloyd Garrison, had become his political antagonist.[22] The opposition of her husband and the majority of the male reformers stunned Elizabeth Cady Stanton. Outraged by the injustice of the outcome and the hypocrisy of the abolitionists, she later cited the London meeting as the event that ignited her interest in the women's movement.[23] At the time, however, everyone, not least of all Henry, was surprised that the new Mrs. Stanton sided with the Mott-Garrison faction. As a result, the trio became mutual allies and admirers. Garrison would write to his wife that "Mrs. Stanton is a fearless woman and goes for women's rights with all her soul."[24] In Lucretia Mott especially, Stanton found both a personal role model and a political mentor. Under the tutelage of the older woman, she discussed women's rights, religion, and other social issues. Her personal independence and fledgling feminism were encouraged and reinforced. For the first time Stanton had found in another woman an alternative source of approval and motivation. For forty years Stanton patterned herself on Mott whenever possible.[25]

It would not be possible, however, for Elizabeth and Henry to duplicate the Motts' marriage. James Mott played the supporting role; Henry Stanton would not be willing to do so. Conditioned by the determining factors of Elizabeth's growing sense of herself as an independent human being and Henry's—in actuality—traditional regard for the marital relationship, there would be daily difficulties. The marriage would be strained by money problems, growing domestic responsibilities, Henry's frequent absences (as much as ten months a year for twenty years), and Elizabeth's commitment to the women's movement. Both would also become increasingly unyielding. But at the beginning they were bound by enormous personal attraction—both of them were magnetic individuals—and mutual interest in public issues. Further, Stanton in her early married years was shielded from the domestic demands that would make her chafe in the next decade.

After returning to the United States in December 1840, Henry decided to give up reform work temporarily and read law with his father-in-law, in what may have been an attempt to heal the breach caused by the marriage. The couple lived with the Cadys in Johnstown, following a pattern established by the other daughters and their attorney husbands. In 1842, the Stantons' first child, Daniel Cady (Neal), was born in the Cady home; a second son, Henry (Kit) arrived in their Albany townhouse during the court session in 1844. After Henry passed the Massachusetts Bar in 1843, Judge Cady bought them a house in Chelsea, where Elizabeth took up housekeeping with two sons and three servants. It was her first experience as head of her own household, and she prided herself on her competence and cleanliness.

> I studied up everything pertaining to housekeeping, and enjoyed it all. Even washing day... had its charms for me.... I inspired my laundress with an ambition to have her clothes look white and to get them out earlier than our neighbors, and to have them ironed and put away sooner.[26]

While they had lived in her home she had borne few household responsibilities; she had read widely, studied law informally, and had hesitantly undertaken some reform activity. She had made her first speech on behalf of temperance, organized a Sunday school for black children, and lobbied the New York state legislature for a Married Woman's Property Act.[27] Significantly, she began to insist on being addressed Elizabeth Cady Stanton, rather than Mrs. Henry B. Stanton:

> I have very serious objections... to being called Henry. Ask our colored brethren if there is nothing in a name. Why are the slaves nameless unless they take that of their master? Simply because they have no independent existence. They are mere chattels, with no civil or social rights. Even so with women. The custom of calling women Mrs. John This and Mrs. Tom That and colored men Sambo and Zip Coon is founded on the principle that white men are the lords of all. I cannot acknowledge this principle as just; therefore I cannot bear the name of another.[28]

In Boston she attended public lectures, sermons, "conversations," anti-slavery conventions and bazaars, entertained notables, and shared in the stimulating life of the city. Meanwhile, another son, Gerrit Smith (Gat), was born in 1845.[29] There was no shared political or reform activity. Theirs was a traditional middle-class marriage: "Mr. Stanton announced to me... that his business would occupy all his time, and that I must take entire charge of the housekeeping."[30] Both seemed outwardly content but there were increasing signs of restlessness. She was still searching for an outlet for her brains and energy, and he was searching for a more hospitable political district.[31]

Suffering the chill rebuff of partisan Garrisonians and Boston winters,

Henry decided in 1847 to remove to Seneca Falls, New York, where Judge Cady conveyed another property to them, a house and two acres.[32] Henry became the attorney for several local manufacturers and a specialist in patent law, which required frequent trips to Washington. In 1848 he helped organize the Free Soil Party but renounced it to run in 1849 for the state senate as a Democrat. Reelected by only six votes in 1851, he was nonetheless offered the lieutenant governorship in 1853.[33]

Located in the Finger Lake region west of Syracuse, Seneca Falls was a mill town, population 3000—small, isolated, lacking sidewalks, adequate schools, and cultural resources. Elizabeth Cady Stanton hated it. Her experience as a pampered daughter and Boston bride left her unprepared for the role of rural housewife. For the first time she became concerned about the lives of dependent, overworked, passive wives. As their family grew to seven children (on the average of one baby every two and a half years), her work increased geometrically. Politics and his law career took Henry out of town regularly and their income remained insufficient. As early as 1848 she began voicing her discontent about the isolating, demeaning and unrewarding character of most women's lives, including her own at that time. She later recalled the convictions that overwhelmed her:

> The general discontent I felt with woman's portion as wife, mother, housekeeper, physician, and spiritual guide, the chaotic conditions into which everything fell without her constant supervision, and the wearied, anxious look of the majority of women impressed me with a strong feeling that some active measures should be taken to remedy the wrongs of society in general, and of women in particular. My experience at the World's Anti-Slavery Convention, all I had read of the legal status of women, and the oppression I saw everywhere, together swept across my soul, intensified now by many personal experiences.

What awaited her was the Seneca Falls Convention and its aftermath, the women's movement.[34] The Seneca Falls Resolutions which Stanton drafted did not specifically address the issues of marriage and divorce, but her concern for the circumstances of married women persisted. The move to Seneca Falls was another milestone, like the London meeting in 1840. It marked the beginning of her active involvement in the women's movement and an expanding awareness of the lives of married women in a patriarchal society.

As a middle-class matron, Stanton had some alternatives to domestic drudgery. She knew that birth control was available and chose not to use it, believing that she and Henry were creating a superior tribe. Although complaining that it was inadequate and untrained, she managed to find household help among Seneca Falls' immigrant Irish and eventually added a Quaker housekeeper who stayed thirty years. She also taught her children to wait on table. When worse came to worse, she fled to Johnstown and put the older boys in Theodore Weld's boarding school. While she also complained about Henry's prolonged absences, she relished the role of decision-maker *pro tem,* and encouraged similar independence among her neighbors.[35] She introduced "conversation clubs" and a co-educational gymnasium, and housed lyceum lecturers as they passed through Seneca Falls. She became part of a northeastern network of women's rights activists, and relied on her closest friends, Susan B. Anthony and Elizabeth Smith Miller (Gerrit's daughter) for moral support, political counsel, helping hands, and borrowed bonnets. The friendship of these two women became increasingly important to her as family enthusiasm for her cause waned.

Yet despite these resources, the chores and the children left Stanton little time for her increasing involvement with women's rights.

> Men and angels, give me patience! I am at the boiling point! If I do not find some day the use of my tongue on this question, I shall die of intellectual repression, a women's rights convulsion!... How much I long to be free of housekeeping and children, so as to have time to think and read and write.[36]

After organizing the 1848 meeting, Stanton laid the groundwork for what would become the woman suffrage movement.[37] She identified co-workers and supervised their efforts locally. Unable to attend most meetings, she always sent a letter to be read at the opening session that outlined the goals and tasks to be accomplished, and when possible she sent Susan B. Anthony in her place, with a speech she had written. Stanton recruited Anthony from temperance work to women's issues after meeting her in 1852. Their partnership eventually became the backbone of the woman suffrage movement, and their friendship became an important emotional and political alliance for both of them.

The division of labor between Stanton and Anthony cast Stanton in a behind-the-scenes role: she stayed home drafting speeches, convention calls, agenda, resolutions, and letters to editors and colleagues at her dining room table while Anthony travelled and lectured and organized. With both Susan and Henry adventuring at large while she stayed home with the children, she felt stranded.

The crisis came in 1855 when Stanton announced plans to become a public lecturer and to travel on behalf of woman's rights. As she wrote Anthony wistfully:

> I wish that I were as free as you and I would stump the whole state

> in a twinkling. But I am not.... The pressure on me just now is
> too great. Henry sides with my friends who oppose me in all that is
> dearest to my heart. They are not willing that I should write even
> on the women question. But I will both write and speak....
> Sometimes, Susan, I struggle in deep waters.[38]

Stanton did not join the circuit. She stayed home and had two more children, but she did keep writing and working. It was not an easy compromise for her and she was frequently angry and frustrated, writing in 1856:

> I pace up and down these two chambers of mine like a caged lion,
> longing to bring to a close childrearing and housekeeping cares. I
> have other work at hand.[39]

Not until the early 1860's would Stanton take on her role as philosopher and propagandist full time.

The restraints placed on her reform activity derived from three sources: her husband, her father and family, and herself. Henry, who had once urged her to become involved in reform, resented her growing commitment to women's rights. He complained to her that "you could write much more frequently to me if you did not spend so much time writing speeches and articles."[40] Having been pressured by his father-in-law into giving up elective office because his family and especially his delinquent oldest son needed his attention, Henry thought Elizabeth should supervise the children more and Anthony less.[41]

In this Henry found an ally in Judge Cady, now an associate juctice of the state supreme court and nearly blind. Although Judge Cady had encouraged his daughter's exceptional academic and athletic achievements as an adolescent, he now found her ambition for public activity wholly inappropriate. As she wrote regretfully to Anthony at that time:

> I passed through a terrible scourging when last at my father's. I
> cannot tell you how deeply the iron entered my soul. I never felt
> more keenly the degradation of my sex.... To think that all in me
> which my father would have felt a proper pride had I been a man,
> is deeply mortifying to him because I am a woman.[42]

Family stories have Judge Cady rushing to Seneca Falls in 1848 to confirm his daughter's sanity, refusing to visit her during the bloomer period, and disinheriting her for testifying before the state legislature in 1854 on married women's property rights, but there is little evidence to document these claims.[43]

But just as important was Stanton's own ambivalence about leaving her children. Her children and her novel childraising techniques were a source of great satisfaction to her.[44] She prided herself on easy births, healthy babies, and clever children. In later years she was referred to inside and outside of her family as the Queen Mother. (The reference was only in part to her Victorian rotundity.) At times she used pregnancy to ward off Anthony's incessant demands. She delayed travelling for another decade because, as she joked to Wendell Phillips in 1860, "I am anchored here, surrounded by small craft which I am struggling to tug up life's stream."[45]

Both she and Henry had made compromises and postponed public careers, but it was not an easy resolution. Resentment sometimes overwhelmed her, as on the Fourth of July, 1858:

> Oh how I long for a few hours of leisure each day. How rebellious it makes me feel when I see Henry going about where and how he pleases. He can walk at will through the whole wide world or shut himself up alone, if he pleases, within four walls. As I contrast his freedom with my bondage, and feel that, because of the false position of woman, I have been compelled to hold all my noblest aspirations in abeyance in order to be a wife, a mother, a nurse, a cook, a household drudge. I am fired anew and long to pour forth from my own experience the whole long story of woman's wrongs. I have been alone today as the whole family except Hattie and myself have been out to celebrate our national birthday. What has woman to do with patriotism? Must not some one watch baby, house and garden? And who is so fitting to perform all these duties, which no one else wishes to do, as she who brought sin into the world and all our woe![46]

While outwardly her marriage was on the whole stable, she felt compelled to articulate an attack on marriage and a defense of divorce.

From her own experience, her exposure to the lives of women less well off, and her extensive reading, especially of law texts and the novels of George Eliot, Stanton condemned traditional marriage as unjust for women.[47] She claimed that marriage made women slaves, depriving them of their autonomy, as well as their bodies, children, and wages, inheritance. She found the marriage ceremony degrading and protested the "humiliating" practice of "giving the bride away from one master to another."[48] In her analysis, marriage for women meant burdens rather than benefits. Even henpecked husbands could demand wifely compliance. As she explained to Anthony in 1857:

> [M]an, too, suffers in the false marriage relation, yet what can his suffering he compared to what every woman experiences, whether happy or unhappy?... A man marrying gives up no right, but a woman, every right, even the most sacred of all, the right to her

own person... so long as our present false marriage relation continues, which in most cases is nothing more or less than legalized prostitution, women can have no self-respect and of course man will have none for her.... Personal freedom is the first right to be proclaimed, and that does not and cannot now belong to the relation of wife, to the mistress of the isolated home, to the financial dependent.[49]

Women in these and more desparate straits needed an alternative. For them Stanton urged immediate reform of the divorce laws. But for the majority of women for whom marriage was their livelihood, status, and occupation, Stanton recommended a series of steps to make the arrangement more equitable.

In mid-nineteenth-century America, divorce, like free love and infanticide, was a scandalous subject. Home and family were sacred; divorce was sacrilegious. In the popular mind, only adulterers divorced; even innocent parties became social outcasts. To raise the subject was to risk the condemnation of the community. Yet Stanton was willing to brave such scorn to defend the rights of spouses trapped in "ill-assorted marriages."

I rejoice over every slave that escapes from a discordant marriage. With the education and elevation of women we shall have a mighty sundering of the unholy ties that hold men and women together who loathe and despise each other.[50]

Stanton first advocated liberalizing state divorce codes when she served as President of New York's Women's Temperance Society. In a speech in 1852, she argued that habitual drunkeness should be allowed as grounds for divorce.[51] After several years of conversations and correspondence, she was ready to demand wholesale reform. She made her first comprehensive public statement on the subject at the tenth annual National Women's Rights Convention, which met in New York City in May 1860.[52]

Stanton disrupted that meeting by condemning "man-made marriage," and by urging quick dissolution in "cases of drunkenness, insanity, desertion, cruel and brutal treatment" as well as incompatability. She teased the chief opponent of marriage reform:

I know Horace Greeley has been most eloquent in recent weeks on the holy sacrament of ill-assorted marriages; but let us hope that all wisdom does not live and shall not die with Horace Greeley. I think if he had been married to the *New York Herald* instead of the Republican Party, he would have found some Scriptural arguments against life-long unions where great incompatability of temper existed between the parties.[53]

While she addressed her belief that marriage and divorce were private matters that ought not to be regulated by civil or canon law, if legislators were to interfere she demanded making marriage harder and divorce easier. She was probably the first to advocate "no-fault" divorce, without "delinquencies" or guilty parties.

Stanton spoke at the meeting for an hour. Her audience responded with loud applause but opponents immediately introduced censoring resolutions. Debate raged for an entire session of the convention. Finally Wendell Phillips, hero of the 1840 London meeting, moved to table the entire discussion and to expunge it from the record, asserting that as marriage and divorce affected men and women equally, it ought to be out of order at a woman's rights convention. William Lloyd Garrison wanted to table the discussion but keep it in the minutes. Typically Susan Anthony had the last word in defense of Stanton. The vote was called: the question was tabled and recorded.[54]

Public reaction to Stanton's divorce speech was heated and hostile, as she recalled later:

> The discussion... called down on us severe criticism from the metropolitan and state press. So alarming were the comments on what had been said that I began to feel that I had inadvertently taken the underpinning from the social system. Enemies were unsparing in their denunciations and friends ridiculed the whole proceedings.[55]

Widely censored, she was nevertheless becoming accustomed to disapproval and she would not drop the subject, characteristically convinced that she alone was right—"my reason, my experience, my soul proclaim it."[56] She sent letters to Greeley's *Tribune* and with Lucretia Mott testified the following year on behalf of the Ramsey (divorce reform) Bill. She realized that any attack on marriage or defense of divorce was indeed a blow at a patriarchal social system, and so she kept hammering away. "This marriage question," she wrote, "lies at the very foundation of all progress."[57]

But she was also astute enough to realize that divorce was an unacceptable alternative for most women, depriving them of their reputations, homes, children, and financial security. Her peripheral involvement in a runaway wife case in 1861 (in which the woman was put in an insane asylum by an unfaithful husband, and dragged back after she had escaped), in the McFarland-Richardson murder case of 1870 (in which a husband shot his wife's escort, was acquitted as insane, and then awarded custody of their son), and the 1875 divorce trial of her friends Theodore and Elizabeth Tilton (in which Victoria Woodhull named Henry Ward Beecher as correspondent), emphasized for her the cruel and unsavory aspects of divorce for individuals.[58]

As early as her 1860 address, Stanton had stressed the need for reform of the marriage relation, making it more equitable:

> Horace Greeley in his recent discussion with Robert Dale Owen, said that the whole question had been tried in all its varieties and conditions from indissoluable monogamous marriage down to free love... there is one kind of marriage that has not been tried and that is a contract made by equal parties to lead an equal life, with equal restraints and privileges on either side. Thus far we have had man marriage and nothing more.[59]

Even though Stanton had achieved only mixed results in attempting to meet this standard in her own marriage, she continued to recommend it to her children and friends.[60]

Stanton's model of an ideal marriage combined pragmatic and romantic factors. To be in a position to marry freely and to avoid having to marry out of financial need, young women (legally no less than twenty-five years old) ought to have equal education and employment opportunities. Birth control, property rights, and suffrage would help women achieve equal status and autonomy once married. Athletic training and improvements in maternity care would improve their health as innovations in child care and household management (along the lines later suggested by Charlotte Perkins Gilman) would eliminate drudgery.[61] Nor was "romance" lacking from Stanton's ideal union, but it was a romance rooted in affection, companionship, and equal consideration:

> In a true relation the chief object is the loving companionship of man and woman, their capacity for mutual help and happiness and for the development of all that is noblest in each other. The second object is the building up of a home and family, a place of rest, peace, security, in which child-life can bud and blossom.

> I hold that it is a sin, an outrage on our holiest feelings that anything but deep and fervent love and sympathy constitute marriage.[62]

If not, then liberalized divorce laws would dissolve the bond.

In Stanton's case, whatever "mutual feeling" bound her to Henry during the early years of their marriage, the difficult decade of the 1850's, was less evident after 1865. Under the pressures of continued separation, unemployment, political disagreements, and family problems, their marital bond weakened considerably. Beginning in 1866, she travelled as widely and for periods as long as he had earlier. She lectured to earn money, since Henry, by then an editorial and obituary writer with the *New York Sun,* had trouble finding jobs in the aftermath of a Civil-War bribery scandal.[63] They had disagreed over the Fourteenth and Fifteenth Amendments, and Henry, like most veteran abolitionists, had been appalled by her tactics. Finally, according to family sources,there was some unspecified controversy which caused a major rift and finally separation. When Henry died in 1887 they were apparently at odds, and they had not lived in the same place for nearly twenty years.[64]

Although Stanton's own marriage did not fit her ideal of 1840 or 1860, she did not resort to divorce. The arrangements of the 1870's suited her work and travel schedule. She spent time with the people who were most important to her—Susan B. Anthony, Libby Smith Miller, her daughters Harriot and Margaret, and other female colleagues. She relished the respect due her as a matron and mother (albeit a radical one), and would thrive as a widow and grandmother. The reforms regarding marriage and divorce which she preached were still a generation or more away, so she and many other women made do.

More important, Stanton had always struggled to achieve the kind of autonomy, the "solitude of self," she considered essential for all human beings, women or men, married or single. By the 1890's she was emotionally and physically independent even from Anthony, and able to break with her personally and politically. She decided not to join the Anthony household in Rochester, instead sharing an apartment in New York with her two unmarried children. And she refused to "sing suffrage evermore," because women needed more than the ballot to make them free. Stanton no longer needed another opinion, or anyone else's models; she made her own, as she had on the questions of marriage and divorce.

Notes

1. Elizabeth Cady Stanton (hereafter ECS), "How Shall We Solve the Divorce Problem?" *New York Journal and American,* 12 October 1902. After 1870, ECS wrote annually and sometimes monthly on this subject in major periodicals and papers.

2. ECS to Susan B. Anthony (hereafter SBA), 1 March 1853, in Theodore Stanton and Harriot Stanton Blatch, eds., *Elizabeth Cady Stanton as Revealed in Her Letters, Diary and Reminiscences,* Vol. 2 (New York: Harper Brothers, 1922) pp. 48-49 (hereafter *Letters*).

3. ECS, *Eighty Years and More, Reminiscences 1815-1897* (New York: T. Fisher Unwin, 1898; reprint ed., New York: Schocken Books, 1971), pp. 32-33, 216.

4. Ibid., pp. 220-225.

5. Margaret Livingston Cady (1785-1871) was the daughter of George Washington's Revolutionary aide, Col. Livingston. She married Daniel Cady in 1801. He was a cobbler and teacher turned lawyer. Of their ten

children, only the five daughters survived. ECS rarely mentions her mother in her autobiography but unpublished letters reveal a warm relationship. The loveliest characterization of Mrs. Cady was written by her granddaughter, Harriot Stanton Blatch and Alma Lutz, *Challenging Years: The Memoirs of Harriot Stanton Blatch* (New York: G.P. Putnam's Sons, 1940), p. 26.

6. Tryphena Cady Bayard (1803-1891) was named executrix in Judge Cady's will, filed in Johnstown, October 1859. She was admired but not liked within the family. Blatch, *Challenging Years,* p. 20; *Letters,* p. 273.

7. Edward Bayard had been a classmate at Union College of Eleazar Cady before his death in 1826. Bayard then studied law with Judge Cady and married his oldest daughter. After they moved to Seneca Falls he became a homeopathist healer, treating diseases by the administration of minute dosages of a remedy that would produce the same symptoms, and thus build antibodies. He was in the vanguard of a reform against excessive interference by doctors in natural healing procedures. Many of ECS's health-care and child-rearing practices were influenced by Bayard, who was an important mentor during her adolescence.

The rumors of romance between Edward and Elizabeth originate in Alma Lutz, *Created Equal: A Biography of Elizabeth Cady Stanton, 1815-1902* (New York: John Day Co. 1940), pp. 16-17, 21-23, which was written with the help of Stanton's daughter Harriot. They claim that Bayard, in addition to acting as tutor and friend, several times urged Stanton to marry him, even after he had married her sister.

3. Gerrit Smith (1797-1874) was President of the New York Anti-Slavery Society, founder and presidential candidate of the Liberty Party, a member of Congress, one of John Brown's backers, and one of the most important abolitionists of the era. Gerald Sorin, *The New York Abolitionists: A Case Study in Political Radicalism* (Westport, Conn.: Greenwood Publishing Co., 1971), pp. 26-38.

9. Henry Brewster Stanton (1805-1887), abolitionist, journalist, and politician, was born in Connecticut and moved to New York in 1826. Converted by Charles Grandison Finney in 1830 and influenced by Theodore Weld, he enrolled in Lyman Beecher's Lane Seminary in Cincinnati and with Weld became a leader of the "Lane Rebels." His Ohio activity led to his recruitment by Garrison to be an abolitionist agent in the northeast. The best biographical data on Henry Stanton is in Arthur H. Rice, "Henry B. Stanton as a Political Abolitionist" (Ed.D. dissertation, Teachers College, Columbia University, 1967).

10. ECS, *Eighty Years,* p. 47.

11. Having been encouraged by her father, her minister, her brother-in-law Bayard, her cousin Gerrit Smith, and the revivalist Charles Grandison Finney, ECS had acquired unusual academic and athletic skills but when she tried to find ways to use them, these mentors changed signals on her. The only two women who play an important role before Lucretia Mott

are her mother and Emma Willard, neither of whom gets any credit for inspiration until much later.

12. Henry Stanton to Gerrit Smith, 27 February 1840, The Gerrit Smith Miller Collection, Syracuse University, Syracuse, N.Y.

13. Such marriages were not uncommon among the reformers; see Blanche G. Hersh, "A Partnership of Equals: Feminist Marriages in Nineteenth-Century America," paper presented at the Women Historians of the Midwest Conference, October 1975.

For ECS, the Weld example was not encouraging. Before they sailed for England, the Stantons visited the Welds in New Jersey, where Angelina seemed to have succumbed to poverty, poor health, pregnancy, unending domestic routine and her husband's jealousy of her antislavery activity. The two women began a correspondence that would eventually bring Angelina and her sister into the women's movement. Angelina in turn appreciated Elizabeth's strengths, writing to Gerrit Smith, "We are very much pleased with Elizabeth Stanton... I could not help wishing that Henry was better calculated to mold such a mind." (As it turned out, Angelina's comment was perceptive and prophetic.) Gilbert H. Barnes and Dwight L. Dumond, eds., *Letters of Theodore Dwight Weld, Angelina Grimke Weld and Sarah Grimke, 1822-1844,* 2 Vols. (New York: D. Appleton-Century Co., 1934), 2: 842. See also, Gerda Lerner, *The Grimke Sisters from South Carolina: Pioneers for Women's Rights and Abolition* (Boston: Houghton Mifflin Co., 1967).

14. As ECS described this period later, she was frequently unhappy and uncertain about what she should be doing. ECS, Susan B. Anthony, and Matilda J. Gage, *The History of Woman Suffrage,* 3 Vols. (New York: Fowler and Wells,1881-86; reprint ed., New York: Source Book Press, 1970), 1:419 (hereafter HWS).

15. ECS, *Eighty Years,* p. 60. In her diary from this period, Stanton had copied romantic poems; "Commonplace Book," Manuscript Collection, Boston Public Library, Boston, Massachusetts.

16. "My engagement was not one of unmixed joy and satisfaction.... My father would never consent to my marriage with an abolitionist." ECS, *Eighty Years,* p. 58. Henry refers to the family's "violent opposition"; H. Stanton to Amos Phelps, 17 April 1840, Manuscript Collection, Boston Public Library, Boston, Massachusetts. See also, ECS to "Cousin Nancy," (Anne Fitzhugh Smith), March 1840, ECS Papers, the Library of Congress, Washington, D.C.

17. ECS, *Eighty Years,* p. 71. The same phrase appears in her diary the day Henry died, *Letters,* pp. 235-36. According to Henry, she refused to be left home "in the hands of opposing friends, and wishes to go with me that the storm may blow over while she is absent." Letter to A. Phelps, 17 April 1840, Boston Public Library, Boston, Massachusetts.

18. ECS mistated the date of her marriage in her memoirs, but Henry gets it correctly in his autobiography, *Random Recollections* (Johnstown.: N.Y.

Blunck and Leaning Printers, 1885), p. 37. See also Rice, "Henry B. Stanton," pp. 204-205. ESC, *Eighty Years,* p. 72.

19. Henry had split with Garrison in late 1839 over the direction the American Anti-Slavery Society was taking. Henry favored more direct political action and election of pro-abolition candidates; as a corollary to this, he opposed the involvement of women in the group because it would undermine its public credibility.

20. Rice, "Henry B. Stanton," p. 204; Dumond, *Weld Letters,* 2:828.

21. Lucretia Mott, Sarah Pugh, Mary Grew, Abby Kimber and Elizabeth Neall attended from Philadelphia; Emily Winslow, Abby Southwick and Ann Green Phillips made up the Boston contingent.

22. Henry spoke in favor of Phillips' resolution but there is disagreement about how he actually voted, and what he believed—a characteristic of his politics in later years. ECS and Garrison thought he voted in favor of seating the women, contradicting his earlier position. Lucretia Mott, James Birney, and Elizabeth Neall put him with opponents. See ECS, *Eighty Years,* p. 79; W.P. and F.J. Garrison, *William Lloyd Garrison, 1805-1879* (New York: Century Co., 1885) 2:383; Birney letter to Lewis Tappan, 29 August 1840, in Dwight L. Dumond, ed., *The Letters of James Gillespie Birney* (New York: D. Appleton-Century Co., Inc., 1938) 2:596; and Elizabeth Neall to E. Whittier, 18 November 1840, Packard-Whittier Papers, Houghton Library, Harvard University, Cambridge, Massachusetts.

23. "[W]hat a cause of wonder it will be to recall. . . that the champions of freedom, the most progressive men of the nineteenth century, denied women the right of free speech. . . . If Sambo had been cast out of the convention for any reason, I wonder if Wendell Phillips and George Thompson would have coolly remarked on his discomfiture, 'Well, he is as happy outside as in.'" ECS to SBA, 2 April 1852, *Letters,* p. 41.

24. Mrs. Mott wrote in her diary, "Eliz. Stanton growing daily in our affections." Lutz, *Created Equal,* pp. 30, 25.

25. Stanton would move beyond Mott as she developed her feminist ideology, but she always hoped Mott would approve and legitimize her actions. It was Mott who encouraged her to take over direction of the suffrage movement and to write its history. Mott's approval and support were very important to Stanton, and especially timely in 1840.

26. ECS, *Eighty Years,* p. 136.

27. Sarah Grimke to ECS, 9 April 1842, Theodore Stanton Collection, Douglass College, New Brunswick, N.J.; ECS, *Eighty Years,* pp. 111, 150.

28. ECS to Rebecca Eyster, 1 May 1847, *Letters,* pp. 15-16. The version of this letter published by her children is typically incomplete. The undated copy in the Theodore Stanton papers at Douglass College also says: "Soon after my marriage Theodore Weld said to me: Do not allow any of your correspondents to insult you by addressing your letters Mrs. Henry B. Stanton. . . . Furthermore, I have talked this matter over with my

husband and he says it would be quite *outré* for us to appear in the papers with either titles or men's names." Theodore Stanton Collection, Douglass College, New Brunswick, N.J.

29. One of the complaints Stanton had about Henry, and one of the issues she surrendered on was the naming of children after other people. Their children were named Daniel Cady, Henry Jr., Gerrit Smith, Theodore Weld, Margaret Livington, Harriot Eaton, and Robert Livingston Stanton. ECS to Elizabeth Smith Miller, 22 October 1852, Lutz Collection, Vassar College, Poughkeepsie, N.Y.

30. ECS, *Eighty Years,* p. 136.

31. Henry admitted in his letters to being guilty of "coldness and unkindness," and was criticized among her friends. Elizabeth Neall could not see what Elizabeth saw in Henry; she "personally would pick his eyes out if she were treated so badly." H. Stanton to ECS, 1843, ECS Collection, Library of Congress, Washington, D.C.; E. Neall to A. Kimber, 11 December 1841, Sydney Gay Collection, Columbia University, New York, N.Y.

32. Data on conveyance in manuscript of biography of ECS by her older daughter Margaret Stanton Lawrence, Manuscript Collection, Vassar College, Poughkeepsie, N.Y. This evidence was confirmed by correspondence with the Seneca Falls Museum, and ended speculation that the reason the Stantons stayed so long in Seneca Falls was because they had no equity with which to buy another property.

33. Henry had been a potential candidate since the 1830's when his name was circulated in Massachusetts as an antislavery candidate. He lost a Congressional nomination in 1844 in Boston, and switched to the Democrats when he moved to New York. His close reelection was related to an Erie Canal appropriations bill which was hotly contested, although some critics claimed that the narrow result was caused by ECS's bloomer attire during the campaign.

34. ECS, *Eighty Years,* p. 148.

35. Ibid., pp. 205-210. ECS recounts inspiring her neighbor to purchase a new stove while her husband was away, and to weep daintily when her husband objected.

36. ECS to SBA, 2 April 1852, *Letters,* pp. 41-42.

37. Stanton's role in the growth of the women's movement is detailed in Ellen C. DuBois, *Feminism and Suffrage: The Emergence of an Independent Women's Movement in America, 1848-1869* (Ithaca: Cornell University Press, 1978).

38. ECS to SBA, 10 September 1855, *Letters,* pp. 59-60.

39. ECS to SBA, 10 January 1856, ECS Collection, Library of Congress, Washington, D.C.

40. This is a constant complaint in every letter from Henry to Elizabeth in the Library of Congress Collection.

41. Daniel Cady to H. Stanton, 15 September (1853), ECS Collection, Library of Congress, Washington, D.C.

42. ECS to SBA, 10 September 1855, *Letters,* pp. 59-60.
43. Because so little of their correspondence remains, it is difficult to determine whether these stories were apochryphal or accurate. Stanton was included in the will filed after her father's death, but whether or not she received a share equal to her sisters' is uncertain.
44. Stanton believed in unswaddled babies, fresh air and fresh vegetables, exercise, little discipline, no Puritan God, bran cereals, and cheerfulness at meals. These and other childrearing practices she espoused on her lecture circuit to audiences of mothers.
45. ECS to Wendell Phillips, 18 August 1860, *Letters,* pp. 84-85.
46. ECS to SBA, 4 July 1858, Theodore Stanton Collection, Douglass College, New Brunswick, N.J.
47. *The Mill on the Floss* and *Adam Bede,* among others, made the marriage problem "all absorbing." ECS to SBA, 28 March 1860, *Letters,* p. 79. ECS searched for heroines in literature and found them in Mme. de Stael, Charlotte Bronte, George Sand, and George Eliot, authors who proved "greatness was an option for women."
48. ECS, *Eighty Years,* p. 295.
49. ECS to SBA, 20 July 1857, *Letters,* pp. 69-70.
50. *The Revolution,* 23 December 1869, p. 385, Library of Congress, Washington, D.C.
51. Report of the Second Women's Temperance Convention, April 20, 1852, printed in *The Lily,* May 1852, Vol. 4, no. 5, Library of Congress, Washington, D.C.
52. In 1859 the Indiana legislature passed a controversial divorce reform bill, adding desertion, habitual drunkenness, and cruelty to adultery as grounds for divorce. A similar bill, introduced in the New York legislature in 1860, lost by four votes in the Senate. These developments generated a public discussion of divorce, including an intense debate in the *New York Tribune* between Robert Dale Owen, author of the Indiana bill, and editor Horace Greeley, principal opponent of the New York bill. It was in this atmosphere that Stanton, encouraged by SBA and Lucy Stone, raised the issue. ESC, *Eighty Years,* pp. 215-216.
53. ECS, HWS, 1:717-725.
54. Ibid.
55. ECS, *Eighty Years,* p. 225.
56. ECS to SBA, 14 June 1860, *Letters,* pp. 82-83.
57. ECS to SBA, 1 March 1853, *Letters,* pp. 48-49.
58. ECS, *Eighty Years,* pp. 213-214, 225-226; Lutz, *Created Equal,* pp. 223-230.
59. ECS, HWS, 1:717-725.
60. ECS cautioned her sons to choose wives "with a spine and sound teeth" and her daughters to learn how to cook because they had a responsibility to make pleasant homes. Only two of her children never married, the oldest and youngest sons. Daniel was a rogue and Robert wrote on his Cornell alumnus record that he knew too much about matrimony to try it.

Eighty Years, pp. 331-332; inscription on cookbook, October 1878, Alma Lutz Collection, Vassar College, Poughkeepsie, N.Y.; Xerox Copy of Cornell records.

61. Long before Charlotte Perkins Gilman suggested variations of apartment hotels in *The Home,* Stanton had envisioned major changes in the ways women lived. Inspired by the utopian communities of the 1840's, she urged "associative households," collective arrangements that would allow housewives to share the work load or hire it out. At the end of her life she shared an apartment in New York City with her widowed daughter Margaret and her bachelor son Bob; they had a maid and meals were prepared in a restaurant.

62. ECS, *Eighty Years,* p. 229; ECS to SBA, 1 March 1853, *Letters,* pp. 48-49.

63. Henry had lost his job as Customs Inspector in New York in October 1863 after it was discovered that his son Neal, who was working for him, had taken bribes. It was a complicated scandal, and wrecked his chances to play elder statesman of the abolition movement. Rice, "Henry B. Stanton," pp. 423-460.

64. Stanton's great-granddaughter insists that the couple were estranged for several years before Henry's death, that the fight was one in which the children took sides, and that there was a legacy of rancor that took years to dissolve. There are no clues about the root of the disagreement— whether it was personal or political. When ECS was at home she lived in Tenafly, New Jersey while Henry stayed in New York City with one of his sons, although there were some visits and family events they shared during that twenty-year period. Interview, October 1976, with Rhoda Jenkins, Greenwich, Ct.

Charles E. Strickland

Juliette Low, the Girl Scouts, and the Role of American Women

Erik Erikson has often reminded us to look for the ways in which a crisis in the life cycle of a person joins with, and gains significance from, a crisis in the larger flow of historical events. He has demonstrated how gifted persons have managed to transcend their personal difficulties, by sensing the relation between their personal pain and a malaise in the larger society. In *Young Man Luther,* Erikson comments: "I wished to delineate in his life... one of those life crises which make conscious or unconscious, diagnosed or unofficial, patients out of people until they find a cure—and this often means a cause."[1]

Juliette Low did not, of course, play as large a role on the historical stage as Erikson's subjects, and she is remembered—if she is remembered at all—as the founder of the Girl Scouts.[2] But, like these better known personages, she made creative use of the convergence of personal and historical crises. The personal crisis in Low's life began with a disastrous marriage, which itself was prelude to despair in mid-life. The historical crisis that gave her personal difficulties a larger significance and that provided her with an opportunity to assuage them is more difficult to name, let alone describe, but two developments have particular relevance to her life and to the early history of the Girl Scouts.[3] The first was World War One and the heightened patriotism and nationalism that preceded it.[4] Another and more complex dimension of the crisis had to do with the widespread agitation and uncertainty concerning family life and the proper role of women. At the very time Low founded scouting for girls in America, a writer for the *Ladies Home Journal* commented:

> That there is a change taking place in our American girls and
> women is unquestioned. And it is so elusive, so baffling of

[Charles E. Strickland is an Associate Professor of History at Emory University. Presently involved in a study concerning the family in the art and life of Louisa May Alcott, he has published widely in educational and historical journals.]

description that it is proving the most attractive of subjects for discussion in the newspaper and magazine.[5]

Together, military conflict abroad and agitation for sexual equality at home supplied the context within which the movement for female scouting arose. The Girl Scouts, in turn, provided Juliette Low with a cause and hence with an opportunity to resolve a crisis of identity.

First, let us try to understand Low's personal crisis. Like so many of her generation, she found that she had been prepared by upbringing for one kind of role, only to discover that life presented her with quite another.[6] Her girlhood fitted her for the conventional life of what Anne Scott has called the "Southern Lady."[7] Born in Savannah in 1860, the second child of an affluent and prestigious family, Juliette grew up in a climate of opinion which demanded that the lady confine herself to the home. She was expected to be self-denying, innocent, pious, and totally submissive to the desires of her husband, dutifully bringing up his children and managing his household. Juliette's mother did not adhere in all respects to that image. Nellie Kinzie Gordon, a Chicago-born transplant to the South, often shocked staid Savannah with her eccentric ways, frank opinions, and colorful language.[8] Nevertheless, Nellie Gordon never challenged the fundamental ideas that a woman's place was in the home. She bore and reared six children, managed the household effectively, and usually submitted to her husband's decisions on major affairs. Moreover, she reared four daughters to follow in her footsteps. By the time she was eighteen, Juliette had acquired all the accomplishments suitable to a woman of her position, accomplishments which possessed little value in the marketplace, but which eminently suited her for the roles of wife, mother, and gracious hostess. She made her debut in Savannah society and entered into a round of parties and chaperoned visits to wealthy friends of the family, both in the United States and abroad. Despite a privileged and protected upbringing, Juliette was more shy than her mother, more naive and vulnerable, and lacked her mother's great beauty and poise. Nevertheless, she possessed considerable wit and charm, and she had been well groomed to become the decorative companion of a young man of wealth and position.

The difficulty was that her identity and role as a woman depended entirely on finding the right man, and here she made an unfortunate choice. Willy Low, son of an English multimillionaire, was handsome but thoroughly spoiled. A typical product of British high society in the Victorian era, Willy grew up without work or responsibility, engaged only in the activities associated with the "seasons"—the London Season, the Hunting Season, and the Shooting Season. His idle life seems to have exasperated even his father, who considered him good for nothing. Juliette's father shared this low estimate of Willy, for he believed that the possession of wealth should provide no exemption from hard work, and he worried about the prospect of Willy as a son-in-law. But Juliette was insistent. As she later explained, she simply found Willy "beautiful." With the encouragement of her mother, Juliette married Willy Low in a fashionable Savannah wedding in 1886. For fourteen years, thereafter, she pursued the life of a lady of leisure—hunting, entertaining, and dabbling in sculpture and painting.[9]

Juliette might have lived out the remainder of her years in this fashion, following the footsteps of her mother, save for several circumstances. For one thing, babies failed to appear, and Juliette was denied the role of motherhood. It is not known if the sterility of the marriage can be traced to Willy, but there is no doubt that he was responsible for the increasing loneliness she felt. He began spending more and more time away from his wife, engaged in extensive and lengthy hunting trips abroad. At this point Juliette began to realize that she was far too dependent on Willy, emotionally as well as financially. "I wish," she told her brother, "I was a self-reliant person, but although I ought to make myself do without any special human affection, I find myself each year craving it more."[10] She was, therefore, scarcely prepared for Willy's affair with a beautiful widow, whom he actually invited to stay in the Low home. Utterly humiliated, Juliette left Willy, and there followed four years of pain, marked by bitter wrangling over a divorce. The crowning degradation came in 1905, upon Willy's premature death, when he left the bulk of his fortune to his mistress, with orders for his lover to grant an allowance to his widow. Juliette fought back, contested the will, and at last secured from Willy's estate the equivalent of a half-million dollars.[11]

In the midst of this domestic crisis, at the age of forty, Juliette Low began a desperate review of her role as a woman, a reappraisal that would last for more than a decade. To be sure, the surface of her life revealed little of the inner turmoil. She was financially secure, and she played to the full the role of the merry widow, taking chaperoned trips to Egypt and India, flirting here and there with handsome British officers. It was during this period also that she developed eccentricities, giving rise to anecdotes concerning her poor memory and lack of punctuality that have delighted generations of Girl Scouts.[12] But, try as she might, she could not overcome a humiliating sense of failure. She began to compare herself to other women, especially to her mother, who seemed, in Juliette's eyes, to have fulfilled so perfectly the role of a woman. Juliette feared her mother would think she was inept at "managing" a man, and she spoke apologetically to Nellie Gordon of the "disgrace Willy has brought on me." Her plea was that her mother remember other qualities in her daughter in which she might take pride.[13] And yet, Juliette had to admit that she had little to show to the world, or more specifically, to her mother. "I am," she confessed to Nellie, "just an idle woman of the world, with no real work or duties."[14] Afflicted by deep depressions, and especially troubled by her childlessness, she took to avoiding Christmas gatherings of the family, where she would be sure to meet her sisters and their brood of youngsters.[15] To one of her sisters she explained, "I feel out of it with all the family and their children and I not having any. It may be a selfish view, but I get lonelier at Xmas than at any other time." Occasionally she toyed with the idea of going to Paris to study sculpturing.[16]

Indeed, Juliette might have become a sculptress of minor repute had it not been for events that eventually engulfed her, most notably the rising tide of patriotism that was prelude to the war in Europe. It was not that she paid much attention to world affairs, for her upbringing had taught her to leave such issues as war and politics to men. The turning point in her life came without warning and did not stem from abstract speculations about international politics. Characteristically for Juliette, it was the result of an intensely personal encounter. In the spring of 1911 she met Sir Robert Baden-Powell, who shared her interest in sculpture. He was also middle-aged, handsome, a bachelor, and a hero of the Boer War. Whether she saw in him a future husband is not clear, but she did find him charming. More important, he provided her with an idea for shaping her life which did not involve sculpturing. Sir Robert had recently founded the Boy Scouts, an organization which emerged from a wave of English nationalistic sentiment, concern for "social efficiency," enthusiasm for physical fitness, and a "back-to-nature" movement.[17] For Baden-Powell, a military hero himself, scouting was above all a way to make more efficient use of manpower in the interests of the British Empire. In particular, he saw Scouting as an ideal preparation for military service.[18]

More to the point, as far as Juliette's future was concerned, scouting might be a way to make more efficient use of womanpower as well. When British girls expressed an interest in scouting, Sir Robert had turned to his sister, Agnes Baden-Powell, persuading her to organize the "Girl Guides," in part, it appears, to keep young women out of the scouts. The Girl Guides always remained for Baden-Powell in the nature of an auxiliary unit, but he did admit that girls too could play a useful role in strengthening the British Empire, on the home front, if not on the battlefront.[19] The first handbook for the Girl Guides, appropriately subtitled, *How Girls Can Help Build the Empire,* explained to fledgling Guides:

> It is men's work to defend the Empire in person, and to be
> prepared to fight for their country and their homes. But you must
> not forget that you can play a very important part in holding the
> Empire by becoming experts at ambulance work and nursing.

In addition, the British girls were urged to learn the skills of woodcraft, camping, cooking in the open, and childcare.[20]

⸱ In any event, the British scouting movement provided Juliette Low with a possible way out of her personal crisis. What may have begun as simply a personal attraction to Baden-Powell rapidly developed into a plan for her life. Low admired the military hero because he had found a purpose in life which happened to take the shape of scouting. She compared herself unfavorably to Baden-Powell, confessing to him regret for her "wasted life."[21] She confided in her diary: "A sort of intuition comes over me that he believes I might make more out of life, and that he has ideas which, if I follow them, will open a more useful sphere of work before me in [the] future."[22] Within a year she was heading back to Savannah, carrying with her the English Girl Guide handbook, her head filled with plans for the organization of a similar group in America. On March 12, 1912, the first two patrols of the Girl Guides of America were formed in Savannah.[23]

If Low found in the Girl Guides hope of a cause for her life, there is little evidence that at first she thought of the possible link between scouting for girls and the larger social issue of women's proper sphere. For one thing, she carefully avoided committing herself or her organization in the growing agitation over women's suffrage. When a suffragist organization in Savannah pressured the Girl Scouts to take a stand on votes for women, Juliette counselled strict neutrality.[24] Given to scribbling verses from time to time, she could also advise women:

> Don't shout for votes, let men vote as they please.
> Daily endeavor to train up the young.
> There lies your burden, oh women of ease.[25]

Her advice to the Girl Scouts was in the same vein. The first American handbook for Girl Scouts contained an unmistakably conservative stance on the matter of women's proper sphere. Echoing the handbook of the English Girl Guides, Low's American version said:

> None of us like women who ape men. An imitation diamond is not as good as a real diamond. An imitation fur coat is not as good as real fur. Girls will do no good by trying to imitate boys; you will be only a poor imitation.[26]

A comparison of the early handbooks of the American Boy Scouts and Girl Scouts provides further evidence that scout leaders assumed boys and girls were heading toward different adult roles. Activities at the lower age levels were virtually identical, but as the adolescents grew older sexual differentiation increased, with the Girl Scouts badges heavily weighted toward the domestic sphere.[27]

But if Juliette Low adhered publicly to a traditional view of women's sphere, she was beginning privately to express greater awareness of the disparity in the status and role of the sexes. Shortly after the death of her father, in 1912, she told her brother: "If I had a beautiful and devoted wife, also children, and an absorbing occupation in business... if I was in the prime of manhood with a future stretching before me, I might grieve just as much for Papa but I would not *despair*."[28] Clearly, by 1912, Juliette felt more than a twinge of envy for the opportunities that men enjoyed to make use of their lives outside the family. Moreover, even if she maintained a public stance of neutrality on the issue of women's suffrage, she endorsed the movement privately, drawing a cartoon of herself holding a suffragist placard.[29]

As for her Girl Guides, Low was clearly appealing to what one historian has called that rising female generation who "resisted apprenticeship into ladylike decorum."[30] Wishing girls to be more independent and self-reliant, Juliette contributed a good deal to breaking down conventions about what a proper young lady might do and still remain a proper lady. Soon she had her girls donning uniforms, tying knots, playing basketball, hiking in the woods, doing calisthenics, and learning signalling and first aid.[31] The very idea that girls could survive a camp in the wilderness without the aid of men was in itself a radical idea in 1912, and nowhere more radical than in the South. Of one thing Low was certain: She did not wish girls to become useless and pampered ornaments. She herself had had a bitter taste of that kind of life and was not inclined to recommend it. In another of her verses, she said:

> Women of ease, before it's too late,
> Shoulder your burdens and open your eyes,
> Pleasures that pass cannot compensate
> For the prizes of life you seem to despise.[32]

She even included in her first handbook a brief section on careers for women.[33] But if Juliette Low held up to the girls any model of woman it was the figure of the early American pioneer, who might not seek to compete with men in the public sphere, but who did display strength, courage, and self-reliance. During the early years of girl scouting, Low often related to the girls, as they sat around a campfire, the story of her pioneer great-grandmother, who had survived kidnapping by Indians. Moreover, she advised Girl Scouts that they should learn how to load and fire a gun. "It is," she said, "one of the best means to 'be prepared.'"[34]

What Juliette Low sensed, and what she tried to persuade others of, was that adolescent girls like to do many of the same things as adolescent boys, whatever Victorian conventions might say. As if to underscore this idea, Low quietly changed the name of her organization, within the first few months,

from the "Girl Guides" to the "Girl Scouts." The first secretary of the
Savannah Girl Scouts has testified that the name change was for the purpose
of identifying the girls organization more closely with the Boy Scout
movement.[35] The change was made without Baden-Powell's knowledge or
approval, and it was an innovation that would prove later to be a source of
considerable difficulty for Low. Moreover, the blue uniform copied from the
English Girl Guides gave way to a military khaki outfit, replete with a broad-
brimmed scouting hat, remarkably similar in appearance to the Boy Scout
attire.[36] Low had also designed a uniform for herself and wore it with great
delight.[37]

Not content with these modest gestures toward greater freedom and
equality for girls, Juliette Low made still other changes, thanks largely to the
favorable climate provided by the war in Europe. She was an enthusiastic
Anglophile—not surprising considering her numerous English connections
—and she quickly took up the British cause as if it were her own.[38] Even
before the war, Low's American organization shared the British scout
emphasis on patriotism: the first American handbook was entitled *How Girls
Can Help Their Country*. After the onset of international conflict, the
American Girl Scouts were caught up in the fever of war preparedness. In
1916, a Girl Scout rally in Savannah featured the following scene:

> Girls entered singing the marching song and marched several times
> around the room. Before saluting, they gave the Girl Scout yell,
> and they saluted Mrs. Low, who gave a talk on preparedness. This
> stirring ceremony was followed by demonstrations in knot tying,
> first aid and signalling.[39]

A woman who joined the Scouts in 1917 recalled that these early years saw a
great deal of hiking, carrying knapsacks, and singing of war songs. It was all,
she remembered "very serious."[40] Low also organized a training school for
leaders, featuring such subjects as military marching drill, semaphore and
wigwagging, first aid, surgical dressings, swimming, calisthenics, fire drill and
rescue work.[41]

If the war subtly transformed the character of Girl Scouting, it also was the
key factor in the success of the movement. Without discounting the importance of Low's talents, energy and money—all of which she poured into
Scouting without stint—there can be little doubt that the international
conflict stimulated the interest of Americans in the new organization for girls.
After Juliette had the foresight to move the Girl Scout headquarters to
Washington, D.C., Lou Hoover, wife of Herbert Hoover, took an interest in
the fledgling organization, and Edith Galt Wilson, wife of the President,
agreed to serve as the first honorary president of the Girl Scouts. Some saw
scouting as a way to keep adolescent girls out of trouble in the unsettled

conditions that the impending war seemed to promote, while others saw the organization as a positive way to enlist the energies of girls in war-related activities, such as the selling of liberty bonds or Red Cross work.[42] Membership rolls swelled from a mere 565 in January of 1914 to more than 2000 after the onset of war, to 5000 in 1915, and to 50,000 by 1920.[43]

It appears that Juliette Low was more interested in supplying womanpower for the Allied cause than she was in women's equality. It should be noted, however, that she had already moved quite far from the heritage of her Southern upbringing. It should also be noted that she faced several difficulties which prevented her taking a more radical stance on women's role. In the first place, she was confronted with a rival organization for adolescent girls, which was dominated by men, which was openly endorsed by the Boy Scouts, and which adhered to a philosophy much more conservative than her own. The Camp Fire Girls had been officially incorporated in the same month that Low organized her Girl Guides.[44] Dr. Luther Gulick, a well-recognized leader in the American youth movement, served as first president of the Camp Fire Girls, and he set out, with the assistance of his wife, Charlotte Vetter Gulick, to build an organization for girls that would be clearly distinguishable from the Boy Scouts—a fact which undoubtedly accounts for the enthusiastic support Camp Fire Girls received from males. Gulick's position could not have been clearer: Speaking to a meeting of youth leaders in 1911, Gulick said that for girls to copy the Boy Scout movement would be "utterly and fundamentally evil."[45]

There was, to begin with, the all-important matter of the name. Unlike "Girl Scouts," "Camp Fire Girls" would not be easily confused with Boy Scouts. Moreover, as Charlotte Gulick recalled, the name was settled on because "keeping the fire burning in a camp or in a home is a feminine activity."[46] There was also the matter of dress. Instead of the khaki Girl Scout uniform, which closely resembled the garb of the boys, the Camp Fire Girls wore a "ceremonial gown," which emphasized the girl's role as an Indian maiden, as did the practice of girls' wearing their hair either hanging or in braids over their shoulders.[47] The Camp Fire organization, unlike the Girl Scouts, also made much of training in aesthetic sensibility, for it was Luther Gulick's contention that "beauty" was the peculiar province of women.[48] But the central emphasis of the Camp Fire movement, as Gulick saw it, was to restore to women the "romance" of domestic work. "We have tried," he explained, "to take drudgery and make it a game; to strip the dull gray covering of the common place from the significant acts of daily life."[49] Here, indeed, was a conservative response to the emergence of the "new woman": simply transform her, through a semimystical process, into a charming and dutiful Indian maiden, who will tend the domestic fires. The formula was successful. Although the Girl Scout enrollment increased, Camp Fire enrollment increased even faster, and it was not until 1930, in fact, that the Girl Scouts forged ahead in membership.[50]

The second difficulty Low faced was that her mild gestures toward sexual equality in scouting encountered fierce opposition. Given the philosophy of the Camp Fire Girls, it was not surprising that Gulick's organization—together with the Boy Scouts—found Juliette Low's ideas radical. There emerged a decade-long conflict, featuring on one side Low and her co-workers, and on the other side an alliance of Boy Scout and Camp Fire Girl leaders. The hapless Robert Baden-Powell, *paterfamilias* of the scouting movement, found himself in the middle, attempting from England to keep peace among the American organizations. As early as 1913, Boy Scout officials were objecting to Low's use of the name "scouts" for girls, but it was the growing enrollment of Girl Scouting that finally brought the conflict to a head.[51] Local Boy Scoutmasters were complaining about the effect of the Girl Scouts in "feminizing" scouting, and the Chief Boy Scout Executive carried his complaints to Baden-Powell.[52] The American boy scout leader resented not only the name "Girl Scouts" but also the fact that the Girl Scouts should "just baldly adopt our whole program and undertake to ape our boys in everything they do." Baden-Powell sided with the Boy Scouts and warned Low that parents might assume that girls were doing the same work as boys.[53] Having girls engage in the same activities as boys was, of course, approximately what Juliette had in mind. For his part, Gulick made it clear what he thought of the military garb and activities of his rivals. Speaking in 1918 before a group of Camp Fire Girls, he pointedly reminded them that soldiers returning from the war "will not come back caring to see you in khaki or doing military tactics—they will have had all and more of that than they care for—but to see you and be with you as women, women who are playing their own part rather than trying to play the man's part in the world."[54] Girl Scout officials responded in kind, finding the Camp Fire program "sentimental," its Indian lore "irrelevant," its ritual "pointless," and its ceremonial Indian costume a "fantastic night gown." As for Juliette Low herself, she stuck by her name, her program, and her uniform, and she predicted that the organization would eventually win the enrollment battle.[55]

Only after her death was Low's prophecy realized, but it was clear as early as 1920 that the Girl Scouts would survive and grow as an organization. Given the conservative climate of opinion within which she was reared, and within which she worked, her achievement was an impressive one. In the face of opposition from Camp Fire Girls and the Boy Scouts, she displayed courage by insisting on the right of girls to call themselves "scouts," and by insisting on the ability of girls to do more than keep the home fires burning. By seeking to make girls more independent and self-reliant, Low perhaps contributed in small part to helping later generations of women cope effectively with the kinds of difficulties which she herself had encountered at mid-life. A woman who only twenty years before had been a mere ornament in the home of an English millionaire could in 1919 boast proudly of her organization:

> The result is the development of the undefinable something in Girl Scouts, which we call the scouting spirit, the esprit de corps, and an insistence on fair play, generous dealing, team work, coupled with individual development, which can all be summed up in the one word "character." Girl Scouts of today are the women of tomorrow. Even as young girls they are eager to do their share of the world's work.[56]

Low might have added that in the cause of scouting she had found her own work as well.

Notes

1. Erikson's *Young Man Luther: a Study in Psychoanalysis and History* (New York: Norton, 1958), p. 14.
2. In preparing this essay, the author is indebted to Shirley Carson, Director, and Charlotte Hallock, Archivist, of the Juliette Gordon Low Girl Scout National Center, Savannah (hereafter cited as GSNC); Mrs. Lila Hawes, Director of the Georgia Historical Society, Savannah; Mary Lecat, Librarian/Archivist, National Headquarters, Girl Scouts of the United States of America, New York City; and Carolyn Wallace, Director, Southern Historical Collection, Chapel Hill, N.C. Special thanks are due Mrs. Mary Stuart Platt, Savannah, the niece of Juliette Low; Mrs. Arthur M. Phillips, Savannah, former director of the GSNC; and Mrs. Florence Crane Schwalb, Savannah, one of the original Girl Scouts, for sharing with the author their recollections of Low.
3. For two efforts to analyze historical changes before World War One, see Henry F. May, *The End of American Innocence: A Study of The First Years of Our Own Time, 1912-1917* (New York: Knopf, 1959); and Robert Wiebe, *The Search for Order, 1877-1920* (New York: Hill & Wang, 1967).
4. See, for example, H.C. Peterson, *Propaganda for War: The Campaign Against American Neutrality, 1914-1917* (Norman, Okla.: University of Oklahoma Press, 1939).
5. Dudley Sargeant, "Are Athletics Making Girls Masculine?" *Ladies Home Journal* 29 (March 1912): 11. On the "New Woman," See David Kennedy, *Birth Control in America: the Career of Margaret Sanger* (New Haven, Conn., Yale University Press, 1970), ch. 2; and James McGovern, "The American Woman's Pre-World War One Freedom in Manners and

Morals," in Ronald Hogeland, ed., *Woman and Womanhood in America* (Lexington, Mass.: D.C. Heath, 1973), pp. 153-162. For other aspects of the "woman question" during the period, see Eleanor Flexner, *Century of Struggle: The Women's Rights Movement in the United States* (Cambridge: Belknap Press of Harvard University Press, 1959; rev. ed. Harvard University Press, 1975), ch. 19; Peter Filene, *Him/Her/Self: Sex Roles in Modern America* (New York: Harcourt, Brace, Jovanovich, 1975, 1976 second ed.), chs. 1-4; and Mary Ryan, *Womanhood in America: From Colonial Times to the Present* (New York: New Viewpoints, 1975), pp. 195-249.

6. For Juliette Low's girlhood, see Gladys Shultz and Daisy Lawrence, *Lady from Savannah: The Life of Juliette Low* (Philadelphia: Lippincott, 1958), esp. chs. 8, 9. In addition, Juliette's brother Arthur has provided an especially revealing portrait, "As Her Family Knew Her," in Anne Hyde Choate and Helen Ferris, eds., *Juliette Low and the Girl Scouts* (Garden City, N.Y.: Doubleday, Doran & Co., Inc., 1928), ch. 5.

7. Anne Firor Scott, *The Southern Lady: From Pedestal to Politics, 1830-1930* (Chicago: University of Chicago Press, 1970), esp. Preface and ch. 1.

8. A letter to her son Arthur, dated February 24, 1886, congratulated him for punching a boy in the nose for calling Southerners cowards. Another to Juliette, dated November 9, 1910, hoped a senator would "go to hell" for voting for a tariff. (Letters in possession of Mrs. Mary Stuart Platt, Savannah.)

9. For a portrait of the life of the British elite, see Ralph G. Martin, *Jennie: the Life of Lady Randolph Churchill* (Englewood Cliffs, N.J.: Prentice Hall, 1969-71), pp. 47-49. For Willy's character, see Willy Low to W.W. Gordon, December 18, 1885, Gordon Papers, Southern Collection; Shultz and Lawrence, *Lady from Savannah*, pp. 165-66; and Arthur Gordon, "I Remember Daisy," p. 8, typescript in Savannah Public Library.

10. Juliette Low to Arthur Gordon, August 6, 1901, Gordon Papers, Southern Collection.

11. For the entire episode, see Shultz and Lawrence, *Lady from Savannah*, ch. 15.

12. Especially revealing of her activities during this period is her "Diary (1907-1908)," Gordon Papers, Southern Collection. See also Rowland Leigh, "Our Delightful Companion," in Choate and Ferris, *Juliette Low and the Girl Scouts*, ch. 12; and Schultz and Lawrence, *Lady from Savannah*, p. 268.

13. Juliette Low to Arthur Gordon, February 1, 1901; and Juliette Low to Nellie Kinzie Gordon, November 3, 1903, Gordon Papers, Southern Collection.

14. Juliette Low to Nellie Kinzie Gordon, quoted in Shultz and Lawrence, *Lady from Savannah*, p. 260.

15. Juliette reported a particularly severe siege of "cholera morbus" after her parents' golden wedding anniversary. Juliette Low, "Diary (1907-1908)," p. 4, Gordon Papers, Southern Collection.

16. Juliette Low to Mabel Gordon Leigh, September 29 (1909?), Gordon Papers, Southern Collection.
17. See John R. Gillis, *Youth and History: Tradition and Change in European Age Relations, 1770-Present* (New York: Academic Press, 1974), esp. 142-48; David MacLeod, "Good Boys Made Better: The Boy Scouts of America, Boys' Brigades, and YMCA Boys' Work, 1880-1920," (Dissertation, University of Wisconsin, 1973), esp. ch. 7; and Peter Schmitt, *Back to Nature: the Arcadian Myth in Urban America* (New York: Oxford University Press, 1969), ch. 10.
18. J.O. Springhall, "The Boy Scouts, Class and Militarism in Relation to British Youth Movements, 1908-1930," *International Review of Social History* 17 (1972): 3-23; Gillis, *Youth and History,* p. 146; MacLeod, "Good Boys Made Better," pp. 218-219.
19. For Robert Baden-Powell's views on the female side of scouting, see his letter to Juliette Low, January 16, 1917, Gordon Family Papers, Georgia Historical Society; and his article, "Girl Scouts or Guides?," typescript in Archives, National Headquarters, Girl Scouts of the U.S.A.
20. Agnes Baden-Powell, *The Handbook for Girl Guides, or How Girls Can Help Build the Empire* (London: Thomas Nelson and Sons, 1911), esp. p. 414.
21. Juliette Low, "Diary," June 17, 1911, Archives, GSNC, Savannah.
22. Ibid., June 1, 1911.
23. Nina Anderson Pape, "History of Scouting," p. 1, typescript in the Archives, National Headquarters, Girl Scouts of the U.S.A. Pape was a close Savannah friend with whom Low first discussed her plans for the Girl Guides and who assisted her in the early years of the movement.
24. Juliette Low to Edith Johnston, March 26, 1915, Gordon Family Papers, Archives, Georgia Historical Society.
25. Juliette Low, "A Call," typescript in Archives, GSNC.
26. Girl Scouts of the U.S.A., *How Girls Can Help Their Country* (facsimile of the 1913 edition published by the Girl Scouts of the United States of America, New York, 1972), p. 12.
27. *How Girls Can Help Their Country,* pp. 123-125, 128-136; and William D. Murray, George Pratt, and A.A. Jameson, *The Official Handbook for Boys* (Garden City, N.Y.: Doubleday, Page, 1911), pp. 16-44.
28. Juliette Low to Arthur Gordon, December 1, 1912, Gordon Papers, Southern Collection.
29. The Cartoon is in the Archives, GSNC.
30. Filene, *Him/Her/Self,* p. 15.
31. Girl Guide Headquarters, "Reports," (November, 1912, through April, 1913), Archives GSNC: Sallie Margaret M'Alphin, "Memoirs of the Formative Days of the Girl Scouts," *Savannah Morning News,* October 13, 1937.
32. Juliette Low, "A Call," typescript in Archives, GSNC.
33. *How Girls Can Help Their Country,* pp. 112-13.
34. Ibid., p. 11; Doris Hough, "Juliette Low Goes Camping," in Choate and Ferris, eds., *Juliette Low and the Girl Scouts,* pp. 141-142.
35. Edith Johnston, "Report of the Savannah Organization of Girl Scouts for

Eight Months, from October 15, 1912, to June 15, 1913," p. 3 (typescript in Archives, GSNC).

36. Ibid., p. 4.
37. Josephine Daskam Bacon, "Here and There with Her in Girl Scouting," in Choate and Ferris, eds., *Juliette Low and the Girl Scouts,* p. 167.
38. Shultz and Lawrence, *Lady from Savannah,* pp. 334-335.
39. Savannah Headquarters, Girl Scouts, "Report for June, 1916," Archives, GSNC.
40. Untitled clipping from *Lansing State Journal,* May 17, 1970, which recounts experiences of Mrs. John F. Dye. Archives, GSNC.
41. "First Training Camp for Leaders," *The Rally* 1 (October 1917): 10.
42. Shultz and Lawrence, *Lady from Savannah,* p. 350; Ethel Demady, "Interview with Doris Hough," and "Interview with Anne Choate," both in Archives, National Headquarters, Girl Scouts of the U.S.A.
43. Figures on enrollment are collated from National Headquarters, "Reports," and "Girl Scouts of the U.S.A., Highlights of the First Fifty Years," both in Archives, GSNC.
44. Helen Buckler, et al., *Wo-He-Lo: The Story of the Camp Fire Girls, 1910-1960* (New York: Holt, Rinehart & Winston, 1961).
45. Ibid., p. 22.
46. Ibid., pp. 25-26.
47. Ibid., pp. 138-139.
48. Ibid., p. 23.
49. Gulick, "The Camp Fire Girl Movement and Education," in *The Journal of Education* 75 (June 20, 1912): 700-701.
50. Comparative figures are supplied in *The New International Yearbook for the Year 1931* (New York: Funk & Wagnalls Co., 1932), edited by H.T. Wade, pp. 137, 362.
51. Edith Johnston, "Early History of the Girl Scouts," p. 5 (typescript in Gordon Family Papers, Georgia Historical Society).
52. J.S. Mendenhall to James West, April 9, 1917; and James West to Robert Baden-Powell, April 12, 1917, Archives, National Headquarters, Girl Scouts of the U.S.A.
53. Robert Baden-Powell to Juliette Low, May 14, 1917, Gordon Family Papers, Georgia Historical Society.
54. Quoted in Buckler, et al., *Wo-He-Lo,* p. 156.
55. See correspondence in "Camp Fire Girls" folder in Archives, National Headquarters, Girl Scouts of the U.S.A., especially C.W. Rothschild to Jane Rippen (undated); Juliette Low to Jane Rippen, August 11, 1919; Frances Dodge to Jane Rippen, September 8, 1919; Josephine Bacon to Jane Rippen, July 30, 1919; Jane Rippen to Mrs. Julius Rosenwald, March 4, 1920.
56. Juliette Low, *Girl Scouts as an Educational Force* (Washington, D.C.: U.S. Department of the Interior, Bureau of Education, 1919), Bulletin, N. 33, p. 6.

III. Beyond the Home,
Beyond Womanhood

Introduction

Women did go beyond the home in both thought and action. But how far did and could they go, figuratively and literally, and what were the consequences for themselves and their society? Broadly speaking, this is the subject of the four essays in this section. Given the boundaries of wifehood and motherhood and a society which dictated that woman assume that role as a primary and exclusive obligation, to go beyond the home was in the eyes of many to go beyond womanhood. Posing the question and the subject differently, to determine how far society *let* women go beyond the home and to what extent it facilitated or obstructed women's efforts to do so, is better to understand the nature and significance of "womanhood" for society. Put simply, did women's emergence from the home threaten any elements of the society? Did it challenge the conception of a proper order of being and events?

For women as individuals, the attempt to assume roles beyond domesticity had great significance. Why did they attempt to do so? What were their motivations? The experience of subjection to a rigid definition of being and place obviously had to affect women's sense of self and the possibilities of self, the nature and the degree of their need for fulfillment, and their responses to what was in some respects a new environment. The question needs to be asked, then, how far did women *let* themselves go? And once beyond the home, were their experiences the same as those of men, or different? Did they face the same challenges or did the meaning of womanhood guarantee different challenges? The answers to any and all of these questions can help elucidate the common humanity shared as well as underline the unique quality of women's lives, and contrast, female to male, perceptions, orientations, and experiences.

Blanche Hersh's essay explores the ideology of nineteenth-century feminists. Locating their feminism in its historical context by tracing the roots of their ideology to the human rights philosophy of radical antislavery, Hersh dissolves the apparent paradox of these feminists' demand for equality and their continuing belief in women's distinctive capacities and obligations. Part of the struggle engaged in by these feminist-abolitionists, as Hersh terms them, involved conflicting perspectives on the nature of "True Woman-hood." This early generation of feminists transcended their culture in their rejection of rigidly defined roles and activities assigned on the basis of gender. But they also subscribed to conventional assumptions about the special responsibilities of women as wives and mothers. These seemingly contradic-tory positions were reconciled in the concept of overlapping spheres and dual roles for both sexes whereby women were defined as human beings and citizens of the republic, first, and wives and mothers, second. As Hersh notes, the feminist-abolitionists wanted freedom from psychological and economic dependence upon men with the ultimate goal of granting both sexes unre-stricted self-development and eliminating many gender differences. Short of the attainment of their ideal society, however, by maintaining the traditional view of woman's moral superiority of nature and function while demanding access to man's world, these feminists were saying that more was less.

The women's crusade for temperance during the winter of 1873 and 1874 is the subject of Ruth Bordin's essay. The crusade not only led to the formation of the Women's Christian Temperance Union, but it was also a tributary of the women's movement in late-nineteenth-century America. Temperance advocates, in general, and women, in particular, were motivated in large part by what they perceived to be a direct threat to a proper social arrangement of the sexes. Women were dependent economically and socially upon men, and the exclusivity of public drinking establishments, or saloons, as well as the spectre of drunkenness appeared to them to pose a severe threat to the family and woman's domestic sphere. Women's involvement, then, stemmed direct-ly from traditional interests. Of new and perhaps greater significance, however, as Bordin suggests, was the fact that, having already played an active and public role in post-Civil-War temperance, women, with the eruption of the crusade, became involved in the movement in numbers greater than those for any previous reform effort. Indeed, they dominated temperance for the next three decades, and the WCTU, in turn, became the largest women's organization of the nineteenth century.

Characterized as "a baptism of power and liberty" by a contemporary observer, Bordin argues that the crusade had a great impact upon women's consciousness. Their active involvement in the public sphere, their use of militant tactics, and, not the least important, their success in the achievement of public objectives, laid to rest for many the belief that women would continue to remain subordinate to men and confine themselves to domestici-ty. The crusade demonstrated that women could exercise worldly power and influence public policy for their own ends. Armed with a more aggressive, and for some, unwomanly identity, these women would join the ranks of suffragists to demand full participation in the sphere which had been man's alone.

Winifred Bolin's essay points to the changing character of women's participation in the larger society. Going beyond the home promised new experiences and the opportunity to learn new skills and tasks, but it also promised new problems for both women and society if neither, particularly society, forgot old ways. Larger percentages of women entered the labor force in the early twentieth century and new opportunities emerged with the heightened demand for workers in clerical and service occupations. However, the Great Depression adversely affected these already established patterns, and Bolin shows that the impact upon female employment was both different and more difficult to gauge that that upon male employement. More specifically, working women found it increasingly difficult to enter white-collar and professional occupations. The reasons, Bolin argues, were twofold. Obviously, there was the obstacle of unemployment. While at first glance, the relatively low rate of unemployment in certain categories of female white-collar and professional occupations appears to indicate that the obstacle was not a particularly serious one, closer examination reveals that white-collar workers such as saleswomen tended to be underemployed, while those in professional occupations experienced losses in status as well as money.

The problems of unemployment were compounded by traditional conceptions of woman's role and place. As the lack of support from New Deal legislation indicates, women were not the traditional breadwinners in society, and in part because of that fact and view, women were increasingly hindered from moving into white-collar and professional occupations and the advancement of those already there was retarded. Women could leave the labor force unnoticed, or face part-time work, a drop in wages, and less skilled employment. They also faced antagonism in the marketplace. Women, it was said, were at fault on two counts. Supposedly the beneficiaries of other sources of support, they were working only for "pin money," and even worse, they were displacing males in the labor force. As faulty as these assumptions may have been, Bolin suggests that they adversely conditioned the experiences and opportunities of women. Not surprisingly, the married woman confronted the greatest prejudice. The victim of discriminatory policies, the plight of such women made it clear that society still considered woman's place as in the home.

The commonalities as well as the differences of the female and male experience is an implicit theme of Susan Hartmann's essay examining the ideologies of feminist organizations during the Second World War. Active a century after the beginning of women's involvement in reform movements of the nineteenth century, these organizations pointed to changes as well as continuities in women's experiences. They also provide a means by which two interrelated questions can be addressed. How did the war affect the experiences of women? Perhaps the most obvious impact was the entrance of millions of women into the labor force. Just as obvious, and even more striking, was the employment of women in nearly all occupational strata. These conditions prompt the major question addressed by Hartmann. What was the response of women's organizations to these altered circumstances? Hartmann notes that basic assumptions about women's aspirations and activism have either neglected or distorted important facets of twentieth-century feminism. Historians, for example, have tended to emphasize a supposed decline in feminism beginning with the passage of the Nineteenth Amendment and ending with the protests of the sixties. While Bolin's essay on the years of the Great Depression supports this analysis, Hartmann finds in the forties a broad spectrum of organizations engaged in efforts to broaden women's opportunities for employment and to increase their representation in administrative and policy-making positions.

Historians have also seen disagreement about the Equal Rights Amendment as the major obstacle to a unified feminism and have thereby neglected other equally substantive issues. Hartmann's analysis points to the significant role played by class and race as obstacles to female solidarity and serves as a needed reminder that factors other than those based upon gender contribute to women's perspectives and experiences. Factors of gender separated women's lives from men's, but disparate class and ethnic backgrounds, personalities, and circumstances mandated against a monolithic experience for women as individuals or in groups.

Blanche Glassman Hersh

The "True Woman" and the "New Woman" in Nineteenth-Century America: Feminist-Abolitionists and a New Concept of True Womanhood

"True womanhood" was an ideal subscribed to by both feminists and antifeminists in nineteenth-century America. Those opposed to broadening woman's sphere and granting her equal rights charged that doing so would "unsex" her: she would fall from true womanhood. Feminists argued that true womanhood was a fixed and natural condition; a woman could enter into the man's world of work and political action and still remain a true woman.[1]

These were obviously different conceptions of what constituted the "true woman," reflecting conflicting views of woman's "true" role and "proper" sphere. This essay explores these differences in order to gain new insight into the ideology of the first generation of feminists—the women who first spoke out and organized for women's rights in the antebellum period. I call these women feminist-abolitionists because of their roots in the antislavery movement, and because their feminist belief and rhetoric were strongly influenced by the human rights ideology of radical antislavery. This generation includes women best known for their later suffragist leadership—Susan B. Anthony, Elizabeth Cady Stanton, Lucy Stone—as well as those mentioned in antislavery works—Sarah and Angelina Grimké, Lucretia Mott, Lydia Maria Child, Abby Kelley Foster. Also important are women whose names barely appear in the literature of either movement—Antoinette Brown Blackwell, Amelia Bloomer, Mary A. Livermore, Paulina Wright Davis, and others.[2]

The essay is part of the process of unraveling a paradox discovered in an earlier study of fifty-one feminist-abolitionists.[3] The world-view of this group

[Coordinator of the Women's Studies Program at Northeastern Illinois University, Blanche Glassman Hersh has recently published *The Slavery of Sex: Feminist-Abolitionists in America*. She is also the author of several articles on nineteenth-century feminism. The essay reprinted here originally appeared in the *Maryland Historian*.]

incorporated an apparently contradictory set of values and beliefs. The central demand of the antebellum movement was the right of a woman to define her own sphere and not have it defined for her by men; she was to be free to do whatever she wished and was capable of doing. "Emancipation" meant access to the world outside the home, and freedom from economic and psychological dependence on men. In their own lives, the early feminists had a remarkable degree of freedom compared with other nineteenth-century women. Fourteen of the fifty-one remained unmarried and defended their right to do so, a defiant act for their day. Twenty-eight of the remaining thirty-seven married women chose men who were also feminists. As a result, they were able to continue their involvement in reform after marriage. A few traveled widely, leaving children and home in the care of husbands.

However, "emancipation" did not mean renunciation of the rights and duties of the true woman. The feminists expressed a firm belief that woman's highest and most sacred duty was to the home, and they shared society's view of woman as moral guardian of the family and the nation. Their passion for sexual equality seemed to be inconsistent with their belief in woman's moral superiority and special domestic obligations. How did they reconcile these diverse commitments?

It is necessary to attempt also to root these feminists more firmly in their own culture. The women's movement of the 1960's and 1970's has been happily reclaiming these lost heroines, but the excitement of discovery has often been accompanied by an ahistorical uprooting of the women from their cultural and ideological soil. An analysis of their beliefs, in the context of the norms of their own day, should help us to regain a historical perspective.

The popular ideal of womanhood—as depicted in sermons, ladies' magazines, educational tracts, and other prescriptive literature—has been documented by Barbara Welter in a now-classic essay, "The Cult of True Womanhood, 1820-1860."[4] Here Welter describes the cardinal virtues expected of the true woman, who would also be a true wife: piety, purity, submissiveness, and domesticity. This ideal woman existed within a societal framework in which women and men were assigned narrowly defined roles and separate spheres of action, predicated on presumably immutable, divinely ordained sex differences. The relationship between the sexes was based on an unequal division of power and status, also viewed as part of the natural order.

The feminist-abolitionists demanded important alterations in this conceptual framework, and accepted the assigned feminine attributes only insofar as they were compatible with their own perspective. Rejecting society's rigid role definition and separation of the sexes (described as "a perfect caricature of the true business of life"[5]), they developed an alternative concept of overlapping spheres and flexible, dual roles for women and men.

This position was never brought forth fully developed at a given moment in time, but was an assumption behind most of the movement's arguments and demands. It evolved naturally from the feminists' commitment to sexual equality as well as from their belief in women's special moral and domestic responsibilities, and it reconciled these apparently inconsistent views.

The feminists' conception of sexual spheres was derived from the distinction between women's primary existence as human beings and citizens of the Republic, and their secondary function in their social roles as wives and mothers. As explained by Elizabeth Cady Stanton, principal philosopher and propagandist of nineteenth-century feminism: "Womanhood is the great fact, wifehood and motherhood its incidents."[6] The basis for Stanton's statement can be visualized as two circles overlapping with the result that there appear one large area and two smaller areas. The large area is the one shared by women and men in their primary function. Here they occupy the same role, and their rights and responsibilities in both family and society are identical. Innate sex differences are here unimportant. The two smaller, peripheral areas are assigned one to each sex. In their respective areas, women and men function in their unique social roles, dictated by natural differences, duties, and talents. Woman's function is to nurture and preserve the family, man's to provide for the family by his labor in the outside world. In these roles, each would give priority to her or his special obligations while also being free to serve in other areas.

The concept of women as citizens and spiritual beings first, lay at the heart of the new feminist ideology. It reflected the influence of abolitionist thought and Enlightenment ideas from which it derived, as well as the direction in which the feminists' religious beliefs were developing. Women were citizens of the Republic first, and wives and mothers second; as citizens, they had natural, God-given rights that were the same for both sexes and extended to all areas of life—family as well as government. As spiritual beings, women, as well as men, were enhanced by a divine presence which enabled them to transcend their earthly limitations and strive for the ideal state, both as individuals and as human beings committed to the achievement of a perfect society. The spiritual being was greater than the social being; one was a whole, the other only a part.

The earliest public defense of this concept was made by Sarah Grimké, an important forerunner of nineteenth-century feminism, whose 1837 *Letters on the Equality of the Sexes* anticipated much of the movement's ideology. She defended the right of antislavery women to speak publicly by arguing that the spheres and duties of women as citizens and as spiritual beings were identical with those of men; only in their narrower social roles were their responsibilities different. Her sister, Angelina, made this idea more explicit: "Rights and duties depend *not* on *sex* but on our *relations* in life; as women we have *no* peculiar duties, but as mothers, wives and daughters we have." Women and men had identical areas of freedom and responsibility in regard to moral issues which affected them as human beings, but different provinces when they functioned in specific sex roles.[7]

The most eloquent expression of the feminist-abolitionist view of woman's dual roles appeared at the end of the century in Elizabeth Cady Stanton's celebrated speech "The Solitude of Self." Stanton reminded her audience that a woman could be considered in four separate ways. As an individual human soul, Protestantism granted her the right of individual conscience and judgment. As a citizen in a republic, she was due the same rights as all others. As a woman, her rights and duties were still the same as a man's—individual happiness and development. Only in her fourth role, in her "incidental relations of life, such as mother, wife, sister, daughter," did she acquire special duties and training.[8]

This basic construct gave rise to two major themes of antebellum feminist rhetoric: women shared with men a common humanity and therefore a common sphere of action; women, as the mothers of the race, were the morally superior sex and therefore had special obligations and functions. ("Does not the maternity of woman give her a nearer resemblance to God?" asked Harriot Hunt, the beloved "little doctor" of the group.[9]) Both themes appeared in the arguments for broadening woman's sphere: emancipation would enable her to develop her human potential to the fullest, and would also permit her "civilizing" influence to have broader scope.

Both themes appear in virtually all antebellum feminist speeches. Frances Gage, mother of eight and fervent worker for her "triune cause" (abolition, temperance, women's rights), addressed the first Ohio women's rights convention (1851) and demanded an equal position for women in society. "Are not the natural wants and emotions of humanity common to, and shared equally by, both sexes?" she asked rhetorically. Man could not call on nature for the authority to assign woman to an inferior position because "Nature made woman his superior when she made her his mother." It followed that women, freed from their bonds, would "purify, elevate, ennoble humanity."[10]

Lucy Stone, who became in the 1840's the first antislavery agent to lecture solely on women's rights, was the prototypical feminist-abolitionist. All her speeches reflected the duality of woman as citizen/human being and as wife/mother. "What is the sphere of woman?" she asked in an early speech. Her answer was clear: "God has defined it by making her a human being. . . by virtue of her humanity, all the rights and duties which belong to any human being belong to her. . . . As moral and responsible beings, God has given the same sphere of action to man and woman. . . ." She demanded for every woman the right to develop every faculty she possessed, but argued that education was needed to "make women better wives and mothers" as well as "fuller human beings." Her philosophy was summed up in a speech to the 1853 national women's rights convention in which she defended woman's domestic role while urging her to enter business and the professions: "Any woman who stands on the throne of her own house, dispensing there the virtues of love, charity, and peace... occupies a higher position than any crowned head. However, woman could do more...."[11]

Given this new perspective, what would be the attributes of a "true woman" in society? Here, too, the feminist-abolitionists made significant modifications in the popular ideal, as described by Welter. They accepted the standards of "piety," "purity," and "domesticity"—but with important qualifications. The virtue of "submissiveness" in women was totally rejected as inconsistent with the sexual equality they demanded. These departures from the norm serve to dispel further the apparent inconsistencies of the developing feminist ideology.

The feminists placed a high value on piety and purity, especially since they shared society's view of woman as naturally more endowed with the "higher" elements of human nature and less susceptible to the "lower" passions. Sarah Grimké noted that "the strength of the moral world lies in woman... in her heart religion has found its home." Even Elizabeth Cady Stanton, iconoclast supreme, supported the conventional wisdom that woman was "superior to man in the affections, high moral sentiments, and religious enthusiasm."[12]

But the feminists added an important qualification to the popular prescription for true womanhood: true *men* ought to be as pious and pure as true women. Though they accepted the idea of inherent sex differences, they were first and foremost reformers committed to the romantic belief in human perfectibility. Women and men could, and indeed should, improve themselves. The emancipation of women and slaves would be only part of the moral regeneration of the whole human family. Women would be the leaders in this crusade, but the goal was to abolish the double moral standard of society and elevate man to woman's naturally higher spiritual level. Amelia Bloomer, whose *Lily* (1849-1856) was one of the few antebellum newspapers committed to women's rights, wrote often of the part to be played by proper childrearing in "making the world better." Mothers were beseeched to "impress indelibly upon the minds of their children, the idea of the perfect equality of the sexes." Instead of the "false notions of purity and honor," a son should be taught that "the same purity, delicacy and refinement, which he admires in the girl, should characterize him in all his words and actions."[13]

In other ways, too, women and men were encouraged to perfect themselves, and all of these improvements served to forward the abolition of separate sexual spheres and functions, and the minimization of sex differences. Men were to become more affectionate, gentle, and sensitive like women; women would give up their dependence and timidity and become more self-reliant and courageous like men. Sarah and Angelina Grimké were among the first to point to the opportunities for self-improvement and the perfection of society that would be achieved by the establishment of equality within a common sphere of activity. Angelina explained that this equality would benefit men as well as women. "Woman has been used," she charged, "as a drudge or cared for like a spoiled child, and man has inflicted no less an injury on himself in thus degrading *us,* for some of the noblest virtues are too generally deemed *unmanly.*" Equality promised the development of the best talents of both sexes: women could develop their physical and intellectual abilities like men; men could be free to act in their highest moral capacities, like women.[14]

All the women agreed that the "perfect" woman or man of their ideal society would combine both "masculine" intellect and "feminine" affection. This utopia itself was often described as one which combined both masculine and feminine elements. Lydia Maria Child, who moved in the 1830's from popular writer to abolitionist editor and propagandist, declared: "God intended a participation of the masculine and feminine elements in every relation and every duty of life. Politics form no exception to this universal rule." Frances Gage similarly noted: "So long as woman is required to take care of the morals of the Community and man to take charge of the politics. . . we shall have a strange and incongruous state of affairs."[15]

The feminist-abolitionists recognized that at least some of the apparent differences between the sexes were due to cultural factors rather than to biology. For example, all of them believed that women were the victims of educational neglect, but were potentially the intellectual equals of men. Susan B. Anthony, who grew up in an enlightened Quaker family and received the same education as her brothers, argued in an 1853 speech that if women were given the same education as men, one might find that differences were not God-ordained but the result of "false education and conventional-isms." Lydia Maria Child suggested on a number of occasions that woman's apparent moral superiority and intellectual weakness, as well as other qualities, were only due to the role she was forced to play.[16] Emancipation from restrictive roles and spheres would permit self-development and erase many sex differences.

It is important to note that even the more daring of the feminists did not envision an androgynous society. Though benefiting from a blending of the strengths of both sexes, women and men would not be identical even in their highest state of development. Instead, they would be equal and complementary parts of the human family. Antoinette Brown Blackwell, who later developed this idea in her treatise *The Sexes Throughout Nature,* described the sexes as different physically, mentally, and spiritually, as "two halves of a great whole." Women would continue to be endowed with superior endurance, compassion, gentleness, and other qualities which especially suited them for childrearing, nursing, and other nurturing roles.[17] (One of the professions considered particularly compatible with women's talents was the ministry. Blackwell herself was the first woman ordained in the Congregationalist church; she later rejected orthodox Protestantism and turned to Unitarianism.)

One of the major tasks of these feminists was to reassure their audiences constantly that "true womanhood" would survive emancipation. They pointed to women like Lucretia Mott, the revered elder stateswoman of the group, who had remained a devoted wife and mother, and superior housekeeper, in spite of her frequent travels as a Quaker minister to preach on abolition and women's rights.[18] Mary A. Livermore, the first editor of the *Woman's Journal* and an important lecturer in the postwar period, asserted that women would not be "unsexed" by entering male occupations. "A woman's nature will never be changed," she insisted, "Men might spin, and knit, and sew, and cook, and rock the cradle for a hundred centuries, and not be women.... God does his work better than that."[19]

Although the feminists called for high standards of piety and purity for both sexes, they were unconventional in the kind of religion they practiced and urged on others. Theirs was a special kind of piety. Strongly influenced by the evangelical fervor of their day, they felt "called" to a sacred mission and were moved by a millennialist vision that directed all their efforts. However, virtually all of them rejected the dogma and rituals of orthodox Protestantism. They moved away from Calvinist theology because they found it intolerably narrow and binding on the spirits of all people, but especially women. Though not a unique phenomenon in this period, it was a striking characteristic of this group. They retained a Calvinist sense of duty and vision of life as a battle with evil, but they moved to an eclectic, nondoctrinal faith strongly influenced by Quakerism and Transcendentalism as well as by the liberal, rationalist religions of the day. For most in the group, reform became their main religion, and reform work replaced formal churchgoing as a means of expressing their faith. This process was hastened by the hostility of the churches to abolitionism and feminism. Susan B. Anthony was an outstanding illustration of this marriage of reform and religion. Single-mindedly devoted to her cause, she said in later years that work and worship had been one with her—she prayed every second of her life, but with her work rather than on her knees: "My prayer is to lift woman to equality with man."[20]

The commitment to equality voiced by Anthony and shared by her cohorts made inevitable their rejection of submissiveness which was a staple ingredient in society's prescription for the true woman. Submissiveness was not only anathema to the feminist-abolitionists, but society's demand that women adopt that posture became a singular target in their critique of traditional marriage. Their experience with antislavery led them to apply the human-rights ideology of abolitionism to the relationship between women and men. In this light traditional marriage was regarded as comparable to a state of slavery for women. As Elizabeth Cady Stanton put it: "The moral principle which forbade man to hold property in man applied to marriage as well as to slavery."[21] The parallel between woman and slave was the most frequent one resorted to in antebellum feminist rhetoric. Lucy Stone declared: "Marriage is to woman a state of slavery. It takes from her the right to her own property, and makes her submissive in all things to her husband." And Antoinette Brown Blackwell protested that, "The wife owes service and labor to her husband as much and as absolutely as the slave does to his master."[22]

The term "slavery" encompassed a multitude of evils. Publicly the efforts of the feminists were directed primarily at gaining for married women the right to own property and obtain guardianship of their children; privately they all agreed that "the right of a wife to her own person," that is, her right not to submit to her husband's sexual advances, was at the heart of her emancipation. Elizabeth Cady Stanton openly declared that this "marriage question" lay "at the foundation of all progress" and Lucy Stone privately agreed that the abuse in question was "perfectly appalling" and that "the question underlies the whole movement."[23] The control of a husband over his wife's body was the "slavery of sex" in its most urgent form.

The conception of traditional marriage as a state of slavery was responsible for the decision of some feminists to postpone marriage themselves or remain unmarried. It did not, however, discourage them from idealizing a happier kind of marital union and advocating "domesticity" for women, the last of the virtues of true womanhood described by Welter. They did, in fact, romanticize the family unit as "the conservator of national virtue and strength" and "the central and supreme institution among human societies."[24] The feminists were able to advocate domesticity because their ideal domestic setting was an unconventional one, and because they rejected the notion that woman should be limited to the private sphere. Their ideal family was built upon a marriage which was a union of two people who would be equal and autonomous partners, sharing property, responsibilities, and decision-making.[25]

The principle of dual roles and overlapping spheres underlay this feminist conception of marriage. The wife bore the prime responsibility for the home, especially during the childbearing years; the husband's obligation was to provide for the family. However, neither was restricted to this role, and, indeed, both had obligations in the broad sphere they shared in common. Repeated over and over by feminist leaders, this theme was echoed by the women who responded to their appeals. Letters to the *Una,* a women's rights newspaper, expressed sentiments similar to those of one indignant reader: "The true woman *will* be a good wife and mother but when her job is done she ought to be free to enter public affairs or any other field of endeavor."[26]

The obligations of both sexes in this shared sphere was a central concern of the feminists. Women as citizens had an obligation to the broader society as well as to the family; men as citizens had a responsibility to the home as well as to the world outside. Just as the father's role in the family was vital, so the influence of woman in government was essential. Jane Grey Swisshelm who left her own husband because she felt imprisoned by their traditional marriage, wrote a series of "Letters to Mothers" for the *Lily,* explaining that husbands and wives were equal partners: the husband's business included spending time with his children; the wife's work entailed understanding and helping her husband with his work, at the very least offering sympathy and advice. The rearing of children, especially, was seen as the sacred obligation of both sexes.[27]

The same sentiments were echoed in the *Lily's* successor, the *Woman's Journal,* by Mary A. Livermore, whose own marriage was a life-long partnership of equals. (Daniel Livermore, a Universalist minister, was an active "woman's rights man" who shared both home duties and reform work with his wife. In 1870, he gave up a pastorate in Chicago so that she could return to Boston to edit the new journal.[28]) In the *Journal,* Livermore expounded her belief in the sexes' dual roles and overlapping spheres, emphasizing especially that childrearing was the responsibility of father as well as mother. To the charge that women would neglect their sacred home duties if granted equal rights, she responded: "What are the sacred home duties of woman as distinguished from man? Is there any one... which does not belong jointly, with her, to the husband and father?"[29]

The large majority of the feminist-abolitionists enjoyed marriages more like Livermore's than Swisshelm's. In these unions, they achieved a notable degree of equality and sharing. The models of egalitarian marriage they created represented a pivotal reform in the nineteenth-century women's movement which has gone unnoticed by historians.[30] Most of the feminists— Mary A. Livermore, Antoinette Brown Blackwell, Lucy Stone, Amelia Bloomer, Lucretia Mott—were able in their day-to-day lives to implement their unconventional concept of flexible roles and spheres. Though the wife assumed more of the responsibility for the care of the home, family decisions were made jointly, property was held in common, and there were broad areas in which they collaborated on an equal basis, notably childrearing and reform work. In one family, that of Abby Kelley Foster and Stephen Foster, actual role reversal occurred. Abby, more in demand as an antislavery speaker, traveled for long periods of time while Stephen remained at home tending the farm and caring for their daughter.[31]

Though all the feminists urged women to pursue both their domestic and public roles, most assumed that these tasks would be carried out sequentially —as domestic burdens eased, more time could be devoted to other work. Antoinette Brown Blackwell was unique in translating the group's ideas about flexible roles and spheres into a detailed life plan, one which she followed successfully in her own life. Her plan was based on the assumption that a woman's primary sphere of action normally would alternate, at different stages of her life, between her specialized role in the home and her broader role outside. According to Blackwell's scheme, each young woman would educate herself for a profession, marry late (between twenty-five and thirty) and choose a husband who would respect his wife's independence in marriage. Twenty years would be spent dividing her time between her domestic life and her work, sharing the responsibilities of childrearing with her husband. The remaining twenty prime years would be free "to give the maturity of all her best powers to some noble life purpose."[32] Though quite idealistic and less practical for others—Blackwell was middle-class, gifted, and lived to the age of ninety-six—the plan provided one concrete illustration of the feminist conception of true womanhood.

Other alterations in the popular prescription for domesticity were proposed that were even more radical in design. In one significant departure from the norm, the feminists insisted on the right of a woman to remain unmarried if she so chose, and to continue in the public sphere of action rather than retreat into domesticity. As was the case with their call for equality in marriage, this demand was expressed early and publicly in the 1830's and 1840's by the Grimkés, Abby Kelley, Lucy Stone, and others. Although "true marriage," conceived as a partnership of equals, was the most desirable state of affairs for both sexes, these early feminists argued that most women were forced into unhappy unions because of economic dependence and social pressures. One of the goals of the movement was to enable women to achieve the financial independence that would allow them the freedom to enter into equal marriages or, lacking that opportunity, to remain celibate.

The feminist-abolitionists, then, made significant alterations in their society's ideal of true womanhood. They concurred in the emphasis upon religious and moral standards for women, but they insisted that men aspire to this same high level of morality and, in addition, condemned the established churches for their failure to abide by the true principles of Christianity. Glorifying the role of home and family in preserving the moral fabric of society, they called for equality for women within the family. Acknowledging the special role that woman was destined to play in the home by virtue of her moral and domestic gifts, they demanded that she not be restricted to this role but be free to function in the broader public sphere as a right of all human beings and citizens of the Republic. This proved to be an ideal even more difficult to achieve than the more popular prescription, but the changes they demanded provided future feminists with alternative models of true womanhood.

Notes

1. See, for example, Susan B. Anthony's 1854 speech on women's rights, Anthony Papers, Arthur and Elizabeth Schlesinger Library on the History of Women in America, Radcliffe College, Cambridge, Massachusetts.
2. This essay stems from my book *The Slavery of Sex: Feminists-Abolitionists in America,* (Urbana: University of Illinois Press, 1978).
3. See *The Slavery of Sex,* especially Chapter 6.
4. Barbara Welter, "The Cult of True Womanhood, 1820-1860," *American Quarterly* 18 (Summer 1966): 151-175.
5. Samuel J. May, *The Rights and Condition of Women* (Syracuse: Stoddard and Babcock, 1846), pp. 9-10.
6. Paulina W. Davis, *A History of the National Woman's Right Movement* (New York, 1871; reprint ed., New York: Source Book Press, 1970), p. 63.
7. Sarah Grimké, *Letters on the Equality of the Sexes, and the Condition of Woman* (Boston: Isaac Knapp, 1838; reprint ed., New York: Source Book Press, 1970). Angelina Grimke to Amos A. Phelps, September 2, 1837, Amos A. Phelps Papers, Boston Public Library, Boston, Massachusetts.
8. Stanton speech, "The Solitude of Self," 1892, Elizabeth Cady Stanton Papers, Library of Congress, Washington, D.C.
9. Harriot K. Hunt, *Glances and Glimpses* (Boston: John P. Jewett and Co., 1856), p. 305.
10. *History of Woman Suffrage,* eds. Elizabeth Cady Stanton, Susan B. Anthony, Matilda Joslyn Gage (New York: Fowler and Wells, 1881), 1: 112-13.
11. Lucy Stone speech, "The Province of Woman," undated, and "Women's Rights," Cincinnati *Daily Times,* October 28, 1853. Both are found in Blackwell Papers, Library of Congress, Washington, D.C. *History of Woman Suffrage,* 1: 554.
12. *Lily,* October 1, 1856; June 1851.
13. Bloomer, "Address to the Women of the State of New York," *Lily,* October 1850. The "short dress" which was the invention of Elizabeth Smith Miller but bears Bloomer's name, was only one of Bloomer's many reform projects.
14. Angelina Grimké to Amos A. Phelps, September 2, 1837, Amos A. Phelps Papers, Boston Public Library, Boston, Massachusetts.

15. *Letters of Lydia Maria Child* (Boston: Houghton, Mifflin and Co., 1883), p. 243, *Una,* February 1, 1853.
16. Anthony 1854 speech previously cited. *Letters of Lydia Maria Child,* pp. 243-44.
17. *Una,* August 15, 1855; February 1, 1853.
18. See, for example, *History of Woman Suffrage,* 1: 736-37.
19. *Woman's Journal,* April 16, 1870.
20. Ida Husted Harper, *Life and Work of Susan B. Anthony* (Indianapolis: Bowen-Merrill Co., 1898-1908), 2: 859.
21. *Liberator,* June 1, 1860.
22. *Una,* April 1854. *History of Woman Suffrage,* 1: 580. See also D.C. Bloomer, ed., *Life and Writings of Amelia Bloomer* (Boston: Arena Pub. Co., 1895), p. 105.
23. *Elizabeth Cady Stanton as Revealed in her Letters, Diary and Reminiscences,* 2 Vols., eds. Theodore Stanton and Harriot Stanton Blatch (New York: Harper and Bros., 1922; reprint ed., New York: Arno Press, 1969), 2: 82. Lucy Stone to Elizabeth Cady Stanton, August 14, 1853, Elizabeth Cady Stanton Papers, Library of Congress, Washington, D.C. and to Antoinette Brown, July 11, 1855, Blackwell Papers, Library of Congress, Washington, D.C.
24. *History of Woman Suffrage,* 1: 719. *Una,* February 1855.
25. See, as one of many examples, Lucretia Mott's 1849 "Discourse on Woman," in *James and Lucretia Mott: Life and Letters,* ed. Anna Davis Hallowell (Boston: Houghton, Mifflin and Co., 1884).
26. *Una,* February 1, 1853.
27. *Lily,* March 1850.
28. Mary A. Livermore, *The Story of My Life* (Hartford, Conn.: A.D. Worthington and Co., 1899).
29. *Woman's Journal,* April 16, 1870.
30. See Blanche Glassman Hersh, "A Partnership of Equals," *University of Michigan Papers in Women's Studies* 2 (1977): 39-62, also *Slavery of Sex,* ch. 7.
31. Ibid.
32. Antoinette Brown Blackwell to Olympia Brown, undated but in the 1860's, Olympia Brown Papers, Arthur and Elizabeth Schlesinger Library on the History of Women in America, Radcliffe College, Cambridge, Massachusetts. See also "Antoinette Brown Blackwell, the First Woman Minister," ed. Claude U. Gilson, Typescript in Blackwell Family Papers, Schlesinger Library.

Ruth Bordin

"A Baptism of Power and Liberty": The Women's Crusade of 1873–1874

Throughout the winter of 1873 and 1874 a grass-roots women's temperance crusade swept through Ohio, the Midwest and parts of the East. Thousands of women marched in the streets, prayed in saloons, and organized their own temperance societies in hundreds of towns and cities. The "crusade," as it was called by contemporaries, had an immense impact on these women. Cut loose from the quiescence and public timidity that was their prescribed role, the crusade gave to many Amercan women a new sense of identity, a taste of collective power, and an acquaintance with the larger world of civic leadership and the public platform. "We have had no wonderful Crusade in England," observed British temperance worker Margaret Parker to her American sisters, a decade later, "no such baptism of power and liberty." Parker claimed that unlike their American sisters, English women still believed that "woman's voice should only be heard within the four walls of her own home."[1]

Parker correctly saw the crusade as a watershed in the participation of American women in the temperance movement. Before the crusade of 1873-1874, American women, much like their British counterparts, played a relatively minor and passive role, but for twenty-five years afterwards, until the growth of the Anti-Saloon League at the turn of the century, women provided the major and most creative leadership for the temperance movement. Their organization, the Women's Christian Temperance Union (WCTU), which emerged as a result of the crusade, in turn provided the single most effective vehicle for the growing women's movement.

The crusade began almost accidentally. On December 22, 1872, a professional lecturer, Diocletian Lewis, well into his fall tour, gave a public address

[Ruth Bordin is a research affiliate of the Bentley Library, University of Michigan, and a Lecturer in history at Eastern Michigan University. In addition to other publications, her articles have appeared in a variety of journals including *Church History, American Archivist,* and *The Business History Review.* The essay reprinted here was originally published in *Ohio History.*]

called "Our Girls" at the Music Hall in Hillsboro, Ohio. Educated at Harvard and trained in homeopathic medicine, Lewis had founded a physical training school for girls and was a leading advocate of physical exercise and an active life for women. Lewis was also an ardent temperance man. Convinced that legal prohibition would not be feasible, he preached voluntary total abstinence. His appearance in Hillsboro was part of the regular winter course of lectures sponsored by the local lyceum association. Lewis had a free day before he was to appear in a neighboring town, and someone in his audience suggested that he give a temperance lecture in Hillsboro the next evening, Sunday, December 23. Eager to further a cause in which he believed, he agreed to do so. Indeed, it was his practice to give free temperance lectures on Sunday. This particular Sunday he called his address "The Duty of Christian Women in the Cause of Temperance." That evening Lewis told his customary story about his own family. Forty years ago, he related to his audience, his father had been a drinking man, and his mother, sorely distressed by his father's regular patronage of a local saloon in Saratoga, New York, had appealed in desperation to the owner to cease selling spirits, prayed in the saloon with several of her friends, and actually succeeded in getting the saloon keeper to close his doors. If his mother had been able to do this many years ago, Lewis asked, why could not the women of Hillsboro do the same in 1873?

There was nothing new in Lewis' message. In fact, it was substantially the same speech he had prepared for his initial venture on the lecture circuit twenty years before in 1854. By that December evening in Hillsboro he had articulated his vision about the power of women's prayers in the grog shops approximately three hundred times, and the plan he outlined had already been tried in some twenty instances. As early as 1858, he inspired fifty women to march praying into the saloons of Dixon, Illinois. Their nonviolent assault had continued unabated for six days until all the community's saloons had closed. Two months later in the same year, women had tried the scheme in Battle Creek, Michigan, with temporary success. Most recently, Lewis had made the same speech ten days before in Fredonia, New York. Over two hundred women heeded his words and marched to the saloons the following day for prayer and song. The next morning they organized a temperance society, but their marching came to an end.[2]

Before Hillsboro, the results of Lewis' appeal had always been temporary and local, but this time his words fell on more fertile ground. The women in the audience took up the challenge with enthusiasm. Early the next morning nearly two hundred lined up outside the church in a column of twos, the shortest leading the way, and began to march on local saloons singing "Give to the Winds Thy Fears." Marching that Christmas Eve day on the cold and sunless streets of Hillsboro, these women touched off a mass movement which soon engulfed hundreds of towns and cities in Ohio, the Midwest, and to a lesser extent, in the Northeast and West.[3]

The typical local crusade began with a public meeting in a church or hall where an audience, composed chiefly of women, prayed together and listened to temperance speakers, frequently women. Within a day or two they deployed throughout the community in what were called "praying bands" for street work, which could involve the methodical circulation of temperance petitions or, more spectacularly, the march of a mass delegation to confront one or more sellers of liquor. On rare occasions the women were accompanied by sympathetic men, but Lewis himself discouraged male participation in the praying band, suggesting the presence of men would reduce the movement's moral force. In small towns and cities the women's demonstrations were accepted peacefully, but in larger cities hostile crowds often harassed the marchers. When crusaders entered a saloon they usually prayed together for a moment, then asked the proprietor to pour out his stock and close his business. Mark Twain renders, albeit in satirical fashion, the full fervor and determination of the crusaders. After being accosted by the crusaders and presented with a "special petition," Twain wrote, the saloon keeper

> has to stand there meekly behind his bar, under the eyes of a great concourse of ladies who are better than he is and are aware of it, and hear all the iniquities of his business divulged to the angels above, accompanied by the sharp sting of wishes for his regeneration.... If he holds out bravely, the Crusaders hold out more bravely still....[4]

Within three months of Hillsboro, such campaigns had successfully, if temporarily, closed thousands of saloons and driven the liquor business out of more than two hundred fifty American communities. Women took to the streets in one hundred thirty Ohio towns and cities; Michigan had thirty-six crusades, Indiana thirty-four, Pennsylvania twenty-six, New Jersey seventeen. The movement spread to twenty-three states in all.[5] While the crusade began in small cities and towns in agricultural areas, it soon spread to a number of larger cities. Cleveland, Cincinnati, Chicago, Philadelphia and Brooklyn were among the metropolitan centers which experienced crusades. Before summer was over, 750 breweries closed. The production of malt liquor dropped over five and one-half million gallons in 1875, and federal excise taxes dropped sharply in some districts.[6] Although most saloons were open again by fall, and the results were transitory, this was the first women's mass movement in American history. Women were taking to the streets in significant numbers using methods they had never before used on such a scale.

What had happened? Why did this crusade catch fire during the winter of

1873-1874, when for years the same techniques had been used occasionally with little effect? The answer in not an easy one, and probably lies at least in part in the local Ohio political scene, for the temperance movement was nearly a century old in 1873 and temperance had become a national issue buoyed by one of the great antebellum reform movements of the Jacksonian era. By the 1830's some temperance advocates turned from concern with individual abstinence to advocacy of legal prohibition, and several states adopted statutes prohibiting or regulating the sale of alcohol in the years before the Civil War. Temperance agitation declined during the great conflict, but quickly revived in the reform atmosphere that accompanied the early reconstruction years.[7] Membership in the Ohio branch of the Independent Order of Good Templars rose from 3,755 in 1865 to nearly 28,000 in less than three years.[8]

A more immediate impetus toward reform came with Ohio's 1873-1874 constitutional convention which heatedly debated the liquor license issue and the regulation of the liquor traffic in general. At this time Ohio did not license liquor dealers and forbade the selling of spirits in saloons, where only beer and wine could be vended. Moreover, under existing Ohio law, an individual could be refused permission to buy liquor or beer if a relative asked that they not be served. Liquor interests wanted the constitutional convention to license saloons to sell spirits, but Ohio's temperance forces furiously opposed such regulation on the grounds that licensing of drink implied the government's approval of intemperance and drunkenness. Divided over the issue, the convention shifted resolution of the licensing amendment to the voters. In the August 1874 election Ohioans defeated licensing, but at the same time turned down the new constitution which would have enforced the decision. Although the end result was a frustrating stalemate, the public debate had kept the temperance question in the public mind all through 1873 and 1874.[9]

However none of this directly explains why the crusade became a *women's* movement. Before the early 1870's women's role in temperance agitation had always been subordinate to that of men, especially in the public or political realm. This reflected the nineteenth century's dominant sexual ideology which assigned to men and women sharply defined spheres of activity. Men functioned in the world of politics and commerce; women presided over the spiritual and physical maintenance of home and family.[10] Women's role at home or in society was to practice moral suasion and set a good example. As long as temperance agitation emphasized individual redemption and personal abstention, women worked easily, if quietly, within the movement. Expected to use their influence to convert their husbands, sons and brothers to total abstinence, they could also offer assistance and counsel to the wife and children neglected by a drunken male. However, those who sought to play a public role were quickly rebuffed. Susan B. Anthony, for example, was denied the right to speak at a convention of New York temperance societies. Informed by the presiding officer that she and her sisters were there not to speak but only to listen and learn, Anthony responded by organizing the first state all-woman temperance society in New York in 1852.[11]

But the drink issue itself was to prove subsersive to the maintenance of a strict division between the sexual spheres. Once the temperance movement had shifted its attention from moral suasion to legislative coercion, involving either local option or prohibition, reformers directed much of their effort toward closing the public saloons, which were growing rapidly in numbers in the generally prosperous era immediately after the Civil War. By 1873 Ohio supported as many as one such establishment for every 150 or 200 people. If one excludes women, children and teetotaling men, each saloon catered to an average of only thirty adult men.[12]

Temperance advocates in general, and women in particular, held the saloon to be a mortal threat to home and hearth. Only a minority of families were actually undermined by the poverty and debauchery of drunken husbands, but almost all women felt threatened by the agressively male atmosphere of the saloon and tavern. It represented an alternative nexus of sociability, separate from and counterposed to, the circle of family, relatives, and friends over which women traditionally exercised influence. In a society in which women were still economically and socially dependent upon men, public drinking establishments eroded ways of life that lent legitimacy and dignity to women's social relationships. To the extent that the saloon encouraged actual drunkenness, women accurately perceived it as a direct threat to themselves and their families.[13] Addressing a convention of the National American Woman Suffrage Association in 1875, Susan B. Anthony emphasized that the virtuous women who were in legal subjection to their drunken husbands were the greatest sufferers from intemperance.[14] Any reading of letters, diaries, newspaper articles, and books written by women in the 1870's reveals that Anthony was merely echoing the widely held belief that drink was a threat to the home. The sudden panic of 1873, which left rural areas and small towns in a troubled condition, probably reinforced the sense of social disorder and economic instability which women already identified with saloon culture.

To many women, therefore, participation in the post-Civil-War temperance movement took place on a basis which did not fundamentally alter the ideology that held women responsible for, and confined to home and family. Yet at the same time, the activism and larger public role that characterized women's temperance work in this era so broadened the narrow definition of women's traditional sphere as to make it, among advanced women, an increasingly anachronistic concept. Thus thirty women were among the five hundred who attended the founding convention of the National Prohibition

Party in 1869. Women were accepted as equal members of the Independent Order of Good Templars, and Martha Brown, later a founder of the Woman's Christian Temperance Union, became a member of the Templar executive board in 1867 and Grand Chief Templar of Ohio in 1872.[15]

The women's crusade fueled this expansion of the legitimate sphere of female activity. Women now joined the temperance movement in numbers that eclipsed their participation in any previous reform. In Hillsboro 200 women marched in a town whose total population was less than 2,000. The village of Franklin had 50 marching against the liquor traffic out of 2,500. In Adrian, Michigan, approximately 1,000 women out of the city's population of 8,000 participated in some way during the crusade, and bands of 150 women were sent out daily over a period of several months. Larger cities too felt the impact: in Chicago in the spring of 1874, 14,000 crusaders petitioned the city council for Sunday closing of saloons.[16]

For the most part these crusaders came from the upper ranks of the society of their towns. Mark Twain characterized them as young girls and women who were "not the inferior sorts, but the very best in their village communities."[17] In a study of ninety-five of the original Hillsboro crusaders who could be identified, Charles Isetts has shown that these women were "socially and economically the dominant force in Hillsboro at that time." All were from households headed by men who were either skilled craftsmen or in white-collar occupations. These families were also the wealthiest in town, and over 90 percent of the crusader households were native white Americans of two generations standing or more. They were the "upper crust of their society."[18]

Why were these essentially conservative women using radical and militant means to achieve their ends? Why were they able to act in ways that at first glance seem so out of character? As a consequence of their high social standing and their sense of righteous womanhood, these crusaders felt a keen sense of the justice of their cause and their own moral superiority. Although few of the women participating in the 1874 crusade favored so radical a demand as suffrage, they did believe their work was in the best interests of the entire society. Certainly this helps to explain their self-confidence and tactical militance. They were also experiencing power and discovering they could force both governmental bodies and individuals to accede to their demands. They marched in the streets, formed picket lines to prevent the delivery of liquor to saloons, took down the names of patrons, and organized and addressed mass meetings. Even though they saw this work as stemming from and in defense of a traditionally defined women's sphere, the radical and public methods to which they subscribed represented a real if only partially conscious commitment to the idea that women could legitimately function in the public realm. Their work was that of an effective pressure group, and in many instances they succeeded in forcing a male-dominated society to yield to their demands, at least temporarily.[19]

A minority of the crusade leaders had already been active in public life, especially in women's missionary societies and in Civil War agencies such as the Sanitary Commission. Eliza Stewart, who led the Springfield, Ohio, crusade had acquired extensive leadership skills while working with the Sanitary Commission. Putting this experience to new use, Stewart brought praying bands into court rooms, organized mass meetings, and eventually became a prominent temperance lecturer whose skill on the podium was hailed in Great Britain as well as in the United States.[20]

But most women who led the crusade had had no previous experience in the public realm. Of the thirty late-nineteenth-century leaders singled out for formal portraits in Frances Willard's *Woman and Temperance,* two-thirds had participated in the crusade; over half of the entire group, eighteen in all, had had no previous experience outside the home.[21] In a score of states women who had previously led quiet lives, who no doubt had always appeared shy and subservient to their husbands, were suddenly organizing, taking to the streets, getting locked into airless, smelly saloons, risking arrest and generally behaving as if nothing in their lives counted except their dedication to temperance. For example, Mary Woodbridge, mother of three by the time she was twenty, had previously devoted herself exclusively to her family. When the crusade came to Ravenna, Ohio, she became overnight a talented, moving speaker in the evangelistic style. Within months Woodbridge was in constant demand as a platform lecturer, and she soon became editor of a temperance paper as well.[22]

Eliza Thompson, who led the Hillsboro crusade, was the daughter of a governor, wife of a judge, and a conservatively inclined housewife and mother. She reported that as she rose to speak at Hillsboro's first crusade meeting, "my limbs refused to bear me," but when the men who were present left the room her strength returned.[23] She was certainly not accustomed to marching on the streets and praying in public (and she always retained some of her original reticence), but she also addressed audiences of hundreds from public platforms for the rest of her life. Another crusader who moved quickly into public life was Amy Fisher Leavitt, wife of a Baptist minister, who joined the movement when it was organized in Cincinnati. There the police arrested her while she prayed on the sidewalk in front of a saloon. As the wife of a minister, Leavitt may have had previous experience in leading prayer meetings, but she certainly had never before run afoul of the law. Nonetheless, she took incarceration in stride and continued her prayers and hymns for the benefit of the inmates of the jail.[24]

The first-hand accounts of the crusade cannot be read without sensing the excitement experienced by these women and their growing conviction that anything was now possible. The women themselves saw the crusade as a watershed, an experience that changed their self-perception. They articulated these convictions at WCTU conventions and whenever and wherever they gathered for the rest of their lives. An editorial in the *Union Signal* in 1889 asserted that the crusade "meant a revolution in women's work and in thousands of women's lives." Eliza Stewart, writing in the same issue of the *Signal,* said that as a result of the crusade, women "who had not dreamed they held such rich gifts in their keeping, were found on pulpits and rostrums with burning words swaying great audiences." Mary Burt, later president of the New York state WCTU, described how she made her first *public* expression in the form of a note to a crusade leader, during the marches in Auburn, New York. Soon after she was giving a public lecture. [25]

The crusade appeared to have had an emotional impact upon women participants equivalent to a conversion experience. It moved them toward feminist principles, even if they did not recognize them as such. Aileen Kraditor has suggested that the aims of feminists, while they varied widely in terms of specific demands, in the last analysis can be summarized as the demand for autonomy. Women wanted to decide for themselves the boundaries of their sphere. [26] Certainly these crusaders shared this perception. They saw their movement as an effort to change an aspect of society which directly affected them as women, and they felt they had a right to work publicly in that cause.

Later, many of the crusaders interpreted their participation as part of a process that helped them realize their true potential as individuals for the first time. On its tenth anniversary in 1883, the WCTU commemorated the crusade at length. WCTU suffragist Mary A. Livermore, argued that the advancement the crusade gave to temperance was far less important than the movement's effect in unifying women, giving them moral courage, and teaching them the power of association. [27] WCTU president Frances Willard thought the crusade "taught women their power to transact business, to mold public opinion by public utterance, and opened the eyes of scores and hundreds of women to the need of the Republic for the suffrage of women and made them willing to take up for their homes' and country's sake the burdens of that citizenship they would never have sought for their own." [28]

In response to the *Union Signal's* query, "What has the Crusade done for you?" anonymous rank-and-file crusaders adopted much the same perspective as leaders Livermore and Willard. They described the crusade's impact upon themselves in terms of personal growth and development. It "startled me into an active thinking life"; it gave me "broader views of woman's sphere and responsibility," reported two participants. One reported that because of the crusade she had "developed a new and grander purpose in life." Another recalled that the crusade had "opened doors of opportunity and tender-hearted fellowship." Still another wrote that the crusade "brought me from

the retirement of my home into public work." Overall reported one partici-
pant, "the Crusade taught women to do noble deeds, not dream them."[29] In
effect, answered these middle-class, church-going women, ten years after the
event, the woman's temperance crusade of 1874 had raised their consciousness.

As the country's largest and most influential nineteenth-century women's
organization, the WCTU reflected the new level at which women now sought
to participate in public life. Founded in 1874 as the institutional expression of
the energies unleashed by the crusade, the WCTU grew to more than 150,000
dues-paying members by 1893. It soon had chapters in every state and major
city of the nation. As in the case of the temperance crusaders of 1873 and
1874, the WCTU's staunch defense of home and family appealed to the
conservatism of middle-class women, but the Union so dramatically broadened the arena in which to carry out this program as to virtually shatter for
thousands the traditional bonds of womanhood. Under Frances Willard's
apt slogan "Do-everything," the WCTU endorsed woman's suffrage by 1883
and came out for a staggering array of other reforms. In addition to
prohibition, the WCTU supported child labor laws, established kindergartens,
paid the salary of municipal police matrons, and aligned itself with the farmer
and labor insurgencies of the 1880's and 1890's.[30]

More than any other single event in nineteenth-century America, the
woman's temperance crusade touched the lives of tens of thousands of
women and legitimized for them a new and expanded role in civic life. It took
large numbers of women out of the home, taught them to confront social
problems directly, and showed them there were ways to make an impact on
society even without the vote. In practice, if not always in terms of formal
ideology, the crusade helped subvert the nineteenth-century idea that women
functioned in a sphere separate from that of men and narrowly confined to
home, family, and religion. As Mary A. Livermore later put it: "That
phenomenal and exceptional rising of women in Southern Ohio ten years ago
floated them to a higher level of womanhood. It lifted them out of a subject
condition... to a plateau where they saw that endurance had ceased to be a
virtue."[31] They had experienced their baptism of power and liberty.

Notes

1. *Union Signal,* December 20, 1883, p. 6. Temperance and Prohibition Papers,
    National Headquarters File of the WCTU (joint Ohio Historical Society-
    Michigan Historical Collections—WCTU microfilm edition, *Union Signal*
    series, roll 1) hereafter cited as *Union Signal.* Margaret Parker was a
    Scots woman who served as president of the first international Woman's

Christian Temperance Union in 1876.

2. Mary Eastman, *Biography of Dio Lewis* (New York, Fowler and Wells 1891), 24-60. Eastman incorporates many of Lewis' reminiscences; see also Francis M. Whitaker, "A History of the Ohio Woman's Christian Temperance Union, 1874-1920" (Ph.D. dissertation, The Ohio State University, 1971), pp. 128-132.

3. Among the many descriptions of the crusade are: Annie Wittenmyer, *History of the Woman's Temperance Crusade* (Philadelphia: Office of the Christian Woman, 1878); Eliza Jane Thompson, *Hillsboro Crusade Sketches and Family Records* (Cincinnati: Jennings and Graham, 1906); Matilda Carpenter, *The Crusade: It's Origin and Development at Washington Court House and Its Results* (Columbus: W.G. Hubbard & Co., 1893); and W.C. Steel, *The Woman's Temperance Movement: A Concise History of the War on Alcohol* (New York: National Temperance Society Publication House, 1874). Most of the issue of December 20, 1883, of the *Union Signal,* the official organ of the WCTU, is devoted to reminiscences and evaluations of the crusade. T.A.H. Brown, reporter for the *Cincinnati Gazette,* who covered the crusade for his paper, wrote a long, partially eye-witness account called "A Full Description of the Origin and Progress of the New Plan of Labor by the Women Up to the Present Time," which appeared in Jane E. Stebbins, *Fifty Years' History of the Temperance Cause* (Hartford: J.P. Fitch, 1876). See also Dio Lewis' account in his *Prohibition A Failure: The True Solution of the Temperance Question* (Boston: James R. Osgood & Co., 1875); and Eastman's *Dio Lewis.*

4. As reprinted in the *Union Signal,* June 4, 1885, p. 5. Techniques very similar to those used in the crusade were used by the New York Moral Reform Society in the 1830's in their campaign against houses of prostitution. In that movement, however, the women hired male missionaries to descend on the brothels and exhort patrons and inmates to give up their ways. The women themselves occasionally invaded the brothels but not without male escorts. They, too, prayed and sang and disrupted normal business. They also used the technique, adopted by crusaders, of writing down the names of patrons, especially those prominent in business and the professions. See Carroll Smith-Rosenberg, *Religion and the Rise of the American City: The New York City Mission Movement, 1812-1870* (Ithaca, N.Y.: Cornell University Press, 1971), ch. 4.

5. *Union Signal,* September 30, 1923. These numbers are probably underestimated. Elizabeth Putnam Gordon, *Women Torch Bearers, The Story of the Woman's Christian Temperance Movement* (Evanston: National Woman's Christian Temperance Union Publishing House, 1924), p. 7, puts the total figure at 250. Actually there were more. Accounts of 255 individual crusades appear in Wittenmyer's *Crusade History* and that record is incomplete.

6. Mary Earhart, *Frances Willard: From Prayers to Politics* (Chicago: University

of Chicago Press, 1944), p. 141; Norton Mezvinsky, "White Ribbon Reform: 1874-1920" (Ph.D. dissertation, The University of Wisconsin, 1958), pp. 54-60. The panic of 1873 may have been partly responsible for this drop in production, but some of it is certainly traceable to the crusade.

7. Alice Tyler, *Freedom's Ferment: Phases of American Social History to 1860* (Minneapolis: University of Minnesota Press, 1944), chapter 13, contains a concise history of the early temperance movement. John Allen Krout's *The Origins of Prohibition* (New York: Knopf, 1925) is the classic work on the pre-Civil War period. Norman Clark's *Deliver Us From Evil* (New York: Norton, 1967) is the best interpretive account and a major contribution to the understanding of the temperance movement as a whole.

8. Whittaker, "Ohio WCTU," pp. 111-112.

9. Charles A. Isetts, "The Woman's Christian Temperance Crusade of Ohio" (M.A. thesis, Miami University, 1971), p. 49; see also Whitaker, "Ohio WCTU," pp. 124-125, 274.

10. The best recent analyses of "woman's sphere" are found in Barbara J. Berg, *The Remembered Gate: Origins of American Feminism: The Woman and the City, 1800-1860* (New York: Oxford University Press, 1978), 67-74, and Nancy Cott, *The Bonds of Womanhood: "Woman's Sphere" in New England, 1790-1835* (New Haven: Yale University Press, 1978). Jed Dannenbaum analyzes this ideology in terms of the temperance movement in his "Woman and Temperance: The Years of Transition, 1850-1870," a paper delivered at the Conference on the History of Women, St. Paul, Minnesota, October 1977.

11. Ida Husted Harper, *The Life and Work of Susan B. Anthony, (Indianapolis: Bobbs-Merrill, 1899) 64-66.*

12. Whitaker, "Ohio WCTU," p. 143.

13. See Clark, *Deliver Us From Evil,* ch. 1, for a discussion of the United States as a drunken society.

14. Susan B. Anthony's address is reprinted in Aileen Kraditor, *Up From the Pedestal: Selected Writings in the History of American Feminism* (Chicago: Quadrangle Books, 1968), 159-161.

15. Whitaker, "Ohio WCTU," pp. 122-123; Frances Willard and Mary A. Livermore, eds., *A Woman of the Century, Fourteen Hundred Seventy Biographical Sketches of Leading American Women (*Buffalo: Charles Wells Mouton, 1893), 127-128.

16. Whitaker, "Ohio WCTU," p. 140; Minutes, 1874, Ladies Temperance Union of Adrian, in the Michigan Historical Collections of the Bentley Library, University of Michigan; Frances Willard, Presidential Address, *Minutes,* 1889, WCTU National Convention, p. 99. WCTU National Headquarters File (joint Ohio Historical Society-Michigan Historical Collections—WCTU microfilm edition) roll 3.

17. *Union Signal,* June 4, 1885, p. 5.

18. Charles A. Isetts, "A Social Profile of the Woman's Temperance Crusade: Hillsboro, Ohio," unpublished manuscript made available to the author by Isetts.

19. These were the arguments the WCTU was to use later to justify its concern with public affairs, especially its demand for woman suffrage. The pattern followed by the suffragists was somewhat different. They began their fight by arguing that a common humanity guaranteed them the same natural rights which the Declaration of Independence claimed for their male brothers. But by the end of the century they were evolving a new set of arguments which stressed women's special qualifications for moral uplift. They were arguing, as the temperance women did earlier, that the necessary social reforms would come only through the votes of women. See Aileen Kraditor, "Ideology of the Suffrage Movement," in Barbara Welter, ed., *The Woman Question in American History* (Hinsdale, Ill: The Dryden Press, 1971), pp. 88-89; and Kraditor, *Ideas of the Woman Suffrage Movement* (New York: Columbia University Press, 1965), pp. 45-56. Gerda Lerner in "New Approaches to the Study of Women in American History," *Journal of Social History* 3 (Fall 1969): 53-62, argues that even without the vote, women effectively used pressure tactics to force political change. Many of their methods were later adopted by civil-rights and other groups.

20. Frances Willard, *Woman and Temperance* (Hartford: Park Publishing Co., 1883), pp. 83-85.

21. Ibid. Of the ten temperance leaders who did not participate in the crusade, three were not Americans, three happened to be abroad when the crusade took place, and four were from areas of the country—New England and the South—where few crusades occurred.

22. Ibid., pp. 103-106. Also see Scrapbook number 7, WCTU microfilm edition, roll 30, frame 405.

23. Thompson, *Crusade Sketches*, p. 61.

24. Willard, *Woman and Temperance*, p. 28.

25. *Union Signal,* December 12, 1889, pp. 5, 9.

26. Kraditor, *Up From The Pedestal,* pp. 7-9.

27. *Union Signal,* December 20, 1883, p. 8.

28. Willard in her introduction to Wittenmyer, *History of the Crusade*, pp. 15-21. Earhart credits the crusade with ushering in a new woman's movement. See *Willard*, p. 143.

29. *Union Signal,* December 20, 1883, p. 12.

30. June Sochen would include these women among her "pragmatic feminists" whom she describes as identifying the specific grievances from which women suffered and trying to do something about them. See *Movers and Shakers: American Women Thinkers and Activists* (New York: Quadrangle, 1973), pp. 65-66. William O'Neill calls this same group the "social feminists." See *Everyone Was Brave: A History of Feminism in America* (New York: Quadrangle, 1971), p. 51. For a description of the

way in which the WCTU's home-based ideology introduced heretofore conservative women to extradomestic, feminist concerns, see Anne Firor Scott, *The Southern Lady: From Pedestal to Politics* (Chicago: The University of Chicago Press, 1970), ch. 6. Ellen DuBois analyzes the relationship between the suffrage movement and the WCTU in "The Radicalism of the Woman Suffrage Movement: Notes Toward the Reconstruction of Nineteenth-Century Feminism," *Feminist Studies* 1 (1975): 63-71. See also Ellen DuBois, *Feminism and Suffrage: The Emergence of an Independent Women's Movement in America* (Ithaca: Cornell University Press, 1978). Janet Giele, "Social Change in the Feminine Role: A Comparison of Woman's Suffrage and Woman's Temperance, 1870-1920" (Ph.D. dissertation, Radcliffe, 1961), analyzes in detail the depth and breadth of WCTU social concerns. Gilman Ostrander sees the WCTU as the only effective temperance organization, 1874-1894, and the WCTU as more effective in winning the vote for women than the suffrage movement itself. See *American Civilization in the First Machine Age* (New York: Harper & Row, 1970), p. 56.

31. *Union Signal,* June 4, 1885, p. 5.

Winifred D. Wandersee Bolin

American Women and the Twentieth-Century Work Force: The Depression Experience

The first decade of the twentieth century witnessed a restructuring of the work opportunities available to American women. The economic develop-ments of this period created new jobs in the service and clerical occupations, and although it may be disputed as to whether the shift in the occupational structure of the female labor force represented actual advancement for women workers as individuals, it seems clear that most women saw white-collar work as a standard of occupational and social mobility.[1] Because of important changes in the occupational characteristics of the female work force, it is necessary to go beyond a description of economic distress when analyzing the impact of the Great Depression upon working women. The bread lines, the labor strikes, the New Deal—all of these were symbols of the 1930's, but none of them really expressed what happened to women workers during these years. Women stood in the bread lines, participated in the strikes, and benefited from the New Deal, but women workers felt the long-range impact of the Depression in a different and less measurable way than men. In particular, women's movement into white-collar and professional work was retarded. Not only were women unemployed, but they were discouraged both materially and psychologically from advancing themselves in the world of work. The antagonism toward the woman worker, which had always been present, even in times of prosperity, was greatly intensified by the Depression, and it had its greatest impact on the white-collar woman worker, especially if she happened to be married.

The 1930's saw a definite decline in the rate of movement into white-collar occupations. The figures in Table I, based upon data from 1910 through 1940 census reports, indicate the rate of change in the percentage of female workers of three broad occupational categories—manufacturing and indus-

[Winifred Bolin's article, "The Economics of Family Life: Working Women of Middle-Income Familes and the Great Depression," appeared in a recent issue of the *Journal of American History*. That article and the essay printed here stem from a study on women, work, and the family, 1920-1940.]

Table I. Rate of Change by Decades in the Distribution of the Female Labor Force, 1910–1940

Year	White Collar	
	DISTR. %	RATE OF CHANGE
1910	23.5	
1920	38.6	+64.3
1930	44.0	+14.0
1940*	44.9	+ 2.1

Year	Domestic and Personal Services	
	DISTR. %	RATE OF CHANGE
1910	31.3	
1920	25.6	-18.2
1930	29.6	+15.6
1940*	28.9	- 2.4

Year	Laborers and Semiskilled Operatives	
	DISTR. %	RATE OF CHANGE
1910	45.2	
1920	35.8	-20.8
1930	26.5	-26.0
1940*	23.9	- 9.8

*The 1940 figures of distribution total only 97.7% because 2.3% of all working women did not report an occupation.

Source: H. Dewey Anderson and Percy E. Davidson, *Occupational Trends in the United States* (California: Stanford University Press, 1940), p. 19; *Fifteenth Census of the United States: 1930. Population.* Vol. V. *General Report on Occupations* (Washington, D.C.: Government Printing Office, 1933), Table 2, p. 39; and *1940 Census,* Vol. III, Part I, Table 61, p. 87.

try, domestic and personal service, and white-collar occupations. (The latter would include clerical, sales, business, and professional work—or, in other words, jobs that were usually perceived as a reflection of occupational advancement.) Although the rate of movement into *each* of these three general categories declined somewhat during the thirties, the reasons were different in each case. The decline in terms of manufacturing and industry was part of a long-term trend away from manual and unskilled labor. Even then, movement away from this kind of work slowed down during the Depression. The category of domestic and personal service is a special case, since it covers such a wide range of occupations.[2] No doubt women in industry and in domestic and personal service suffered more severely in material terms than white-collar workers during the Depression. But because the purpose of this essay is to analyze a down-turn in earlier occupational advancement, the emphasis will be upon the decline in the rate of movement into white-collar and professional work.

The rate of movement into white-collar work had already begun to decline in the 1920's, probably as part of a natural slowing-down process after years of unusually rapid growth. Also, the movement of more married women into the labor force had a somewhat negative effect upon the occupational pattern, since married women were more likely to be concentrated in low-status work. (Table II shows the rate of movement of married women into the labor force.) Finally, it has been argued that women's relatively slow occupational progress after 1920 was due to the rapid expansion of fields in which women were underrepresented, such as the scientific and engineering professions, college teaching, and high-paying managerial occupations.[3] Although all of these factors may have had a bearing upon occupational distribution in the thirties, the evidence indicates that the twin burden of unemployment and economic discrimination during the Depression hindered individual advancement and retarded the occupational mobility of women as a group.

The most obvious factor limiting the opportunities of all American workers was the problem of unemployment. Throughout most of the Depression the proportion of unemployed women was smaller than that of unemployed men, although this situation varied from year to year as well as place to place. In the early years of the Depression, women seeking work had several advantages over men. In particular, they were likely to work more cheaply, simply because women workers had always been paid less than men. Then too, much of women's work, such as domestic service, secretarial and

Table II. Married Women Workers, Fifteen Years and Over: Percent Gainfully Employed, Percent Female Labor Force, and Rate of Increase, 1910–1940

Year	Gainfully Occupied %	Rate of Increase	Female Labor Force %	Rate of Increase
1910	10.7		24.7	
1920	9.0	-15.9	23.0	- 6.7
1930	11.7	+30.0	28.9	+25.7
1940	15.3	+30.8	35.5	+22.8

Source. *Labor Force: Its Growth and Changing Composition,* Census Monograph Series (New York: John Wiley and Sons, 1958), Table 28, p. 45.

Table III. Percentage of Women Workers Seeking Employment in Particular Occupational Fields, July, 1936

Normally Employed (1930 Census)	Distr. %
Domestic and Personal Services	29.6
Clerical Occupations	18.5
Professional Service	14.2
Trade	9.0
Other	11.2
Total	100.0

Seeking Employment (1936)	Distr. %
Service Workers	50.9
Clerical Workers	15.5
Manuf. and Mech.	10.8
Salespersons	4.8
Other	12.3
Total	100.0

Source. Mary E. Pidgeon, *Women in Economy of the United States: A Summary Report,* U.S. Department of Labor, Women's Bureau Bulletin No. 155 (Washington, D.C.: Government Printing Office, 1937), p. 37.

clerical work, and some kinds of factory work, was so stereotyped that it was virtually closed to men. Women's attitudes toward work also tended to be more flexible than men's, particularly if they were forced to work because of the unusual circumstances of the Depression. They were likely to see their plight as a temporary aberration rather than a permanent condition.[4]

Perhaps another reason for the relatively low unemployment rate was the self-perception and behavior of women. Rather than seeing themselves as an unemployed part of the labor force, they simply viewed themselves in terms of their traditional nonworking role. For example, Margaret H. Hogg, an economist who surveyed a group of families in New Haven, Connecticut in 1931, noted that women tended to drop out of the labor market when work was unobtainable. Thus, it is possible that there were many women who did not appear in the unemployment statistics, but may well have accepted a job had there been one available.[5]

In spite of a relatively lower unemployment rate, women were nonetheless directly and severely affected by the Depression. In 1937 an enumerative check was conducted as part of the Census of Partial Employment, Unemployment, and Occupations. This report estimated that there were over three million totally unemployed women workers in November of that year. (The total female force in the 1930's was about 11 million.) An additional 398,000 women were estimated to be working on WPA and other emergency jobs, making a total of about 3.5 million women without normal employment. Another 1.5 million had intermittent or part-time employment.[6] Throughout most of the thirties women in domestic and personal service carried the burden of unemployment in proportionately greater numbers than women in other fields.[7] Table III, which is based upon figures from a 1937 Women's Bureau study, shows the percentage of women in particular occupations who were seeking employment. In the case of professional women and salespeople, unemployment rates were relatively low, but not all white-collar workers fared as well. The second highest percentage of women seeking work was in the clerical occupations.

Clerical work had long been the goal of lower-middle-class, young women who had to earn their livings, as well as that of large numbers of young women who merely wanted to work for a few years before marriage. But by the 1930's the field no longer offered the wide-open opportunities for employment that had been characteristic of the previous decades. Almost every good-sized American city during these years had its business school, tempting patrons with slogans such as "take our six months course and prepare yourself for a career," or "positions guaranteed to all graduates." But the guarantee became increasingly hard to make good with the lessened need for clerical workers. Exacerbating this situation was the fact that in many cities the only public-school trade course open to women was the high school "commercial course."[8]

A special census of unemployment in Massachusetts in 1934 reported nearly 9,500 young women who had received vocational training but had never worked. Of this number, 7,500 were trained for clerical work. A Women's Bureau study pointed out that in New Bedford, Massachusetts, 663 girls were enrolled in commercial courses in 1934-1935, but only thirty-four members of the June, 1934, graduating class were placed in clerical positions. A report of the U.S. Employment Service showed 177,000 women seeking clerical work in November, 1937, but only 5,300 were placed in such jobs, and half of these were temporary positions.[9]

Temporary and part-time work was often the only work available to women who desperately needed a job. Thus the unemployment figures understated the economic straits of many working women who, although listed as employed, were actually underemployed. Saleswomen were typical in this respect. Many of them worked part-time during the peak hours of business. For some women, particularly married women, this was a convenient arrangement. But for others who needed full-time employment, the job was taken simply because there was no full-time work to be had.

Saleswomen also faced total unemployment, of course. In November of 1937, nearly 58,000 women were registered for sales positions with the U.S.

Employment Service, but only 4,800 were placed, and well over half of these were in temporary jobs. Data on the employment of women in stores varied from state to state, but in general, by 1935 the level of employment was above the low point of 1929. And, as Table III indicates, saleswomen did not have the high unemployment rates of other occupational groups, in spite of, and perhaps because of, the fact that many were underemployed.[10]

Professional women also had low unemployment rates in comparison to other occupational groups, but the case of the professional worker is one that requires special attention, for the statistical evidence probably understated the impact of unemployment to a greater extent than was true for any other occupational group. For one thing, professional women often possessed sufficient skills to enable them to move into other occupations, so that while they were not actually unemployed, they were probably not working in the job of choice and might well have experienced a loss of status.[11] Also, professional women were often able to simply drop out of the labor market when work was not available to them—either because they were married to men with professional positions, or because they had other family support. This is not to suggest that all professional women in the 1930's were financially independent apart from their work. Nonetheless, they were more likely to have resources to fall back upon, and more likely to be working for reasons other than strictly economic need than was the average woman worker.

In 1934, Lorine Pruette did a study of employment and unemployment among the members of the American Woman's Association, which had a membership of 4,000 women, more than 75 percent of whom were actively engaged in a business or professions. The AWA was not representative of the country as a whole, since about 90 percent of its membership were either residents of New York City or lived within a ninety-mile radius. Nonetheless, the study suggested the extent to which professional and business women were affected by the Depression. Although AWA members were in a very favorable position compared to working women as a whole, during the three years covered by the survey, unemployment was a reality at one time or another for 29 percent of those responding to Pruette's questionnaire. The evidence which Pruette compiled indicated that even temporary unemployment resulted in a loss of professional status. And re-employment did not guarantee a return to former status. Even during the affluent years of earlier decades, professional women had to be better than their male competition when applying for good jobs. With the tightening up of the job market, women were more likely to be pushed down into the lower occupational levels.[12]

In addition to loss of occupational status there was an obvious loss of money. On the average, these unemployed women lost sixteen months out of a possible working period of four years and eight months. Seventy-five percent were unemployed for at least three months and almost 10 percent were out of work at least three years. The longest average duration was twenty-two months, reported by twenty-five women who were unemployed at the end and the beginning of the period, with some employment in between. The shortest average of unemployment, 9.7 months, was found among women who were employed at the beginning and at the end, but not by the same organization.[13] Naturally such extended periods of unemployment resulted in considerable financial loss for the women involved. But there was also the matter of declining salaries with which to contend. Over 60 percent of the women responding reported a salary decrease between 1929 and 1933. (Unfortunately, the amount of the decreases were not reported, so there is no way of knowing if they exceeded the decline in the cost of living during these years.) Also, the general feeling of insecurity, which was present even among those who had not been unemployed or lost earnings, led the overwhelming majority—97.7 percent—to cut their budgets.[14]

Perhaps the most important effect that the Depression had upon professional women was that it undermined their self-confidence and forced them to readjust their career aspirations—a particularly tragic development since for many of them, their careers were their main interest in life. The majority of them were not married, and as Pruette pointed out, they were members of the generation that had stressed the importance of jobs and exulted in their own economic independence. A very proud group, they were not likely to advertise either their insecurity or their economic need.

> We shall probably never know the humiliation and disruptive shifts
> that educated women have resorted to in order to hide their
> economic distress... And to recall that these are the women who
> by their age and training and marital status largely belong to the
> women who have sought major satisfactions in their jobs,
> renouncing marriage and working years to reach their vocational
> achievements.[15]

Although it is apparent that professional and business women did not suffer to the same extent as other classes of women workers during the Depression, the economic hardships which they faced discouraged and retarded the expansion of their occupational fields. And furthermore, business and professional women, along with other white-collar working women did not receive the same support and encouragement from the New Deal legislation, which substantially advanced the interests of other classes of women workers.

New Deal labor legislation left out large groups of women workers at the bottom and the top of the economic ladder. For instance, the Fair Labor

Standards Act specifically exempted from its provisions many job categories, such as domestic service. The National Recovery Act (NRA) codes applied only to industries in, or affecting, interstate and foreign commerce, and they covered only about half of all employed women—mainly those in the manufacturing industries, trade, communications, clerical work, and certain large service groups. Many women who were not covered by the codes were working in occupations in which the worst employment conditions prevailed, the most obvious example being that of household employment. Other groups of similarly low status were also excluded from code provisions. They included laundresses not in laundries, dressmakers and seamstresses not in factories, and women in agriculture and public service.

At the other end of the occupational spectrum were the 1.5 million women who were also neglected in the NRA codes. Clerical workers also received only limited benefit from the codes. Though many of them were technically covered, most of them were located in industries where they received very little benefit, and some were not covered at all. Codes were not approved either for telephone workers, 235,000 of whom were women, or for insurance companies, where about 150,000 women worked.[16] In general, although clerical workers made a much higher weekly wage than workers in production or service, their hours and working conditions were not as favorable as the public impression of them. A typical work week was forty-four hours, and the clerical worker might be paid anywhere from $15 to $25, depending upon the type of office and its regional location. But most important, as already noted, was the unemployment of office workers during the 1930's—a problem that might have been partially met by unionization, unemployment benefits, and government programs, had there been support for these approaches.

White-collar and professional workers also failed to benefit from Section 7(a) of the National Industrial Relations Act (NIRA), the provision that revitalized the labor movement for workers in industry by protecting the rights of unions to organize free of employer interference. Thus, the formation of the Committee for Industrial Organization (CIO) in 1935 marked another advance for the industrial woman worker that was not extended either to the domestic and service worker or to the business and professional woman.[17]

The emergency public employment programs, administered and financed by the federal government, were of little help to white-collar and professional women workers. Women did not participate in the work relief programs to the same degree as men, at least partly because these programs were aimed at the male breadwinner as the mainstay of family life in America. And more than half of the 372,000 women participating in the Works Project Administration (WPA) were employed on projects which emphasized menial domestic work.[18] Thus, garments and supplies made by these women were distributed to relief clients and to hospitals and other public institutions; preserved, canned, and dried surplus food, also produced by them, went to needy families and for school-lunch projects.[19] Many of the women involved in work relief under WPA were in a special program set up in July, 1937, called the Household Service Demonstration Project. The program provided training for women who were seeking domestic employment, but it also provided for the employment of women who acted as teachers and demonstrators in the courses. Some 1,700 women were involved in giving a two-month training course (later extended to three months) in methods of cooking and serving food, care of the house, care of children, washing, ironing, and marketing. The WPA also employed another 30,000 women on housekeeping-aid projects. Women who were good homemakers, but had no other skills, were sent into the homes of needy families to help out in times of illness or other distress. In addition, during the 1937-1938 school season, 8,000 women were employed on school-lunch projects.

Obviously all of these tasks were a reflection of women's traditional domestic roles. None of them really developed skills that could be transferred to other sectors of the economy. However, women were also employed in the various professional and white-collar projects. In fact, although in general not as many women participated in WPA projects as did men (only 17.5 percent of all WPA workers were female, at a time when women made up about 24 percent of the total labor force), their occupational distribution was much more favorable than their male counterparts. That is, women on WPA projects were more likely to be placed in a white-collar occupation than were men. Nearly one-third of all women working on WPA projects were employed as clerical workers, professional and technical workers, or project supervisors and foremen.[20] An obvious reason for this relatively strong representation in white-collar work was that a high proportion of women in the actual work force were in white-collar occupations. Therefore, it was logical that they were well represented among those seeking work in government-funded projects.

As late as 1940 there were still 1,250,000 women seeking work and another 450,000 employed in public emergency work. Along with unemployment, women workers had to face the additional obstacle of prejudice and discrimination on the part of their prospective employers and co-workers. The hostility toward the woman worker, always a factor regardless of economic circumstances, was heightened by the crisis of the thirties. The white-collar woman worker, especially if married, faced the most severe antagonism.

The basic argument that emerged during the Depression was that women were taking jobs away from unemployed male workers. Actually, this was not the case. In direct response to the theory that the entrance of women into gainful occupations had displaced men, the National Industrial Conference Board published a study in 1936 entitled *Women Workers and Labor Supply* which concluded that there was little evidence that female workers were substituting for male workers, or that women were encroaching upon male occupations. Instead, the increase in women workers during the twentieth century resulted from the fact that the male population of working age was not large enough to supply the labor force needed for new service occupations or to meet the expansion of old ones. Most of the increase in the number of women gainfully employed took place in distribution and service occupations. Meanwhile, the proportion of women workers in the production industries, particularly manufacturing and mechanical industries, was definitely on the decline.[21]

A corollary to the theory that women were displacing men was the assumption that most women did not really have to work because they had someone to support them and were therefore working only for "pin money." The "pin-money theory" served also as a justification for lower wages. Even during the early decades of the century and, indeed, in the nineteenth century as well, the argument was advanced by antifeminists and others who felt threatened by women's changing roles. Voiced by almost everyone except those involved in social and labor reform, the "pin-money theory" proved a significant obstacle to the aspirations of working women. Mary Anderson, Director of the Women's Bureau, felt that the "pin-money theory" was one of the most exasperating problems facing those who tried to advance their cause.[22]

The dispute over women's right to work was bound to have a negative effect upon women's attitude toward their role in the world of work, and yet the overall effect was not entirely negative. The interest in women workers did result in the collection and interpretation of a large amount of data concerning the economic status of women, which brought about an increased awareness of women's economic role. Still, the attitudes expressed were manifestations of a climate of opinion that must have had its impact upon women workers, immeasurable though that impact might have been. Of course, for the great majority of women, who had to work for their economic sustenance, a debate between economists, business leaders, and social workers was of little direct concern. But it certainly narrowed their opportunities on the job market, and of course it directly affected their wages. Even the NRA codes reflected the general view that women needed less money than men. By September 1, 1934, 233 NRA codes had been approved, and of these 135 fixed minimum rates for women in production work lower than for men for at least some occupations. As a general comparison, in three codes women's wage rates were 6.3 percent below men's. This was the smallest difference found.

The greatest difference was 30 percent, found in one code. In eighteen codes the difference was less than 10 percent, and in twenty-five codes the difference was 20 percent or more.[23]

Most women working in production, or other unskilled or semiskilled occupations, had little choice in their economic roles. But for those women who were in a position to make decisions regarding their career, the hostile environment of the thirties was undoubtedly discouraging. Such was especially true for married women wishing to pursue a career or simply work to raise their family's standard of living. All women workers were suspect, but those who were married were the objects of outright discrimination through the actions and policies of employers. Direct discriminatory action was the logical extension of the "pin-money theory" and the married woman worker, who presumably had a husband to support her, was the natural victim.

Private employers, particularly those in large service industries, and state and federal governmental agencies, were the most likely to adopt policies discriminating against the married woman worker. The New England Telephone and Telegraph Company discharged married women in January, 1931, and the Northern Pacific Railroad Company followed suit exactly nine months later. Public school teachers were often subject to immediate dismissal if they were married. The National Education Association made a survey of 1,500 cities in 1930-1931 and found that in 63 percent of the cities a woman teacher was dismissed as soon as she married. Seventy-seven percent of them did not employ married women as new teachers.[24]

Legislative attempts to restrict the employment of married women were plentiful, but not particularly successful. However, as the Depression wore on, efforts along these lines intensified. The National Federation of Business and Professional Women's Clubs reported in 1940 that bills directed against married women workers had been introduced in the legislatures of twenty-six states during the previous few years.[25] The bills differed in content, but their intent was obvious—to keep the middle-class, married woman out of the job market. Some bills would have barred the married woman only if her husband earned a certain amount, such as $100 a month, or $1,200 or $1,500 a year. But in one state the amount was set at $800 a year, although a WPA study of the cost of living reported that $1,243 was the minimum for family maintenance in a city of that state.[26]

The federal government took more direct discriminatory action than did the state governments. On June 30, 1932, Congress passed the Federal Economy Act which stipulated that no two persons in any family could be employed in government service. The language used in the bill applied to "persons" rather than "women" as such, and theoretically it was antinepotist rather than discriminatory, but in application it discriminated against women. Before the act was repealed in January, 1935, 1,603 employees were discharged; three-fourths of them were women.[27]

Although public sentiment in general was opposed to the married woman worker in business and the professions, particularly during the Depression, in the end the private employer made the hiring and firing decisions. Private policymakers had three considerations to balance: public sentiment as expressed through the attitudes of customers and clients; the simple economics of running a business in terms of efficiency and labor supply; and the private feelings of the individual employer himself. Often a conservative conscience led an employer to believe that he was undermining family life by hiring wives and mothers. The oversupply of applicants for his job, and the fact that many of these applicants were totally dependent upon their job for a livelihood, also led him to underestimate or deprecate the needs of the married woman who seemingly had a husband to support her.

A study published in 1939 by the National Industrial Conference Board showed that most private employers considered merit more important than marital status, but at the same time, they were influenced to some extent by the prevailing opinion that the unemployment would be resolved if married women left the job market. The general practice was to maintain a flexible policy, with a preference for single women. Practically three-fourths of the companies said they had no definite fixed policy concerning women factory employees who married and 60 percent had none regarding their office employees.[28] Discrimination varied in intensity depending upon the type of office work. For example, 84 percent of the insurance companies, 65 percent of the banks, and 63 percent of the public utilities had restrictions against the employment of married women in their offices, but only 14 percent of the manufacturing concerns and 11 percent of the mercantile establishments had such restrictions against office workers. There was also a wide variation from city to city across the nation, depending on which type of industry predominated.[29]

Sales work was another area of white-collar employment that attracted a particularly high proportion of married women workers. In 1920, 21.1 percent of all saleswomen were married and in 1930 the proportion was up to 33.5 percent. By 1940, 42.7 percent were married.[30] The National Federation of Business and Professional Women's Clubs made a survey early in 1930 that revealed that only a small number of department stores refused employment to married women. However, in 1939, the *Department Store Economist* had reported that the sentiment against married women was growing strong. Opposition came from customers, labor organizations, women's clubs, and miscellaneous groups of the unemployed. Despite this opposition, most department store managers were not eager to announce an official policy against hiring or retaining married women. Their hesitancy was partly a matter of public relations and partly a matter of simple economics. Married women's employment was advantageous to department stores because the necessary part-time arrangements were convenient for both parties.[31] In the end, convenience and efficiency were both more important to these employers than the doubtful and debatable principles espoused by those who opposed the married woman's right to work.

Despite the fact that policies varied widely according to locale, type of industry, and attitude of the employer, it is obvious that married women workers, who had always met with a certain amount of hostility, faced the double burden of job shortage and intensified discrimination during the Depression. Single women faced less direct discrimination, perhaps, but certainly they were not presented with opportunities for responsibilities and advancement that most of their male colleagues took for granted. The damage that must have been done to this generation of women can never be measured. Perhaps Lorine Pruette came closest to the truth when she speculated that the achievements reached by women in the earlier decades of the century might stand as the high-water mark for many years. The Depression had its impact not only upon the mature women who learned to settle for less, but on the young girls who had never known more.

> The lost generation of girls has been marking time in a world that allowed them neither security nor opportunity. They have not had to confront the earlier feminist choice of career versus home of their own for many of them had a chance at neither.[32]

Recent interpretations of American women's experiences during the interwar years suggest that this was a period of stagnation—politically, socially, and economically.[33] So far as the thirties are concerned, this essay certainly supports that perspective. The responsibility for the decline of feminism, social activism, and careerism has often been placed upon American women themselves. And yet, given the social and economic obstacles that they faced, it is not surprising that so many women retreated from the challenges of an earlier generation and sought security in home and family. And in spite of the relative decline in the occupational status of women during these years, the Depression experience made certain truths self-evident. For instance, by the thirties it was apparent that women were in the labor market to stay, no matter what the economic conditions or the state of public opinion. This fact was an inevitable response to long-range changes in American economic structure which created a demand for female labor; women met this demand because their own needs could no longer be met through work in the home.

More surprising, perhaps, was the staying power of married women workers as a group. In spite of overt prejudice and blatant discrimination, married women increased their work-force participation both absolutely and proportionately. Perhaps it was a matter of how they sought security, for at a time when men of all economic levels were insecure in their jobs, it is possible that within the family, at least, there was a gradual acceptance of the working wife.[34]

Finally, the changing economic basis of family life beginning in the nineteenth century and accelerating in the twentieth century, from a unit of production to one which emphasized consumption, meant that the male wage-earner was not always able to support his several family members, in spite of the efforts of reformers, economists, and labor unions. Additional wage-earners have always been important to the American family, and with the decline of child labor in the 1920's and 1930's this responsibility often fell upon the married woman. Thus, the woman worker, both married and single, could hold dear the values of family life, security, and material comforts, but at the same time move into the labor market to protect those values.[35]

The experience of women in the Depression of the 1930's was discouraging, but it was not a complete reversal of the long-term trends affecting their lives that had emerged with the industrialization of the nation. The women who overcame the economic conditions and the discriminatory policies of the Depression to remain in the work force were never a majority of all American women, but they carried out a pattern of combined work and family roles that was to predominate in the post-war years.

Notes

1. For women's perception of white-collar work at the turn of the century, see Lynn Weiner, "A Woman's Place Is in the Home: American Working Women and the Ideology of Domesticity, 1865-1978" (dissertation in progress, Boston University). See also, William L. O'Neill, ed., *Women At Work* (Chicago: Quadrangle Books, 1972), especially his introduction, which is a comparison of the unskilled manual labor available to women early in the twentieth century and the white-collar work which was typical of most women workers by mid-century. Joseph F. Kett, *Rites of Passage: Adolescence in America, 1790 to the Present* (New York: Basic Books, 1977), pp. 150-153, also points to the white-collar sector of the economy as offering new opportunities for middle-class and working-class youth. For a detailed discussion of the shift in the occupational distribution of the female labor force during the decades before World War II, see Winifred D. Bolin, "The Changing Nature of the Female Labor Force, 1920-1940," paper presented at the Conference on the History of Women, St. Paul, Minnesota, October 24-25, 1975.
2. See Winifred D. Wandersee Bolin, "Past Ideals and Present Pleasures: Women, Work, and the Family, 1920-1940" (Ph.D. dissertation, University of Minnesota, 1976), pp. 27-29, for a description of the nature

of domestic and personal service in the early decades of the twentieth century.

3. See Alan L. Sorkin, "On the Occupational Status of Women, 1870-1970," *American Journal of Economics and Sociology* 32 (July 1973): 238-239.

4. For a discussion of the wage differential between men and women during the 1930's, see William H. Chafe, *The American Woman: Her Changing Social, Economic, and Political Roles, 1920-1970* (New York: Oxford University Press, 1972), p. 61; and Elizabeth Faulkner Baker, *Technology and Woman's Work* (New York: Columbia University Press, 1964), pp. 398-401, and 404-411.

5. Margaret H. Hogg, *The Incidence of Work Shortage: Report of a Survey by Sample of Families Made in New Haven, Connecticut in May-June, 1931* (New York: Russell Sage Foundation, 1932), pp. 24-25.

6. "Findings of the Unemployment Census," *The Woman Worker* 17 (November 1938): 4.

7. See Mary E. Pidgeon, *Employment Fluctuations and Unemployment of Women: Certain Indications from Various Sources, 1928-31,* U.S. Department of Labor, Women's Bureau Bulletin No. 113 (Washington, D.C.: Government Printing Office, 1933), for 1930-1931 figures.

8. Elisabeth D. Benham, *The Woman Wage Earner: Her Situation Today,* U.S. Department of Labor, Women's Bureau Bulletin No. 172 (Washington, D.C.: Government Printing Office, 1939), p. 20. See also, U.S. Department of Labor, Women's Bureau, *Office Work and Office Workers in 1940,* Bulletin No. 188 (Washington, D.C.: Government Printing Office, 1942), p. 1. Frances R. Donovan, *The Saleslady* (Chicago: University of Chicago Press, 1929) talks about the appeal of office work to young girls in the 1920's.

9. Benham, p. 20.

10. Ibid.

11. Ibid., p. 50.

12. Lorine Pruette, *Women Workers Through the Depression* (New York: Macmillan Company, 1934), pp. 144-145, and pp. 21-22.

13. Ibid., pp. 22-23.

14. Ibid., pp. 126-130.

15. Ibid., pp. 21-22.

16. Mary E. Pidgeon, *Employed Women Under N.R.A. Codes,* U.S. Department of Labor, Women's Bureau Bulletin No. 130 (Washington, D.C.: Government Printing Office, 1935), pp. 7 and 31.

17. Chafe, *The American Woman,* pp. 82-83. See also, Amy Hewes, "Women Wage-Earners and the N.R.A.," *American Federationist* 41 (February 1935): 164, for a discussion of unionism.

18. "Women and the W.P.A.," *The Woman Worker* 18 (September 1938): 8. See also, Ellen S. Woodward, "W.P.A.'s Program of Training for Housework," *Journal of Home Economics* 31 (February 1939): 86-88; and Florence Kerr, "Training for Household Employment: The W.P.A.

Program," *Journal of Home Economics* 32 (September 1940): 437-440.

19. Kerr, p. 439; and "Women and the W.P.A.," p. 8.

20. "Occupations of W.P.A. Workers," *Monthly Labor Review* 49 (August 1939): 355-356.

21. National Industrial Conference Board, *Women Workers and Labor Supply* (New York, 1936).

22. Mary Anderson, *Woman at Work* (as told to Mary Winslow) (Minneapolis, Minnesota, 1949), p. 139.

23. Pidgeon, *Employed Women Under NRA Codes*, pp. 140-141.

24. Pruette, *Women Workers Through the Depression*. See also, Ruth Shallcross, *Should Married Women Work?* National Federation of Business and Professional Women's Clubs, Public Affairs Pamphlet No. 49, 1940.

25. Shallcross, *Should Married Women Work?*, pp. 5-6.

26. "Work of Married Women Seriously Menaced," *The Woman Worker* 29 (May 1939): 3-4.

27. Anderson, *Woman at Work*, pp. 155-156; and Samuel A. Stouffer and Paul E. Lazarsfeld, *Research Memorandum on the Family in the Depression*, Social Science Research Council, Bulletin No. 29 (New York, 1937), p. 56.

28. Shallcross, *Should Married Women Work?* p. 9: and "Married Women and Private Industry," *The Woman Worker* 20 (May 1940): 14-15.

29. Shallcross, *Should Married Women Work?* p. 9; and "Married Women and Private Industry," pp. 14-15. See also, U.S. Department of Labor, Women's Bureau, *Office Work and Office Workers in 1940*, Bulletin No. 188 (Washington, D.C.: Government Printing Office, 1942), pp. 55-57.

30. U.S. Department of Commerce, Bureau of the Census, *Fifteenth Census of the United States, 1930, Population*, Vol. V, *General Report on Occupations*, Chapter V, Table IX, p. 279; and *Sixteenth Census of the United States, 1940, The Labor Force*, Part I, *U.S. Summary*, Table 68, p. 111.

31. Shallcross, *Should Married Women Work?* pp. 6-7.

32. Pruette, *Women Workers Through the Depression*, pp. 5-6.

33. The best recent interpretations of women's experience in the twentieth century are Chafe; Lois Banner, *Women in Modern America: A Brief History* (New York: Harcourt, Brace, Jovanovich, 1974); and William L. O'Neill, *Everyone Was Brave: A History of Feminism in America* (Chicago: Quadrangle Books, 1969). See especially, Chafe, pp. 92-93, and Chapter 5; Banner, pp. 191-196; and O'Neill, Chapters 8 and 9.

34. Banner, p. 196.

35. For a discussion of the economic basis of married women's work during the Depression, and the changing economic function of the American family, see Winifred D. Wandersee Bolin, "The Economics of Middle-Income Family Life: Working Women During the Great Depression," *Journal of American History* 65 (June 1978): 60-74. The relationship between child labor and women's work was the topic of a paper: Bolin, "Modernization

of the American Family as an Economic Unit: The Role of Women and Children," presented at the Organization of American Historians Annual Meeting, New Orleans, April 11-14, 1979.

Susan M. Hartmann

Women's Organizations During World War II: The Interaction of Class, Race, and Feminism

The tendency of historians to emphasize the decline of feminism between 1920 and the 1960's and to focus on conflict over the proposed Equal Rights Amendment as the great barrier to feminist solidarity has led to an overly simplistic view of female consciousness and activism in twentieth-century America. The assumption that feminism died out after the suffrage victory not to be reborn again until the 1960's prevents our understanding of both the continuities and discontinuities between the two movements. If by feminism we mean the consciousness of women as a distinct group and their collective efforts to remove socially-imposed barriers to their full development, then feminism was very much alive during the war years. The traditional emphasis on the divisiveness of the Equal Rights Amendment has also left unexplored the complexity of women's responses to their oppression. Such a focus both overlooks the ability of women, despite disagreement over the amendment, to forge coalitions around certain goals, and it ignores other issues on which class and race differences inhibited feminist solidarity. It is the purpose of this essay to analyze ideologies and priorities of women's organizations during World War II, and thereby to measure the shifting considerations of gender, class, and race which defined the nature of their activism.[1]

The groups considered here were autonomous: not affiliated with male-dominated bodies, their programs were exclusively women-defined. Although each spoke for only a minority of women, taken together they did represent active, politically conscious women across a broad spectrum of class, race, economic participation, and educational background. White, middle-class and professional women were represented by two organizations.[2] The American Association of University Women (AAUW) represented an elite of 70,000 to 80,000 educated, professional women, about half of whom were employed outside the home. The National Federation of Busi-

[An Associate Professor in the Department of History at the University of Missouri-St. Louis, Susan M. Hartmann's publications include *The Marshall Plan* and *Truman and the 80th Congress* as well as articles on women in the twentieth century.]

ness and Professional Women (BPW) spoke for 70,000 members, more than 90 percent of whom were in the labor force, concentrated in the areas of clerical work, education, and trade.[3]

Lacking the sizeable independent organizations available to professional and white-collar workers, women in blue-collar jobs were represented by the Women's Bureau of the Department of Labor and by the National Women's Trade Union League (NWTUL). Despite its declining membership and funds, the NWTUL retained its function as the voice for women in industrial and service occupations. Connected to the NWTUL by their common history, ideology, and even personnel, the Women's Bureau supported the League's public policy objectives.[4]

With 800,000 members in eighteen national organizations and fourteen metropolitan councils, the National Council of Negro Women (NCNW) was the largest black women's organization in the 1940's. Founded in 1935 by educator and New Deal official Mary McLeod Bethune, the Council afforded a formal structure for Bethune's already-recognized role as leader of the masses of black women. While class differences among black women were reflected in their organizational patterns, the common experience of racial oppression led black women more readily to transcend the barriers which divided their white sisters. The nation's oldest black women's sorority, Alpha Kappa Alpha (AKA), was affiliated with the NCNW and ordered its priorities in much the same way as the larger organization. Representing some three to five thousand college-educated, professional black women, AKA had moved from its original social orientation to a program encouraging race consciousness and political activism on behalf of the race.[5]

While all of these organizations had addressed women's issues during the 1930's, World War II dramatically altered the context in which they functioned and, as a result, the content of their goals. The Depression had put women on the defensive: their organizations struggled to resist intensified discrimination arising from the economic crisis. World War II allowed women to take the offensive. The public depiction of the war as a struggle for freedom and democracy afforded women symbols to turn to their own advantage. More importantly, the critical labor shortage opened doors to women in almost all occupational strata, lent a new legitimacy to the woman worker, and made government, employers, and labor unions more willing to consider the needs of women. Finally, the influx of millions of women into the labor force sharpened the contradiction between women's traditional family obligations and their new responsibilities and compelled women's organizations to confront that contradiction to an unprecedented degree.

United in their determination to expand female participation in the public sphere and to improve the conditions of such participation, women's organizations nonetheless revealed sharp differences in the order of their priorities.

The primary cleavage, that of class, was reflected in the two forms which feminism took during the war years. One strain of World-War-II feminism focused on elevating women's general status, on gaining popular recognition of women as fully competent and equal participants in all aspects of public life. The other centered on issues of day-to-day survival and sought to promote opportunities for women that would meet their basic material needs. The first emphasis was that of elite, predominantly white, women's organizations and was manifested principally in the movement for female participation in policymaking. The second focus was that of working-class women and embraced such issues as labor standards, child care, and domestic service. Black middle-class women were represented in both status-oriented and survival-oriented feminism, but their allegiance rested primarily with the latter.

Although representatives of black and working-class women frequently supported the goals of status-oriented feminism their priorities differed considerably from those of groups like the BPW and AAUW. Similarly, while middle-class women confronted problems of primary concern to blue-collar women, their race and class position prompted resolutions which often posed them against their working-class sisters. These tensions reflected the middle-class insularity of professional women, their failure to recognize the immediate needs of blue-collar women, and their insensitivity to the weight of racial oppression on their black sisters.

Women displayed the greatest solidarity in their efforts to expand economic opportunities for themselves. Throughout the war representatives of women's organizations met to design programs to promote the training, equal treatment, and full utilization of women in war production and to plan for the retention of women's gains after reconversion. The Women's Bureau functioned as linchpin for these endeavors by sponsoring conferences and by working bilaterally with individual organizations. While the National Council of Negro Women was represented at Women's Bureau conferences there is little record of collaboration, in part, no doubt, because of the Bureau's resistance to black women's attempts to get a black woman on its professional staff. The Bureau did work closely with the Federation of Business and Professional Women, assisting with the establishment of a master file of Federation members available for war work and cooperating to secure defense training for women and to promote equal pay. The Federation in turn pressured Congress for increased appropriations for the Bureau. The American Association of University Women also lobbied for Women's Bureau funding and received assistance from the Bureau for its program concerning the problems of industrial women. But in its goals and focus on blue-collar women, the Women's Bureau's closest allies were the National Women's Trade Union League and the female representatives of various unions. This alliance was personified in Elizabeth Christman, vice-president of the NWTUL, who was hired by the Bureau when its wartime activities necessitated additional personnel. Efforts by the BPW and AAUW to draw more attention to white-collar and professional women failed to shift the Bureau's priorities. Nonetheless employment issues, and especially the drive for equal pay legislation, evoked significant cooperation among women's organizations.[6]

The demand that the door be opened to policymaking positions was a second issue which mobilized each of the organizations, but which also reflected even greater diversity in motivations and objectives. Their relative material security freed middle-class women to focus on this goal, which represented the epitome of status-oriented feminism. Professional women took the initiative in organizing coalitions to press for government posts for women and ranked it among their top priorities. Even before the war the AAUW had initiated a program to analyze the current status of women and to increase their participation on governing boards and in administrative posts. In 1942 the BPW reported dismal statistics on the number of women in federal war agencies and launched a campaign to increase their representation. These efforts were motivated in part by the belief that only female participation in decision making would ensure that women's needs were addressed. In this regard they acted from the same considerations as did representatives of lower-class women. But elite women also felt the stinging rebuke to their self-esteem when the capabilities of women like themselves went unrecognized. Thus, they sought symbolic affirmation that their worth and ability equalled that of men. Not only was their feminism limited by their concentration on a goal of direct benefit only to well-educated women, but it was also disguised by their insistence that they were not struggling for women's rights or special favors, and mitigative as well was their use of sentimental arguments based on women's presumed moral superiority. Indeed, the two largest coalitions concentrated on obtaining appointments of women to the international postwar conferences, endeavors which promised little of immediate benefit to most women. For elite women representation in decision-making positions was as much an end in itself as it was a means to securing the more basic interests of women.[7]

Although representatives of working-class women also insisted on the right of women to opportunities for full development, they placed more emphasis upon the practical benefits of female government appointments. While the Women's Bureau and the National Women's Trade Union League supported the drives for women's representation in international conferences, their major efforts concerned domestic agencies whose policies affected women. Mary Anderson, director of the Women's Bureau, cooperated with the NWTUL and the BPW to press for female representation on the War

Manpower Commission, but in the end was less pleased than the leaders of those organizations with the results of this struggle. Refusing women a seat on its Management-Labor Policy Committee, the War Manpower Commission instead created a Women's Advisory Committee. The BPW initially celebrated this decision and the appointment of its vice-president Margaret Hickey to chair the committee. Anderson, however, recognized the difference between symbolic recognition and actual power to implement women's interests. Objecting to women being put "off in a corner," she was also disturbed about the composition of the committee in which representatives of middle-class women outnumbered allies of blue-collar women.[8]

Representation in policymaking and administrative positions was also a major concern of black women, but the imperatives of race shaped a different approach and rationale. In general, black women pressed more for representation of their race than for their sex. And even when they worked specifically for the appointment of black women, they displayed less interest in symbolic representation than in the desire to address the basic needs of the total black population. Alpha Kappa Alpha's campaign for the appointment of black women to the professional staff of the Women's Bureau produced an avalanche of letters whose central argument emphasized the high incidence of black women workers and the necessity for representation to insure that their specific problems would be considered. In a different context, National Council of Negro Women member Marjorie McKenzie made explicit the differences between white and black women. At the bottom rung of the economic ladder, most black women could only view the goals of white women as "special privileges" and "window dressing." Black women, McKenzie argued, perceived their problems as stemming less from sex discrimination than from "the paramount consideration of race and the casteline...."[9]

Class and race differences were also apparent when women's organizations addressed the issue of female participation in the military. Leaders in the drive for equal status in the armed services, the AAUW and BPW, looked upon women's opportunity for military service as an essential step toward the recognition of their competence and right to equal participation in the war effort. Reflecting the perspective of their own constituency, the National Women's Trade Union League lent their support to equal status, but did not campaign actively for it. Black women were not among the advocates of the establishment of women's corps in the military branches, but once they were created, both the NCNW and AKA insistently pressured the Navy to admit blacks into the Waves and demanded the end of segregation and discrimination in all of the women's corps. The AAUW and BPW ignored military discrimination against black women while they concentrated on opening the Medical Reserve Corps to women physicians. Impervious to the wholesale discrimination against their black sisters, white women sought the expansion of professional opportunities for a few privileged women and elimination of the insulting aspersions cast upon women by the military's exclusion of female doctors. [10]

Elite white women ignored other issues of primary concern to black women, who found their most consistent support among representatives of working-class women. Elizabeth Christman of the National Women's Trade Union League sought in vain the inclusion of a special section on the problem of black women workers in the Women's Advisory Committee report and recommendations on women in the postwar period. Only the NWTUL continuously advocated bills to eliminate lynching, abolish the poll tax, and establish a permanent Fair Employment Practices Commission—three cardinal items on the agendas of Alpha Kappa Alpha and the National Council of Negro Women. The American Association of University Women endorsed a permanent FEPC in its 1945 platform, but this was the extent of white women's efforts to transcend racial barriers. Indeed, publicity concerning the discriminatory practices of local affiliates forced both the AAUW and the National Federation of Business and Professional Women to disavow exclusionary policies. Even the Women's Bureau rebuffed the pleas of Alpha Kappa Alpha for the appointment of a black woman to its staff. [11]

World War II intensified the disagreement among women's organizations over the proposed Equal Rights Amendment, a conflict which had begun with the amendment's introduction into Congress in 1923. Advocates sought to exploit the need for female participation in the defense effort as well as the rhetoric which portrayed the war as a struggle for freedom and equality, while the national emergency made defeat of the amendment seem even more imperative to opponents. The National Woman's Party led the drive for the Equal Rights Amendment; of the organizations studied here only the BPW supported the amendment. On this issue, the AAUW reached across class lines and joined the Women's Bureau and the National Women's Trade Union League in vigorous opposition. Alpha Kappa Alpha registered mild opposition and the National Council of Negro Women was represented on the National Committee to Defeat the Un-Equal Rights Amendment. However, the involvement of black women in this controversy was minimal, no doubt, because the vast majority of black women worked in occupations excluded from coverage by protective legislation. [12]

Opposition to the amendment centered on its threat to protective legislation for women. Already on the defensive as employers sought to meet production goals through exemptions from laws limiting hours and prohibiting night work for women, the Women's Bureau and the National Women's Trade Union League redoubled their efforts against the Equal Rights Amendment. The significance of the dispute over the amendment was not that it represented an irrevocable breach among women's organizations. On the contrary, the BPW continued to cooperate with the Women's Bureau and sister organizations on other issues of mutual interest. More importantly, opponents of the amendment diverted a large degree of collective female energy to an issue where defeat of the amendment simply preserved the status quo. Indeed, more space in the historical records of the NWTUL was devoted to the Equal Rights Amendment than to any other woman's issue.[13]

Disagreement over protective legislation was only one manifestation of the extent to which economic and class differences inhibited feminist activism. Despite some attempts at solidarity, women were unable to breach the gap between white collar women and those in industrial and service occupations. Although the AAUW worked against the Equal Rights Amendment, its Committee on the Legal and Economic Status of Women rejected a member's proposal that the Association seek closer ties with industrial women's organizations by concerning itself with female union membership. The AAUW's General Director displayed a similar myopic vision when she voiced concern at a Women's Bureau conference on women workers that too little attention was being paid to professional and business women. Margaret Hickey, president of the BPW, did urge her organization to reach out to production workers, noting that some clubs had members in defense plants, and the organization's journal wrote favorably about unions and female labor leaders. But the BPW resisted the principle of unionization of office workers, objected to the Women's Bureau's insistence on maintaining labor standards during the national emergency, and continued to press for the Equal Rights Amendment. From the point of view of Rose Schneiderman, President of the National Women's Trade Union League,

> higher salaried women too often allow their concern over the special discriminations against women in their group to obscure the more fundamental problem which millions of working men and women face—that of securing jobs with decent wages, decent hours, and decent living conditions.

Elizabeth Christman, one of the three representatives of blue-collar women on the Women's Advisory Committee to the War Manpower Commission, expressed a similar perspective. Commenting on the Committee's recommendations for women in the postwar period, she objected to the report's emphasis on professional women.[14]

Christman referred specifically to the issue of domestic service, an issue which sharply delineated the class and race divisions among women. Women's organizations recognized the contradiction between women's domestic obligations and their participation in the public sphere, but they sought to resolve that contradiction in different ways. Elite women had traditionally done so by employing household workers, but they were acutely aware that the war-generated economic expansion had sharply reduced the supply. These women attempted to reverse this situation by persuading unskilled women that household employment was a war service and by elevating the wages and conditions of domestic work. Black women, on the other hand, celebrated the opportunity to move from white women's kitchens into better paying jobs: an article on this mobility reprinted in *The Aframerican Women* was entitled, "The Whip Changes Hands." But experience tempered their optimism, and recognizing that many black women would remain in domestic service while many others would be forced to return there after the war, they too sought improved conditions in that employment. Unlike privileged white women, their primary concern was the plight of the employee and their solution unionization. The Women's Trade Union League supported this effort since the organization of household workers had been a special concern even before the war. Differences between elite women and blue-collar women were not limited to their respective emphases on household employer and employee. While privileged women found the solution to married women workers' problems in better domestic help, Christman pointed out their failure to recognize that such a solution was beyond the means of the average female worker. Elite women were insufficiently sensitive both to the needs of the household worker and to the problems of married women in other low-wage employment. The result was a failure to define a common ground upon which women could address a basic element of their subordinate status.[15]

Similar divergence characterized women's perspectives on the contradiction between women's traditional responsibility for childrearing and their participation in production. All of the organizations endorsed federal funding of child-care centers, but the nature of their support was as much related to class and race interests as it was to feminist concerns. The fundamental division was between an emphasis on the needs of the working mother and on those of the child. Neither the AAUW or the BPW addressed day care as an issue of direct interest to their members as working mothers. A large portion of AAUW members did not work outside the home, while most of the BWP membership was not married. Women in these two organizations who were both mothers and employed were in the minority, and apparently most of them had the financial resources for a personal solution. Day-care received little attention from the BPW, but it was a high priority issue for the AAUW. As early as 1942 more than sixty AAUW branches were involved in establishing child-care centers, and the organization actively lobbied for national legislation. But the Association defined the issue as a community problem, not as a woman's problem, and its discussion of the issue revealed both a measure of self-interest and a lack of confidence in the desire or ability of working mothers to plan for the welfare of their children. In an article on day-care published during the war, the AAUW criticized the earlier New Deal WPA nursery program for its focus on providing jobs in day-care centers for unemployed women and queried: "Why had young college-trained women prepared themselves for professional careers in the field of nursery education, if at the drop of a hat... they could be replaced by untrained women or women of questionable employment background?"[16]

The concern of elite women's organizations for professionalism in child-care services was apparent in the controversy over the jurisdiction of federal programs. They vigorously—though unsuccessfully—supported transfer of that control from the Federal Works Agency, an emergency agency whose primary function was administration of federally-financed construction, to the Children's Bureau and Office of Education and their state counterparts. While liberals supported such a move since it promised a high-quality program administered by experts in child development, proponents of the transfer ignored black women's concerns over racial discrimination. Alpha Kappa Alpha objected vigorously to the legislation reorganizing the federal child-care program. Its representative pointed to the positive record of the Federal Works Agency in ensuring an equitable distribution of funds to centers for black children, arguing that the records of both the Children's Bureau and the Office of Education were "full of instances of injustices to Negroes and a lack of concern for their welfare." To black women the primary imperative of securing services for parents and children of their race overshadowed the question of which agencies could improve the quality of child-care services.[17]

The Women's Bureau and the NWTUL remained neutral in the debate regarding jurisdiction over the federal child-care program, but their blue-collar constituency insured a perspective on child-care which embraced the problems of the mother as well as the interests of the child. Unlike elite women who often addressed the issue in terms of child neglect, union women consistently emphasized working mothers' anxiety over the security of their children and defended child-care programs as essential for both "the welfare of the child and the peace of mind of the mother." Moreover, blue-collar women were well aware that middle-class women tended to view working mothers with disapproval and to suspect them of child neglect. The tendency of privileged women to advocate child-care more as a means of social control than as a way to solve women's problems and promote female opportunities demonstrated again the class barriers to feminist solidarity.[18]

The behavior of women's organizations during World War II revealed both the extent to which feminist consciousness survived more than twenty years after the suffrage victory and the impediments to the creation of a united female front. In mobilizing around the issues of women's employment, female participation in public affairs, and the reconciliation of domestic obligations with activities outside the home, women's organizations confronted female oppression at a number of its most critical points. But white middle-class women, who had contributed much of the leadership to earlier feminist campaigns, remained captured by a perspective shaped by race and class that left unfulfilled the potential for feminist solidarity. Not surprisingly, black women devised their goals and strategy in line with their acute experience of racial oppression. Elite white women's organizations not only largely ignored race discrimination in general—so evident in the debate over the federal child-care program—but they likewise neglected the specific problems of black women, for example, their treatment by the military.

A contributing impediment to transracial cooperation, class differences posed even more formidable barriers to collective activity among women. Relative material security along with possession of education and training influenced middle-class white women in the establishment of wartime agendas that emphasized the appointment of women to policymaking positions. They thereby promoted the direct interests of women like themselves, those with the experience and skills to qualify for such positions. Moreover, they revealed the extent to which middle-class feminism concentrated on the symbolic manifestations of status.

By offering public affirmation of women's competence and rights, visibility of women in decisionmaking posts was of potential benefit to all women. Working-class women, however, confronted the more pressing needs of providing adequate income and care for themselves and their children. Privileged women addressed these problems, but they brought to them a perspective which derived as often from economic class as from gender. Open disagreement was limited to the Equal Rights Amendment and the issue of protective legislation. Less overt differences appeared when women dealt with the problem of reconciling family maintenance with work outside the home. Middle-class women tended to work out individual solutions for themselves by hiring household workers. Thus they viewed the issue of domestic service from the standpoint of the employer. And they dealt with child-care from the perspective of their economic class, demonstrating more of a concern for social order than an identification with the blue-collar working mother. Politically active women during World War II evinced dissatisfaction with the conditions of womanhood and labored to change those conditions, but they were unable to transcend class and race barriers to fashion a feminist program and strategy capable of channeling that discontent into a powerful social movement.

Notes

1. An earlier version of this essay was presented at the Organization of

American Historians meeting in April, 1978. I am grateful to Karen Anderson, Ann Lever, Jeane Mongold and Leila Rupp for their comments and critique. The most extensive treatment of twentieth-century feminism is William Chafe, *The American Woman: Her Changing Social, Economic and Political Roles, 1920-1970* (New York: Oxford University Press, 1972). His able analysis of the conflict over the Equal Rights Amendment is not extended to other issues which divided feminists. While he emphasizes World War II in this book and in *Women and Equality: Changing Patterns in American Culture* (New York: Oxford University Press, 1977), he pays little attention to women's organizations and none at all to those representing black women. In an unpublished paper, "'The Forgotten Woman': Working Women, The New Deal and Women's Organizations," Lois Scharf has recently demonstrated that in the 1930's white women's organizations displayed considerable unity in their defense of women workers despite disagreement over the Equal Rights Amendment.

2. On the basis of my research on the National League of Women Voters I have excluded it from this study. Although its program depended upon and encouraged women's participation in public affairs and although it continued to press for jury service for women and to attack economic discrimination against married women, the League abolished its Department on Government and Legal Status of Women in 1938, an action symbolic of its diminished feminist consciousness. The League's wartime agenda ignored the specific needs of women even when it addressed such issues as labor resources and planning for reconversion. Explicitly disavowing any connections with feminism, the League also refused in most instances to work closely with other women's organizations even on issues it endorsed. See Edith Valet Cook, "Department of Government and the Legal Status of Women: Twenty Years," April 24, 1940, Papers of the National League of Women Voters, Schlesinger Library, Radcliffe College, Cambridge, Mass. Box 7; National League of Women Voters, Platforms and Programs, 1940-1948, Ibid., Box 2; Kathryn H. Stone, *Twenty-five Years of a Great Idea: A History of the National League of Women Voters* (Washington, D.C.: National League of Women Voters, 1946), pp. 15-16, 27-29, 31-33. For an example of the League's "unilateralism" see Minnie L. Maffett to Marguerite Wells, December 2, 1939, and Wells to Maffett, December 15, 1939, Papers of the League of Women Voters, Library of Congress, Box 423.

3. Dorothy Elizabeth Johnson, "Organized Women and National Legislation, 1920-1941" (Ph.D. dissertation, Western Reserve University, 1960), surveys the white women's organizations considered in this essay. AAUW membership figures are given in the General Director's Letter, Vol. VII-XII (1940-1945), Schlesinger Library; Susan M. Kingsbury, *Economic Status of University Women in the U.S.A.* (Washington, D.C.: Government Printing Office, 1939), p. 3. BPW membership statistics are

given in "How Federation Members Earn," *Independent Woman* 29, (July 1940): 206. (Of those employed, 30.9 percent were in clerical work; 19.9 percent in education; and 17.7 percent in retail trade, insurance, and real estate).

4. Chafe, *The American Woman*, pp. 74-76; Mary Anderson with Mary N. Winslow, *Woman at Work: The Autobiography of Mary Anderson* (Minneapolis: University of Minnesota Press, 1951), pp. 247-252; Bertha M. Nienburg, "War History Statement," n.d., Women's Bureau Records, National Archives, RG 86, Accession number 55-A-485, Box 2; Memo, "Assignment of Elizabeth Christman for the Duration," April 6, 1942, Ibid., Box 4. (Women's Bureau records with accession numbers refer to documents which were being stored at the National Archives Records Branch at Suitland, Maryland, when part of this research was in progress. Most of these records were subsequently moved to the National Archives in Washington, D.C.)

5. Jeanne L. Noble, "The American Negro Woman," in John P. Davis, ed., *The American Negro Reference Book* (Englewood Cliff, N.J.: Prentice-Hall, 1966), p. 544; Rackham Holt, *Mary McLeod Bethune: A Biography* (Garden City, N.Y.: Doubleday, 1966), pp. 181-183, 232-234; "Negro Women Organize for Unity of Purpose and Action," *The Southern Frontier* 4 (December 1943): 2, 4; "Mrs. Jeannetta Welch Brown, Speaks for the Council," *The Aframerican Woman's Journal* 3 (Summer 1943): back page; Annabel Sawyer, "The Negro Woman in National Defense," Ibid., 2 (Summer and Fall, 1941): 2-5; Mary McLeod Bethune, "Annual Report to the National Workshop-Convention," Ibid. 3 (1943): 2-4; "Excerpts from the Report Presented by the Executive Secretary," Ibid., pp. 6-10; Marjorie H. Parker, *Alpha Kappa Alpha: Sixty Years of Service* (Alpha Kappa Alpha Sorority, 1966), pp. 1, 7, 19, 120-123; Zatella R. Turner, "Alpha Kappa Alpha Sorority's Wartime Program," *The Aframerican Woman's Journal* 3 (Summer 1943): 22-23; Memo, Miss Ware to Flora Y. Hatcher, November 27, 1941, Office of Price Administration, Records of the Information Department, Consumer Division, RG 188, Box D-6 (Other memos in this file set AKA membership at 5,000 and 6,000: Anne Mason to Oliver A. Peterson, February 28, 1945, Box D-7, Oliver Peterson to Robert R.R. Brooks, May 12, 1945, Box D-8); Alpha Kappa Alpha Legislative Release, April, 1944-January, 1946, Schomberg Collection, New York Public Library, New York, N.Y.

6. "Statement of Mary Anderson, dictated November 17, 1944," Records of the Women's Bureau, Accession Number 55-A-485, Box 4; "Program as to Women's Work in a Period of Economic Upturn," September 1939, Ibid., Accession Number 56-A-260, Box 1; Correspondence between Mary Anderson and BPW officers, 1940-1944, Records of the Women's Bureau, Box 840; Louise Stitt to Frances Speek, December 5, 1941, Ibid., Box 839; Memo, "Assignment of Elizabeth Christman for the Duration,"

April 6, 1942, Records of the Women's Bureau, Accession number 55-A-485, Box 4; Comments by Kathryn McHale, "Verbatim Proceedings of the Conference on Post-War Adjustments of Women Workers, December 4-5, 1944," Ibid., Box 900, pp. 143-146; U.S. Senate, Committee on Education and Labor, *Equal Pay for Equal Work for Women,* Hearings, by Subcommittee on S. 1178, October 29-31, 1944 (Washington, D.C.: Government Printing Office, 1944); Mary Anderson to Matthew J. Connelly, August 17, 1945, Papers of Mary Anderson, Schlesinger Library, Folder 57; "In Behalf of Equal Pay," *Independent Woman,* Vol. 23, No. 11 (November, 1944), pp. 331, 349-350.

7. Susan M. Kingbury and Frances V. Speek, "Women on Governing Boards," March, 1942, Status of Women Historical File, American Association of University Women Archives, Washington, D.C., Folder 30; "AAUW News and Notes," *Journal of the American Association of University Women* 38 (Fall 1944): 43-44; Minnie L. Maffett, "We too Must Fight this War," *Independent Woman* 21 (August 1942): 227-228, 246-247; "Underuse of Womanpower Slows War Effort," Ibid., 22 (August 1943): 230-231; "Conference at the White House," Ibid. 23 (July 1944): 225; Minnie L. Maffett to Paul G. Hoffman, February 15, 1943, Records of the Women's Bureau, Accession Number 55-A-556, Box 1; Margaret E. Burton, "The Committee on Women in World Affairs," December 18, 1946, Lucy Somerville Howorth Papers, Schlesinger Library, Box 7; Lucy Somerville Howorth, "Women Step Forward," Ibid., Box 9; "The White House Conference: How Women May Share in Post-War Policy Making," Ibid.; "Results of the Washington White House Conference," *Journal of the American Association of University Women* 38 (Spring 1945): pp. 178-179.

8. Eleanor F. Straub, "Government Policy toward Civilian Women During World War II" (Ph.D. dissertation, Emory University, 1973), pp. 43-63; Mary Van Kleeck to Mary Anderson, December 14, 1942, Records of the Women's Bureau, Accession Number 55-A-556, Box 13; Anderson to Van Kleeck, January 6, 1943, Ibid.; Anderson to Van Kleeck, September 24, 1943, Anderson Papers, Schlesinger Library, Folder 37; Mary Anderson, *Women at Work,* p. 249.

9. "The Report of the Committee on Findings, Council Workshop Convention, October 15-17, 1943," *The Aframerican Woman* 3 (1943): 11; Pauline Redmon Coggs, "Community War Challenges to Negro Women" Ibid. 3 (summer 1943): 9; Letters from members and chapters of Alpha Kappa Alpha to Frances Perkins and Mary Anderson, November-December, 1941, Records of the Women's Bureau, Box 881; Marjorie McKenzie, "Against the Lean Years," *The Aframerican Woman* 3 (Summer 1943): 6.

10. "Women's Joint Congressional Committee Legislative Programs of Member Organizations," December, 1942, Women's Joint Congressional Committee Papers, Library of Congress, Box 5; "Women's Joint Congressional Committee Legislative Committees as of March 1, 1943,"

Anna Kelton Wiley Papers, Library of Congress, Box 218; Mildred H. McAfee to Chief of Naval Personnel, August 6, 1943, Records of the Bureau of Naval Personnel, General Correspondence, Record Group 24, National Archives, Box 2330; "Statement on the Admission of Negro Women into the Auxiliary of the Navy, July 21, 1943," Ibid.; Letters from black organizations regarding women and racial discrimination in the military in Ibid., Boxes 2329-2331; Jessie Parkhurst Guzman, ed., *Negro Year Book, 1941-1946* (Tuskegee Institute, 1947), p. 374; Holt, *Mary McLeod Bethune,* pp. 233-34; "Why Women Physicians Should Be Commissioned in the Medical Corps of the U.S. Army and Navy," n.d., pamphlet in Anna Kelton Wiley Papers, Library of Congress, Box 217; "Position of the AAUW on Women in Military Service from 1941 to Date," October 13, 1947, AAUW Archives, Status of Women Historical File, Folder 4; U.S. Congress, House Committee on Military Affairs, *Appointment of Female Physicians and Surgeons in the Medical Corps of the Army and Navy,* Hearings before Subcommittee No. 3 on H.R. 824 and H.R. 1857, March 10, 11, and 18, 1943 (Washington: Government Printing Office, 1943).

11. Elizabeth Christman to Virginia Price, December 26, 1944, Records of the Women's Advisory Committee to the War Manpower Commission, Record Group 211, National Archives; "Women's Joint Congressional Committee Legislative Programs of Member Organizations," December 1, 1942, Wiley Papers, Box 218; National Women's Trade Union League of America, "Condensed Proceedings, Thirteenth Convention, May 19-22, 1947, p. 25; American Association of University Women, *General Director's Letter* 12 (January 1945): 53-54; "News Afield," *Independent Woman* 22 (May 1943): 151-154; Mrs. Clarence F. Swift, "Facts about Mrs. Mary Church Terrell's Application for Membership in the Washington Branch, A.A.U.W.," October 24, 1946, Mary Church Terrell Papers, Library of Congress, Box 13; A.A.U.W. Press Release, December 11, 1946, Ibid.

12. Alma Lutz to Anna Kelton Wiley, June 4, 1942, Alma Lutz Papers, Schlesinger Library, Box 6; Helen Hunt West to Caroline L. Babcock, April 21, 1940, Caroline L. Babcock-Olive E. Hurlburt Papers, Schlesinger Library, Folder 24; National Committee to Defeat the Un-Equal Rights Amendment, "Statement of Opposition to the Equal Rights Amendment," n.d. (c. 1946), Papers of the National League of Women Voters, Library of Congress, Box 698; Alpha Kappa Alpha National Non-Partisan Council on Public Affairs, *Legislative Release,* Vol. III, No. 6 (November, 1945-January, 1946), p. 3; U.S. Senate, Committee on the Judiciary, *Equal Rights Amendment,* Hearing before a Subcommittee on S.J. Res. 61 (Washington, D.C.: Government Printing Office, 1945).

13. Eleanor Straub, "Government Policy Toward Civilian Women During World War II," pp. 230-238; Elizabeth Christman to Local Unit Secretaries, February 6, 1942, Papers of the National Women's Trade Union League,

Library of Congress, Box 9; Christman to Executive Board Members, August 9, 1944, Ibid.; New York Women's Trade Union League, *Annual Report, 1942-1943,* Baker Library, Harvard University, pp. 2-3.

14. Lucy S. Howorth, "Questions for Consideration by the A.A.U.W. Committee on Economic and Legal Status of Women," September, 1944, AAUW. Archives, Status of Women Historical File; "Minutes of the AAUW Committee on Economic and Legal Status of Women, September 14, 1944," Ibid., p. 7; "Verbatim Proceedings of Conference on Post-War Adjustment of Women Workers, December 4-5, 1944," Records of the Women's Bureau, Box 900, p. 143; Press release, National Federation of Business and Professional Women's Clubs, "A Statement from Margaret A. Hickey," July 28, 1944, Record of the Women's Advisory Committee to the War Manpower Commission, Record Group 211, National Archives, Box 161; Alice Mary Kimball, "Careers on the Labor Front," *Independent Woman* 21 (February 1942): 34-36, 62-63; Minnie L. Maffett to Mary Anderson, n.d. (c. February, 1942), Records of the Women's Bureau, Box 840; Rose Schneiderman, "Common Goals for Women's Organizations," n.d. (c. 1936), Records of the Women's Bureau, Box 850; Elizabeth Christman to Virginia Price, December 26, 1944, Records of the Women's Advisory Committee to the War Manpower Commission.

15. Ruth W. Tryon, *The American Association of University Women, 1881-1949* (Washington, D.C.: American Association of University Women, 1950), pp. 40, 44; Virginia Price to Minnie L. Maffett, July 7, 1944, Records of the Women's Advisory Committee to the War Manpower Commission, Box 166; Margaret Hickey, "The Task Ahead for Women," *Independent Woman* 24 (August 1945): 214, 237; "Verbatim Proceedings of Conference on Post-War Adjustment of Women Workers, December 4-5, 1944," Records of the Women's Bureau, Box 900, pp. 75-76, 157-174; Dora Jones, "Self-Help Program of Household Employees," *The Aframerican Woman* 2 (Summer and Fall 1941): 26-31; "Report of the Commission on Findings of the National Council of Negro Women," Ibid. 2 (Winter 1941-1942): 6; Christman to Price, December 26, 1944, op. cit., pp. 1, 6, 8-9.

16. Harriet Ahlers Houdlette, "For Our Children, Understanding and Protection," *Journal of the American Association of University Women* 36 (Fall 1942): 15; Houdlette, "Straight Thinking on Services for Children," Ibid. 37 (Spring 1944): 152-155; Ruth W. Tryon, *The American Association of University Women,* p. 39.

17. Straub, "Government Policy Toward Civilian Women During World War II," pp. 263-285; Women's Joint Congressional Committee, Subcommittee on the War Area Child Care Act of 1943 (S. 1130), "Child Care in War Areas," n.d. (c. 1943), Wiley Papers, Box 189; U.S. Senate, Committee on Education and Labor, *Wartime Care and Protection of Children of Employed Mothers,* Hearings on S. 876 and S. 1130, June 8, 1943

(Washington, D.C.: Government Printing Office, 1943), pp. 54, 75-79; U.S. House of Representatives, Committee on Public Buildings and Grounds, *Community Facilities,* Hearings on H.R. 2936, June 29 and 30, 1943 (Washington, D.C.: Government Printing Office, 1943), pp. 3, 81-83.

18. Christman to Price, December 26, 1944, op. cit., pp. 3-4; R.J. Thomas, "Report of UAW-CIO Women's Conference, December 8-9, 1944," January 22, 1945, Papers of the United Auto Workers, War Policy Division, Archives of Labor History, Wayne State University, Box 27; National Women's Trade Union League, "Condensed Proceedings, Thirteenth Convention, May 19-22, 1947," p. 40; Untitled report on United Electrical Workers conference on the problems of women workers, n.d., Records of the Child Care Center Parents Association of New York, Schlesinger Library, Folder 11.

IV. Deviancy:
Conflict and Resolution

Introduction

The more universally propounded and widely accepted, the more rigid and rigidly applied the standard, the stranger the deviancy or the more threatening the rebellion will be—or appear to be. Catharine Maria Sedgwick, a deviant herself in the nineteenth century not only as a popular writer but as an unmarried woman, noted in her journal that "there is more individuality in single than in married women—their position is singular and forced. There is something peculiar in their history." As the two essays in this concluding section again attest, deviancy or rebellion can shed as much or more light upon a society's values as so-called normalcy. They attest as well to the fact that socialization can produce identity crises and vocational conflict and trauma as much as it can lead to resolution and harmony. The existence of social standards can falsely and superficially connote a uniformity of perspective and interests upon the part of a society. The appearance of conflict, frustration, or paralysis in the individual psyche or in group behavior can be merely a reflection of contradiction and distortion in society's values. And, finally, given American society's rigid demand and expectation of the past that middle- and upper-class women fulfill the roles of wifehood and motherhood within the home, the fact that some women both within the home and without deviated from the norm or resisted or rebelled against it, attests to a singular impact if not single experiences.

Lee Chambers-Schiller's essay concerns the woman who chose to remain unmarried in nineteenth-century America and thereby assured for herself the status of a statistical oddity during a century in which nine out of ten women married. The life of her spinsters was uncommon in more ways than one. Having already challenged the prescriptions concerning wifehood and motherhood by remaining single, she compounded her deviancy when she left behind the sphere deemed appropriate for women and actively engaged in social reform. How did such a woman escape the cultural dictates of her time? The answer, says Chambers-Schiller, is that she didn't, she *was* vulnerable to those dictates. Indeed, her deviancy made her all the more sensitive to the obligations of true womanhood.

However much the unmarried woman might try to transfer the demand for service to others from the private to the public sphere, she yet encountered dictates concerning woman's being and woman's place and, suspended between the two spheres, her sense of self remained conflicted. The spinsters examined by Chambers-Schiller oscillated between involvement with reform which they perceived as their desired vocation and submergence in domesticity which denied that vocation. Caught between apparently mutually exclusive demands, these single women reformers were unable to develop as complete and fulfilling a sense of expertise, confidence, and accomplishment that might have come with consistent dedication to their chosen vocation. There were personal costs as well. Their truncated, divided existences not only reaped tension, frustration, and depression, but contributed in some cases to invalidism. For all, there was an erosion of self-esteem. The rejection of wifehood and motherhood notwithstanding, the experience of single women reformers underlines the strength and force of cultural dictates in antebellum America.

As Chambers-Schiller found conflict to be a primary motif among antebellum spinsters involved in reform, Sharon O'Brien locates tension and trauma in the lives of adolescent girls in the later nineteenth century. Against the background of post-Civil-War advice literature, her essay explores the conflicts that engulfed three nineteenth-century tomboys during adolescence. As O'Brien demonstrates, the purveyors of advice enmeshed themselves in contradictions that could only invite individual frustration and conflict: having begun by encouraging a free, active childhood that promised the development of self-reliance, strength, and competence, considered necessary for the demands of wifehood and motherhood, they followed by dictating that submissiveness and other attributes of domesticity be inculcated with the onset of puberty.

Indeed, the experiences of Frances Willard, Willa Cather, and Louisa May Alcott reflect the same discontinuity implicit in the literature. Adolescence, at least for these three, was marked by confrontation between their assertive, independent personalities and expectations of feminine behavior. Resolution of the contradictions inherent in their culture's dictates varied from individual to individual. Frances Willard forged a merger of identity and vocation that met her need for autonomy and still enabled her in part to maintain traits deemed womanly. Willa Cather, the most deviant of the three, and perhaps the most successful in achieving resolution, rejected rigid definitions of woman's nature and role, without rejecting her sex, by projecting conflict outward and into her work and role as an artist. Louisa May Alcott was not so fortunate. Unable to either abandon or submit to the dictates of femininity, her adult life was characterized by emotional and psychological turmoil.

Regardless of the outcome, O'Brien's analysis looks from the adolescent girl to the adult woman and suggests answers and an understanding of the behavior of the female in a world that offered little choice.

Lee Chambers-Schiller

The Single Woman: Family and Vocation Among Nineteenth-Century Reformers

Women formed the backbone of antebellum reform. While they were seldom regarded as leaders, they performed the tasks necessary for the organization and growth of the movement and the spread of its ideas. They passed petitions, raised money, sold newspaper subscriptions, attended meetings, organized boycotts, and distributed tract literature. Yet many aspects of female participation remain unclear. For example, did marital status affect the mode of female activism, or even the act of female participation? Although no broadly based study exists, historians have assumed that the majority of female reformers were single. It has seemed logical that the single woman would have had more time and energy than the married woman to engage in such work; would have faced fewer obligations within the home that hindered her participation; and would have felt a greater need for a socially useful vocation.[1] Yet in exploring the parameters of female reform activity,[2] it has become clear that the antebellum spinster[3] shared many of the domestic and cultural encumbrances of her married sister.

By the cultural standards of her day, the single female reformer was an uncommon woman. She refused matrimony when nine out of ten women married, and so rejected the womanly calling of motherhood. As a reformer, she chose to leave the private sphere of home and family for the decidedly public and unfeminine roles of activist and publicist. Yet despite her "un-womanly" status, the unmarried woman was free neither of the constraints of the domestic role, nor of the prescriptions of the cult of true womanhood. In spite of the critical nature of the social evils which they sought to eradicate, the high moral value which they placed on their activity, and the positive experiences of commitment, these women, perhaps more than their married sisters, found the domestic role compelling. Their lives reflect an emotional

[On leave from the Department of History and the Directorship of the Women's Studies program at the University of Colorado, Boulder, Lee Chambers-Schiller is currently a Research Associate at the Mary Bunting Institute at Radcliffe College. Her essay is part of a large project on single women in nineteenth-century America.]

and financial dependence on the family through which their reform work was mediated. Their reasons for remaining single varied: some valued independence and vocational freedom more than marriage; some idealized marriage and never found a suitably noble mate; some experienced family pressure to remain in the parental home. Whatever the reasons, the positive value they ascribed to their callings and causes outweighed the opprobrium attached to spinsterhood. Yet the unmarried woman felt her deviancy and was therefore all the more conscious of the duties and role of the unattached woman in American society. Her public activism followed a cyclical pattern in which long periods of submersion in domesticity separated times of participation. Both internally and externally, the single-woman reformer had to confront competition and even conflict among the varying demands made of her: the culturally imposed duties to God and family, and the personally generated need for self-actualization. The dedication of single women to reform came at some personal cost and for complex personal, social, and ideological reasons. The purpose of this essay is to elucidate the encumbrances which hampered the public role of those very women who, at first glance, seemed most liberated from the social and cultural constraints of antebellum womanhood.

Two cultural concepts affected the participation of women in antebellum reform: the cult of true womanhood and the concept of vocation. A true woman was delicate of body, pure of mind, devoted to religion and the home, compassionate, selfless, nurturing, and submissive. In a world increasingly dominated by the qualities of materialism, competition, and individualism, women ensconced in their refuge-like homes were held to embody the old virtues of love, spirituality, selflessness, harmony, and service. The female was believed to have a specific social role and a vocation of some significance. Religion and patriotism demanded that women marry and raise children. By their example, and through their teaching, mothers formed goodly and godly future citizens.[4]

Like other antebellum women, single women reformers acknowledged the prescriptions of this ideology. They felt the deviancy of their unmarried state. Catharine Maria Sedgwick's *Married or Single?*, a novel published in 1857, detailed the popular view of spinsters as "inconvenient," and of their lives as "helpless, joyless... almost ridiculous."[5] Sarah Pugh, a Philadelphia abolitionist and feminist, wrote to another spinster about the upcoming marriages of two young women friends saying, "well, that is the way of the world, save in exceptional cases."[6] And Emily Howland, a Quaker and an abolitionist, described her private struggle to make peace with her decision not to marry. "I have found my place," she wrote in her journal, "and I feel sure it is the right one." Yet her "darkest self" scorned her self-assurance:

Why then do you have to pit yourself against your pitiless logic to

convince yourself of a self-evident truth? You take the position of a
single woman voluntarily, why falter at the consequences, why care
for slights, for lack of caste and place or be chilled by isolation, are
you not with the right, if you've got it stronger than the slighters?
Are you sure you're not living a mistake? I, Earth, teach you in
every lesson I give, that isolation is wrong. Marriage is the law.[7]

This sense of the deviancy of spinsterhood corroded the self-esteem of these
women and deeply affected the energies and concentration which they were
able to marshal for their reform activity.

Perhaps because they lacked the usual accoutrements of womanhood—
husband and children—these spinsters felt their subjection to other measure-
ments of femininity that much more strongly. Mary Grew, the inspired
speaker and editor of the abolitionist journal, *The Pennsylvania Freeman*,
turned down an invitation to speak at an American Antislavery Association
anniversary meeting for "want of sufficient voice to fill the Tabernacle."[8]
Delicacy and softness were understood to be distinctly feminine qualities.
Perhaps in her own mind, Grew balanced her unfeminine vocation with her
feminine style. And Catharine Sedgwick, who on occasion freely admitted
her literary ambitions, who stood in awe of the "egotism" exhibited by such
women writers of her age as Margaret Fuller and Harriet Martineau, denied
that authorship constituted her primary identity, denigrated the care and
craftsmanship with which she approached her work, and de-emphasized the
emotional and financial investment it embodied when she wrote, according
to the dictates of feminine humility and submissiveness:

My *author's* existence has always seemed something accidental,
extraneous, and independent of my inner self. My books have been
a pleasant occupation and excitement in my life. The notice, and
friends, or acquaintances they have procured me, have relieved me
from the danger of ennui and blue devils, that are most apt to
infest a single person. But they constitute no portion of my
happiness.[9]

The adherence of these women to the cult of true womanhood, an adherence
revealed by their emphasis upon that which their culture deemed feminine,
often limited their contributions to reform and made their vocational
commitment a conflicted and guilt-ridden experience.

A second cultural concept which deeply affected the lives of antebellum
women was that of vocation. A vocation provided the vehicle by which a
good citizen participated in God's work and society's progress. It served a
number of valued individual, social, and religious functions in a person's life:
a vocation set one on the road to perfection; it enabled one to develop fully

God-given talents which might otherwise find no outlet; it provided a means by which one could compose a psyche made anxious by rapidly changing social mores through traditionally approved constructive works; and it proffered a physical regimen and an emotional discipline deemed necessary for the well lived life. Yet, despite the value placed on vocation for the upper and middle classes, it was, in the popular mind, a sex-linked concept. Emily Howland recalled that on hearing of Myrtilla Miner's Washington, D.C., school for black girls, she felt a sense of calling. Writing that she was "leading the aimless life that was required of young women," she bemoaned the fact that "the more imperative necessity of being employed to insure health of body and mind was neither recognized nor understood."[10] Having a wide variety of possible choices before him, a young man searched for and reverenced his calling as part of the process of social and personal maturation. No such act was deemed necessary on the part of a young woman. She had only to assume the inherent, biologically rooted vocation in which all of her sex were expected to serve their race, God, and country.

In motherhood even more than marriage lay the female calling. Such a vocation was overtly closed to the spinster. Yet the power of the idea may be seen in the behavior of many single women reformers in the nineteenth century who either formally or informally adopted daughters. Elizabeth Blackwell adopted an orphaned Irish immigrant. Noting that "I desperately needed the change of thought she compelled me to give her," she recalled, "It was a dark time [1854, when despite her medical degree, she was banned from New York hospitals] and she did me good—her genial, loyal Irish temperment suited me."[11] At the time, hate mail and newspaper editorials attacked Blackwell and her occupation as "unwomanly." This virulent opposition may have increased Blackwell's sense of her deviant behavior as both spinster and doctor. Perhaps, at least in part, the adoption of a child stemmed from insecurity and represented Blackwell's need to legitimate herself in a role deemed appropriate for a woman. Certainly, it would enable her critics to see her as more conventionally female. Emily Howland consciously trained and educated a spiritual and professional heiress in Suzy Baker when she informally adopted her young black student. She played an important role in the girl's personal as well as professional life, even sharing, albeit in an uneasy alliance, with Suzy's biological mother the nursing of her fatal illness.[12] Howland deeply valued the young woman's affection and admiration. Other single women too—Ellen Blackwell, Catharine Sedgwick, and Mary Grew— spoke of the daughters of friends or relatives as their own, and participated significantly in raising them.

Yet motherhood was for these women neither a necessary nor a sufficient vocation. However much they valued the rearing of a future generation, they could not delegate their moral responsibility for the state of their own souls, nor those of their neighbors or their nation. Many believed that the Lord allowed no spiritual surrogates—neither husband nor children could pay their way for them. Hence some women, particularly but not solely those of more liberal Quaker or Unitarian background, took seriously the significance of a calling beyond motherhood in all of its personal, spiritual, and social ramifications. The vocational impetus of the antebellum reformer was couched therefore in religious terms. Author Catharine Sedgwick quoted Sir James Mackintosh on the value of fiction as being "one of the great instruments employed in the moral education of mankind, because it is only delightful when it interests, and to interest is to excite sympathy for the heroes of fiction—that is. . . to teach men the habit of feeling for each other."[13] She justified her calling as a novelist by deeming herself God's instrument:

> When I feel that my writings have made any one happier or better,
> I feel an emotion of gratitude to Him who has made me the
> medium of any blessing to my fellow-creatures. And I do feel that I
> am but the instrument.[14]

Elizabeth Blackwell's rationale was similar. Responding to her mother's fears that in taking on a medical career she jeopardized her spiritual welfare, she asked, "bless the dear mother, what am I doing else but living religion all the time?"

> Isn't it my meat and my drink to do the good will of God; didn't I
> use to sit in the lecture-room and send up a whole cannonade of
> little prayers; and didn't a whole flood of answers come straight
> down from the throne of grace? And what am I doing now? Do
> you think I care about medicine? Nay, verily, its just to kill the
> devil, who I hate so heartily—thats the fact, mother; and if that
> isn't forming Christ in one, the hope of Glory, why I don't know
> what is.[15]

Female gender implied certain responsibilities, roles, and tasks with regard to God as well as to domesticity. Woman was pious and pure as well as domestic, and so was granted a particular duty to guard the morality of family and community. Moral reform or humanitarian service might provide a culturally sanctioned social role for the unmarried woman.

However, the religious imperatives of vocation conflicted with certain strains of the cultural prescriptions of the cult of domesticity. While neither concept should be reified by the historian, one can see in these lives the very real pain caused by a sense of competing prescriptions and of deviancy from the norm. Ultimately, the culture upheld submissiveness as the most feminine of virtues. Both a patriarchal family structure and a patriarchal religion demanded of women the submission of the self to the will of others, whether

God, the clergy, father, brother, or husband. Submission and duty were ruling principles of female culture, but to whom should one submit, and to which duty? Emily Howland, twenty-nine years of age and hardly a child, begged her mother for permission to respond to her calling by teaching in Miner's school:

> May I give a little of my life to degraded humanity? May I work a little while for that class which has so long enlisted my closest sympathies? May I try if I really can to make the world a little better for having lived in it? Can't thee spare me a while to do what I think my portion? I want to do something which seems to me worthy of life, and if all my life is to go on as have the last ten years, I know I shall feel at the end of it as tho' I had lived in vain, others with perhaps not as much capacity had reared noble, worthy families, contributed their share to the world and I had done nothing, dwindled away.[16]

Howland's moving plea embodied the contradictory values held by the culturally attuned antebellum woman. No matter how acutely she felt the obligations of her personal calling, she also recognized her domestic responsibilities. Howland had for some years cared for her parents and their mutual home, recognizing this as a filial responsibility. Her decision to remain unmarried meant that she could not participate in the noble task of child-rearing. But, as Elizabeth Blackwell put it, "bright visions of usefulness" floated around her, and she sought a way to serve and to embody those visions.[17] She felt unfulfilled, and capable of doing and feeling far more than her limited sphere had so far provided. Clearly, however, her course must be sanctioned by her parents, and her domestic responsibilities forgiven as they were foregone. This letter, written after all arrangements for joining Miner were made, after a period of teacher training at a nearby school, and after some seventeen months of knowing that her calling was to teach, still reflected hesitancy and the unspoken acknowledgment that without parental approval, Howland would not go.

Here lay the conflict for many single women reformers. Autonomy, although an important developmental stage for young antebellum men, was not valued in young women, for whom the crisis of puberty meant curtailing the will and submitting to dependence. How could one submit, most often to the family as the most immediate and pressing force in their lives, and yet somehow meet the urgent need within for self-expression, self-fulfillment, and self-actualization? Most were unable to understand, as did Catharine Beecher, that their struggle was one of role conflict, a cultural and social issue of profound significance for their society, sex, and class.[18] Rather, they internalized the contest and sought to control their willfulness, their unfeminine desire for a substantive life, in an effort to adopt genuine female submissiveness.

The internal conflict of the single woman reformer was exacerbated by the social role expected of unattached women. It consisted of family duties and social responsibilities. Family claims left little time for more substantive study or work. Parents, siblings, nieces and nephews, aunts, uncles and cousins clearly expected a spinster to have no particular occupation and therefore freely sought from her companionship, business assistance, nursing, housekeeping, and babysitting services. Social conventions of the early and mid-nineteenth century required that young, middle-class, unmarried women spend part of every day engaged in social visiting. The task of maintaining a family's social connections continued to be the responsibility of the adult spinster, an important function as the nuclear family increasingly turned in upon itself during the eighteenth and nineteenth centuries. As the closely knit hierarchy, homogeneity, and connectedness of New England village life gave way to the more impersonal, heterogenous, loosely organized city, families lost their sense of shared community values and their sense of being an integral part of religious and political life. The institution of visiting provided a forum in which middle-and upper-class women came together to impart information, to refine values, to conduct business, to discuss community needs and doings, to make matches, to arrange care or companionship, and to guide behavior through censure or praise.

Such an occupation was a trial to some. Emily Howland, for example, despaired at a life characterized by light domestic chores, social visiting, nursing, studying French, and looking for wild flowers and herbs with which to build a herbarium. She acknowledged "vain, bitter regrets for misspent lost time, yes, lost time squandered what no price can recover, no useless repinings can recall one single moment of the squandered years!"[19] And Sarah Pugh, comparing herself to her reformer friends, admitted wistfully:

> My days are one long holiday. Mary [Grew] assures me that the *work* will come—and meanwhile tries to pursuade me that I need rest!!—which I go on...reading a *little* writing a little and then as a refreshment from the *labor* walk or drive! Cannot you see me in my round of petty employments?[20]

The problem was not the lack of genuine reform work to do, but rather the inability of these women to leave behind the petty responsibilities that ate away at both time and will.

Abigail Kimber, Pugh's cousin and co-abolitionist, well understood the ennervating nature of the domestic and social duties required of the unmarried.

> This frittering away of life, this abrasion from the veriest triffles
> is... very much like walking over a soft sandy plain—you leave no
> foot prints that the next breeze will not efface—you make no
> progress—you feel your strength wasted without seeing that you
> have done anything more today than was done yesterday, and will
> be done tomorrow.

Gradually Kimber felt herself demoralized, or perhaps tranquillized, to the point where she no longer felt "as though any change was desirable." "Then," she said, "you sink into placidity and stupidity—and seem to be good sort of folks, because you have just energy enough to be gladdened when good active folks are busy in the world around you and are *doing* while you are wishing to do."[21] Women's work consisted of rendering services rather than producing results. And while they saw something wrong in the way most women submitted so totally to what was, within limits, a noble and necessary occupation, they themselves were unable to set appropriate constraints. Because her services, both domestic and social, were ongoing in nature, because they were constantly renewable, the spinster could never feel that her obligations were met and her time her own. The majority of married women of these classes had domestic help, often the unpaid services of the family daughter or maiden aunt. The unmarried remained on call throughout her life.

The conflict between one's womanly duties and one's desire for a substantive life, whether dedicated to God, humanity, or culture, was deeply painful for these women. The cult of domesticity taught women that they would find self-fulfillment through self-abnegation. Experience told them that this was not so and that self-actualization required the exercise of their talents. Sarah Pugh described her work in the antislavery cause as the "blessing of my life," and her role as family caretaker as "less responsible and not so calculated to call forth the powers of my being."[22] Participation in reform work provided an opportunity for personal growth, liberation from domestic routine, intercourse with interesting people, a sense of civic usefulness, and productive labor. These were necessary for the self-esteem and mental health of these women. Yet none could fully accept the validity of their experience and reject the restrictive dictates of the dominant culture. Periodically, the spinster re-immersed herself in self-sacrifice, usually in the form of dedicated domesticity, as if to expunge from her record her self-centered vocational drive. Feeling herself pull away from woman's proper sphere, the single woman, defined by her culture as "unnatural" and "unwomanly," bound herself the more tightly to it.

The internal conflict of the single woman reformer was made more painful because the domestic services which she rendered were provided for people whom she loved. The neglect of her responsibilities, whether real or imagined, necessary or exorbitant, resulted in shame and sorrow. In a deep depression following the death of her mother, Sarah Pugh went to England to visit her antislavery colleague Mary Estlin. There Estlin encouraged her to undertake an active role in the movement by helping to edit the *Anti-Slavery Advocate*, organizing local female antislavery associations, and maintaining the Bristol family's antislavery correspondence. Pugh spent two years with Estlin during which she came to feel a deep satisfaction in her work and a new sense of self-worth. But with her mother and father dead, when her extended family asked her to return to Philadelphia, she did. She found one cousin dying. While nursing this relative, she was called away to attend a sick aunt. Still another lay ill requiring care not far away. "Very thankful am I," wrote Pugh to Estlin, "that I am here to share—and in a degree to lighten the labors of love that have been crowded into these last weeks. I have never felt that I staid away too long, yet very often that it was well that I came home last autumn."[23] Although Pugh's return ended her full time antislavery work, and one of the most rewarding and productive periods of her life, she could not have borne the guilt of rejecting her family's needs for her own interests, or even for those of her cause.

Sarah Pugh, Emily Howland, and Abigail Kimber each submerged herself periodically in domesticity. It is evident that for them, the family proved to be a conservative influence on middle-class women's public activity. Kimber, for example, was a member of the Philadelphia Female Anti-Slavery Society, one of the more radical abolitionist and more outspokenly feminist organizations in antebellum America. With Pugh, Mary Grew, and Quaker minister Lucretia Mott, Kimber crossed the Atlantic in 1840 to attend the World Anti-Slavery Convention. It was a momentous experience for these women individually, as it was to prove pivotal for the women's movement. The convention rejected the credentials of female American delegates, raising in Britain the question of female participation which had so divided American abolitionists. For Kimber the convention was a time of expanding horizons. She traveled on the continent with Sarah Pugh; she met and talked with outstanding British women such as Harriet Martineau, Elizabeth Pease, and the Ashurst sisters; she defied and debated the pre-eminent men in Anglo-American reform; and she cemented a commitment to the cause of human freedom.

Yet throughout her life, Kimber was unable to give more than passing attention to her cause. Her father dominated her, alternately seducing her help with pleas of familial love and using his authority as *paterfamilias,* to tie her to him and his work. Kimber taught in his school at Kimberton, Pennsylvania. She helped with its administration. She kept house for her mother and father, and was frequently called upon to nurse sick relatives.

Whenever Kimber could leave the school, she came to Philadelphia to stay with her cousin and to participate in the deliberations of the Anti-Slavery Society. But opportunities were irregular. When her father became seriously ill, Kimber took on full responsibility for the school in addition to nursing her father despite the pleas of Pugh that she hire a nurse.

Like other single-women reformers, Kimber was tied financially as well as emotionally to her family. Few antebellum middle-class women held money in their own right, nor had they many opportunities to earn any. Other than school teaching, few jobs were both available and respectable. Pugh taught school briefly while living with her brother and jointly contributing to the care of her mother, and housekeeping for the assortment of older relatives who moved in with them. Thereafter, she lived off the largess of her brother and other relatives. Surely this contributed to her willingness to serve as family caretaker, which was for the next ten years her primary vocation. Emily Howland had an allowance from her father to help support her career of teaching black women, nursing, and providing social services for the blacks interned around Washington, D.C., during and after the Civil War. When Howland wanted to organize a black communal farm in Virginia, for the purpose of showing that free black men and women could support themselves, her father contributed the capital necessary to buy the land. She, like Pugh and Kimber, returned this support in recurring family service.

For these women, in both youth and middle age, the salient identity was that of daughter. In pleading for her mother's approval of her calling, Emily Howland wrote:

> I know thy health is very poor but I can do nothing for it, and as long as no one would think of its deterring me from marrying and leaving home forever if I choose, (Most think very strange that I do not, doubtless) it certainly can no more be urged against my taking a few years or months perhaps, for a benevolent enterprise.[24]

For some nineteenth-century women at least, it would seem that marriage offered a step toward autonomy, and a step away from paternal domination. Lucretia Mott devoutly wished that Abigail Kimber would marry and so have a socially (and paternally) acceptable reason for leaving her father's house. "Her father," said Mott, "has a great idea of being 'monarch of all he surveys,' and has ever kept his family in greater subjection to his will than accords with my view of right." After all, thought Mott, when a daughter reached the age of forty, her independence should be respected, particularly when what she had gained in position and livelihood was "the product of [her] own labor."[25] Whatever her age, the unmarried daughter remained a child in the eyes of her society, her parents, and to some extent herself. The emotional and financial strings with which she was bound were an inherent part of the social role of the spinster.

It is not surprising then, that despite her deep desire to work in a cause, the single woman had difficulty in balancing the mutually exclusive demands of her domestic role with those of her vocation. This inability to clearly define priorities and to claim adequate time for herself and her calling, resulted in several serious consequences. Perhaps most important, she found herself unable to make the full-time commitment necessary to excel in any field of endeavor. She experienced interruptions which proved distracting, time consuming, and enervating. Sarah Pugh lamented the many movement-related letters which remained unwritten due to claims of friends and family. She compared her own lack of productivity with the ninety-two letters written in one month by her friend and British abolitionist Mary Estlin. "This," said Pugh, "in contrast to what I myself accomplish seems immense."[26] The expertise and accompanying confidence that came with constant partici-pation also eluded these women. Mary Grew, who held a well-deserved reputation as a local speaker, refused to take the stand at national meetings. "My gift for speaking," she said, "is not for such occasions."[27] This sense of mediocrity eroded the spinster's ability to contribute and in turn trapped the single woman reformer in a debilitating cycle of self-castigation and loss of ambition. Looking back on her life at the age of sixty, Sarah Pugh could only regret: "What has been my life? Alas! without record save as one crowned with blessings." Despite her "earnest longing for light and truth," she found her behavior characterized by,

> the continued sense of inability to accomplish anything beyond the
> petty trivialities of the day, the dwelling in little things, not from
> the love of them, but from the want of effort and the feeling of
> power to escape from them; for these little things must be done to
> make the lives of others and my own comfortable, and why should
> I not accept them as my work, as gifts for accomplishing greater
> things are not mine?[28]

The spinster's inability to make a consistent commitment to her work, coupled with subsequent frustration and demoralization, undermined her physical and mental health.

For Abby Kimber, Mary Grew, Emily Howland, and Catharine Sedgwick, illness proved to be one cost of flouting conventional womanhood. Sedgwick, for example, suffered all her life from dyspepsia and nervous headaches. She found no cure in the continued success of her novels or in the caring support and affection of her siblings. After a particularly bad winter in which she endured "mental paralysis," depression, and morbidity, she ruminated on the roots of her dysfunctionalism. She felt her "solitary condition" to be "unnatural," and feared it to be unchanging. "Hope now seems to turn from me," she wrote. "The best sources of earthly happiness are not within my grasp." She admonished those who would follow her course:

> From my own experience I would not advise anyone to remain unmarried, for my experience has been a singularly happy one. My feelings have never been embittered by those slights and taunts that the repulsive and neglected have to endure; there has been no period of my life to the present moment when I might not have allied myself respectably, and to those sincerely attached to me, if I would.... My fortune is not adequate to an independent establishment, but it is ample for ease to myself and liberality to others. In the families of all my brothers I have an agreeable home. My sisters are all kind and affectionate to me...; their children all love me.... I have troops of friends, some devotedly attached to me, and yet the result of all this very happy experience is that there is no equivalent for those blessings which Providence has placed first, and ordained that they should be purchased at the dearest sacrifice.[29]

While the experience of illness was no doubt both real and painful for these women, a primary cause of their discomfort was psychological stress. In the case of Emily Howland, her cycles of invalidism related to ambivalence about her vocational life. Howland was consumed by the demands of domesticity for an extended period in the 1870's, virtually giving up her calling to work with blacks in order to nurse her sick father. During this decade, she suffered periodic depression and physical invalidism every six months or so, usually in early fall and late winter. The illnesses corresponded to her returns from visits made with members of her female reform network. Shorter depressions occurred at other times, when she received letters of encouragement from these same friends. Howland's biographer believes that she thought of her sense of duty and reform commitment as slumbering for a time. It was, however, a fitful sleep.[30]

Mary Grew habitually succumbed to invalidism when the stress of family or vocation proved too great. She felt keenly any change in personal relationships, as when her mother died and her father remarried within six months. She also sought rest periodically from the demands of her editorial work on the *Pennsylvania Freeman*, her participation in the Philadelphia Female Anti-Slavery Society, her teaching, or her speaking engagements. During the 1840's and 1850's, she patronized the water cure, often spending months at a time in a local hydropathic establishment. A touch of self-conscious martyrdom appeared in the explanations she sent to her friends in the cause:

It is painful to be compelled to comparative inactivity, when there is so much work all around us, to be done; but I do not believe that any one need be wholly useless, or that any life is without influence for good or for evil. I console myself with the reflection that what cannot be helped, must be patiently borne; and strive, as an invalid ought, to be as little burdensome, as possible, to other persons, and as I am not given to low spirits, I think I seldom mar the cheerfulness of healthier people.[31]

While the retreat into illness may be seen as negative, self-destructive behavior, whether conscious or not, it did serve in a positive way to meet some of the spinster's emotional needs. It provided an opportunity for respite from the taxations of reform work, from the inner conflict associated with so public and unfeminine a role, and from the demands of family and social obligation. Sallie Holley, an antislavery agent who drove herself for fifteen years on the lecture circuit, and who referred to herself as a "field-hand" because of the fatigue and hardship which characterized the tour, adjourned to the Elmira, New York, water cure sanitarium for a "brief" respite in the fall of 1861. She stayed for one month and then wrote: "I am inclined to think that when a person is so happy as I am here it should be received as an indication from Providence to remain. It is certainly a rare chance in my life."[32] She remained there for seven months. Illness provided a time in which the woman herself became the subject rather than the provider of care, affection, and attention. Such a course was also a culturally legitimate one, confirming apparently the delicacy of the female constitution. And yet despite the fact that sickness enabled a woman to rest, recuperate, and renew herself, it did nothing to relieve her long-term difficulty.

The reform activity of antebellum women, then, was a double-edged experience. The role that they chose was an alien one in an alien sphere. Political agitation and serious authorship demanded of women behavioral patterns which were considered blatantly unfeminine. Many adopted this behavior piecemeal at the cost of great mental anguish. Mary Grew refused for years to address a mixed audience, and would simply stop speaking if a man appeared at the door.[33] After three years on tour, Sallie Holley still felt uneasy when traveling without an escort in a public conveyance:

> "I'm afloat! I'm afloat!
> The world is my country
> And the 'cause' my bride."

Such are my feelings this morning. As I enter the cars alone and see no familiar face, I often wonder if the other women I see there are as cowardly as I am. Oh I am only an apology for a woman!

Oh for the whole armour of Christianity, that panoply divine![34]

The public sphere in which these women acted was, by definition, not women's sphere. Entering that realm took great courage. How much sager to remain at home untouched by, and uncognizant of abounding social evil. Outcasts of a kind in their rejection of marriage and motherhood, these women found public activism the more difficult because it reinforced the public view of them as "Amazons."[35] Yet despite the constraints of culturally defined femininity, of financial and emotional dependence on the family, of domestic responsibilities, and of the physiological and psychological consequences of her sex-role conflict, the single woman did contribute to the moral reform of her society. And in so doing, she achieved a sense of dignity, fulfillment, and productivity.

While single women in antebellum America resisted certain cultural prescriptions, they also accommodated much of the cult of domesticity. These women valued freedom from interdependent personal relationships. In choosing spinsterhood, they escaped the marital bond only to succumb to, in many cases, the filial one. They valued independence of mind and spirit. Yet in choosing to pursue autonomy through a morally sanctioned and socially useful activity, they indicated an acceptance of the belief that women had a special role in the American family and society. That these women did not maintain consistently their public participation, that they felt compelled to return periodically to the domestic sphere, that their contributions were made in the face of substantial resistance by family and culture, and at a high cost to the health and happiness of the individual, suggests that the social role of the single woman in America prior to the Civil War was primarily domestic in nature.

Notes

1. Harriet Warm Shupf, "Single Women and Social Reform in Mid-Nineteenth Century England: The Case of Mary Carpenter," *Victorian Studies* 17 (March 1974): 301–317.
2. The term "reformer" is used here in its broadest sense. These were women for whom their activity, whether joining a reform society, writing sympathetic tracts or novels, or adopting the role of agent or orator, represented a vocation to which they dedicated time and effort, and which engaged to some extent their identities. They may have sympathized with one or more of a number of antebellum causes: temperance, women's rights, moral purity, antislavery, prison, hospital, or educational reform. The joining of a reform association was for them a rare opportunity to pursue the intellectual. Much of the data for this

essay is the result of previous research on the antislavery women of Britain and America, yet the same themes recur in the lives of other single intellectual and professional women. In the process of studying these women, for a book sponsored by the Lilly Endowment at the Mary Bunting Institute of Radcliffe College, it has become clear that many middle-class spinsters valued what Margaret Adams has defined as the essence of singlehood: a commitment to the pursuit of ideas and intellectual self-realization in preference to close, interdependent personal relationships. As will be seen, they were not always free to single-mindedly pursue that value. Margaret Adams, *Single Blessedness* (Harmondsworth, England: Penguin Books, 1978), p. 23.

3. An objection has been raised by some feminist historians to the use of the term "spinster" as being rooted in male culture and negative in its connotations. The term is used here, with some qualms, because it is an historical one, one which these women would have recognized and used. The denotation and connotation of the word "spinster" has changed greatly over time, paralleling the changing status of single women in their society and their own political consciousness. In the seventeenth century, the term was used generally to refer to the female sex. The task of spinning was part of every woman's daily routine. Late in the century, the word became a legal term for the unmarried woman. Spinning was the prime contribution made by these women to the domestic economy. In the eighteenth century, spinning schools were established by New England's communities to occupy and make socially productive its dependents—orphans, widows, and single women. With the industrial revolution, this socially and economically productive role was lost. The word "spinster" took on the negative connotations of extra, left-over, dried up, and grasping. By late in the nineteenth century, the single woman, particularly of a professional, reform, or intellectual cast, was branded in major medical texts as a "mannish maiden," an Hermaphrodite, no longer strictly female in sex. Yet among themselves, unmarried women used the term "productive spinster," harkening back to a time when the word was used with pride and designated a woman of valued and significant occupation.

4. See Barbara Welter, "The Cult of True Womanhood, 1800–1860," in her *Dimity Convictions: The American Woman in the Nineteenth Century* (Athens: Ohio University Press, 1976), pp. 21–41; Nancy Cott, *The Bonds of Womanhood: "Woman's Sphere" in New England, 1790–1835* (New Haven: Yale University Press, 1977); Linda Kerber, "The Republican Mother: Women and the Enlightenment—An American Perspective," *American Quarterly* 28 (Summer 1976): 187–205.

5. Catharine Maria Sedgwick, *Married or Single?* (New York: Harper and Brothers, 1857), II: 214.

6. Sarah Pugh, Letter to Mary A. Estlin, June 17, 1867, Estlin Papers, Dr. Williams Library, London, England.

7. Judith Colucci Breault, *The World of Emily Howland: Odyssey of a Humanitarian* (Millbrae, California: Les Femmes, 1976), pp. 46–47.

8. Mary Grew, Letter to Sidney H. Gay, April 10, 1848, Sidney H. Gay Papers, Columbia University, New York, N.Y.

9. Catharine M. Sedgwick, Letter to Rev. Dr. Channing, August 24, 1837, in Mary E. Dewey, ed., *Life and Letters of Catharine M. Sedgwick* (New York: Harper and Brothers, 1871), p. 271.

10. Breault, *Emily Howland*, p. 28.

11. Elizabeth Blackwell, *Pioneer Work in Opening the Medical Profession to Women, Autobiographical Sketches* (New York: Schocken Books, 1977), p. 198.

12. Breault, *Emily Howland*, p. 83.

13. Dewey, *Catharine M. Sedgwick*, p. 254.

14. Ibid., p. 271.

15. Elizabeth Blackwell, Letter to her mother, February 25, 1849, in Blackwell, *Pioneer Work*, p. 93.

16. Breault, *Emily Howland*, pp. 4–5.

17. Blackwell, *Pioneer Work*, pp. 82–83.

18. Kathryn Kish Sklar, *Catharine Beecher, A Study in American Domesticity* (New York: W.W. Norton and Co., 1976).

19. Breault, *Emily Howland*, p. 16.

20. Sarah Pugh, Letter to Hannah Webb, August 27, 1852, Antislavery Collection, Boston Public Library, Boston, Mass.

21. A[bigail] K[imber], August 18, 1853, Estlin Papers, Dr. Williams Library, London, England.

22. *Memorial of Sarah Pugh: A Tribute of Respect from Her Cousin* (Philadelphia: J. B. Lippincott Co., 1888), p. 35.

23. Sarah Pugh, Letter to Mary A. Estlin, April 11, 1834, Estlin Papers, Dr. Williams Library, London, England.

24. Breault, *Emily Howland*, p. 5.

25. Lucretia Mott, Letter to Richard and Hannah Webb, 3rd month 23, 1846, Antislavery Collection, Boston Public Library, Boston, Mass.

26. Sarah Pugh, Letter to Mary A. Estlin, November 13, 1853, Estlin Papers, Dr. Williams Library, London, England.

27. Mary Grew, Letter to Sidney H. Gay, April 10, 1848, Sidney H. Gay Papers, Columbia University, New York, N.Y.

28. *Memorial of Sarah Pugh*, p. 97.

29. Dewey, *Catherine M. Sedgwick*, pp. 197–199.

30. Breault, *Emily Howland*, pp. 113–114.

31. Mary Grew, Letter to Helen Benson Garrison, August 19, 1858, Garrison Papers, Boston Public Library, Boston, Mass.

32. Sallie Holley, Letter to Caroline F. Putnam, September 29, 1861, in John White Chadwick, ed., *A Life for Liberty: Anti-Slavery and Other Letters of Sallie Holley* (New York: G. P. Putnam's Sons, 1899), p. 183. For discussion of the water cure and hydropathic establishments in the lives

of antebellum women, see Sklar, *Catherine Beecher*, pp. 205–209.

33. Sarah Pugh, Letter to Elizabeth Neall Gay, November 7, 1847, Sidney H. Gay Papers, Columbia University, New York, N.Y.

34. Sallie Holley, Letter to Caroline F. Putnam, February 4, 1854, in Chadwick, p. 136.

35. *The Mother's Magazine* carried an article entitled "Female Orators" in 1838 in which these women were described as follows: "These Amazonians are their own executioners. They have unsexed themselves in public estimation, and there is no fear that they will perpetuate their race. We treat insanity in all its forms, with allowance." The correlation is thus made between public activism, spinsterhood, and insanity. "Female Orators," *The Mother's Magazine* 6 (1838): 27.

Sharon O'Brien

Tomboyism and Adolescent Conflict: Three Nineteenth-Century Case Studies

If she consulted one of the innumerable advice books addressed to her, a white, middle-class Victorian woman might have been surprised to discover that her life was enviably free of conflict. Unlike her husband or brother, who faced an increasing number of role options as nineteenth-century industrialization and urbanization progressed, she did not have to choose a career and prepare for a demanding, anxiety-provoking struggle in a turbulent, rapidly changing society. No choices were required of her, advisers agreed, for the innate feminine traits of nurturing, piety, dependence, and submissiveness admirably suited her for a protected domestic realm. There, as wife and mother, she would uplift her society without having to enter it through the benevolent influence she exerted upon husband and children. No tension or distress need mar her gentle tranquillity, for the prescriptive literature portrayed the Victorian woman as doubly insulated from conflict: the innateness of feminine characteristics obviated the bothersome choice of social role, and the domesticity for which she was destined was an oasis of ordered peace in the midst of a chaotic world.[1]

Recently, historians of American women have validated the wonderment a middle-class woman might have felt as she read such soothing words. In studying the reality of nineteenth-century women's lives, historians have increasingly found them to be characterized by discontinuity, tension, and conflict instead of calm fulfillment.[2] Individual psychology did not invariably conform to the prevailing definition of woman's nature or mesh with the demands of the domestic role; lack of choice could breed discontent as readily as happiness. Contradictions between the ideal and the real were particularly

[Sharon O'Brien, an Assistant Professor in the Department of English at Dickinson College, was a Visiting Fellow in the Department of American Civilization at the University of Pennsylvania this past year. She is involved in a literary and biographical study of Willa Cather that locates identity formation in a cultural and psychological context. Her articles on Cather have appeared in *Women and Literature* and *Studies in American Fiction*.]

troublesome for assertive women whose natures did not fit the cultural ideal of self-sacrificing feminity, yet who still judged themselves by it. Some women managed to resolve ensuing conflict by turning to reform work, which offered them a legitimate way of leaving the home, expanding their roles, and even attempting to control male behavior under the rubric of service to others.[3]

But not all women found relief from role stress by committing themselves to moral causes. The expanded opportunities wrought by the social, economic, and technological changes transforming post-Civil-War America ironically intensified role stress for some women as the gulf widened between the rigid, unchanging prescriptions they internalized and the new social, educational, and occupational possibilities they saw developing.[4] Hysterical illness became a strategy some employed in resolving the discontinuity between individual nature or aspirations and the limited feminine role. As invalids, these women could legitimately spurn domestic burdens and perhaps covertly express the aggression and self-absorption the feminine ideal denied them.[5]

Contradictions and discontinuities not only pervaded the complex interplay between prescription and behavior that characterized the experience of Victorian women: some were inherent in the prescriptive literature itself. Carroll Smith-Rosenberg has pointed to the dichotomy between the ideal woman and the ideal mother. Although the ideal woman was gentle, passive, dependent, "a born follower," the ideal mother was expected to be "strong, self-reliant, protective, an efficient caretaker in relation to children and home"—in short, a born leader.[6] One major source of hysteria, Smith-Rosenberg theorizes, may have been the conflict endured when the "fragile, sensitive, and dependent child" encountered the demanding responsibilities of the adult female role.[7]

Some Victorian social arbiters seem to have perceived this contradiction between the feminine and the maternal ideal. Perhaps alarmed by the growing number of hysterical and neurasthenic women who abandoned domestic responsibilities, a surprising number of post-Civil-War advice-givers began to recommend free, active, untrammeled childhoods for little girls and even advocated tomboyism.[8] Their prescriptions seemed to promise smoother transitions between the stages of feminine development and ensure more competent mothers than those encouraging children to be fragile, passive, and dependent. An active tomboy would surely develop the resourcefulness, self-confidence and, most important, the physical health required for motherhood. Assuming maternal duties would be far easier for her than for her delicate, pampered counterpart.

Yet in removing one inconsistency that promoted conflict, these prescriptive writers substituted another. Unknown to themselves, they were making stress more likely at an earlier stage in feminine development than marriage and motherhood, for the freedom they encouraged in childhood contrasted sharply with the restrictions they demanded in puberty. Like other Victorian Americans, these advisers expected adolescent girls to conform gracefully to the traditional feminine role and develop the domestic interests thought innate. What they failed to see was that tomboys whose preference for boyish pastimes reflected assertive, competitive, and ambitious natures might easily encounter difficulties when adolescence required a restructuring of identity and interests.[9]

This essay explores the personal consequences of such contradictions by examining the conflicts three nineteenth-century tomboys experienced when they reached adolescence: Frances Willard, Willa Cather, and Louisa May Alcott. These three women have been chosen because their differing behaviors in adolescence suggest the range of options open to tomboys confronting the feminine role. My sample is selective, for I am not attempting to delineate the typical experience of the Victorian tomboy, but to use case studies of three prominent women to raise questions for consideration by historians when studying the childhood and adolescence of Victorian women. My findings may also have relevance for understanding the nineteenth-century female experience in general, for the contradictions characterizing the early stages of the feminine life cycle are related to the stress and conflict historians have found so pervasive in middle-class women's adult lives.

An analysis of the Victorian advice literature advocating tomboyism precedes the case studies and provides a framework within which to consider them. We can neither equate this prescriptive literature with behavior nor hold these promoters of tomboyism responsible for the childrearing attitudes held by the parents of the three girls.[10] But this literature does provide insights into the cultural norms that Victorian girls had to confront. Although these norms influenced individual behavior in diverse ways, they provide the context within which—or against which—Willard, Cather, and Alcott were forced to define themselves. In addition, the advice literature merits consideration because remarkable similarities exist between its implicit contradictions and the stresses the three tomboys experienced both in adolescence and in adult life.

Although the word "tomboy" originated in sixteenth-century England,[11] it does not appear regularly in American advice literature until after the Civil War, when it connoted a noisy, energetic, romping girl who preferred boyish pursuits like climbing trees and running races to playing quietly with dolls and tea sets.[12] Perhaps because they were countering antebellum authors like Harvey Newcomb, who urged parents to curb activity and curiosity in female children,[13] these advice-givers took an indulgent view of the young girl who enjoyed boys' vigorous activities and even encouraged tomboyism. Their sanctioning of an active female childhood was based on the belief that significant sex differences, considered moral and emotional as well as physical, did not emerge in childhood. Little boys and girls were virtually identical, they assumed, and Dr. John Kellogg's advice to mothers is typical: they should treat their daughters like their sons, encouraging them to think, to be independent, and to engage in outdoor play and exercise.[14] Mary Virginia Terhune, the popular sentimental novelist known to her contemporaries as Marion Harland, agreed with such medical advice, for, she contended, "our sons and daughters start even." She went on to articulate the second major premise on which many advisers rested their endorsement of tomboyism: not only were children free of sex differences, but in addition tomboyism was only a very common phase through which little girls would pass on their way to the safe harbor of domestic femininity.[15]

Social arbiters like Terhune and Kellogg consistently integrated their endorsement of tomboyism with a traditional notion of woman's domestic role. The rowdy tomboy would make a better wife and mother than her prissy, housebound sister, they argued, for participation in boyish sports and games would develop the health, strength, independence, and competence she would later need as wife and mother. In supporting this view, Terhune cited the case of a former tomboy who had spent her childhood out of doors romping and adventuring with her brothers. Now happily married, she had borne five vigorous children and was a healthy, active, and effective mother. Meanwhile, Terhune commented tellingly, her proper sisters who had been passive, decorous young girls were now querulous invalids with sickly children.[16] This argument for tomboyism would have been persuasive in late-nineteenth-century America, when Americans became increasingly concerned with the deplorable state of women's health, worrying in particular about sickly women whose enfeebled reproductive organs produced weak or defective children.[17]

Thus in arguing for active tomboy childhoods these advice-givers were seeking to preserve rather than to challenge woman's essential role as wife and mother. Their praise of tomboys reflected a wish to discourage parents from inculcating the passivity, delicacy, and clinging dependency that might cause women to falter under the burdens and responsibilities of motherhood. In trying to promote a vital continuity between childhood and woman's domestic role, however, they unwittingly introduced a crucial discontinuity between childhood and adolescence which made stress and conflict almost inevitable and subtly undermined their goals.

Accepting prevailing Victorian medical views of puberty, both lay and medical advocates of tomboyism conceded that the child's indulgence in masculine activities must cease when puberty commenced. At that crucial turning point, they explained, the mother must cease to treat her daughter like her son. When the grace period of childhood ended, boys and girls rapidly developed the physical, psychological, and emotional traits peculiar to each sex. At this time, Dr. Kellogg insisted, the girl must abandon her childhood romping and forsake the woods and fields where she once roamed with her brothers. More appropriate arenas for activity awaited the budding woman: the "kitchen, washroom, and the garden" which he proclaimed "nature's gymnasia" for adolescent girls.[18] Strenuous outdoor play and excessive studying must be shunned, for the girl needed to channel her vital energies into her developing reproductive system. Rest and carefully-regulated exercise must replace the tomboy's unfettered activity to ensure that energy would not be drained from the all-important uterus and ovaries.[19]

In addition to prescribing rest and curtailed physical and mental activity, advisers saw puberty as the critical period for instilling such proper feminine traits as domesticity and submissiveness. At this time the adolescent girl was unusually plastic and malleable; along with her body, her mind and spirit were taking the shape "in which they must remain ever after."[20] Hence boyish activities were to be doubly shunned: not only were they too strenuous, but they might encourage unfeminine characteristics to develop at this critical stage.

This schema of feminine development was riddled with contradictions. Feminine traits were supposedly innate, yet the mother must be careful to inculcate them when the child reached adolescence. In fact, the very existence of advice literature questioned the notion that the emergence of femininity was an inevitable, natural phenomenon. Paradoxically, these authors expected the ideal woman to be both self-reliant and submissive: self-reliant in relation to children and household duties, submissive in relation to husband and male authority. The most serious contradiction, however, lay in the opposition they created between childhood and adolescence.

Although they described puberty as a period of rapid and far-reaching physical and emotional change, both doctors and lay advisers felt that childhood and puberty were naturally linked stages in the life cycle; one led coherently and smoothly to the other. The floral imagery they inevitably evoked in describing the passage of girlhood into young womanhood implied that the emergence of the young woman was a natural, organic process.[21] It is apparent, however, that the two states imagined in this literature were jarringly different rather than smoothly consistent. The tomboy child need see no distinction between girls' and boys' activities and natures, while the adolescent girl must perceive that certain traits and destinies were male, others female. Moreover, despite the sentimental glorifications of adolescent womanhood that abounded, the transition from the asexual freedom of childhood to the sex-linked restrictions of adolescence required an abrupt passage from activity to passivity, from independence to regulation. Attempting to adjust a personality formed through active, competitive, boyish pastimes to the demands of the socially-restricted feminine role could have brought the tomboy intense conflict rather than womanly delight. The advice-givers who saw tomboyism leading naturally to domestic femininity evidently did not anticipate this potential conflict, not seeing that whole-hearted participation in active sports and games with boys might easily reinforce or foster personality traits alien to the feminine ideal: namely competitiveness, assertiveness, ambition. Doubtless they were blinded to the implications of their own advice by their firmly-held, although inconsistent beliefs that personality was molded in adolescence rather than childhood and that feminine traits were innate.[22]

Frances Willard, Willa Cather and Louisa May Alcott experienced the discontinuity implicit in the advice literature as a social reality. Adolescence for them was not a natural unfolding into domestic femininity; rather, it was a turbulent, stressful period during which they confronted expectations regarding female behavior that did not coincide with the personality and interests they developed during their active tomboy childhoods. Ranging from surface adaptation to overt defiance, their responses to adolescence reveal how these girls coped with the conflicts engendered by the clash between expectations for feminine behavior and their assertive natures; how they formed identity without abandoning totally their tomboy selves; and anticipate how in adult life they would resolve, or fail to resolve, the resultant role stress.

Frances Willard experienced a classic tomboy childhood years before advice-givers began to recommend the phenomenon. Born in Churchville, New York, in 1839, she spent her childhood years on a Wisconsin farm where she delighted in outdoor play and active sports. Frances (or "Frank," as she was then called) joined her older brother Oliver in most of his recreations, which included climbing trees, playing with stilts, and running races. She also displayed a preference for boyish activities when she played with her younger sister Mary. The lively Frank consistently took the male role in the childhood dramas the two sisters invented, while Mary was content to be the wife, the mother, or the hostess. Unlike her domestic sister, Frank "could not abide" a "needle and a dishcloth," far preferring to spend her time whittling and working with carpenter's tools while Mary embroidered and cooked.[23]

Young Frank's delight in active sports and her preference for male personae in her childhood playacting coexisted with an ambitious spirit that would have distressed Victorian prescriptive writers. Her vision of her future role was cloudy at this time, but even then it went beyond wifehood and motherhood. Frank dreamed of vague, heroic destinies in which she would change the course of human history rather than preside over the quiet pleasures of hearth and kitchen. "I never knew what it was not to aspire, and not to believe myself capable of heroism," she recalled in her autobiography.

"I always wanted to react upon the world about me to my utmost ounce of power; to be widely known, loved, and believed in—the more widely the better" (688). As a child, Willard confessed, she had thought the hymn couplet "Make me little and unknown/ Loved and prized by God alone" contemptible. How absurd to desire only divine recognition; other girls might prefer such a humble destiny, but Frank Willard intended to be "loved and prized" by multitudes.

The isolated farm life and concomitant freedom from the socializing pressures of school and peers doubtless fostered Frank's independent nature, but her mother was the crucial factor in encouraging her boyish activities and unconventional aspirations. Believing that children should be left free to develop their own personalities, Mary Willard did not teach her son and daughters that certain activities were male, others female. Consequently she did not praise one daughter's domestic interests more than another's tomboyish ones. "Mother did not talk to us as girls, but simply as human beings," Willard recalled. "It never occurred to me that I ought to 'know housework' and do it. Mary took to it kindly by nature; I did not, and each one had her way" (25). Although their mother believed in allowing her children to develop in an atmosphere "free from restraint" (664), she was nevertheless aware of the norms regarding feminine conduct; she just neglected to impose them during Frank's childhood. A comment Mary Willard made later suggests that her disregard of prescriptions for feminine behavior may have been more an unconscious preference than a conscious policy: "I wonder sometimes that I had the wit to let her do what she preferred instead of obliging her to take up house work as did all the other girls of our acquaintance" (4).

But some cultural norms Mary Willard finally did enforce. Although she let Frank pursue her tomboyish activities and maintain an unfeminine appearance well into the critical stage of puberty, far longer than even the most liberal advice book would have recommended, when her daughter became seventeen the mother told her that she could "hardly forgive herself" for having let Frank "run wild" so long. She must now adopt a more feminine appearance by doing her hair up "woman-fashion" and exchanging the boyish clothes she loved for a womanly long dress (69). Frank's entry in her journal on her seventeenth birthday, which she dramatically referred to as the "day of her martyrdom," reveals the trauma she experienced in obeying her mother. The change in hair and dress became the emblem of a lamentable passage from freedom to confinement, activity to passivity, strength to weakness:

> [H]ere I sit like another Samson "shorn of my strength." That
> figure won't do, for the greatest trouble with me is that I never
> shall be shorn again. My "back" hair is twisted up like a corkscrew;

> I carry eighteen hair-pins; my head aches miserably; my feet are entangled in the skirt of my hateful new gown. As for chasing sheep...it's out of the question, and to climb to my "Eagle's nest" seat in the big burr oak would ruin this new frock beyond repair. Altogether, I recognize the fact that my "occupation's gone." (69)

Although Mary Willard demanded some changes in her tomboy daughter, the contradiction in her view of acceptable feminine behavior in childhood and in adolescence was not as deep as that contained in the prescriptive literature. Consequently she did not require the restructuring of personality and interests demanded by Kellogg, Terhune, and others. Because Mary Willard had internalized some of her culture's notions of femininity, she ultimately required Frank to look and act like a lady. But the mother did not equate femininity with submissiveness or domesticity; instead of urging Frank to marry, she actively encouraged her spirited daughter to seek an active, powerful role in the world, although she again revealed her acceptance of nineteenth-century views of woman's nature in hoping that Frank's chosen role would be womanly, "beneficent," and socially useful (688). She considered education the key to "open the world" for her daughter and prepare her for a nondomestic, although womanly, social role (76), so after the fateful birthday she urged Frank to channel her energies into schooling: "Your mind is active; you are fond of books and thoughts, as well as of outdoors; we must provide the means for you to make up for the loss of your girlish good times" (10). With this support, Frank overcame her father's objections to formal schooling for women and entered Milwaukee Female College in 1857.

Her mother's encouragement of education made the loss of "girlish good times" bearable, and curtailment of freedom was also less wrenching than it might have been because, despite her nickname and appearance, the adolescent Frank was not male-identified. She enjoyed being active and free but did not associate these impulses with maleness. In her advice book for young women written in 1888, Willard explained that a tomboy phase should not be confused with male identification: "Perhaps some of you may have thought you wanted to be a boy, but I seriously doubt it. You may have wanted a boy's freedom, his independence, his healthful, unimpeding style of dress, but I do not believe any true girl could ever have been coaxed to be a boy."[24]

The likelihood that Frank would continue to be independent and self-assertive despite her adoption of womanly attire was foreshadowed on her eighteenth birthday. She wrote a poem entitled "I am Eighteen," a jubilant celebration of liberation from parental constraints in which she exulted "And now I feel that I'm alone and free / To worship and obey Jehovah only" (71). Her subsequent behavior revealed that her declaration of independence was directed toward her father, who held far stricter notions of feminine propriety than did her mother. Openly challenging her father's male authority, Frank proclaimed that she would no longer observe his commandment to shun novel-reading: "I am eighteen—I am of age—I am now to do what *I* think is right" (71).

Frances Willard would also defy her father's preferences in seeking a career, for he felt that woman's sphere was unquestionably the home, but her mother's "liberality of soul" effectively countered his "old-time conservatisms."[25] Even with Mary Willard's support of her goals, however, Frank suffered a crisis of vocation after she left school. What course in life was open to a woman who wanted power, prominence, and the affection of multitudes as well as to be unselfish and womanly? What "beneficent" profession was there in which Frank would not "climb by others' overthrow" and yet fulfill her need for significant achievement in the world (688)? She first chose the profession most open to women, teaching, but the choice never brought her deep satisfaction. Not until she reached her mid-thirties did she discover the vocation in which she would realize her childhood ambitions. That vocation became temperance.

It was a happy choice. Elected president of the Women's Christian Temperance Union (WCTU) in 1879, she retained the position until her death in 1898. Willard served herself as well as her cause. In devoting herself to temperance, she could be both ambitious and womanly, attaining the prominence and autonomy she had long desired without seeming unfeminine to herself or to others. Legitimated by her virtuous cause, standing behind the unassailable WCTU motto, "For God, Home, and Native Land," and expressing the praise-worthy feminine traits of purity and piety, Willard could receive respect and admiration from her contemporaries despite her pursuit of a career. She also gained her mother's approval, for in crusading for the sanctity of the home and assisting the unfortunate, Willard was being both "womanly" and "beneficent," fulfilling herself through dedication to the cause of others.

Unlike many Victorian women, Willard managed to forge an identity and pursue a social role that deviated from the norm with a minimum of psychological conflict. The advice books she wrote for young girls reveal an interesting inconsistency, probably unconscious and perhaps inherited from her mother, that suggests why her expansion of the feminine role was relatively free of conflict.[26] On the one hand, Willard argues that neither personality traits nor social roles are inherently "male" or "female," but have merely been assigned to the sexes by social custom, to the detriment of women who have been confined to the home and encouraged to be passive and dependent. Hence a woman has as great a need for success in the world as a man and should be given equal opportunity to attain her goals. On the other hand, Willard reveals her acceptance of some contemporary views of woman's nature in also insisting that women are more pure, selfless, and loving than men. She uses this inconsistency to enhance women's stature and possible roles: women should be allowed to pursue all the professions normally alloted to men, since the passivity and dependency supposedly characteristic of them are socially inculcated, not innate, but women are especially suited for professions like nursing and social work since their superior traits of nurturing and compassion are innate, not socially inculcated. Seemingly unaware of this paradox, Willard could argue that women were both equal to men and superior to them.

This inconsistency in her thinking explains why reform work provided a particularly conflict-free choice. Willard could channel her ambitions into an adult role that combined power and autonomy with the superior womanly traits of piety and compassion that her mother and her society taught her to value. Because she retained some traditional notions of woman's nature, Willard could integrate her assertive self into an adult female identity without great difficulty. On her traumatic seventeenth birthday she equated femininity with passivity and weakness, mourning the loss of her childhood "occupation," but in temperance work she found an occupation that allowed her to realize her ambitions while expanding woman's role in an acceptable way.

Like Frances Willard, Willa Cather was a childhood tomboy who dreamed of heroic destinies far beyond the domestic sphere and displayed "boyish" traits and interests. Born into a small farming community in the Shenandoah Valley of Virginia in 1873, Willa Cather also led an active rural childhood, roaming the fields surrounding the Cather farmhouse and playing with her two younger brothers. Years later she characterized her young self as a "rude" and "dirty" little girl given to "tomboyish proceedings" who detested her well-behaved female cousins with their prim manners and their curly hair.[27] Willa's parents were relatively indulgent in their treatment of their tomboyish daughter. Her gentle, chivalrous father adored her and evidently almost always let her have her own way. Proud of Willa's intelligence, Charles Cather encouraged her to show off her learning. Nebraska friends later remembered a common scene that captures the father's delight in the daughter's quick mind: the nine-year-old Willa sitting in the Red Cloud general store, surrounded by adults, and "discoursing with some prompting from her father, on Shakespeare, English history, and life in Virginia."[28] Willa's strong-minded, imperious Southern mother, who dominated the family and overshadowed her easy-going, accomodating husband, did not approve of her daughter's tomboyish manners and would have preferred Willa to be a gracious, well-groomed Southern lady like herself. But in common with Mary Willard, Virginia Cather believed that children should develop their own personalities and goals without maternal interference. Willa's mother "had a most unusual sympathy and understanding of her children's individuality—gave them almost complete freedom," remembers Edith Lewis, Cather's long-time companion.[29] So although she occasionally clashed with Willa over questions of dress and appearance, Virginia Cather encouraged her daughter's imaginative and creative interests. When Willa decided that she passionately wanted to attend the University of Nebraska, her younger sister later recalled, "mother was on her side."[30]

When the Cather family emigrated to the Nebraska Divide in 1883, Willa gained even more freedom. During the eighteen months she spent there, Willa delighted in riding her pony across the prairies, talking with immigrant farmwives about their lives and customs, and exploring her new surroundings with her two younger brothers. The free Western atmosphere reinforced her development of traits then associated with the male sex: she was adventurous, curious, strong-willed, and self-sufficient. Like Frank Willard, Willa was also dreamily ambitious, imagining exciting, nondomestic destinies that involved individual achievement. Eventually she focussed her aspirations on the medical profession. Because of the rural isolation of her childhood and her understanding parents, Willa evidently did not feel that such a goal was unfeminine.

But when the Cathers moved into the small railroad town of Red Cloud in 1884, Willa discovered society's rigid distinctions between the sexes and learned that her personality, interests, and ambitions were masculine. Her first encounter with the socializing forces of town life, incarnated in neighbors, peers, and school, occurred just when she was entering the critical period of puberty when the community would stress expectations for proper feminine behavior. Willa's first response to these expectations was a declaration of contempt for the female sex. Her candid entries in a friend's album book are laden with disdain for feminine symbols: her choice for the category "my Idea of real Misery" was "doing fancy work" and she defined the "greatest folly of the nineteenth century" as "dresses and skirts."[31]

Sometime during her fourteenth year Willa decided to broaden her rejection of femininity. She had always enjoyed taking male parts in plays and charades, but now she assumed the male role in earnest. She cropped her hair to crew-cut length, donned boyish dress, sported a derby hat and a cane, and loudly declared the superiority of the male sex—and her own membership in it. Her childhood nickname had been "Willie," but now she made her name more explicitly masculine, proclaiming herself "William Cather, Jr." or, reflecting her career aspirations that now seemed male, "William Cather, M.D." One childhood acquaintance later said that he remembered Willa most for the "masculine habits and dress" she adopted during her teenage years. He recalled that any semblance of masculine activity "brought the accusation of 'tomboy'" during those years, but Willa "seemed impervious to any criticism along this line and even boasted that she preferred the masculine garb" as well as the masculine sex.[32]

There were several sources for this unusual behavior. In part, Willa was defying her mother's standards of ladylike conduct; in part, she was declaring her contempt for the conventional, narrow-minded citizens of Red Cloud by adopting an extreme pose in order to shock the bourgeoisie.[33] But the major source of her four-year period of male impersonation was the sexual polarization she encountered in her society. Unable to separate the qualities and opportunities she admired and wanted for herself, Willa chose to abandon her gender rather than her goals. When she could not establish an inner continuity between the self formed in childhood and the available social roles, she chose defiance rather than adaptation. A semiautobiographical short story she wrote a few years later, "Tommy the Unsentimental," illuminates the cultural source of her male impersonation. Cather's opposition of a boylike, competent heroine and a silly, childlike female reveals association of strength, intelligence, and assertiveness with men and weakness, helplessness, and mindless domesticity with women.

Escaping the narrow world of Red Cloud did not immediately cause Willa Cather to abandon her preference for the male sex, as "Tommy the Unsentimental" suggests. Friends at the University of Nebraska persuaded her to grow her hair and wear dresses, but this external change did not symbolize an acceptance of a feminine identity. During these years Willa was beginning to aspire to a lofty vocation as a literary artist, and her journalism of the period reveals her belief that "woman" and "artist" were mutually exclusive identities.[34] It seemed to her that the egotism, ambition, and intense commitment to a craft required of the artist could not coexist with the selflessness, submissiveness, and domesticity supposedly inherent in woman's nature.

But after she left college and began to meet several opera singers, actresses and writers who combined femininity with devotion to art, Willa Cather gradually realized that a woman could choose a single life of artistic commitment without identifying with men. These role models helped her to accept a feminine identity by demonstrating that women could reject Victorian definitions of woman's role and nature without rejecting their sex. By the time she began to compose her first novels in the second decade of the twentieth century, Willa Cather combined an egotistic, passionate commitment to her art with an acceptance of her femininity, a union accomplished only by her ability to reject the nineteenth-century definition of femininity and form her own. The heroines of *O Pioneers!* (1913), *The Song of the Lark* (1915), and *My Antonia* (1918) reflect her shift in perspective. They are strong, competent, and creative, but unlike the "aggressively masculine and professional" heroine of "Tommy," they are not portrayed as manlike.

Although Louisa May Alcott also possessed an intense drive for a vital, productive life outside the domestic sphere, she was never able satisfactorily to balance her need for self-realization with an adult female identity; as her recent biographer demonstrates, her inability either to rebel or fully to accept the self-sacrificing feminine role left her a smouldering, resentful, emotionally-damaged woman.[35] In striving to attain the feminine ideal of selflessness and humility, Alcott tried unsuccessfully to repress the urge for autonomy and assertiveness her tomboy period expressed. Because she never saw these traits as legitimate, and because they would not dissipate despite her attempts at repression, she never escaped psychological and emotional turmoil.

Her childhood relationship with her father was a major source of later conflict. Taking responsibility for the rearing of Louisa and her older sister Anna, Bronson Alcott set out with romantic optimism to bring his children as close to human perfection as possible. Considering physical punishment an improper inducement to obedience because it did not appeal to the child's moral nature, Bronson sought to inculcate self-control through the potent force of his disapproval and withdrawal of affection. His aim was breaking the child's resistant will, but his means were perhaps more effective in Louisa's case than straightforward corporal punishment. Instead of rebelling definitively against a father who continually used physical force, Louisa sought to please a father whose love seemed conditional on her good behavior. She also internalized Bronson's condemnation of her passionate, assertive nature (he was distressed to find that even at two years old Louisa was "obstinate, ungovernable, rude, aggressive, and—at times—even violent") and continually struggled to subdue her unfeminine, un-Christian wilfulness.[36]

Louisa's beloved mother, Abba Alcott, did not provide a countering force to her husband's values despite her close relationship with her daughter, whom she viewed as an alter ego. Like Louisa, Abba was a wilful, strong-minded woman who sought to subdue an assertive nature because she accepted the Victorian ideal of self-sacrificing, domestic femininity; after her marriage to Bronson she tried, with much struggle and conflict, to cultivate "submission, docility, and gentleness."[37] She helped to transmit her conflict to Louisa; unlike Mary Willard or Virginia Cather, she believed that children should be inculcated with proper ideals, not left to evolve their own personalities, and she agreed with Bronson that the qualities important to encourage in her daughters were the ones she tried to attain herself—selflessness, submissiveness, self-control.

But her parents' efforts to inculcate submissiveness did not seem too oppressive at first, and Louisa had a relatively "free, happy" childhood.[38] A self-confessed tomboy, she scorned female dress and pastimes and threw herself into active outdoor play in the rural surroundings of Concord, Massachusetts. "I was born with a boy's spirit under my bib & tucker," she commented later. "I always thought I must have been a deer or a horse in some former state, because it was such a joy to run. No boy could be my friend till I had beaten him in a race, and no girl if she refused to climb trees, leap fences, and be a tomboy."[39] Alcott's childhood memory reveals not only a love of outdoor play and boys' activities, but also a wish to compete with— and moreover defeat—boys at their own games. Assertiveness and competitiveness were intertwined with her love of physical activity.

Louisa's free childhood ended in puberty, however, when her parents expected more feminine behavior from her and she developed a more active conscience. Instead of rebelling as did Willa Cather, Louisa strove to exhibit the docile, lady-like behavior her parents desired. When she was fourteen she wrote a poem that reveals her internalization of their standards in its condemnation of her wilfulness and unruliness:

MY KINGDOM

A little kingdom I possess
Where thoughts and feelings dwell,
And very hard I find the task
Of governing it well;
For passion tempts and troubles me
A wayward will misleads,
And selfishness its shadow casts
On all my words and deeds.[40]

A diary entry she made at the same age similarly reveals Louisa's interest in curbing self-assertion: she lists as desirable virtues "Patience, Obedience, Industry, Love, Generosity, Respect, Silence, Perserverance, Self-Denial" and as "vices" to be purged "Impatience, Selfishness, Wilfulness, Impudence, Activity, Vanity, and Pride."[41] But hers was a divided self. At the same time that Louisa condemned her assertiveness, like Frank Willard and Willa Cather she dreamed of heroic achievements: "I'll be rich and famous and happy before I die," she promised herself, "see if I won't."[42]

Although she struggled to control her vices in adolescence, Louisa was not able to eradicate them completely. During her teenage years she expressed the forbidden urges by acting the male role in the melodramatic plays she wrote for herself and her sisters. These dramas represented her way of coping with the demands for submissive behavior that she tried to meet during this time, as they provided a veiled outlet for her unfeminine, passionate, and ambitious self. The plays reveal that Louisa's attitude toward her assertive nature was one of ambivalence rather than of unconflicted condemnation. On the level of plot, these dramas generally endorse the conventional expression of a woman's power; they frequently concern the triumph of a good, pure woman over a proud, passionate male villain (as in "Norna; or, the Witch's Curse") or a long-suffering woman's successful capturing of a formerly indifferent man's love (as in "The Greek Slave" or "The Unloved Wife, Or, Woman's Faith").[43] But Louisa was able to have it both ways in these dramas. She wrote plays in which woman's strength was derived from the approved traits of self-sacrifice and self-regulation, but in performance she enthusiastically enacted the role of the defiant, passionate male villains. But her criticism of this submerged part of her personality is as evident as its expression, for she gives the ultimate victory in the power struggle to the virtuous, long-suffering women as the Byronic villain/heroes end crushed by remorse or despair.

As these adolescent plays foreshadowed, Alcott was never able satisfactorily to combine the energetic, assertive self represented by her tomboy period with an adult female identity. To some extent she channeled her need for achievement into a profession sanctioned for women when she became a writer, which also allowed her to remain within the domestic sphere as financial support and nurse for her aging parents. But the content of her fiction demonstrates the continuance of her adolescent conflict, showing Alcott's attraction to defiant, rebellious, or strong-minded characters whom she finally judges as less worthy than characters who exemplify selflessness or patient forebearance.

Her recently-discoverd thriller fiction, which she published anonymously and pseudononymously from 1863 to 1869, reveals that her tomboy self never disappeared despite her attempts at repression.[44] Several of these melodramatic tales feature proud, passionate, and wilful women who seek to control, manipulate, and even destroy men. In her imagination, freed by the pseudonym and the fanciful plots, Alcott could release the part of herself condemned by her society, her parents, and her conscious mind in portraying women as assertive, untamed, and defiant—women who without conflict express the traits she tried to eradicate. But although Alcott's characterization reveals admiration for her heroines' fiery spirits and proud individualism, she repudiates them on the level of plot. The stories end with a conventional imposition of poetic justice as the wilful heroines find their purposes thwarted.

Alcott's children's fiction, although far more overtly moral and conventionally didactic than her thrillers, similarly reveals an ambivalence toward the hidden strain in her nature that emerges most fully in her conflicted portrayals of tomboys, who are invariably versions of her untamed youthful self. Whereas Willard had exalted her tomboy days, praising them as a natural expression of feminine independence, Alcott forces her boyish heroines to convert to the feminine role and adopt such feminine characteristics as noncompetitiveness, selflessness, and nurturing. Hence wild, rebellious girls like Jo March, *Little Women*s archetypal tomboy, Bab in *Under* *the Lilacs*, and Jill in *Jack and Jill* eventually learn to be patient, submissive, and self-sacrificing little women by regulating their spirited natures. But despite her moralism, Alcott's portrayals of tomboys are riddled with ambivalence. Although her "wild girls" convert to the feminine role, they are more engagingly and lovingly drawn in their unregenerate state. Once again, Alcott's characterization belies her moralizing. But in the end she must repudiate her tomboy alter egos, for they represent the passion and aggressiveness she sought to quell in herself.

As might be expected, the case studies do not conform to the model of feminine development explicitly proposed in the prescriptive literature. None of the tomboys naturally channeled her energies into domestic interests when she reached adolescence; none adapted without conflict and submissively to the feminine role. But the adolescent experiences of Willard, Cather, and, to a lesser extent, Alcott reflect the discontinuity between a free, tomboy childhood and a regulated adolescence implicit in the advice books.[45] The stress and conflict they experienced belies the advice books' optimistic assumption that energies unleased in active childhoods could be smoothly accomodated within the traditional feminine role. Tomboy childhoods may have produced the physical and emotional strength Victorians wanted mothers to possess, but they also encouraged the development of personality traits that did not mesh with selfless femininity.

The adolescent conflicts the three girls experienced differed, however, as did their adult resolutions. But in each case, the adolescent girl's response to requirements for feminine behavior foreshadows the ways she would later resolve—or fail to resolve—role stress. When Mary Willard required Frank to cease her childhood romping and cultivate a feminine appearance, her daughter suffered intense despair at the loss of girlish freedom. But her independent behavior on her eighteenth birthday reveals that adolescent conflict would neither be debilitating nor enduring. Frank Willard's teenage combination of adaptation with assertiveness would characterize her future role as the leader of the Women's Christian Temperance Union, a position in which she could crusade aggressively for the sanctity of the home and continue to defy male authority without appearing deviant. Whereas Frank adapted to the external demands of femininity, the adolescent Willa Cather went to the other extreme in rebelliously adopting a male persona. Although Cather would not continue male impersonation in adulthood, the flagrant defiance of her William Cather period anticipates the individualism and unorthodoxy of her adult resolution of role stress. Unlike Willard, who broadened the role and retained some traditional notions of woman's nature, Cather rejected the feminine ideal entirely, fashioning a new role and identity as a woman artist egotistically devoted to her craft rather than selflessly concerned with other people. Since Cather's solution was more radical, its attainment was understandably more difficult and time-consuming. But because Cather projected conflict outward into a contest between self and society, rather than internalizing it, she escaped the enduring psychic scars of a divided self. Louisa May Alcott was not as fortunate. Unlike Willa Cather, as a teen-ager she could not flout the wishes of parents or defy her community; unlike Willard, she could not regard ambition and assertiveness as legitimate components of feminine identity, although she could not dispell them. Her self-division, revealed in her diary entries and adolsecent plays, anticipated the continuance of adult conflict.

Why were Willard and Cather able to resolve adolescent stress more satisfactorily than Alcott? Some suggestive patterns emerge in considering the three cases that may have larger implications. Although neither Willard nor Cather transcended her culture completely, both could finally disentangle their strong personalities and ambitious goals from identification with the male sex. Thus they were not forced to regard feminine identity and professional aspirations as mutually exclusive. Alcott, on the other hand, could not reject the equation of femininity with selflessness and ego-regulation, so her dreams of significant worldly attainments always seemed vaguely suspect.

The mother's contribution to the daughter's ability to express an assertive, ambitious nature without conflict seems to have been crucial here.[46] Mary Willard and Virginia Cather allowed their lively daughters to develop their own personalities and encouraged their intellectual ambitions, whereas Abba Alcott assisted Bronson in his efforts to inculcate submissiveness and self-denial in Louisa. In addition, although Willard and Cather's mothers differed in personality, they were both confident, strong women who did not find their assertive natures in conflict with femininity. The model of feminine strength they presented, although expressed in the traditional role, may have given Frances and Willa an unconscious resource to draw on later. By contrast, Louisa's model of femininity was a conflicted woman who tried to repress her own rebellious instincts and encouraged her daughter to do the same.

Finally, it is significant that both Willard and Cather forged close, supportive bonds with a group of professional women who were similarly redefining or rejecting the feminine role: the temperance workers who formed the leadership of the WCTU and the actresses, opera singers, and writers Cather discovered in Pittsburgh and New York. Membership in a female community provided emotional and psychological support for women who had turned away from the domestic role, and—particularly in the case of Willa Cather—made behavior that may have seemed deviant to the larger society normative within the context of a subgroup. Alcott, by contrast, never left her parents, the original source of her psychological conflict. Although she occasionally fantasized about communities of artistic and professional women in her fiction, she never attained real-life membership in one. Literally and figuratively unable to escape her parents, she died one day after Bronson.

These case studies raise some questions for historians to consider in undertaking future investigations of the female experience in Victorian America. It would be interesting to see, for example, whether the correlation found here between childhood tomboyism and adult public achievement was common. But it is likely that tomboy periods were not restricted to girls who achieved public recognition. They may even have been as frequent as Mary Virginia Terhune hinted when she said that it was unusual to "meet a woman who... would not own that at some period of her life, she had wished she had been born a boy."[47] If so, questions like the following may help us in analyzing female childhood and adolescence in Victorian America: How common was tomboyism? How often was fondness for boyish pastimes linked with "unfeminine" character traits? Did tomboys generally encounter stress or conflict in adolescence? Did tomboys characteristically expand, redefine, or reject woman's domestic role in adult life? If answers to these questions can be found in studying diaries, letters, journals, and other primary data, we may gain new insights into the experience of adult women as well. It would be interesting to see whether John Demos' hypothesis that childrearing practices contribute to the formation of adult modal personality is relevant for Victorian women.[48] Certainly the stress-arousing discontinuities between tomboy freedom and adolescent socialization parallel, if they do not account for, the stresses, tensions, and conflicts historians are finding so pervasive in Victorian women's adult lives.

Whatever the future answers to these questions, the lives of Frances Willard, Willa Cather, and Louisa May Alcott attest to the problems spirited young women confronted in a society as sexually polarized as Victorian America. The preferences for the male sex or delight in male activities these girls expressed reflect dramatically the contemporary assignment of human traits like curiosity and ambition to the male sex. Given Victorian society's rigid separation of male and female traits and spheres, it is impossible to attribute even such extreme behavior as Willa Cather's male impersonation period solely to individual psychodynamics. A woman writing in the late nineteenth century eloquently described the reasons why adolescent girls may have declared their preference for the male sex or revelled in boyish pastimes, agreeing with Frances Willard that such girls wanted to be fully human, not masculine:

> During the whole history of the human race up to the present
> generation the male has declared unchallenged... "I am the human
> being." Man is the person, woman is the female of the species....

The woman who wants to be a man—what is it that she really wants? And is it really impossible?... She wants to be what she may be and ought to be, a fully developed human being... not to be a male. It is man who keeps insisting on the distinction of sex,—woman would willingly forget it.[49]

Notes

1. The classic analysis of the prescriptive literature is Barbara Welter's "The Cult of True Womanhood," *American Quarterly* 18 (1966): 151-174. An analysis of the male anxiety behind the development of nineteenth-century professionalism can be found in Burton J. Bledstein, *The Culture of Professionalism* (New York: Norton, 1976).
2. Carroll Smith-Rosenberg, "Beauty, the Beast and the Militant Woman: A Case Study in Sex Roles and Role Stress in Jacksonian America," *American Quarterly* 23 (1971): 562-584 and "The Hysterical Woman: Sex Roles and Role Conflict in Nineteenth-Century America," *Social Research* 39 (1972): 652-678; Nancy Cott, *The Bonds of Womanhood: "Woman's Sphere" in New England, 1780-1835* (New Haven: Yale University Press, 1977), in particular "Domesticity," pp. 63-100; Anne Scott, *The Southern Lady: From Pedestal to Politics 1830-1930* (Chicago: University of Chicago Press, 1970), pp. 4-79; Martha Saxton, *Louisa May: A Modern Biography of Louisa May Alcott* (Boston: Houghton Mifflin Company, 1977); Mary Ryan, *Womanhood in America from Colonial Times to the Present* (New York: New Viewpoints, 1975), pp. 139-191; Mary Kelley, "A Woman Alone: Catharine Maria Sedgwick's Spinsterhood in Nineteenth-Century America," *New England Quarterly* 51 (June 1978): 209-225; "At War with Herself: Harriet Beecher Stowe as Woman in Conflict in the Home," *American Studies* (Fall 1978): 23-40. "The Sentimentalists: Promise and Betrayal in the Home," *Signs: Journal of Women in Culture and Society* 4 (Spring 1979): 434-446.
3. Smith-Rosenberg, "Beauty, the Beast and the Militant Woman " For a related argument, see Glenda Gates Riley's development of the "moral guardian" theory in "The Subtle Subversion: Changes in the Traditionalist Image of the American Woman," *Historian* 22 (1970): 210-227.
4. This argument is made in Smith-Rosenberg, "The Hysterical Woman," 658-659 as well as in Carroll Smith-Rosenberg and Charles Rosenberg, "The Female Animal: Medical and Biological Views of Woman and Her Role in Nineteenth-Century America," *Journal of American History* 60 (1973): 338-339.
5. In addition to Smith-Rosenberg, "The Hysterical Woman," see Anne Douglas Wood, "'The Fashionable Diseases': Women's Complaints and Their

Treatment in Nineteenth-Century America," *Journal of Interdisciplinary History* 4 (1973): 25–52.

6. "The Hysterical Woman," p. 656.

7. "The Hysterical Woman," p. 658.

8. My sample consisted of approximately forty advice books, fifteen written in the antebellum period and twenty-five after the Civil War. None of the post-Civil-War books recommended passive, delicate childhoods, although not all of them simultaneously recommended tomboyism. Thirteen of them did, however, although not all used the term "tomboy" in describing the active, rambunctious child they praised. The advice books advocating active childhoods were written by both men and women, most of whom were doctors, although there was a sprinkling of ministers and sentimental novelists. Most of them went through several editions, indicating their popularity. My main spokespeople in this essay are Dr. J.H. Kellogg, author of *Ladies' Guide in Health and Disease* (Des Moines, 1883) and Mary Virginia Terhune, author of *Eve's Daughters: Or, Common Sense for Maid, Wife, and Mother* (New York, 1882). They reflect the views held by the other post-Civil-War proponents of tomboyism.

9. Carroll Smith-Rosenberg discusses medical views of puberty in "Puberty to Menopause: The Cycle of Femininity in Nineteenth-Century America," in *Clio's Consciousness Raised*, ed. Mary Hartman and Lois Banner (New York: Harper-Torchbooks, 1974), pp. 23–29. The medical literature, she concludes, implies that adolescence was a traumatic period that required "an often painful restructuring of intrafamilial and social identities" (28). Her argument is based on medical literature, however, not on case studies of adolescent girls. Joseph Kett's recent study of adolescence, *Rites of Passage: Adolescence in America, 1790 to the Present* (New York: Basic Books, 1977) does not fill in this gap, for despite the inclusiveness of his title, he in fact is concerned almost solely with male adolescence.

10. The methodological problems involved in using advice manuals have been discussed by Jay Mechling in "Advice to Historians on Advice to Mothers," *Journal of Social History* 9 (1975): 44–63.

11. According to the *Oxford English Dictionary*, the term originally meant a "bold, immodest" girl, which implies an element of sexual allure absent in the second, and dominant, definition of a "wild, romping" child. Perhaps the link between the two is female aggressiveness which is expressed in different ways.

12. Fiction featuring a tomboy heroine—Louisa May Alcott's children's literature and Susan Cooledge's *What Katy Did* series—is also a post-Civil-War phenomenon. The reasons for the emergence of tomboyism as a popular concept in the late nineteenth century remain to be explored. Were there more tomboys as the century wore on because little girls increasingly rebelled against restrictions on feminine behavior? Or did active little girls

who enjoyed boys' pastimes merely become more noticeable as sexual polarization became more rigid? Or, as the population shift from rural areas to urban centers progressed, did the energy that farm girls had channelled into country activities and farm work seem boyish when expressed by urban and suburban girls in competitive play with male companions? The term itself, of course, reflects a concern with appropriate sex-role behavior that transcends American culture.

13. Harvey Newcomb, *How to Be a Lady: A Book for Girls* (Boston, 1852) p. 10.
14. *Ladies' Guide*, p. 118.
15. *Eve's Daughters*, p. 46.
16. *Eve's Daughters*, p. 44.
17. See Smith-Rosenberg, "Puberty to Menopause" and Charles Rosenberg, *"No Other Gods: On Science and American Social Thought* (Baltimore: Johns Hopkins University Press, 1976), pp. 54–71.
18. *Ladies' Guide*, p. 188.
19. Smith-Rosenberg, "Puberty to Menopause," p. 27.
20. Tullio Verdi, *Mothers and Daughters: Practical Studies* (New York, 1877), p. 74.
21. Advice-givers continually rhapsodized about sweet, budding childhood blossoming into lovely maidenhood.
22. Their untroubled holding of contradictory views may have partly resulted from the compartmentalized view of the human personality they accepted: the self-reliance an active childhood encouraged would be channeled into maternal relationships, never tainting the rest of the ideal feminine personality.
23. Frances E. Willard, *Glimpses of Fifty Years: The Autobiography of an American Woman* (Chicago: 1889; rpt. Source Book Press, 1970), p. 17. Subsequent page references are included in the text.
24. *How to Win: A Book for Girls* (New York, 1894), p. 52.
25. *How to Win*, p. 17.
26. It is possible to argue, of course, that Willard was aware of the inconsistency in her thinking but was using it to advance the cause of women. My opinion is that she was unaware of it. It is always easier to notice the contradictions in others' thinking than in our own.
27. *The World and the Parish: Willa Cather's Articles and Reviews, 1893–1902,* selected and edited with a commentary by William M. Curtin (Lincoln: University of Nebraska Press, 1970), I: 363.
28. Mildred Bennett, *The World of Willa Cather* (Lincoln: University of Nebraska Press, 1951; rpt. 1961), p. 1.
29. Edith Lewis, *Willa Cather Living* (Lincoln: University of Nebraska Press, 1953), p. 6.
30. Bennett, *World of Willa Cather*, p. 233.
31. Bennett, *World of Willa Cather*, p. 112.
32. Elmer Thomas, *Eighty Years in Webster County* (Hastings, Nebraska, 1953), p. 114.

33. A fuller discussion of the psychological sources of Willa Cather's male impersonation appears in the literary/biographical study I am writing on her reconciliation of femininity with the demands of art.

34. *The World and the Parish*, p. 56.

35. Saxton, *Louisa May*.

36. Charles Strickland, "A Transcendentalist Father: The Childrearing Practices of Bronson Alcott," *History of Childhood Quarterly* 1 (1973): 29. I am indebted to Strickland for my understanding of Bronson Alcott's childrearing philosophy and techniques.

37. Saxton, *Louisa May*, p. 66.

38. "Those Concord days were the happiest of my life." *Louisa May Alcott: Her Life, Letters and Journals,* ed., Ednah D. Cheney (Boston: Little Brown, 1928), p. 21.

39. Cheney, *Louisa May Alcott*, p. 20.

40. Cheney, *Louisa May Alcott*, p. 22.

41. Cheney, *Louisa May Alcott*, p. 36.

42. Saxton, *Louisa May Alcott*, p. 167.

43. Louisa May Alcott, *Comic Tragedies Written by "Jo" and "Meg" and Acted by the "Little Women"* (Boston, 1893).

44. Collected in *Behind a Mask: The Unknown Thrillers of Louisa May Alcott*, ed. Madelaine Stern (New York: William Morrow, 1975) and in *Plots and Counterplots: More Unknown Thrillers by Louisa May Alcott*, ed. Madelaine Stern (New York: William Morrow, 1976).

45. Although Alcott experienced a relatively free and happy childhood, which she later thought of nostagically, her parents attempted to regulate her behavior from infancy. So there was continuity in parental attitude.

46. This contrasts to the family pattern Barbara Welter notes in the lives of woman suffragists: a father who encourages the daughter's education and a distant invalid or "nurse-housekeeper" mother. Barbara Welter, *Dimity Convictions: The American Woman in the Nineteenth Century* (Athens: Ohio University Press, 1976), p. 6.

47. Terhune, *Eve's Daughters,* p. 76.

48. John Demos, "Developmental Perspectives on the History of Childhood," in *The Family in History*, ed. Theodore K. Rabb and Robert I. Rotberg (New York: Harper-Torchbooks, 1973), pp. 127–139.

49. Annie L. Mearkle, "The Woman Who Wants to be a Man," *Midland Monthly* 9 (1898): 176.